Hossein Bidgoli

INFORMATION SYSTEMS LITERACY
Windows 3.1

Macmillan Publishing Company
New York

Maxwell Macmillan Canada
Toronto

Maxwell Macmillan International
New York   Oxford   Singapore   Sydney

**To so many fine memories of my brother, Mohsen,
for his uncompromising belief in the power of education.**

Cover photo: Copyright © Douglas E. Walker/Masterfile. Cover photo insets courtesy of International Business Machines Corp.
Editor: Charles Stewart
Production Editor: Christine M. Harrington
Art Coordinator: Peter A. Robison
Photo Editor: Chris Migdol
Text Designer: Anne Flanagan
Cover Designer: Russ Maselli
Production Buyer: Pamela D. Bennett

This book was set in Baskerville by Carlisle Communications, Ltd. and was printed and bound by Semline Inc., a Quebecor America Book Group Company. The cover was printed by Phoenix Color Corp.

Copyright © 1993 by Macmillan Publishing Company, a division of Macmillan, Inc.

Printed in the United States of America

All rights reserved. No part of this book may be reproduced or transmitted in any form or by any means, electronic or mechanical, including photocopy, recording, or any information storage and retrieval system, without permission in writing from the Publisher.

The Publisher offers discounts on this book when ordered in bulk quantities. For more information, write to: Special Sales Department, Macmillan Publishing Company, 445 Hutchinson Avenue, Columbus, OH 43235, or call 1-800-228-7854.

Macmillan Publishing Company
866 Third Avenue
New York, New York 10022

Macmillan Publishing Company is part of the
Maxwell Communication Group of Companies.

Maxwell Macmillan Canada, Inc.
1200 Eglinton Avenue East, Suite 200
Don Mills, Ontario M3C 3N1

Bidgoli, Hossein.
    Information systems literacy : Windows 3.1 / Hossein Bidgoli.
       p.   cm.
       Includes index.
       ISBN 0-02-309533-4 : $6.00
       1. Windows (Computer programs)   2. Microsoft Windows (Computer file) I. Title.
QA76.76.W56B54 1993
    005.4'3—dc20   92-38278
                                                                   CIP

Printing: 2 3 4 5 6 7 8 9   Year: 3 4 5 6 7

Preface

Information Systems Literacy: Windows 3.1 is a component of a modular series of textbooks developed for use in introductory computing courses. This Windows text is written for first courses that include operating systems that use Windows or for use in any course where a Windows tutorial is required.

Chapter 1, *The World of Microcomputers,* takes a comprehensive look at microcomputer hardware, software, and their applications. The chapter provides a thorough discussion of the types of application software and provides the foundation for the hands-on sections of the text.

Chapters 2 through 4 provide a detailed discussion of MS-DOS and PC-DOS. This presentation will help students use their PCs and Windows software more effectively.

The software tutorials in Chapters 2 through 13 are designed to give students comprehensive training and a reference text. All material is broken down into manageably sized chapters. This approach gives the instructor a choice about which and how many topics to cover and gives students a valuable reference to use long after the class is completed. Advanced topics not covered in many texts are included, as a growing number of students come into introductory courses with some software literacy. This book allows students to go further in their studies.

The software chapters were designed with students in mind:

- The Introductory chapters explain, in basic terms, what the software is, why it was developed, and how it is used. Too many books "jump right in" without presenting a sense of context.
- Computer screens appear frequently to augment written instruction.
- Each chapter ends with 18 to 25 review questions, 5 to 8 hands-on experience assignments, and 10 multiple choice and 10 true/false questions.
- Each chapter includes a list of key terms and key computer commands.
- Most chapters have a unique section titled Misconceptions and Solutions. Common errors, improper operating procedures, and ways to avoid/solve them are highlighted.
- A unique appendix provides guidelines for file transfer among the most popular software packages. This coverage should make computer data more portable than ever!

Answers to selected review questions, which can be found in Appendix A, are provided to assist students in their studies.

In any hands-on computer lab, an accurate text makes managing the lab far easier. The best way to make a text accurate is to use it. In the six years that I took to develop this series, I received corrections and suggestions that make this book one that is easy to use and reliable.

This text is accompanied by a complete instructor's manual with lecture outlines, transparency masters, answers to review questions/exercises, additional projects, and a test bank.

Acknowledgments

Several colleagues reviewed different versions of this manuscript and made constructive suggestions. Without their help the manuscript could not have been refined. The help and comments of the following reviewers are greatly appreciated: Kirk Arnett, Mississippi State University; Tom Berliner, University of Texas—Dallas; Glen Boswell, San Antonio College; Carolyn Scott Budd, University of North Carolina—Greensboro; Paul Chase, Becker College; Michael Davis, Texas Technical University; Steve Deam, Milwaukee Area Technical College; Beth Defoor, Eastern New Mexico University—Clovis; Richard Ernst, Sullivan Junior College; Barbara Felty, Harrisburg Area Community College; Pat Fenton, West Valley College; Phyllis Helms, Randolph Community College; Nancy Houston, Grove City College; Mehdi Khosrowpour, Pennsylvania State—Harrisburg; Candice Marble, Wentworth Military Academy; John Miller, Williamsport Area Community College; Charles McDonald, East Texas State University; Sylvia Meyer, Community College of Vermont; Barbara Minnick, Indiana State; J. D. Oliver, Prairie View A&M University; Greg Pierce, Penn State University; Eugene Rathswohl, University of San Diego; Herbert Rebhun, University of Houston—Downtown; R. D. Shelton, Loyola College; Sandra Stalker, North Shore Community College; Maureen Thommes, Bemidji State University; G. W. Willis, Baylor University; and Judy Yeager, Western Michigan University.

Many different groups assisted me in completing this project. I am grateful to over five thousand students who attended my executive seminars and various classes in information systems and software productivity tools. They helped me fine-tune the manuscript during its various stages. My friend Bahram Ahanin helped me to improve many concepts of hardware/software and put them in a non-technical and easy-to-understand format. My colleague and friend Dr. Reza Azarmsa provided support and encouragement. I am grateful for all of his encouragement. My colleague Andrew Prestage assisted me in numerous trouble-spots by running and debugging many of the screens presented in the book.

I am indebted to Jacki Lawson, Denise Candia, Julie Gunn, and Vivian Cochneuer, who typed and retyped various versions of this manuscript. Their thoroughness and patience made it easier to complete this project. They deserve special recognition for all this work.

I also thank Inset System Inc. and Wendy Schulman for providing the HiJaak package for capturing the screens included in this text.

A team of professionals from Macmillan Publishing Company assisted me in this venture, including Charles Stewart, senior editor, and Christine Harrington, production editor.

Finally, I want to thank my family for their support and encouragement throughout my life. My two sisters, Azam and Akram, deserve my very special thanks and recognition. My wife, Nooshin, has been very supportive and patient. My little baby, Morvareed, has been very patient throughout this work. I extend my deepest love and appreciation to both.

Dr. Hossein Bidgoli is professor of management information systems at California State University, Bakersfield. He holds a Ph.D. degree in systems science from Portland State University with a specialization in design and implementation of MIS. His master's degree is in MIS from Colorado State University. Dr. Bidgoli's background includes experience as a systems analyst, information systems consultant, financial analyst, and he was the Director of the Microcomputer Center at Portland State University, where the first PC Lab in the United States was started.

Dr. Bidgoli, a two-time winner of the MPPP (Meritorious Performance and Professional Promise) award for outstanding performance in teaching, research and university/community service is the author of twenty-six texts and numerous professional papers and articles presented and published throughout the United States on the topics of computers and MIS. Dr. Bidgoli has also designed and implemented over twenty executive seminars on all aspects of information systems and decision support systems.

Contents

1
The World of Microcomputers — 1

1–1	Introduction	2
1–2	What Is a Microcomputer?	2
1–3	More on the Keyboard	5
1–4	Other Auxiliary Devices	5
1–5	Types of Primary Memories	6
1–6	Conventional, Expanded, and Extended Memories	7
1–7	Types of Secondary Memories	9
1–8	Memory Capacity and Processor Speed	11
1–9	General Capabilities of Microcomputer Software	13
1–10	Guidelines for Successful Selection of a Microcomputer	18
1–11	Taking Care of Your Microcomputer	20
1–12	Advantages of Microcomputers Compared with Mainframes	21
1–13	You and Your PC: A Hands-On Session	21
1–14	What Is a Computer File?	22
1–15	Types of Data	22
1–16	Types of Values	23
1–17	Types of Formulas	23
1–18	Priority (Precedence) of Operations	23

2
You and Your PC: The First Official Meeting — 29

2–1	Introduction	30
2–2	Turning On Your PC	30
2–3	DOS Prompts	31
2–4	DOS File Specifications	31
2–5	The DIR Command	31
2–6	Using DIR with Switches	33
2–7	Important Keys in the DOS Environment	34
2–8	The FORMAT Command	34
2–9	Different Versions of MS-DOS and PC-DOS	36

Contents

3
Commonly Used DOS Commands   43

3-1	Introduction	44
3-2	FORMAT Command	44
3-3	LABEL Command	46
3-4	DISKCOPY Command	47
3-5	DISKCOMP Command	48
3-6	CHKDSK Command	48
3-7	SYS Command	50
3-8	COPY Command	50
3-9	COPY Versus DISKCOPY	51
3-10	COMP Command	52
3-11	RENAME Command	52
3-12	DELETE and ERASE Commands	53
3-13	ATTRIB Command	53

4
Directories and Subdirectories   59

4-1	Introduction	60
4-2	Defining a Directory	60
4-3	Important Commands for Directories	61
4-4	Example 1: Directory Creation	62
4-5	Example 2: Copying to Directories	63
4-6	Example 3: Copying from One Subdirectory to Another	64
4-7	Example 4: Removing a Directory	64
4-8	Hard Disk Management	65
4-9	Partitioning a Hard Disk	65
4-10	Preparing a Hard Disk	66
4-11	Backing Up a Hard Disk	66
4-12	Restoring a Crashed Hard Disk	67

5
Windows 3.1: An Overview   73

5-1	Introduction	74
5-2	Advantages of Windows	74
5-3	Understanding Windows Terminology	75
5-4	Getting In and Getting Out of Windows	75
5-5	Using a Mouse in the Windows Environment	78
5-6	Using the Keyboard in a Windows Environment	81
5-7	Running Windows in Different Modes	82
5-8	Getting Help	83
	5-8-1 Help Facility	83
	5-8-2 Help on a Specific Topic	85

Contents

		5-8-3 Tutorial Facility	85
5-9		Different Parts of a Windows Screen	88
5-10		Upgrading to Windows 3.1	89

6
Windows Paintbrush — 95

6-1	Introduction	96
6-2	What Is Paintbrush?	96
6-3	Getting In and Getting Out of Paintbrush	96
6-4	The Paintbrush Screen	97
6-5	Drawing a Simple Illustration	98
6-6	Selecting Foreground and Background Colors and Line Width	98
6-7	Working with the Toolbox	99
6-8	Undoing Your Last Change	101
6-9	Entering Text Into Your Drawings	101
6-10	Printing Drawings	102
6-11	Working with Cutout Tools	103
6-12	Using the Toolbox for Drawing Lines and Shapes	105
	6-12-1 Straight Lines	105
	6-12-2 Curved Lines	106
	6-12-3 Boxes	106
	6-12-4 Circles and Ellipses	107
	6-12-5 Polygons and Filled Polygons	107
	6-12-6 Airbrush	108
6-13	Paintbrush Menus	108
	6-13-1 File Menu	108
	6-13-2 Edit Menu	110
	6-13-3 View Menu	110
	6-13-4 Text Menu	112
	6-13-5 Pick Menu	112
	6-13-6 Options and Help Menus	112

7
Windows Write — 119

7-1	Introduction	120
7-2	Starting Windows Write	120
7-3	Your First Electronic Document	121
7-4	Saving a Document	122
7-5	Retrieving a Saved Document	124
7-6	Moving Around in a Document	125
	7-6-1 Using the Keyboard	125
	7-6-2 Using the Mouse	125

Contents

7-7	Inserting and Deleting Text	126
7-8	Printing Text	126
7-9	Selecting Text	127
7-10	Find and Replace Operations	127
7-11	Cut and Paste Operations	129
7-12	Moving Text	131
7-13	Undoing Your Last Action	131
7-14	Line Spacing	131
7-15	Enhancing Text	132
7-16	Inserting Page Breaks	134

8
Windows Basic Operations   141

8-1	Introduction	142
8-2	Menu Conventions	142
8-3	Opening the Control Menu	142
	8-3-1 For an Application Window or Icon	142
	8-3-2 For a Document Window	144
	8-3-3 For a Dialog Box	144
8-4	Control-Menu Commands	144
8-5	Moving a Window	146
8-6	Moving an Icon	147
8-7	Modifying the Size of a Window	147
8-8	Reducing a Window to an Icon	148
8-9	Enlarging a Window	148
8-10	Restoring an Icon to a Window	148
8-11	Navigating Through Screens Using Scroll Bars	148
8-12	Closing a Window	150
8-13	Different Parts of a Window	151
8-14	The Task List	151

9
Working with Applications and Documents   159

9-1	Introduction	160
9-2	The Program Manager	160
	9-2-1 What Is the Program Manager?	160
	9-2-2 Parts of the Program Manager Window	160
9-3	Starting Applications	162
	9-3-1 From the Program Manager	162
	9-3-2 From the File Manager	162
	9-3-3 By Using the Run Command	162
	9-3-4 By Using the MS-DOS Prompt	163
9-4	Running Two or More Applications at the Same Time	164

Contents

9-5	Switching Between Applications		164
9-6	Selecting Text		165
9-7	The Clipboard		166
	9-7-1	Moving or Copying Information to the Clipboard	166
	9-7-2	Transferring Information from the Clipboard	166
	9-7-3	Working with the Clipboard Viewer	167
	9-7-4	Saving the Contents of the Clipboard to a File	167
	9-7-5	Retrieving a Clipboard File	168
	9-7-6	Clearing the Contents of the Clipboard	168
9-8	Quitting an Application		169
9-9	Working with Documents		169
	9-9-1	Opening Files	169
	9-9-2	Saving Files	170
	9-9-3	Switching Between Documents	170
	9-9-4	Working with Text	170
	9-9-5	Moving Around in Text	171
	9-9-6	Correcting Mistakes	171

10
Customizing Windows Environments 177

10-1	Introduction		178
10-2	Working with Groups		178
	10-2-1	Opening a Group Window	179
	10-2-2	Reducing a Group Window to an Icon	179
	10-2-3	Rearranging Group Windows	179
	10-2-4	Organizing Group Icons	180
	10-2-5	Organizing Program-Item Icons	180
	10-2-6	Creating New Groups	181
	10-2-7	Deleting a Group	183
	10-2-8	Changing the Description of a Group	183
10-3	Working with Program Items		184
	10-3-1	Creating a Program Item	184
	10-3-2	Creating a Program Item for a Document	185
	10-3-3	Deleting a Program Item from a Group	186
	10-3-4	Copying Program Items from One Group to Another	186
	10-3-5	Moving a Program Item to Another Group	186
	10-3-6	Changing an Icon	187
10-4	Starting an Application When You Start Windows		188
10-5	The Control Panel		188
	10-5-1	Starting the Control Panel	188
	10-5-2	Displaying Custom Wallpaper	190
	10-5-3	Using a Screen Saver	191
	10-5-4	Installing and Configuring a Printer	191

11
Managing Files and Floppy Disks Using the File Manager — 197

11–1	Introduction	198
11–2	File Manager: Getting Started	198
11–3	What Is a Directory Window?	198
11–4	Selecting Files and Directories	200
	11–4–1 Selecting Several Files or Directories That Are in Sequence	200
	11–4–2 Selecting Several Files or Directories That Are out of Sequence	200
	11–4–3 Deselecting Files or Directories	201
11–5	Changing Drives	201
11–6	Sorting the Contents of a Directory	201
11–7	Specifying the Type of File to Be Displayed	202
11–8	Naming a File or a Directory	203
11–9	Creating a Directory	204
11–10	Searching for a File or a Directory	205
11–11	Deleting a File or a Directory	205
11–12	Renaming a File or a Directory	207
11–13	Copying or Moving a File or Directory	207
11–14	Using Multiple Windows in File Manager	209
11–15	Associating Files with a Software Application	209
11–16	Printing a File	212
11–17	Formatting a Disk	212
11–18	Labeling a Disk	213
11–19	Copying a Disk	214
11–20	Creating a system Disk	214

12
Additional Windows Accessories — 221

12–1	Introduction	222
12–2	Calculator: An Overview	222
	12–2–1 Performing Simple Calculations	223
	12–2–2 Correcting Mistakes	223
	12–2–3 Using Operators and Symbols	224
	12–2–4 Conducting Simple Operations	224
12–3	Calendar: An Overview	225
	12–3–1 Layout of the Calendar Screen	225
	12–3–2 Performing a Simple Task	227
	12–3–3 Using Cursor-Movement Keys	229
	12–3–4 Setting an Alarm for an Event	230
	12–3–5 Calendar File Menu	231
	12–3–6 Calendar Edit Menu	232
	12–3–7 Calendar View Menu	233

Contents

	12–3–8	Calendar Show Menu	233
	12–3–9	Calendar Alarm Menu	233
	12–3–10	Calendar Options Menu	234
	12–3–11	Calendar Help Menu	234
12–4	Clock: An Overview		236
12–5	Cardfile: An Overview		237
	12–5–1	An Application of the Cardfile	239
12–6	Notepad: An Overview		241
12–7	Terminal: An Overview		243
	12–7–1	Components Required to Use Terminal	243
	12–7–2	Starting the Terminal Application	244
	12–7–3	Terminal Application	245
12–8	Character Map, Media Player, Recorder, and Sound Recorder		246

13
Advanced Features of Windows 3.1   253

13–1	Introduction		254
13–2	Recorder		254
	13–2–1	Starting the Recorder	254
	13–2–2	Example 1 —A Macro for Typing a Centered Title	255
	13–2–3	Example 2 —A Printing Macro	257
	13–2–4	Example 3 —A Macro for Formatting a Disk	257
13–3	Object Linking and Embedding		258
	13–3–1	Embedding an Object Versus Linking an Object	259
	13–3–2	Example of Object Linking	259
	13–3–3	Hands-On Example of Object Embedding	260
	13–3–4	Hands-On Example of Object Linking	261
	13–3–5	Dynamic Data Exchange Versus OLE: What's the Difference?	264
13–4	Print Manager		265
13–5	PIF Editor		267
13–6	Object Packager		270

APPENDIX A
Answers to Selected Review Questions and Review of System Files   277

A–1	Answers to Selected Review Questions	277
A–2	Review of System Files	280

APPENDIX B
File Transfer Among Popular Software Packages   287

B–1	Introduction	287
B–2	Why Use File Transfer?	287
B–3	What Is an ASCII File?	288
B–4	File Transfer and DOS	288

Contents

B–5	File Transfer and WordPerfect 5.1	288
B–6	Importing Files into WordPerfect: A Second Method	289
B–7	File Transfer and Lotus 1-2-3	290
B–8	File Transfer and dBASE	290
B–9	File Transfer and 1-2-3 PIC Files	291
B–10	File Transfer and Quattro Pro	293
B–11	File Transfer and Paradox	294
B–12	File Transfer and BASICA	295

Index 299

The World of Microcomputers

1-1 Introduction
1-2 What Is a Microcomputer?
1-3 More on the Keyboard
1-4 Other Auxiliary Devices
    1-4-1 Disk Drives
    1-4-2 Adapter Cards
1-5 Types of Primary Memories
1-6 Conventional, Expanded, and Extended Memories
1-7 Types of Secondary Memories
    1-7-1 Magnetic Storage Devices
    1-7-2 Optical Technologies
1-8 Memory Capacity and Processor Speed
1-9 General Capabilities of Microcomputer Software
    1-9-1 Word Processing Software
    1-9-2 Grammar Checker Software
    1-9-3 Spreadsheet Software
    1-9-4 Database Software
    1-9-5 Graphics Software
    1-9-6 Communications Software
    1-9-7 Desktop Publishing Software
    1-9-8 Financial Planning Software
    1-9-9 Accounting Software
    1-9-10 Project Management Software
    1-9-11 Computer-Aided Design Software
    1-9-12 Other Popular Software for Microcomputers
1-10 Guidelines for Successful Selection of a Microcomputer
1-11 Taking Care of Your Microcomputer
1-12 Advantages of Microcomputers Compared with Mainframes
1-13 You and Your PC: A Hands-On Session
1-14 What Is a Computer File?
1-15 Types of Data
1-16 Types of Values
1-17 Types of Formulas
1-18 Priority (Precedence) of Operations

1-1
INTRODUCTION

In this chapter we concentrate on microcomputer fundamentals. Hardware and software for micros are explained. Different classes of application software are introduced. Guidelines for successful selection and maintenance of micros are highlighted. A brief section points out the advantages of micros compared with mainframes. The chapter includes a hands-on session with a microcomputer. All of this knowledge will help you to be more effective when you use a microcomputer.

1-2
WHAT IS A MICROCOMPUTER?

The terms *personal computer, PC, micro,* and *microcomputer* refer to the smallest type of computer, when measured by such attributes as memory, cost, size, speed, and sophistication. Although small, microcomputers are so powerful that sometimes the difference between them and larger computers is blurred. Since the beginning of the microcomputer era, roughly in 1975, the capability of microcomputers has improved beyond imagination. Still, some experts believe that this is only the beginning and there is a lot more to be done by these computers.

   A typical microcomputer consists of input, output, and memory devices. Figure 1–1 illustrates a typical system. The input device is usually a keyboard. A PC keyboard is similar to a typewriter, with some additional keys. Figure 1–2 displays an IBM standard keyboard and an enhanced keyboard. In the future, voice input devices may be on the market. Other input devices include the mouse, touch technology, light pens, graphics tablets, optical character readers, magnetic ink character recognition readers, cameras, sensors, and bar code readers.

   The common output devices for microcomputers are a CRT (sometimes called VDT) and a printer. The output generated on the monitor is called soft

Figure 1–1
Typical microcomputer system (courtesy of International Business Machines Corp.).

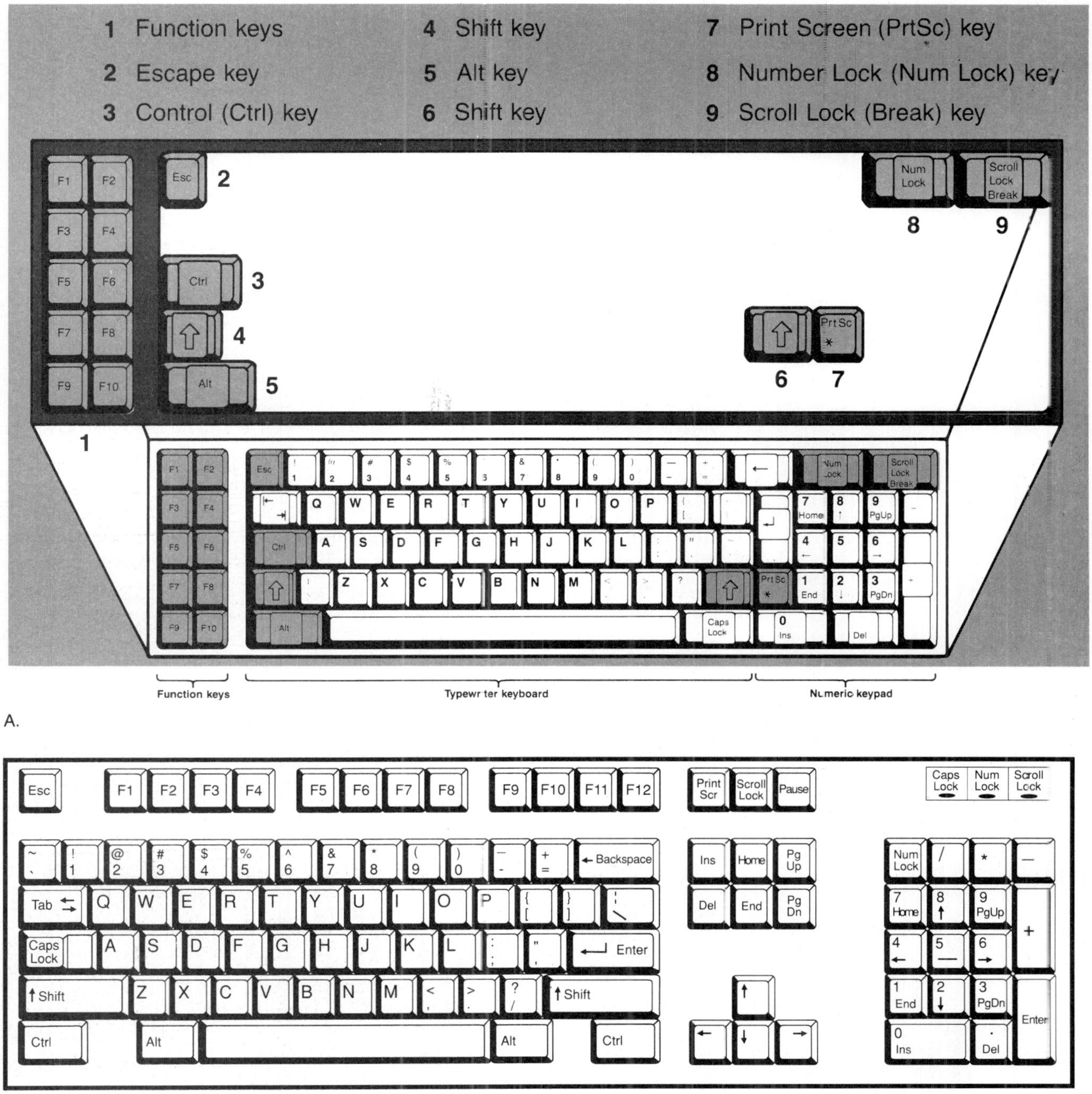

Chapter 1 The World of Microcomputers

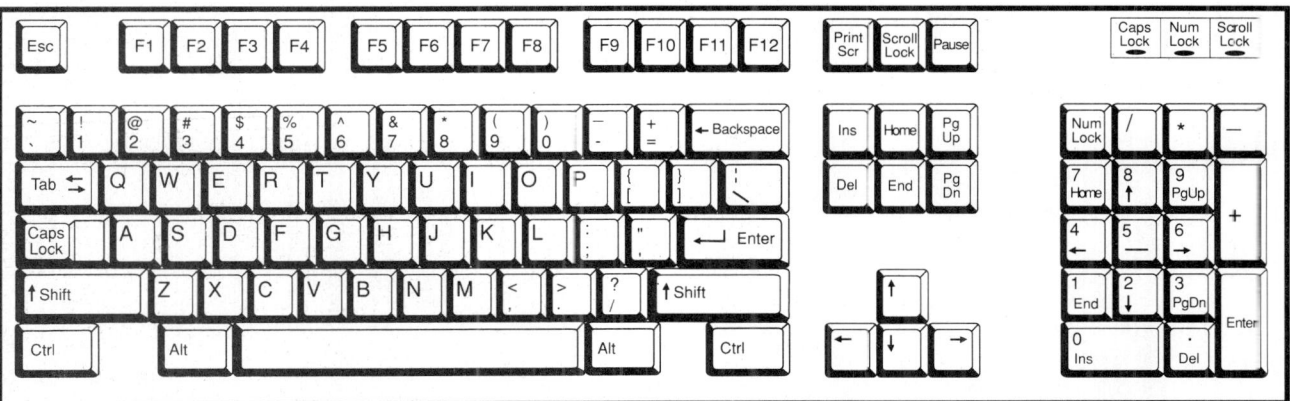

Figure 1-2
A. IBM standard keyboard. B. IBM enhanced keyboard (courtesy of International Business Machines Corp.).

copy and the printed output is referred to as hard copy. Other output devices include cameras and plotters.

Two types of monitors are common to microcomputers. Some micros have a monochrome screen, which generates one color, typically green although some screens are amber (orange). Monochrome screens can generate graphic output if accompanied with a graphics card or graphics adapter. The other type of monitor is called a color monitor (sometimes referred to as a RGB monitor for red green blue). It shows data in a color format.

Color monitors come in various levels of resolution that are referred to as CGA, EGA, VGA, super VGA, and XGA. The sharpness of images on the display monitor is the resolution. Color Graphics Adapters (CGAs) display 320-by-200 (pixels) resolution in four colors. The intersection of a row and a column is called a pixel. The higher the number of these pixels, the higher the resolution. Enhanced Graphics Adapters (EGAs) display 640-by-350 resolution in 16 colors. More advanced versions of EGA display 640-by-480 resolution in 16 colors and 320-by-200 resolution in 256 colors. Video Graphics Array (VGA) displays 640-by-480 resolution in 16 colors or 320-by-200 resolution in 256 colors. This add-on board was introduced in 1987 for the IBM PS/2 series of computers. Super VGA and XGA monitors display more than 640-by-480 resolution in many different colors. The exact resolution depends on the specific type of the monitor.

The processing part of a microcomputer, its CPU or the microprocessor, includes three components:

1. Main memory stores data, information, and instructions.
2. Arithmetic/logic unit performs arithmetic and logical operations. Arithmetic operations include addition, subtraction, division, and multiplication. Logical operations include any types of comparisons, such as sorting (putting data into a particular order) or searching (choosing a particular data item).
3. The control unit serves as the commander of the system. It tells the microcomputer what to do and how to do it.

Figure 1–3 illustrates two different microprocessor chips, or microchips.

Microcomputers are getting smaller but more powerful. Among the various types are portable (laptop) micros and notebook micros (see Figure 1–4).

A.

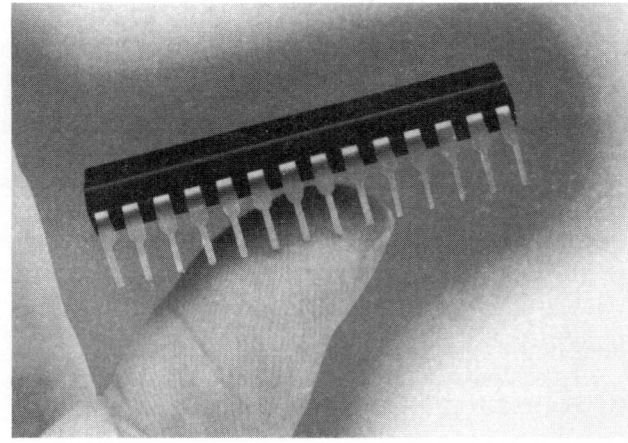

B.

Figure 1–3
A. Motorola MC 68020 microprocessor in its protective ceramic package (courtesy of Motorola, Inc.). B. AT&T Bell Labs microprocessor (courtesy of Radio Shack, a division of Tandy Corp.)

Chapter 1 The World of Microcomputers

A.

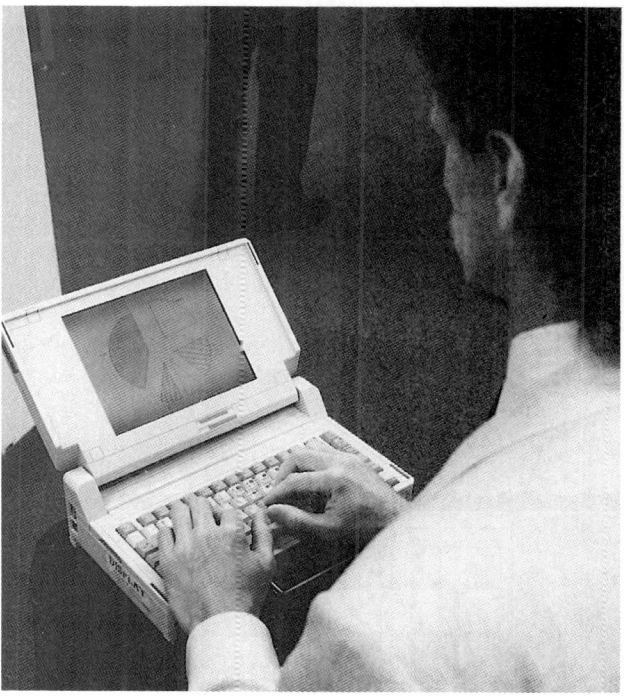
B.

Figure 1–4
A. Portable (laptop) computer; B. notebook computer (courtesy of Cobalt Productions/Macmillan).

1–3 MORE ON THE KEYBOARD

As you can see in Figure 1–2, an enhanced keyboard is divided into three sections. On the top there are 12 function keys (some keyboards have the function keys on the left). With most application software, these keys perform special functions, or they can be programmed to perform a particular task. For example, Lotus 1-2-3, Quattro Pro, dBASE, and WordPerfect effectively use 10 keys (F1 through F10) for performing different tasks.

The middle part of the keyboard is similar to a typical typewriter. It contains, however, some special keys that a typewriter does not have (e.g., the Alt key).

The right section is a numeric key pad similar to that of an adding machine. These keys facilitate numeric data entry (when the Num Lock key is pressed down) or cursor movement.

The purpose of function keys and some of the special keys varies in different application programs. For example, the F1 key in WordPerfect performs "undelete" operations. In Lotus 1-2-3, Quattro Pro, and dBASE, it accesses the on-line HELP command.

1–4 OTHER AUXILIARY DEVICES

Besides the typical input/output devices, some additional devices are required for effective use of a microcomputer. Two of these devices are disk drives and adapter cards.

Windows 3.1

1-4-1 Disk Drives

Disk drives are used to read and store data or information from and to the disk into main memory. Disk drives come in various capacities, and you may have one or more disk drives for your micro. Your micro may also have a hard disk drive. As you will see later, hard disks are capable of storing masses of information. The capacity of a hard disk is many times greater than that of a floppy diskette. A floppy diskette can hold from 360 kilobytes (K) to 1.44 megabytes (MB) of information. Some new floppies are capable of storing even more. The capacity of a hard disk varies from 5 to 300 MB or more.

The capacity of a storage device, either main or auxiliary, is measured in terms of bits or bytes of information stored on that device. Table 1–1 summarizes the memory equivalents.

1-4-2 Adapter Cards

Adapter cards are installed in expansion slots (channels) inside the system unit of the micro (see Figure 1–5). These cards are added so that a particular option can be attached to the system unit. Typical adapter cards are summarized in Table 1–2.

The original IBM PC had five expansion slots; the IBM XT and IBM AT have eight slots. Adapter cards usually have outlet ports that are accessed at the back of the system unit. It is important to remember that the new PCs do not require as many adapter cards. Ports, which are either parallel or serial, are used to connect devices to the system. Serial devices transfer one bit of data at a time; parallel devices transfer a set of bits of data at a time. Remember, you must connect a serial device to a serial port and a parallel device to a parallel port.

1-5 TYPES OF PRIMARY MEMORIES

There are two kinds of memory: **main memory,** or **primary memory,** and auxiliary, or secondary, memory. Main memory, the heart of the microcomputer, is usually referred to as **RAM** (random-access memory). This is a volatile memory: data stored in RAM will be lost in the event of a power failure. To avoid such a loss, always save your work in a permanent memory such as a diskette.

Three other types of memory can be referred to as main memory, but the user does not have direct control over them. **ROM** (read-only memory) is provided on a prefabricated chip supplied by vendors. This memory stores some general-purpose instructions or programs. For example, some DOS commands and the BASIC language are stored on ROM chips. (DOS is the popular disk operating system for IBM PCs and compatibles.) **PROM** (programmable read-only memory) allows users to program it by using a special device. Once programmed, however, this type of memory cannot be erased. **EPROM** (erasable programmable read-only memory) can be programmed by the user and, as the name indicates, erased and programmed again.

Table 1–1
Memory equivalents

0 or 1 is equal to one bit
8 bits is equal to one byte
1,024 (2^{10}) bytes is equal to one kilobyte
1,048,576 (2^{20}) bytes is equal to one megabyte
1,073,741,824 (2^{30}) bytes is equal to one gigabyte
10,995,627,776 (2^{40}) bytes is equal to one terabyte

Chapter 1 The World of Microcomputers

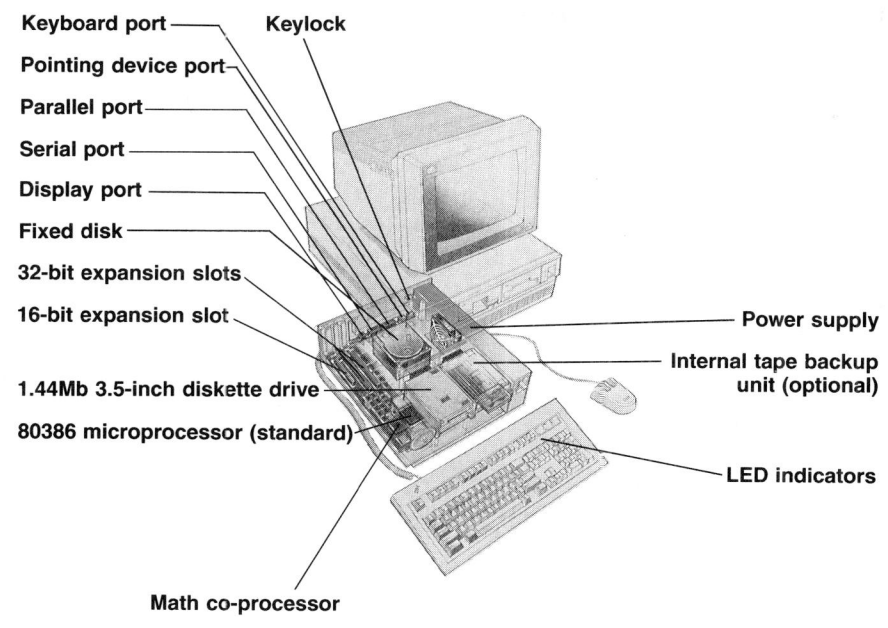

A.

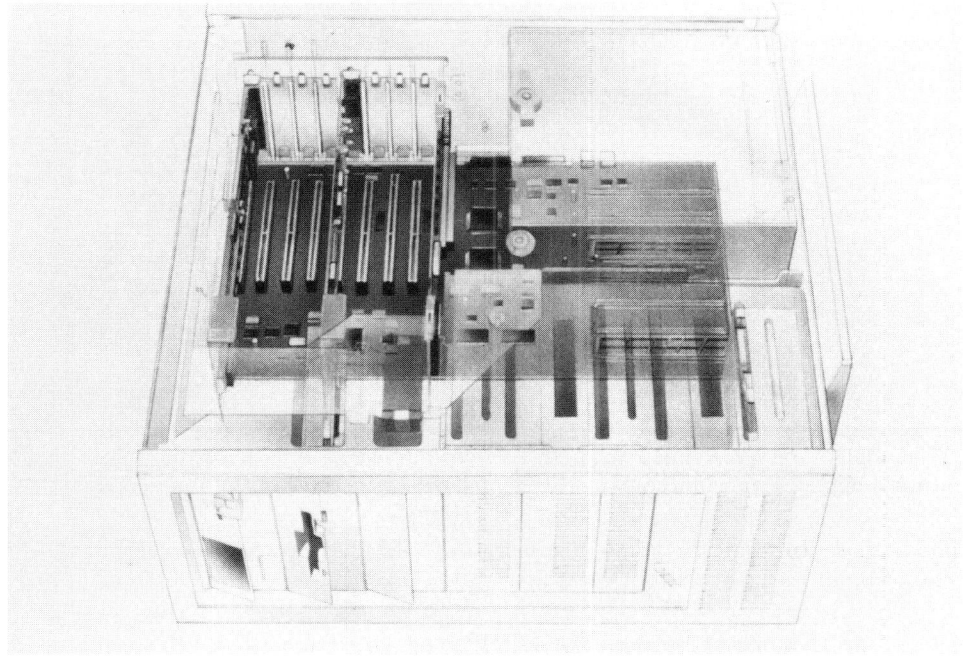

B.

Figure 1-5
A. Port and expansion slots in a microcomputer (courtesy of International Business Machines Corp.). B. Inside a microcomputer. This model is IBM's PS/2 95XP 486. (courtesy of International Business Machines Corp.).

1-6 CONVENTIONAL, EXPANDED, AND EXTENDED MEMORIES

In recent years, with the introduction of microcomputers based on the 286, 386, and 486 chips, two new types of main memory have entered the market and have made the memory discussion more confusing. Next we briefly discuss these two memories and differentiate them from so-called conventional memory.

Conventional memory (i.e., RAM) is the first 640 K of the memory of your computer. The majority of IBM XT and compatible machines come with

Windows 3.1

Table 1-2
Commonly used adapter cards

Disk drive card for connecting disk drives to the system unit
Display card for connecting the CRT to the system unit
Memory card for connecting additional RAM to existing memory
Clock card for connecting a clock to the system unit
Modem card for connecting the PC to the outside world
Printer interface card for connecting a printer to the system unit
Fax interface card for connecting a computer to a fax machine, thereby allowing information to be sent to and received from other locations

1 MB of memory; however, DOS can only directly reach the first 640 K of this memory. The other 384 K (1,204 K − 640 K) is used by ROM BIOS (Basic Input/Output System), adapter ROM, video memory, and EMS (Expanded Memory Specification) window (see Figure 1–6).

Expanded memory, which is located outside of conventional memory, works based on a technique called bank switching. Three companies, Lotus, Intel, and Microsoft (LIM), devised the LIM expanded memory specification (EMS) for expanded memory. It is more like a memory storage area on an EMS-compatible expansion card inside your computer. To use expanded memory, you need both an EMS-compatible memory expansion card and a device driver known as expanded memory manager (EMM). The EMM assists microprocessors to find a page (or pages) of data that your software is looking for and puts it into a 64 K-page frame as four 16 K pages, so DOS can find it and then your application program can use it. This is very useful for designing large spreadsheets. See Figure 1–6.

Figure 1-6
Conventional, extended, and expanded memories

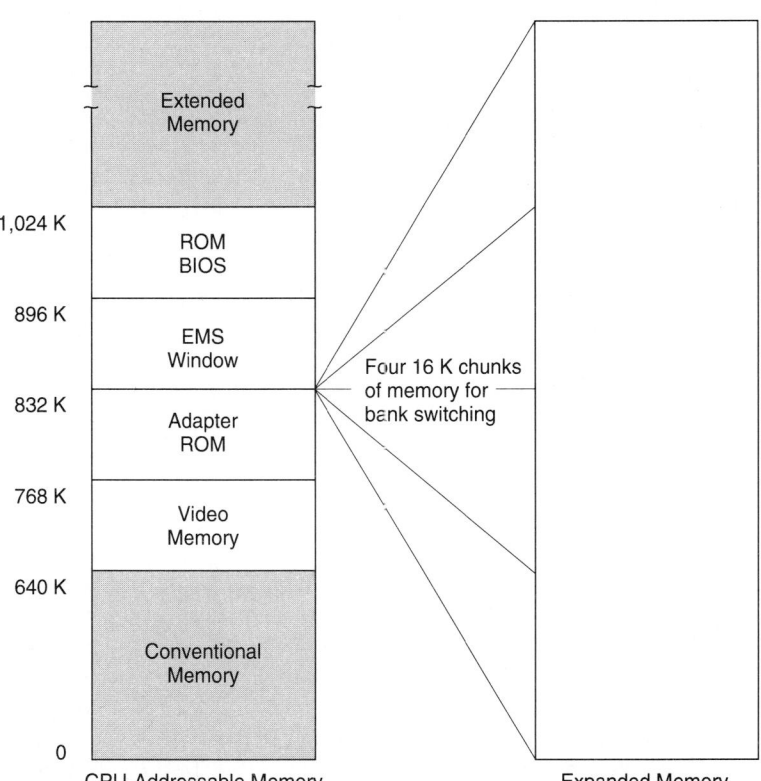

Chapter 1 The World of Microcomputers

Extended memory is also outside of conventional memory, but it is basically treated as more RAM and is accessible to your computer directly. No bank switching is involved with extended memory. This means that after DOS addresses the first 640 K of conventional memory, then it automatically accesses the next chunk of the memory, which is the extended memory (see Figure 1–6). A 286-based PC can access up to 16 MB of RAM and PC based on the 386 and 486 chips can access up to 4,096 MB of RAM.

Which memory should you get, expanded or extended? Well, the software you are using dictates the type of memory you need. Earlier software products requested expanded memory. Today's graphic environments, such as Windows, prefer extended memory.

1-7 TYPES OF SECONDARY MEMORIES

Since the main memory of a microcomputer is limited, expensive, and volatile, **secondary memory,** or secondary storage, is used for mass data storage. Secondary storage is nonvolatile. Secondary storage devices are broadly classified into magnetic and optical.

Magnetic Storage Devices

1-7-1

Magnetic storage devices include the **floppy diskette,** mini floppy diskette, **hard disk,** and Bernoulli box. The capacity of a diskette or a hard disk depends on its technical features. The three types of standard diskettes, classified by diameter, are $3\frac{1}{2}$ inches, $5\frac{1}{4}$ inches, and 8 inches. The most recent floppy, just entering the market, is 2 inches. Diskettes can be single density, double density, or high density. Density refers to the amount of information that can be stored on a disk. Diskettes can also be single sided or double sided. A $5\frac{1}{4}$-inch, single-sided, single-density floppy can hold roughly 125 K; a $5\frac{1}{4}$-inch single-sided, double-density floppy can hold roughly 250 K; a $5\frac{1}{4}$-inch double-sided, double-density floppy can hold roughly 360K; and a high-density (sometimes called quad-density) can hold up to 1.2 MB. A $3\frac{1}{2}$-inch, low density floppy diskette can store 720 K; a high density can store 1.44 MB on a double-sided diskette.

A hard disk, fixed disk, or Winchester disk can be either 14, 8, $5\frac{1}{4}$, or less than 4 inches in diameter. The capacity of these devices varies from 5 MB to 1 gigabyte.

A Bernoulli box is a removable medium; that is, after finishing your computer work, you can pull this device out and store it in a safe place. This is not possible with a hard disk. A Bernoulli box uses high-capacity floppy diskettes to store 10 MB or more of information. Generally speaking, it is less prone to damage than a hard disk. This is true because the Bernoulli box drive head does not move as a hard disk head moves, which often causes head crashes. In a Bernoulli box the floppy diskette moves toward the stationary read/write head through air currents. Figure 1–7 displays a Bernoulli box.

At the present time, the most commonly used secondary storage device is the $3\frac{1}{2}$-inch floppy diskette. At the beginning of the PC era, the $5\frac{1}{4}$-inch floppy was the most common secondary storage device. A $5\frac{1}{4}$-inch diskette is enclosed in a permanent vinyl jacket to protect it. The $3\frac{1}{2}$-inch diskette has a hard protective coating. A floppy diskette is made of plastic material coated with magnetic material. Always protect your diskettes from dirt and dust. Don't place your fingers on exposed portions of the diskette or data loss may result. Figure 1–8 highlights important areas of a $5\frac{1}{4}$-inch diskette and Figure 1–9 displays the features

Figure 1-7
Bernoulli Box

Figure 1-8
A $5\frac{1}{4}$-inch floppy diskette

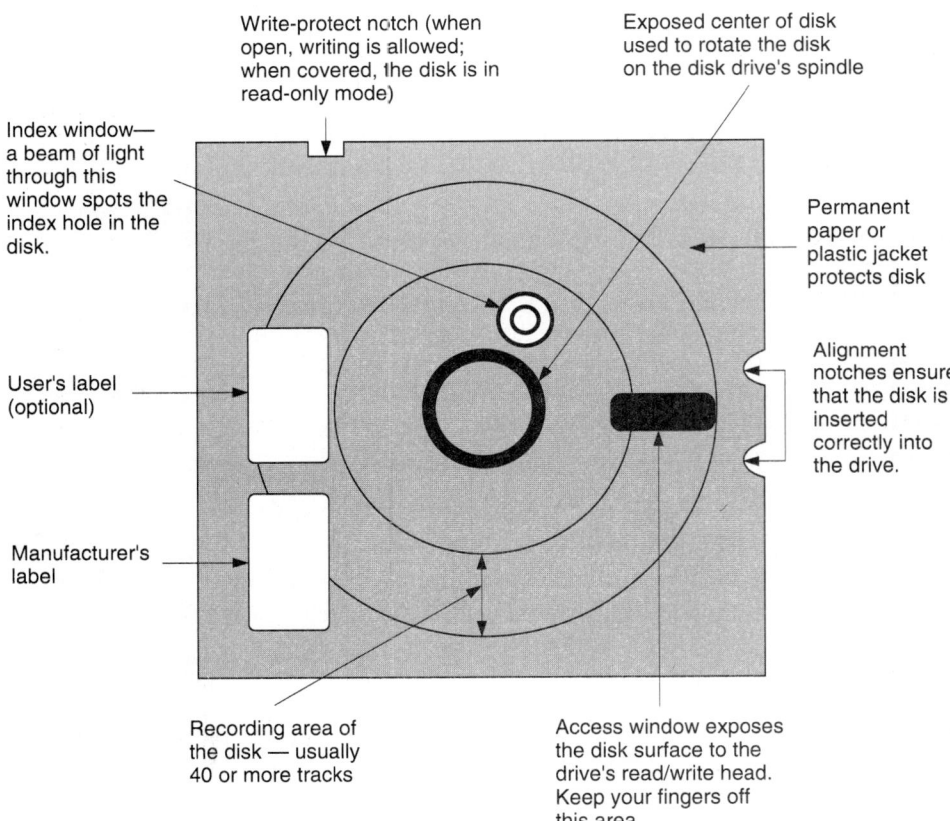

of a $3\frac{1}{2}$-inch diskette. The $3\frac{1}{2}$-inch diskettes are more durable and easier to handle than the $5\frac{1}{4}$-inch diskettes; they also store more data.

1-7-2 Optical Technologies

Three types of optical storage have attracted much attention in recent years: CD ROM, WORM, and erasable optical disk. Figure 1-10 illustrates each. The major advantages of optical technology devices are durability and massive stor-

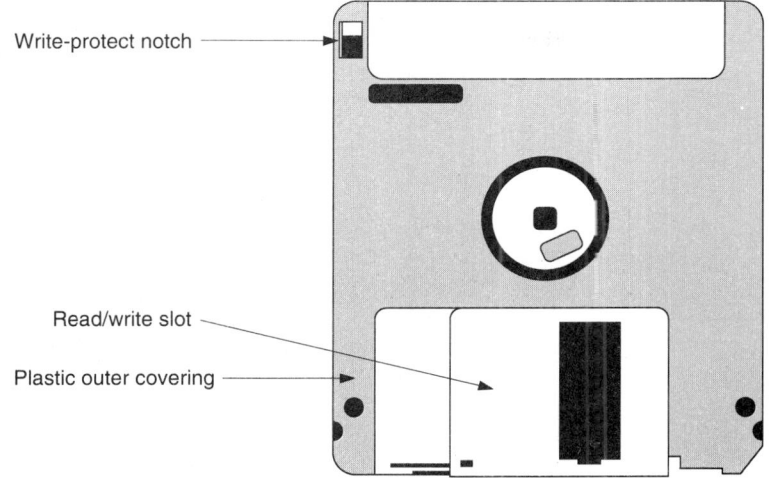

Figure 1-9
A $3\frac{1}{2}$-inch floppy diskette

age capacity. The major drawback of the technology is its slow speed, although vendors are working rapidly to improve this characteristic. Let us briefly consider each type.

CD ROM (compact disk read-only memory), as the name indicates, is a permanent device. Information is recorded once. The CD ROM is similar to an audio compact disk. The major application for CD ROMs involves large permanent databases, for example, public domain databases such as libraries, real estate information, and corporate financial information. A CD ROM can be duplicated and distributed throughout an organization.

The **WORM disk** (write once, read many) is also a permanent device. Information can be recorded once and cannot be altered. Its major drawback compared with CD ROM is that the disk cannot be duplicated. Its major application is for storing information that must be kept permanently, for example, information related to annual reports, nuclear power plants, airports, and railroads.

An **erasable optical disk** allows high-volume storage and updating. Information can be recorded and erased repeatedly.

1-8 MEMORY CAPACITY AND PROCESSOR SPEED

Microcomputer RAM capacity usually starts at 512 K or 640 K. Now PCs with capacities of 1 to 4 MB are becoming more common, and in the future they will approach the capacity of minicomputers.

To plan for the present and the future, you should be able to calculate the memory requirements for your computing needs. If you have a PC with 640 K of RAM, all of it may not be accessible to you. A large portion of this memory may be used up by your application software. As an example, Lotus 1-2-3 Release 2.01 uses almost 200 K of RAM. So in your 640K PC, you are left with only 440 K of user memory (640 − 200 = 440).

Another consideration regarding memory is speed. The speed of the processor is measured in megahertz (MHz) and usually varies from 4 to 50 MHz. Vendors are rapidly extending this technology, and soon speeds of 100 MHz or more will be available. The higher the processor speed, the faster the computer. Another factor that has a direct impact on speed is the word size of the processor.

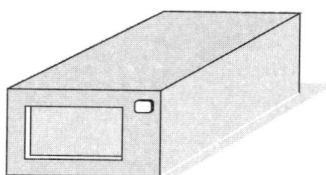
WORM disk

CD ROM

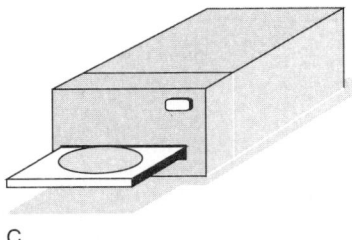
Erasable optical disk

Figure 1–10
Optical storage devices for microcomputers. A. Disks and disk drive (courtesy of NEC). B. Close-up of CD-ROM disk (courtesy of Radio Shack, a division of Tandy Corp.). C. Erasable optical disk.

Word size indicates the number of characters that can be processed simultaneously. Word size varies from 8 to 32 bits for microcomputers. The bigger the word size, the faster the computer. The speed of your microcomputer may have a direct impact on your business operation. With a faster computer, you can process more information in a shorter period of time. However, always consider the additional cost incurred by buying the more powerful PC and the marginal benefit to be gained.

1-9 GENERAL CAPABILITIES OF MICROCOMPUTER SOFTWARE

A microcomputer can perform a variety of tasks by using either commercial software or software developed in-house. In-house software is usually more expensive than commercial software; however, because it is customized, it should better fit users' needs. Several thousands of software packages are available for PCs. For any task that can apply to several users, there is a software package on the market. Typical commercial packages and applications available for microcomputers are discussed next.

1-9-1 Word Processing Software

A microcomputer that functions as a word processor is similar to a typewriter with a memory. With such a facility, you can generate documents, make deletions and insertions, and "cut and paste." **Word processing software** can save hundreds of hours of working time. Think of an organization that wants to send the same letter to many of its customers. The only difference in the letters is the name and address of the customer. A word processing program allows the main part of the letter to be typed just once. Only the customer's name and address need to be changed for each new letter.

Numerous word processing programs are on the market. And they are getting more sophisticated: some of them provide limited graphics and data management features. Some of the popular ones are WordPerfect (WordPerfect Corp.), Word (Microsoft Corp.), AmiPro (Lotus Development Corp.), Wordstar (MicroPro International Corp.), and PC-write (Quicksoft).

1-9-2 Grammar Checker Software

The ever-increasing speed and memory of microcomputers are promoting a new brand of software. **Grammar checker software** allows users to correct a document grammatically. Most word processing software now includes spelling checkers, which can correct most of the typos in a document. The next challenge is the creation of documents that are characterized by correct verbs, subjects, adjectives, and a smooth writing style. Also, creation of simple and easy-to-read sentences is often important.

Grammar checkers evaluate text through linguistic analysis, parsing, and rule matching. Parsing is simply breaking long sentences into shorter ones. The more sophisticated software includes more sophisticated parsers. Grammar checkers can play a specially important role when multiple authors are involved in a project. In such cases, the software can create uniformity of tone, level, style, and usage. This type of software is not 100 percent perfect yet, but it has come a long way. Among the more popular programs are Grammatik Windows and

Grammatik IV (Reference Software International), PowerEdit (Artificial Linguistics, Inc.), and Correct Grammar for DOS (Writing Tools Group, Inc.).

1-9-3 Spreadsheet Software

A spreadsheet is a table of rows and columns. **Spreadsheet software** can be broadly classified into two types. The first type is a dedicated spreadsheet, which means that the program performs *only* spreadsheet analysis. (VisiCalc was a good example.) The other type of spreadsheet package is integrated software, which means it can perform more than one type of analysis. Lotus 1-2-3, for example, is capable of performing spreadsheet analysis as well as database and graphics tasks. Some experts do not consider Lotus 1-2-3 a truly integrated package because it does not offer word processing and communications. Although this criticism is true, Lotus 1-2-3 can easily incorporate these features from other software. Other popular integrated packages include Electronic Desk (Software Group, Inc.), Framework (Ashton-Tate), Smart Software System (Innovative Software, Inc.), Symphony (Lotus Development Corp.), UniCalc (Lattice, Inc.), Excel (Microsoft Corp.), SuperCalc 5.0 (Computer Associates International, Inc.), and Quattro Pro (Borland International).

The number of jobs that can be performed by a spreadsheet program is unlimited. Generally speaking, any application suitable for a row-and-column analysis is a candidate for a typical spreadsheet. Say you use a spreadsheet to prepare a budget. As soon as you have completed the budget, you can perform some impressive what-if analyses. This means you can manipulate variables on the spreadsheet. For example, reduce your income by 2 percent and ask the spreadsheet to calculate the effect of this change on other items in your budget.

1-9-4 Database Software

Database software is designed to perform operations such as file creation, deletion, modification, search, sort, merge, and join (combining two files based on a common key). A file is a collection of a series of records. A record is a collection of a series of fields. A field is a collection of a series of characters. Popular database programs include Business Filevision (Telos Software Products), dBASE III Plus and IV (Ashton-Tate), PC-File III (Buttonware, Inc.), Q&A (Symantec), Paradox (Borland International), Omnis Quartz (Blyth Software), DataEase (DataEase International), FoxBase (Fox Software), and R:BASE (Microrim Corp.).

A database can also be compared to a table of rows and columns. The rows correspond to the occurrence of a record. The columns correspond to the fields within the record. Two common applications for a database program are sorting and searching records. In sort operations, the user enters a series of records in any order then asks the database management program to sort the records in ascending or descending order based on the data in the fields. Search operations are even more interesting. You can search for data items that meet certain criteria, for example, all the computer students who have grade-point averages greater than 3.60 and are under 20 years of age. Some databases (such as Q&A) allow you to search for key words within a text file.

1-9-5 Graphics Software

Graphics software is designed to present data in graphic format. Data can be converted into a line graph to show a trend, into a pie chart to highlight the

Chapter 1 The World of Microcomputers 15

components of a data item, and into other types of graphs for different analyses. Masses of data can be converted to one graph and, in a glance, the user can discover the general pattern of the data. Graphs can easily highlight patterns and correlations of data items. They also make data presentation a more manageable job. Graphics can be done with integrated packages, such as Lotus 1-2-3 or Symphony, or with dedicated graphics packages. Five of the most popular packages are Aldus Persuasion (Aldus Corp.), Hollywood Graphics (IBM Corp.), Harvard Graphics (Software Publishing Corp.), Freelance (Lotus Development Corp.), and Power Point (Microsoft Corp.).

Communications Software　　　　　　　　　　　　　　　　　　1-9-6

If you have a modem and **communications software,** your microcomputer can easily connect you to a wealth of information available in public and private databases. In business, several managers can simultaneously work on the same report in different states or countries by using communications software. The report is sent back and forth to each location until it is completed. Communications software and a modem make data entry from remote locations an easy task. A modem converts computer signals (digital signals) to signals transferrable on a telephone line (analog signals). Some packages, such as Symphony, include a communications program within the package itself. Among the many communications software products on the market are Crosstalk (Microstuf, Inc.), On-Line (Micro-Systems Software, Inc.), Pfs: Access (Software Publishing Corp.), and Smartcom II (Hayes Microcomputer Products, Inc.).

Desktop Publishing Software　　　　　　　　　　　　　　　　　1-9-7

Desktop publishing allows production of professional-quality documents (with or without graphics) using relatively inexpensive hardware and software. All that is needed is a PC, a desktop publishing software package, and a laser or letter-quality printer. Desktop publishing has evolved as a result of three major factors: inexpensive PCs, inexpensive laser printers, and sophisticated and easy-to-use software.

　　Desktop publishing enables a user to produce high-quality screen output, then transfer it to the printer—"what you see is what you get" (WYSIWYG). The major application for desktop publishing is creating newsletters, brochures, training manuals, transparencies, posters, and books. See Figure 1–11.

　　There are several desktop publishing software packages available on the market. Pagemaker (Aldus Corp.) and Ventura Publisher (Xerox Corp.) are two popular ones.

Financial Planning Software　　　　　　　　　　　　　　　　　1-9-8

Financial planning software works with large amounts of data and performs diverse financial analyses. These analyses include present value, future value, rate of return, cash flow, depreciation, and budgeting. Several packages for financial planning on the market: DTFPS (Desk Top Financial Solutions, Inc.), Excel (Microsoft Corp.), Finar (Finar Research Systems, Ltd.), Javelin (Javelin Software Corp.), Micro-DSS/Finance (Addison-Wesley Publishing Co.), Lotus 1-2-3 (Lotus Development Corp.), Quattro Pro (Borland International), IFPS (Execucom Systems), and Micro Plan (Chase Laboratories, Inc.).

　　Use such packages to plan and analyze your financial situation. For example, you can learn how much your $2,000 IRA is worth at 10 percent

Figure 1-11
A. Desktop publishing combines text, graphics and illustrations (courtesy of Aldus). B. With desktop publishing, business professionals can prepare high-quality documents on their own (courtesy of Ashton-Tate Corp.).

A.

B.

interest in 30 years, or you can discount all future cash flows into today's dollar. You can learn how much you have to deposit in the bank to save $60,000 in 10 years for your child's education.

1-9-9 Accounting Software

In addition to spreadsheet software, which has widespread applications in the accounting field, there is dedicated **accounting software.** The tasks performed by this software include general ledgers, account receivables, account payables, payrolls, balance sheets, and income statements. Depending on the price, these software packages vary in sophistication. Some of the popular accounting software packages are On-write Plus 2 (Great American Software), Business Works PC (Manzanita Software Systems), 4-in-1 Basic Accounting (Real World Corp.), Peachtree (Peachtree Software, Inc.), and DacEasy (Accounting by Dac Software, Inc.).

Project Management Software   1-9-10

A project consists of a series of related activities. Building a house, designing an order entry system, and writing a thesis are examples of projects. The goal of **project management software** is to help decision makers keep the time and budget of projects under control by resolving scheduling problems. Project management software helps managers to plan and set achievable goals. It highlights bottlenecks and the relationships among different activities. It allows the user to study the cost, time, and resource impact of any change in the schedule. Several project management products are in the market: Harvard Total Project Manager (Software Publishing Corp.), Micro Planner 6 (Micro Planning International), Microsoft Project (Microsoft Corp.), Superproject Expert (Computer Associates), and Time Line (Symantec).

Computer-Aided Design Software   1-9-11

Computer-aided design (CAD) software is used for drafting and designing. It has replaced traditional tools such as the T-square, triangle, paper, and pencil. It is being used extensively in the architectural and engineering industries (see Figure 1–12). CAD software no longer belongs only to the large corporations. Because of the 386- and 486-based PCs and significant price reduction, small companies and individuals can afford this software. These new PCs have a larger memory and are significantly faster than the earlier PCs. With their enhanced power and sophistication, they are able to take advantage of the majority of features offered by CAD programs. There are several CAD programs on the market: AutoCAD (Autodesk), Cadkey (Cadkey), and VersaCAD (VersaCAD).

Other Popular Software for Microcomputers   1-9-12

In addition to the aforementioned 11 groups of software, there is yet more software commonly used with microcomputers. Let us briefly introduce these programs.

UTILITY SOFTWARE. These programs, or utilities, provide various disk operating system operations. Their goal is to simplify DOS operations for PC users. Depending on the sophistication of the program, tasks vary from hard disk management to recovering a damaged disk or file to menu design to condensing a hard disk, and so forth.

TERMINATE AND STAY RESIDENT (TSR) SOFTWARE. These programs are loaded when the PC is started and stay in the background while other software applications are being used. The programs offer features such as screen printing, calendar, memo pad, and online calculator.

INVESTMENT ANALYSIS SOFTWARE. In addition to spreadsheet programs, several other types of software are designed for investment analysis. They allow the user to track stocks, bonds, and other investment portfolios. Some of the programs are able to download financial data from public databases

A.

B.

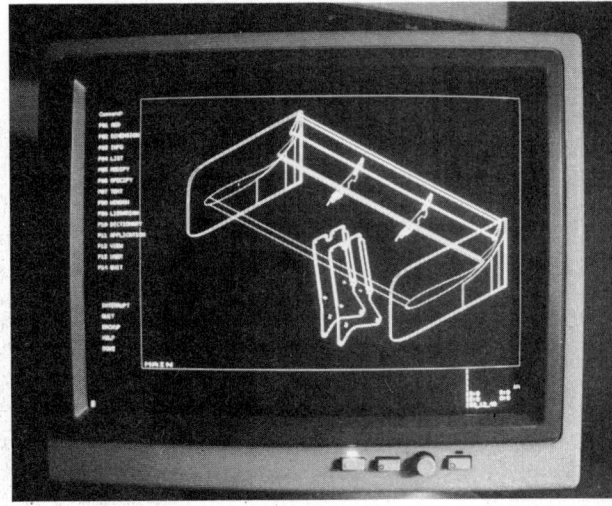

C.

Figure 1-12
A. CAD system for detailed architectural design (Larry Hamill/Macmillan). B. CAD system for design of a multicomponent product (courtesy of International Business Machines Corp.). C. CAD-supported design of aircraft landing gear (courtesy of International Business Machines Corp.).

or stock exchanges. Others allow the user to input his or her own financial data, then perform the financial analysis.

TAX PREPARATION SOFTWARE. This software assists PC users in preparing their taxes in a fairly straightforward manner. Some of the programs enable users to electronically download a prepared tax statement to an IRS office.

GAMES SOFTWARE. Games are probably the oldest type of software for microcomputers, and they include a broad range. Although they are losing popularity, they are still played by many PC users.

1-10 GUIDELINES FOR SUCCESSFUL SELECTION OF A MICROCOMPUTER

Because of the many microcomputers on the market, making a selection is a difficult task. The general guidelines regarding the purchase and maintenance of a microcomputer provided here may help you choose a suitable computer and maintain it more easily.

Before you start the selection process, define your requirements. Sometimes this is called the "wish list" approach. You should have a clear idea of the microcomputer that you need and the specific applications you want it to handle.

After you have defined your needs, think about software. Remember, if commercial software is available, there must be hardware to run it. In contrast, hardware may be available without the ability to run the software you need. After defining your software and hardware needs, look at technical support and vendor reputation.

Important factors regarding selection and maintenance of a microcomputer are summarized next.

Software Selection
Good software should

- Be easy to use
- Be able to handle your business volume
- Have good documentation
- Have training available
- Have updates available (free of charge or for a minimum charge)
- Have local support
- Come from a reputable vendor
- Have a low cost

Hardware Selection (Processor and Keyboard)
Good hardware should

- Have a comfortable keyboard
- Have function keys
- Have a general operating system (e.g., OS/2, MS-DOS, PC-DOS, Windows, or UNIX)
- Have 16-bit or bigger processor (word) size
- Have a high speed
- Be expandable (memory and peripheral)
- Have enough channel capacity or expansion slots (for peripherals to be attached to)
- Have a low cost

Hardware Selection (CRT)
A good monitor should

- Have a separate CRT (not a built-in one)
- Be easy to read (high resolution, super VGA or higher)
- Have a standard number of characters per row and column

Hardware Selection (Disk Drive and Hard Disk)
A good disk drive should

- Have a built-in, not separate, disk drive
- Have adequate storage capacity (to load and run popular software)
- Have a hard disk option

Hardware Selection (Printer)
A good printer should

- Have a standard printer interface (without additional devices)
- Produce quality output
- Have high speed
- Have a reasonable amount of noise suppression
- Let you change tape, ribbons, or toner cartridge easily
- Have a low cost

Vendor Selection
A good vendor should

- Have a good reputation
- Have a knowledgeable staff
- Have training available for hardware and software
- Have a hot line available
- Support newsletters and user groups
- Provide a "loaner" in case of breakdown
- Provide updates (e.g., trade-in options)

Maintenance Contract Selection
A good contract should

- Have a warranty period
- State a flexible time for repair
- Limit downtime and inconvenience by providing flexible repair visits and timely repair of the computer
- Have reasonable terms for contract renewal
- Allow relocation and/or reassignment of the present contract
- Observe confidentiality issues

1-11 TAKING CARE OF YOUR MICROCOMPUTER

To maintain the health of your microcomputer, consider the following factors:

- Protect your microcomputer against dirt, dust, and smoke.
- Make backups for security reasons and keep backups in different locations.
- Avoid any kind of liquid spills.
- Maintain steady power. Use surge protectors for power fluctuations and use lightning arresters in mountainous areas.
- Protect the machine from static by using humidifiers or antistatic spray devices.
- Do not start your computer with a disk that you are not familiar with. (Avoid computer virus—a deadly program that erases and/or corrupts all your data.)
- Do not download information to your computer from unknown bulletin boards. Downloading means importing information from other computers through a telephone line.
- Acquire insurance for your computer equipment.

1-12 ADVANTAGES OF MICROCOMPUTERS COMPARED WITH MAINFRAMES

Generally speaking, microcomputers offer several advantages compared with the larger mainframe computers. Because of extended memory and increased speed, microcomputers can perform many of the tasks performed by a mainframe on a smaller scale. The advantages of microcomputers compared with mainframes are listed next.

- They are easier to use.
- They are less threatening to those who are not computer experts. (They are smaller.)
- They allow the user more control.
- They are relatively inexpensive.
- They can be portable.

1-13 YOU AND YOUR PC: A HANDS-ON SESSION

If DOS is in drive A, when you turn the computer on your microcomputer will ask for the date. Remember, any IBM or IBM compatible comes with a DOS disk. Either type the date in the desired format or press the Enter key. The computer then asks you for the time. Either type the time in the desired format or press the Enter key. Now you are at the A> prompt. If your computer has a hard disk, this procedure is slightly different. You will get the system started from the hard disk and your prompt will be C> instead of A>. This is used in this text. Our DOS disks are stored in drive C. See Figure 1–13. In any case, from this mode, the disk operating system mode, you can go to any application software. For example, put the Lotus system diskette into drive A and type 123 and press the Enter key. This will load Lotus 1-2-3 into RAM. From DOS you can access any other application software.

When you are at the C> prompt, you are in RAM. We call this area a working, or temporary, area. This means any work done in this area will disappear if you turn the computer off. To make your work permanent, you have to transfer it to a **permanent area.** The permanent area can be a floppy diskette, hard disk, or cassette. Your work stays in the permanent area until you erase it.

While you are the C> prompt, you can send any data to RAM by using the keyboard. This data can become permanent by saving it into a permanent medium. Remember, any application program includes a command for saving your work.

Beginning computer users are always worried about making mistakes! What happens if you make a mistake? Don't panic. Your mistake can be easily corrected. Some computers and application programs have an "UNDO" command. This means that if you make a mistake, you can always change your mind and recover from the mistake by using the UNDO feature. Any application

```
C>
```

Figure 1–13
Getting the system started

program includes a feature for correcting mistakes. In the worst case, you can retype the correct statement by typing over your previous material. Remember, any address or cell in the computer memory can hold only one value at a time. As soon as you type a new value, the old one disappears.

1-14
WHAT IS A COMPUTER FILE?

A **computer file** is basically an electronic document. One way to create a document is to enter it using the keyboard. As soon as you save the document, you have generated a computer file.

To differentiate one file from another, you must save each file under a unique name—a file name. A file name is any combination of up to eight valid characters. Valid characters include letters of the alphabet (uppercase or lowercase), digits 0 through 9, underscore, and some special characters. If you provide a name longer than eight characters, some application programs give you an error message and others truncate the name and accept only the first eight characters. In addition to a file name, a file is usually saved with a file extension as well. A file extension uses the same type of characters as a file name, but up to three. Some application programs automatically provide a file extension as soon as you save the file. In other application programs, providing a file extension is the user's responsibility.

Several characters have special meanings in different application software. The asterisk (*) can represent any number of characters up to eight. The question mark (?) can represent any single character. These two characters are called **wildcard** characters, and they can significantly improve your efficiency while working with application programs. For example, all your Lotus graphic files are identified by *.PIC. The * represents any file name and the PIC indicates that your file is a Lotus graphic file. In DOS, if you want to COPY all your Lotus graphic files from the disk in drive A to the disk in drive B, the command is COPY *.PIC B: (followed by pressing the Enter key). If you do not have this feature, the COPY command must be repeated as many times as the number of the graphic files. The file BRANCH?.* represents BRANCH1, BRANCH2, and so on. For example, in DOS if you type DIR *.WK?, your Lotus files from version 1 and 1A (WKS) files, version 2 (WK1) files, version 3 (WK3) files, and student version (WKE) files will be displayed. The * as the file extension indicates that the file can have any extension. Your entire disk can be identified by *.*. For example, in DOS to copy the entire disk in drive A to drive B the command is Copy *.* B: (press Enter).

1-15
TYPES OF DATA

Any application program or computer language accepts different types of data. There are several commonly used data types. **Numeric data** includes any combination of the digits 0 through 9 and decimal points. Numeric data can be integer or real. Integer data includes only whole numbers without any decimal points. For example, 656 or 986. Real data includes digits and decimal points. For example, 696.25 or 729.93. Real data is sometimes called floating-point data. Floating point means that the decimal point can move from right to left. For example, 222.2, 22.22, 2.222. Another type of real data is fixed-point data, meaning that the decimal point is always fixed.

Nonnumeric data, or alphanumeric data (sometimes called labels), includes any types of valid characters. For example, Jackson or 123 Broadway Street. Remember, you cannot perform any arithmetic operations with nonnumeric data or labels.

1-16 TYPES OF VALUES

Computers usually handle two types of values: variables and constants. **Variables** are valid computer addresses (locations) that hold different values in different times. For example, in A = 65, A is the variable and 65 is the **constant.** In B = Brown, B is the variable and Brown is the constant. A variable holds a given value at any given time. As soon as you enter a new value into this variable, the old value disappears. The constant is always fixed. See Figure 1-14.

1-17 TYPES OF FORMULAS

Computers handle two types of formulas or functions: user defined and built-in.

User-defined formulas or functions are a combination of computer addresses designed to perform a certain task. For example, the area of a triangle can be presented as A = B*H/2, that is, base multiplied by height divided by 2. In this case, A is a formula or a function. When you enter different values for B and H a different value for A, the area of the triangle, will be calculated.

Built-in formulas or functions are already available within the application program or the computer language. As soon as the user provides values for a given variable or variables, the application program or the computer language dynamically calculates these formulas. For example, SQRT(X) is a function that calculates the square root of a variable, X. The X, or any other information needed by these functions, is called an argument(s). As soon as you provide a value for X, the square root is immediately calculated. For example, SQRT(25) is equal to 5. Function FV(payment,interest rate,term) calculates the future value of a series of equal payments with a given interest rate over a period of time (term).

1-18 PRIORITY (PRECEDENCE) OF OPERATIONS

When application programs perform arithmetic operations, they follow a series of rules. These priority rules, called **priority of operations,** are as follows:

1. Expressions inside parentheses have the highest priority.
2. Exponentiation (raising to power) has the next highest priority.

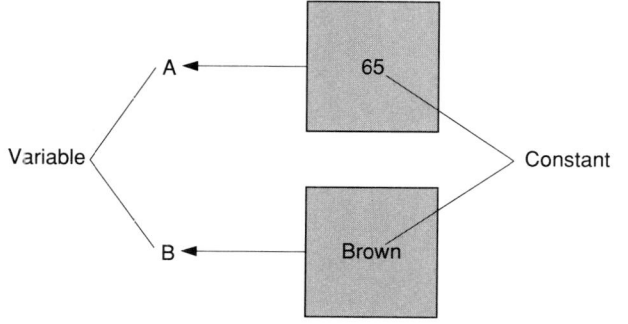

Figure 1-14
Example of a variable and a constant

3. Multiplication and division have the third highest priority.
4. Addition and subtraction have the fourth highest priority.
5. When there are two or more operations with the same priority, operations proceed from left to right.

The following examples should make these rules clear. First, an application program uses * (asterisk) for multiplication, ^ (caret) for exponentiation (raising the power), and / (slash) for division. If A = 5, B = 10, C = 2, calculate the following:

1. A + B/C = 10
2. (A + B)/C = 7.5
3. A*B/C = 25
4. (A*B)/C = 25
5. A^C/2 = 12.50

SUMMARY

In this chapter we focused on microcomputers. Input, output, primary memory, and secondary memory devices for micros were explained. The general capabilities of micros were introduced and their advantages compared with mainframes were described. To help you actually choose a microcomputer, guidelines for successful selection and maintenance were presented. To help you use your microcomputer, an introductory hands-on session was outlined. The chapter concluded with explanations of computer files, types of data, types of values, types of formulas, and priority of operations.

REVIEW QUESTIONS

*These questions are answered in Appendix A.

1. What is a microcomputer? What should a computer have to be called a micro?
*2. What are some typical input devices for a micro?
3. What are some typical output devices for a micro?
4. What is the difference between a primary memory device and a secondary memory device?
5. What is RAM? ROM? PROM? EPROM?
*6. What are the most commonly used secondary memory devices for a micro?
7. What are optical technologies? What are their advantages? Disadvantages?
8. How do you measure the memory capacity of a micro?
9. Besides memory, what other attributes are important when you buy a micro?
10. What is the difference between a floppy and a hard disk?
11. What is the speed range for a typical microcomputer?
*12. What is the memory size of a typical micro?
13. What is a good software?
14. What is a good hardware?
15. What is a good contract? Who are the good vendors?
*16. How do you care for your micro?
17. What are some application programs for a micro?
18. What are some of the advantages of a micro compared with a mainframe computer?
19. What is permanent memory in a PC? What is temporary memory?

Chapter 1 The World of Microcomputers 25

20. How do you send information from RAM to a floppy or hard disk?
*21. How do you correct your mistakes?
22. What is a computer file?
23. What is a wildcard character?
24. What are different types of data?
25. What is a variable? A constant?
*26. What does priority of operations mean?
27. What symbols are used for arithmetic operation?
28. Turn on a PC. What do you see? Turn it off.
29. At the C> prompt, type DATE and press the Enter key. Insert the correct date. What happens if you make a mistake?
30. Type DIR and press the Enter key. What is displayed at this time?
31. How many generations of micros have we seen? What are the most powerful PCs on the market?
32. What type of PCs do you have on your campus? Describe different input/output devices used by the PCs in your school micro lab. Do you have Bernoulli box in the lab? What are some of the advantages of Bernoulli box over a hard disk?
33. What are the most commonly used disks on your campus—$3\frac{1}{2}$ or $5\frac{1}{4}$? Compare and contrast these two types of storage devices.
34. Consult computer magazines to find out which computers are currently using optical disks.
35. Of the 12 application software packages introduced in this chapter, which are available on your campus? What are the applications of each?
36. If you want to buy a PC for your personal use, how do you start shopping? What attribute(s) makes a PC attractive?

KEY TERMS

Accounting software
Built-in function or formula
CD ROM
Communications software
Computer-aided design (CAD) software
Computer file
Constant
Database software
Desktop publishing
EPROM
Erasable optical disk
Expanded memory
Extended memory
Financial planning software
Floppy diskette
Grammar checker software
Graphics software
Hard disk
Main memory
Nonnumeric data (label)
Numeric data
Permanent area
Primary memory
Priority of operations
Project management software
PROM
RAM
ROM
Secondary memory
Spreadsheet software
User-defined formula or function
Variable
Wildcard
Word processing software
WORM disk

ARE YOU READY TO MOVE ON?

Multiple Choice

1. Choose the correct ranking of monitor display resolutions from lowest to highest:
   a. VGA, CGA, EGA
   b. EGA, VGA, CGA

c. EGA, CGA, VGA

d. CGA, EGA, VGA

e. XGA, CGA, EGA

2. Which of the following is *not* a typical adapter card?

   a. printer interface card

   b. clock card

   c. disk drive card

   d. display card

   e. punch card

3. Of the various types of main memory, the user has direct control over

   a. ROM

   b. EPROM

   c. RAM

   d. PROM

   e. all of the above

4. At the present time, the most commonly used secondary storage device is the

   a. $5\frac{1}{4}$-inch floppy diskette and a hard disk

   b. $3\frac{1}{2}$-inch floppy diskette and a hard disk

   c. Bernoulli box and a hard disk

   d. hard disk with no floppy diskette

   e. none of the above

5. The major advantage(s) of optical storage technology is (are)

   a. storage capacity

   b. cost

   c. durability

   d. both a and c

   e. all of the above

6. When we refer to memory and storage capacity sizes, we use K (as in 360 K). 1 K equals approximately

   a. 1 byte

   b. 1,000 bytes

   c. 1,000,000 bytes

   d. 1,048,576 bytes

   e. none of the above

7. Word size directly affects

   a. the speed of the computer

   b. the ability of the user to understand what is being said

   c. the maximum amount of data that can be displayed on the CRT

   d. the choice of which type of disk drive to use

   e. the meaning of the function keys on the keyboard

8. Which of the following are disadvantages of mainframes when compared with microcomputers?

   a. They are more difficult to use.

   b. They are more threatening to non-computer users.

   c. The user has less control.

   d. They are relatively more expensive.

   e. all of the above

Chapter 1 The World of Microcomputers

9. After "booting" the computer with the DOS disk (loading DOS and entering the date and time), you are at
   a. the Lotus access menu
   b. the DOS prompt (A> or C>)
   c. the parallel/serial interface
   d. the BASIC prompt
   e. none of the above
10. An example of alphanumeric data is
    a. 123
    b. 123.
    c. LOTUS-123
    d. A = (123-2)/4
    e. none of the above

True/False

1. The terms *personal computer, PC,* and *microcomputer* refer to different types of computers.
2. A typical microcomputer consists of input, output, and memory devices.
3. Monochrome CRTs cannot generate graphic output.
4. The purpose of function keys and special keys on a computer keyboard does not vary in different application programs.
5. The capacity of a hard disk is greater than the capacity of a floppy diskette.
6. A WORM drive can be recorded and erased repeatedly when high-volume storage and updating are essential.
7. Typical microcomputer software packages and applications include spreadsheet, database, graphics, communications, and word processing.
8. The first step in selecting a microcomputer is to define your needs, then think about software.
9. The commands DIR *.* and DIR ????????.??? produce the same results.
10. Expressions inside parentheses have the lowest priority when it comes to performing arithmetic operations.

Multiple Choice	True/False	ANSWERS
1. d	1. F	
2. e	2. T	
3. c	3. F	
4. b	4. F	
5. d	5. T	
6. b	6. F	
7. a	7. T	
8. e	8. T	
9. b	9. T	
10. c	10. F	

You and Your PC:
The First Official Meeting

2-1 Introduction
2-2 Turning On Your PC
2-3 DOS Prompts
2-4 DOS File Specifications
2-5 The DIR Command
2-6 Using DIR with Switches
2-7 Important Keys in the DOS Environment
2-8 The FORMAT Command
2-9 Different Versions of MS-DOS and PC-DOS

2-1
INTRODUCTION

In this chapter we consider the basics of the disk operating system (DOS) and define the differences between internal and external DOS commands. The system date and time are explained, and file specifications in the DOS environment are described. Important keys in the DOS environment, and the DIR and FORMAT commands, are highlighted. The chapter concludes with a review of different versions of MS-DOS and PC-DOS.

2-2
TURNING ON YOUR PC

All the commands introduced in this book work on all versions of MS-DOS and PC-DOS, unless specified otherwise. For purposes of simplicity, DOS 5.0 is used for all screens throughout Chapters 2 through 4.

When you access a personal computer, the computer is either off or on. If the computer is off, put the **disk operating system** (DOS) disk in drive A and turn on the computer. This procedure is called a **cold boot** (boot means getting the computer started). If the computer is already turned on, insert the DOS disk in drive A and press the Ctrl, Alt, and Del keys simultaneously (Ctrl-Alt-Del). This procedure is called a **warm boot**. A warm boot is faster than a cold boot because the computer does not check its memory when you do a warm boot.

In some cases DOS is already installed in the C drive (the **hard disk** drive) when you use the computer, and this is the situation assumed in the examples in this book. If DOS is installed in the C drive, when you press Ctrl-Alt-Del you will see the C prompt (C>).

When the computer is booted, it asks you to enter the current date. Enter the date in the format requested (mm-dd-yy) and press Enter. Your PC next asks for the current time. Enter the current time in the format requested (hh:mm:ss) and press Enter. (Note that DOS operates on a 24-hour clock, 2:30 p.m. is 14:30, 9:15 p.m. is 21:15, and so on.) Some computers have an internal clock and you do not need to enter the date and time—the computer keeps track automatically. This is the case in the examples in this book.

Now you should see the C> **DOS prompt,** which indicates that the necessary portions of DOS have been loaded into primary memory (RAM) and drive C is the default drive. The default drive is the disk drive that the PC will access if no other disk drive is specified. This is the drive the computer accesses for executing commands. For example, if you try to save a file, your file will be saved to this drive. If you ask for a directory listing, the directory of this drive will be highlighted. At this point, you should be able to access any internal or external DOS commands.

At boot-up time, if you do not want to enter date and time, you can bypass the prompts by pressing Enter twice. It is a good practice to enter both correct date and time when you start the PC. Your PC uses both the **system date** and **system time** when saving your files. The correct date and time will help you to determine the most or least recent versions of the files in the directory. A directory is a listing of all your files.

If you forget to enter the current date and time at boot-up, or if you decide to change date and time, you can enter this information any time by using the DATE and TIME commands. At the C> prompt type either DATE or TIME and press Enter to enter the information. The computer registers this information in its memory where it will be updated automatically until you turn off the PC.

Internal commands (sometimes called memory-resident commands) are those commands that are loaded into the computer memory at boot-up. Internal commands can be used without the DOS disk in any disk drive. CLS (clear screen) is an example of an internal DOS command. If you type CLS and press Enter, the screen will be cleared (erased).

External commands (sometimes called nonmemory-resident commands) are those commands that can be executed only when the DOS disk is in one of the drives. These commands, which are sometimes called DOS utilities, are separate programs stored on the DOS disk. For example, DISKCOPY is an external DOS command. We will talk about these commands in detail in the next chapter.

2-3 DOS PROMPTS

Depending on how you get your PC started, you may see different prompts. If you have a hard disk in your system and you start the system from the hard disk, your prompt may be C>. The prompt indicates the current default drive. If a file is located on a disk that is not in the default drive, the default must be changed or the disk drive containing the file must be specified. Changing the default is an easy task. At the C> prompt type *A:* (remember the colon) and press Enter. Now the prompt is A>, which indicates that drive A is the default. You can change the default drive back to C> by typing *C:* and pressing Enter.

2-4 DOS FILE SPECIFICATIONS

DOS files follow the same conventions discussed in Chapter 1: File names can be up to eight characters long. File names can contain digits 0 through 9 and some special characters such as underscore (__) and the pound sign (#). File extensions can be up to three characters long and contain the same characters used in file names. Important extensions in **DOS file specifications** include the following:

- BAK (Backup). **Backup files** are generated by some word processing, spreadsheet, and database management programs. These files are backup copies of the original files.
- BAT (Batch). **Batch files** are text files generated by the user. This type of file contains DOS commands and statements that are executed when the name of the file is typed.
- COM (Command). This extension identifies **command files,** which can be executed by typing the name of the file.
- EXE (Executable). Like COM files, **executable files** can be executed by typing the file name.
- SYS (System). This extension identifies **system files,** which can be used only by DOS.

2-5 THE DIR COMMAND

With the DOS disk in drive C, you can generate a listing of your current directory by using the DIR command. If you type *DIR* and press Enter, information similar to that in Figure 2–1 is presented. At the top of Figure 2–1, the listing indicates that the volume in drive C is MS_DOS_5. This is the internal name for this disk.

Figure 2-1
Directory listing of DOS 5.0

```
C>DIR

 Volume in drive C is MS-DOS_5
 Volume Serial Number is 18C6-6309
 Directory of C:\DOS

.            <DIR>      06-06-92  12:24p
..           <DIR>      06-06-92  12:24p
COUNTRY  SYS     17069  06-13-91   5:00a
EGA      SYS      4885  06-13-91   5:00a
FORMAT   COM     32911  06-13-91   5:00a
KEYB     COM     14986  06-13-91   5:00a
KEYBOARD SYS     34697  06-13-91   5:00a
NLSFUNC  EXE      7052  06-13-91   5:00a
DISPLAY  SYS     15792  06-13-91   5:00a
EGA      CPI     58873  06-13-91   5:00a
HIMEM    SYS     11552  06-13-91   5:00a
MODE     COM     23537  06-13-91   5:00a
SETVER   EXE     12007  06-13-91   5:00a
ANSI     SYS      9029  06-13-91   5:00a
DEBUG    EXE     20634  06-13-91   5:00a
EDLIN    EXE     12642  06-13-91   5:00a
EMM386   EXE     91742  06-13-91   5:00a
FASTOPEN EXE     12050  06-13-91   5:00a
FDISK    EXE     57224  06-13-91   5:00a
MEM      EXE     39818  06-13-91   5:00a
MIRROR   COM     18169  06-13-91   5:00a
RAMDRIVE SYS      5873  06-13-91   5:00a
SHARE    EXE     10912  06-13-91   5:00a
SMARTDRV SYS      8335  06-13-91   5:00a
SYS      COM     13440  06-13-91   5:00a
UNDELETE EXE     13924  06-13-91   5:00a
UNFORMAT COM     18576  06-13-91   5:00a
XCOPY    EXE     15804  06-13-91   5:00a
DOSKEY   COM      5883  06-13-91   5:00a
DOSSHELL VID      9462  06-13-91   5:00a
DOSSHELL INI     12231  06-13-91   5:00a
DOSSHELL COM      4623  06-13-91   5:00a
DOSSHELL EXE    235484  06-13-91   5:00a
DOSSHELL GRB      4421  06-13-91   5:00a
DOSSWAP  EXE     18756  06-13-91   5:00a
PACKING  LST      2507  06-13-91   5:00a
PRINT    EXE     15656  06-13-91   5:00a
DOSSHELL HLP    161763  06-13-91   5:00a
EDIT     HLP     17898  06-13-91   5:00a
RECOVER  EXE      9146  06-13-91   5:00a
DOSHELP  HLP      5651  06-13-91   5:00a
HELP     EXE     11473  06-13-91   5:00a
QBASIC   HLP    130810  06-13-91   5:00a
```

The DIR command displays the name and extension of each file, the size of the file in bytes, and the date and time that the file was created. At the end of the listing, the DIR command tells you the number of files and the amount of bytes available on this particular disk. To erase the screen, type *CLS* and press Enter.

The DIR command can be used with wildcard characters. Wildcard characters function as place holders for other characters in the file name or file extension. The two valid wildcards used by DOS are * and ?. The * takes the place of one or more characters in the file name or extension. For example, *.COM refers to any file name with the extension COM. The ? takes the place of only one character in the file name or extension.

```
EDIT     COM        413  06-13-91   5:00a
MONEY    BAS      46225  06-13-91   5:00a
MSHERC   COM       6934  06-13-91   5:00a
QBASIC   EXE     254799  06-13-91   5:00a
GORILLA  BAS      29434  06-13-91   5:00a
4201     CPI       6404  06-13-91   5:00a
4208     CPI        720  06-13-91   5:00a
5202     CPI        395  06-13-91   5:00a
APPEND   EXE      10774  06-13-91   5:00a
ASSIGN   COM       6399  06-13-91   5:00a
ATTRIB   EXE      15796  06-13-91   5:00a
BACKUP   EXE      36092  06-13-91   5:00a
COMP     EXE      14282  06-13-91   5:00a
DISKCOMP COM      10652  06-13-91   5:00a
DISKCOPY COM      11793  06-13-91   5:00a
DRIVER   SYS       5649  06-13-91   5:00a
FC       EXE      18650  06-13-91   5:00a
FIND     EXE       6770  06-13-91   5:00a
GRAFTABL COM      11205  06-13-91   5:00a
GRAPHICS COM      19694  06-13-91   5:00a
GRAPHICS PRO      21232  06-13-91   5:00a
LABEL    EXE       9390  06-13-91   5:00a
MORE     COM       2618  06-13-91   5:00a
NIBBLES  BAS      24103  06-13-91   5:00a
REMLINE  BAS      12314  06-13-91   5:00a
RESTORE  EXE      38294  06-13-91   5:00a
SORT     EXE       6938  06-13-91   5:00a
EXE2BIN  EXE       8424  06-13-91   5:00a
EXPAND   EXE      14563  06-13-91   5:00a
JOIN     EXE      17870  06-13-91   5:00a
LCD      CPI      10753  06-13-91   5:00a
LOADFIX  COM       1131  06-13-91   5:00a
PRINTER  SYS      18804  06-13-91   5:00a
REPLACE  EXE      20226  06-13-91   5:00a
SUBST    EXE      18478  06-13-91   5:00a
TREE     COM       6901  06-13-91   5:00a
README   TXT      23692  06-13-91   5:00a
APPNOTES TXT       8660  06-13-91   5:00a
KEYBHP   COM      15997  06-13-91   5:00a
MODEHP   COM      23232  06-13-91   5:00a
SSTOR    SYS      37260  06-13-91   5:00a
MOUSE    COM      32864  06-13-91   5:00a
MOUSE    SYS      32730  06-13-91   5:00a
COMMAND  COM      47863  06-13-91   5:00a
B        BAT         46  06-06-92   1:53p
       89 file(s)    2210960 bytes
                   110641152 bytes free

C>
```

Figure 2-1
(continued)

You can use these wildcard characters in various combinations. For example, DIR *.COM displays all COM files. DIR *.PIC displays all Lotus 1-2-3 graphics files. DIR *.WK? displays 1-2-3 WK1, WKS, WK3, and WKE files. It also displays WKQ files.

2-6 USING DIR WITH SWITCHES

You can use the DIR command with different switches (parameters) to provide different types of listings. DIR/W provides a wide (horizontal) directory listing. In this case, only file names and extensions are listed. Figure 2-2 shows a wide

```
C>DIR/W

 Volume in drive C is MS-DOS_5
 Volume Serial Number is 18C6-6309
 Directory of C:\DOS

[.]              [..]             COUNTRY.SYS      EGA.SYS          FORMAT.COM
KEYB.COM         KEYBOARD.SYS     NLSFUNC.EXE      DISPLAY.SYS      EGA.CPI
HIMEM.SYS        MODE.COM         SETVER.EXE       ANSI.SYS         DEBUG.EXE
EDLIN.EXE        EMM386.EXE       FASTOPEN.EXE     FDISK.EXE        MEM.EXE
MIRROR.COM       RAMDRIVE.SYS     SHARE.EXE        SMARTDRV.SYS     SYS.COM
UNDELETE.EXE     UNFORMAT.COM     XCOPY.EXE        DOSKEY.COM       DOSSHELL.VID
DOSSHELL.INI     DOSSHELL.COM     DOSSHELL.EXE     DOSSHELL.GRB     DOSSWAP.EXE
PACKING.LST      PRINT.EXE        DOSSHELL.HLP     EDIT.HLP         RECOVER.EXE
DOSHELP.HLP      HELP.EXE         QBASIC.HLP       EDIT.COM         MONEY.BAS
MSHERC.COM       QBASIC.EXE       GORILLA.BAS      4201.CPI         4208.CPI
5202.CPI         APPEND.EXE       ASSIGN.COM       ATTRIB.EXE       BACKUP.EXE
CHKDSK.EXE       COMP.EXE         DISKCOMP.COM     DISKCOPY.COM     DRIVER.SYS
FC.EXE           FIND.EXE         GRAFTABL.COM     GRAPHICS.COM     GRAPHICS.PRO
LABEL.EXE        MORE.COM         NIBBLES.BAS      REMLINE.BAS      RESTORE.EXE
SORT.EXE         EXE2BIN.EXE      EXPAND.EXE       JOIN.EXE         LCD.CPI
LOADFIX.COM      PRINTER.SYS      REPLACE.EXE      SUBST.EXE        TREE.COM
README.TXT       APPNOTES.TXT     KEYBHP.COM       MODEHP.COM       SSTOR.SYS
MOUSE.COM        MOUSE.SYS        COMMAND.COM      B.BAT
         89 file(s)    2210960 bytes
                     117313536 bytes free

C>
```

Figure 2–2
Wide directory listing obtained with DIR/W command

listing. The DIR/P command displays one screen of the file listing at a time. You press a key to see another screen. Figure 2–3 shows a listing using the /P switch.

The DIR command can be used to provide a listing of files in any drive. You only have to specify the drive. For example, if the current drive is C, you can use the command DIR A:/W to display a wide directory of the files on drive A. Remember that there must be at least one space between the DIR command and the drive name when you issue the command.

2–7
IMPORTANT KEYS IN THE DOS ENVIRONMENT

Examine the picture of a typical keyboard presented in Figure 2–4. Several of the keys perform special tasks in the DOS environment. Table 2–1 briefly explains these keys.

2–8
THE FORMAT COMMAND

To use a newly purchased blank disk on your PC, you first must format the disk. To format a disk, put the blank disk in drive A, type *FORMAT A:* and press Enter. When the process is finished, DOS asks whether you would like to format another disk. If you answer Y, you are prompted to insert a new disk. If you answer N, the C> prompt returns.

When you format a disk, the operating system checks the entire disk for defective spots. It tells you whether your disk is usable. The FORMAT command

```
C>DIR/P

 Volume in drive C is MS-DOS_5
 Volume Serial Number is 18C6-6309
 Directory of C:\DOS

.            <DIR>      06-06-92  12:24p
..           <DIR>      06-06-92  12:24p
COUNTRY  SYS      17069 06-13-91   5:00a
EGA      SYS       4885 06-13-91   5:00a
FORMAT   COM      32911 06-13-91   5:00a
KEYB     COM      14986 06-13-91   5:00a
KEYBOARD SYS      34697 06-13-91   5:00a
NLSFUNC  EXE       7052 06-13-91   5:00a
DISPLAY  SYS      15792 06-13-91   5:00a
EGA      CPI      58873 06-13-91   5:00a
HIMEM    SYS      11552 06-13-91   5:00a
MODE     COM      23537 06-13-91   5:00a
SETVER   EXE      12007 06-13-91   5:00a
ANSI     SYS       9029 06-13-91   5:00a
DEBUG    EXE      20634 06-13-91   5:00a
EDLIN    EXE      12642 06-13-91   5:00a
EMM386   EXE      91742 06-13-91   5:00a
FASTOPEN EXE      12050 06-13-91   5:00a
FDISK    EXE      57224 06-13-91   5:00a
Press any key to continue . . .

(continuing C:\DOS)
MEM      EXE      39818 06-13-91   5:00a
MIRROR   COM      18169 06-13-91   5:00a
RAMDRIVE SYS       5873 06-13-91   5:00a
SHARE    EXE      10912 06-13-91   5:00a
SMARTDRV SYS       8335 06-13-91   5:00a
SYS      COM      13440 06-13-91   5:00a
UNDELETE EXE      13924 06-13-91   5:00a
UNFORMAT COM      18576 06-13-91   5:00a
XCOPY    EXE      15804 06-13-91   5:00a
DOSKEY   COM       5883 06-13-91   5:00a
DOSSHELL VID       9462 06-13-91   5:00a
DOSSHELL INI      12231 06-13-91   5:00a
DOSSHELL COM       4623 06-13-91   5:00a
DOSSHELL EXE     235484 06-13-91   5:00a
DOSSHELL GRB       4421 06-13-91   5:00a
DOSSWAP  EXE      18756 06-13-91   5:00a
PACKING  LST       2507 06-13-91   5:00a
PRINT    EXE      15656 06-13-91   5:00a
DOSSHELL HLP     161763 06-13-91   5:00a
EDIT     HLP      17898 06-13-91   5:00a
RECOVER  EXE       9146 06-13-91   5:00a
DOSHELP  HLP       5651 06-13-91   5:00a
Press any key to continue . . .

(continuing C:\DOS)
HELP     EXE      11473 06-13-91   5:00a
QBASIC   HLP     130810 06-13-91   5:00a
```

Figure 2-3
Directory listing obtained with DIR/P command

divides a disk into tracks and sectors and creates the **file allocation table** (FAT). The FAT indicates where data is saved on a disk.

When you format a disk, remember that disk is completely erased. Make sure the disk you are formatting is either a brand new disk or an old disk with files you no longer need. Figure 2-5 shows the formatting procedure.

Formatting is discussed further in Chapter 3.

Figure 2–3
(continued)

```
EDIT     COM       413 06-13-91   5:00a
MONEY    BAS     46225 06-13-91   5:00a
MSHERC   COM      6934 06-13-91   5:00a
QBASIC   EXE    254799 06-13-91   5:00a
GORILLA  BAS     29434 06-13-91   5:00a
4201     CPI      6404 06-13-91   5:00a
5202     CPI       395 06-13-91   5:00a
APPEND   EXE     10774 06-13-91   5:00a
ASSIGN   COM      6399 06-13-91   5:00a
ATTRIB   EXE     15796 06-13-91   5:00a
BACKUP   EXE     36092 06-13-91   5:00a
CHKDSK   EXE     16200 06-13-91   5:00a
COMP     EXE     14282 06-13-91   5:00a
DISKCOMP COM     10652 06-13-91   5:00a
DISKCOPY COM     11793 06-13-91   5:00a
DRIVER   SYS      5649 06-13-91   5:00a
FC       EXE     18650 06-13-91   5:00a
FIND     EXE      6770 06-13-91   5:00a
GRAFTABL COM     11205 06-13-91   5:00a
Press any key to continue . . .

(continuing C:\DOS)
GRAPHICS COM     19694 06-13-91   5:00a
GRAPHICS PRO     21232 06-13-91   5:00a
LABEL    EXE      9390 06-13-91   5:00a
MORE     COM      2618 06-13-91   5:00a
NIBBLES  BAS     24103 06-13-91   5:00a
REMLINE  BAS     12314 06-13-91   5:00a
RESTORE  EXE     38294 06-13-91   5:00a
SORT     EXE      6938 06-13-91   5:00a
EXE2BIN  EXE      8424 06-13-91   5:00a
EXPAND   EXE     14563 06-13-91   5:00a
JOIN     EXE     17870 06-13-91   5:00a
LCD      CPI     10753 06-13-91   5:00a
LOADFIX  COM      1131 06-13-91   5:00a
PRINTER  SYS     18804 06-13-91   5:00a
REPLACE  EXE     20226 06-13-91   5:00a
SUBST    EXE     18478 06-13-91   5:00a
TREE     COM      6901 06-13-91   5:00a
README   TXT     23692 06-13-91   5:00a
APPNOTES TXT      8660 06-13-91   5:00a
KEYBHP   COM     15997 06-13-91   5:00a
MODEHP   COM     23232 06-13-91   5:00a
SSTOR    SYS     37260 06-13-91   5:00a
Press any key to continue . . .

(continuing C:\DOS)
MOUSE    COM     32864 06-13-91   5:00a
MOUSE    SYS     32730 06-13-91   5:00a
COMMAND  COM     47863 06-13-91   5:00a
B        BAT        46 06-06-92   1:53p
       89 file(s)    2210960 bytes
                   110641152 bytes free

C>
```

2–9

DIFFERENT VERSIONS OF MS-DOS AND PC-DOS

PC-DOS is used in IBM microcomputers, and MS-DOS is used in IBM compatibles. Both of these operating systems have gone through several revisions from 1.0 to the latest version, 5.0. Each version has added new commands and corrected some of the bugs in the earlier versions. Versions 3.1 and later include

Chapter 2 You and Your PC: The First Official Meeting

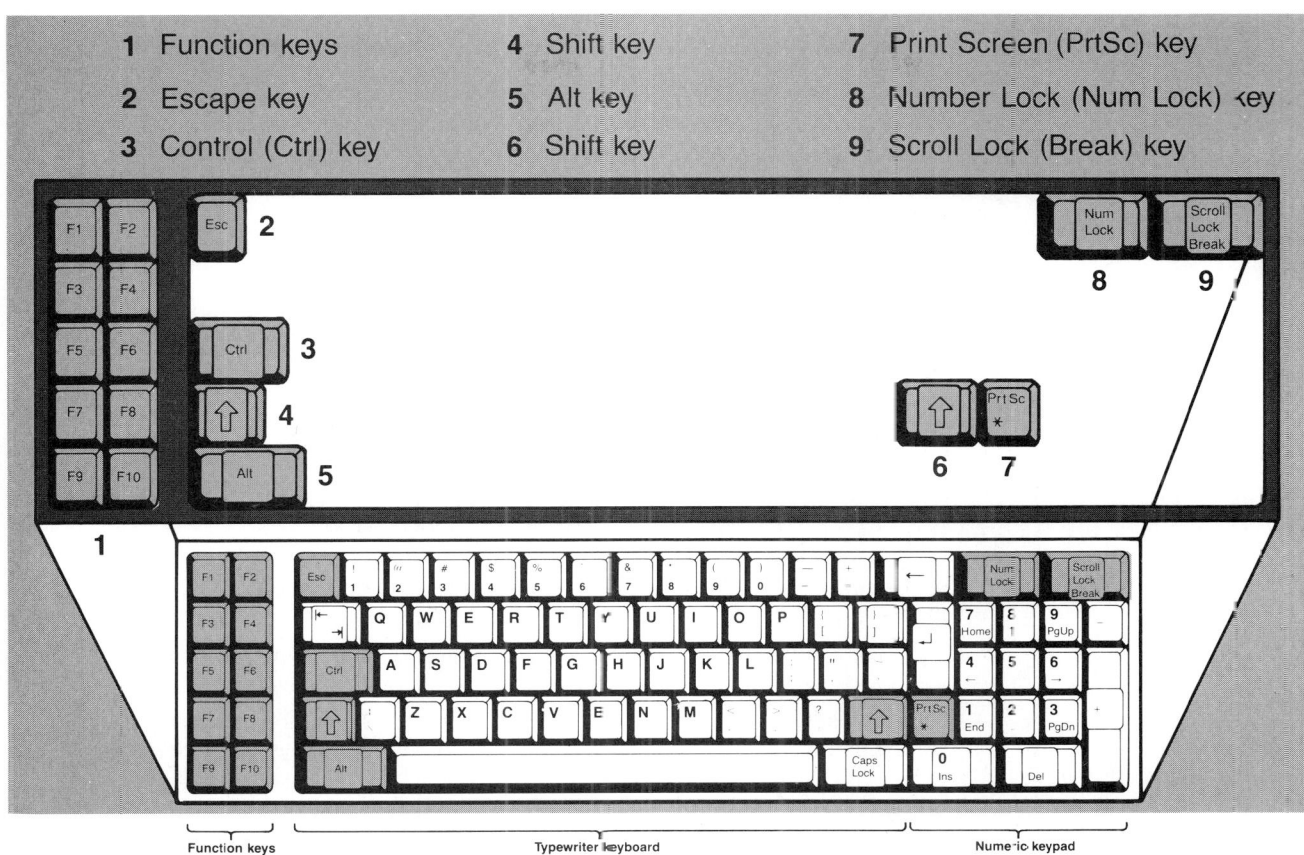

Figure 2-4
IBM PC keyboard

```
C>FORMAT A:
Insert new diskette for drive A:
and press ENTER when ready...

Checking existing disk format.
Formatting 1.2M
Format complete.

Volume label (11 characters, ENTER for none)? N

   1213952 bytes total disk space
   1213952 bytes available on disk

      512 bytes in each allocation unit.
     2371 allocation units available on disk.

Volume Serial Number is 2805-1D02

Format another (Y/N)?N

C>
```

Figure 2-5
Formatting procedure

Table 2-1
Special keys on the keyboard

Keys	Description
Ctrl-Alt-Del	This key combination is used to warm boot the system. This is equivalent to turning your computer off, then turning it back on (without memory check).
Ctrl-C or Ctrl-Break	Cancels a command while it is being executed.
Ctrl-PrtSc or Ctrl-P	Sends a copy of each line on the screen to the printer, as it is being displayed (assuming that you are connected to a printer and the printer is on). This command toggles the printer on, meaning it will remain in effect until you press Ctrl and PrtSc or P again. When the printer is toggled on, everything displayed on screen also is printed on your printer.
Shift-PrtSc	Sends a copy of the screen to the printer. This command does not toggle the printer on. In enhanced keyboards, press the dedicated **Print Screen** key.
Ctrl-S or Ctrl-Num Lock	Pauses the directory listing for viewing.
F1 function key	Displays one character of the previous command with each press. Useful for editing a DOS command.
F3 function key	Displays the previous command. You can perform editing, or just press F3 and Enter to execute the command again.
F6 function key (equivalent to Ctrl-Z)	Marks the end of a batch file. It also stops an autoexec file (an autoexec file starts execution as soon as you start the computer).
Backspace	Backs up and erases the character typed.
Esc	Erases the current command or statement as it is being entered.

commands for the LAN (local area network) environment. Major revisions are indicated by whole numbers (2.0, 3.0, and so on); minor revisions are indicated by fractions (2.01, 3.2, and so forth).

Versions of MS-DOS and PC-DOS are upwardly compatible. All the commands in earlier versions are available in the newer versions, but not vice versa. To a typical microcomputer user, PC-DOS and MS-DOS are almost identical. To find out which version of DOS you are using, type *VER* at the C> prompt and press Enter. This command reveals the current version of DOS in the disk drive. Figure 2-6 illustrates this process. It shows that our version of DOS is 5.0. All the commands discussed in the text work with all versions of DOS unless otherwise specified.

Figure 2-6
Determining your version of DOS

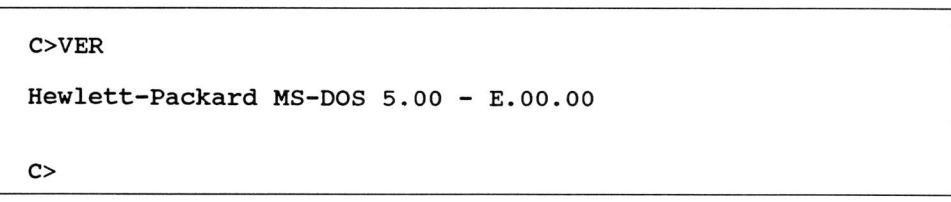

```
C>VER

Hewlett-Packard MS-DOS 5.00 - E.00.00

C>
```

Chapter 2 You and Your PC: The First Official Meeting

SUMMARY

This chapter reviewed elementary DOS operations and explained the difference between internal and external DOS commands. Types of DOS prompts and file name specifications in the DOS environment were highlighted. Use of the DIR command with different switches and important keys frequently used in the DOS environment were introduced. We also examined the FORMAT command. The chapter concluded with a brief discussion of different versions of DOS. In the next chapter, commonly used DOS commands are discussed.

REVIEW QUESTIONS

*These questions are answered in Appendix A.

1. What is a cold boot? Warm boot?
2. What are DOS internal commands? External commands?
3. What is the C> prompt? The A> prompt? How do you change the C> prompt to the A> prompt?
*4. Why should you always enter the correct date and time at boot-up? How do you bypass the date and time prompts?
5. What constitutes a valid DOS file name? An invalid DOS file name?
6. What are three examples of DOS file extensions?
7. What are the applications of the DIR command?
*8. What is the difference between DIR/W and DIR/P?
9. What are the applications of the F1 and F3 function keys in the DOS environment?
10. How do you generate a hard copy of the current screen?
*11. How do you stop the execution of a DOS command?
12. What are the applications of the Esc key?
13. How and where is the Ctrl key used?
14. Why does a new disk have to be formatted before it can be used?
15. What is actually done when you format a disk?
16. What is the first version of DOS? The latest version?
*17. How do you determine which version of DOS you are using?

HANDS-ON EXPERIENCE

1. Turn on your PC. Enter the current date and time. Change the date to January 1, 1995. Change it to the current date. Change the time to 3:30 p.m. Change it to the current time.
2. List the directory of the DOS disk (use the DIR command). Erase the screen and display a wide directory of the disk (DIR/W). Erase the screen and list the directory with the pause switch (DIR/P).
3. Put a blank disk in drive A. Using the FORMAT A: command, format the disk. List the directory of the new disk. What are the contents of the disk?
4. Using a wildcard character, list all system files (system files have COM as their extension). Use the VER command to determine the version of DOS you are using.
5. Try to use all the keys presented in Table 2–1.
6. Display the directory of the default drive. Create a hard copy of this directory. What is the difference between Ctrl-PrtSc and Ctrl-P?
7. Can F1 and F3 perform the same task? If so, how?
8. Why are there many different versions of DOS? By consulting a DOS manual, name two specific improvements of DOS 5.0.

KEY TERMS

Backup file	DOS prompt	Internal command
Batch file	Executable file	System date
Cold boot	External command	System file
Command file	File allocation table	System time
Disk operating system	Hard disk	Warm boot
DOS file specification		

KEY COMMANDS

A:, B:, C: (internal)	DATE (internal)	F3 function key (internal)
Backspace (internal)	DIR (internal)	F6 function key (internal)
CLS (internal)	DIR/P (internal)	FORMAT (external)
Ctrl-Alt-Del (internal)	DIR/W (internal)	Shift-PrtSc (internal)
Ctrl-C (internal)	Esc (internal)	TIME (internal)
Ctrl-PrtSc or Ctrl-P (internal)	F1 function key (internal)	VER (internal)
Ctrl-S or Ctrl-Num Lock (internal)		

MISCONCEPTIONS AND SOLUTIONS

Misconception You turn on your PC, and you see a message that is not familiar to you—non-system disk, for example.

Solution You either forgot to put the DOS disk into drive A, a data disk is in drive A, or you inserted your disk on the wrong side. Insert the DOS disk into drive A properly and reboot the system. If DOS is installed in drive C, remove any data disk from drive A and reboot the system.

Misconception You are trying to format a disk and receive an ATTEMPTED WRITE-PROTECT VIOLATION error message.

Solution The disk in drive A has the write-protection notch covered. Either remove the protection or insert another disk.

Misconception You are using the FORMAT command and receive a DRIVE NOT READY error message.

Solution Either the target drive door is not closed or there is no disk in that drive. Insert a disk in this drive, close the drive door, and press Enter.

Misconception You are using a DOS command and receive a SYNTAX ERROR, BAD COMMAND, or FILENAME error.

Solution Check the spelling of the command. Most likely, you have misspelled a command.

ARE YOU READY TO MOVE ON?

Multiple Choice

1. The procedure known as warm boot means
   - **a.** inserting the DOS disk in drive A and turning on the computer
   - **b.** typing the name of the program to be run and pressing Enter
   - **c.** simultaneously pressing the Ctrl, Alt, and Del keys
   - **d.** formatting a disk
   - **e.** none of the above

Chapter 2 You and Your PC: The First Official Meeting

2. Which of the following prompts are you most likely to see after performing a cold boot with the DOS disk in drive C?
   a. A>
   b. B>
   c. C>
   d. OK
   e. B:/DOS>
3. If the correct date and time are not entered during the boot process or if you want to change them at any time, the commands are
   a. HOUR and DAY
   b. DAY and HOUR
   c. DATE and CLOCK
   d. DATE and TIME
   e. none of the above
4. To change the default drive from drive C to drive A, what should you type at the DOS prompt before pressing Enter?
   a. A
   b. DRIVE=A
   c. B=A
   d. GO TO A:
   e. A:
5. File names with these extensions can be executed by typing the name of the file:
   a. COM and SYS
   b. COM and EXE
   c. EXE and SYS
   d. BAK and SYS
   e. BAK and BAT
6. The command DIR/P will yield
   a. the same as DIR
   b. a wide directory listing
   c. one screen at a time of the directory listing
   d. a hard copy output to the printer
   e. nothing—it is not a valid command
7. The command to format a disk in drive B is
   a. ERASE B:
   b. DELETE *.*
   c. SYS B:
   d. FORMAT B:
   e. a or b
8. The file allocation table indicates
   a. where data is saved on a disk
   b. the maximum number of files that can be saved on disk
   c. how much disk space is available
   d. how much memory (RAM) is available
   e. none of the above
9. A typical computer response to the command VER is
   a. Disk Verified OK
   b. MS-DOS Version 5.00

      c. File Verified OK
      d. Insert new disk and strike Enter when ready
      e. a or b
10. When you format a disk,
      a. all data is erased
      b. a file allocation table is created
      c. the operating system checks for defective spots
      d. the disk is divided into sectors and tracks
      e. all of the above

True/False

1. If the computer is off and the system does not have a hard disk, the DOS disk must be placed in drive A to boot the computer.
2. A cold boot is faster than a warm boot because the computer does not check the memory.
3. Although DOS does not require the current date and time, it is good practice always to enter the correct information.
4. External DOS commands are those loaded into the computer memory at boot-up time.
5. The DOS prompt indicates the current default drive.
6. The DIR command generates a listing of the files in the default directory.
7. DOS wildcards act as placeholders for other characters and include *, ?, @, $, %, and .
8. DIR and DIR/W yield exactly the same information except that DIR/W places it in a wide format.
9. In general, a newly purchased disk cannot be used directly out of the box.
10. Versions of MS-DOS and PC-DOS are not upwardly compatible.

ANSWERS

Multiple Choice	True/False
1. c	1. T
2. c	2. F
3. d	3. T
4. e	4. F
5. b	5. T
6. c	6. T
7. d	7. F
8. a	8. F
9. b	9. T
10. e	10. F

Commonly Used DOS Commands

3-1   Introduction
3-2   FORMAT Command
3-3   LABEL Command
3-4   DISKCOPY Command
3-5   DISKCOMP Command
3-6   CHKDSK Command
3-7   SYS Command
3-8   COPY Command
3-9   COPY Versus DISKCOPY
3-10 COMP Command
3-11 RENAME Command
3-12 DELETE and ERASE Commands
3-13 ATTRIB Command

3-1
INTRODUCTION

In this chapter we discuss some of the most common DOS commands. These commands are used in day-to-day operations and will help you improve your effectiveness while you are working with PCs. Various versions of the FORMAT command are discussed as are the DISKCOPY and COPY commands for copying an entire disk or selected files. The CHKDSK command, which is used for checking the space available on your disk and your PC is also covered. The RENAME (for changing a file name), DEL and ERASE (for erasing a file), and ATTRIB (for making a file read-only) commands are introduced.

3-2
FORMAT COMMAND

Any disk, floppy or hard, must be formatted before it can be used by your PC. **Formatting** a disk means checking the disk for defective spots and preparing storage areas. When the computer formats a disk, the disk is completely erased and a directory is generated that can be accessed by the DIR command. A file allocation table (FAT) is created, which provides the name, extension, size, date, and time a file is created. The FAT determines where data is saved. Remember that the FORMAT command is a destructive command. Be careful!

FORMAT is an external DOS command and has several variations (see Table 3–1). To use any of the commands shown in the table, the DOS disk must be in one of the drives. In our case, it is in the C drive. Although drive A is used in Table 3–1, these variations will work with any drive. Formatting a hard disk is explained in Chapter 4.

Figure 3–1 illustrates an example of the FORMAT command. Insert an empty disk in the A drive. At the C> prompt, type *FORMAT A:* and press Enter. Follow the instructions at the prompt. When the disk is formatted, DOS asks whether you would like to format another disk. Answer N (for no). Remember, DOS commands are not case sensitive. This means there is no distinction between uppercase and lowercase.

Table 3–1
Various FORMAT commands

Command	Function
FORMAT A:	Format a data disk with 9 or 15 sectors per track
FORMAT A:/S	Format a disk for self-booting. This command transfers system files IBMBIO.COM, IBM.COM, and COMMAND.COM to the newly formatted disk. This disk can then be used to boot the computer. This means the DOS disk is not needed to start up the system.
FORMAT A:/V	Format a disk with a volume label. A volume label is any valid name up to 11 characters. It follows the same conventions as the file name.
FORMAT A:/1	Format a one-sided disk
FORMAT A:/4	Format a double-sided disk in a high-capacity drive
FORMAT A:/8	Format an eight-sector-per-track disk
FORMAT A:/B	Format a disk for eight sectors and leave correct space for system files IBMBIO.COM and IBMDOS.COM. These files can be copied later.
FORMAT A:/F:size (DOS 3.3 and higher)	Specifies the size of the floppy disk to format, such as 360 K, 720 K, 1.2 MB or 1.44 MB and so forth.

Chapter 3 Commonly Used DOS Commands

```
C>FORMAT A:
Insert new diskette for drive A:
and press ENTER when ready...

Checking existing disk format.
Formatting 1.2M
Format complete.

Volume label (11 characters, ENTER for none)? N

    1213952 bytes total disk space
    1213952 bytes available on disk

       512 bytes in each allocation unit.
      2371 allocation units available on disk.

Volume Serial Number is 182C-19DA

Format another (Y/N)?N

C>
```

Figure 3-1
Formatting a data disk

Figure 3-2 illustrates formatting with a **volume label.** Insert a blank disk in drive A. At the C> prompt, type *FORMAT A:/V* and press Enter. Follow the instructions at the prompt. Enter a volume label up to 11 characters (Customers, for example) and press Enter. When you are finished, the computer displays

```
Format another (Y/N)?
```

Answer N to stop the format command. This disk now has a name—CUSTOMERS. When you list the directory of the disk, the volume name is

```
C>FORMAT A:/V
Insert new diskette for drive A:
and press ENTER when ready...

Checking existing disk format.
Saving UNFORMAT information.
Verifying 1.2M
Format complete.

Volume label (11 characters, ENTER for none)? CUSTOMERS

    1213952 bytes total disk space
    1213952 bytes available on disk

       512 bytes in each allocation unit.
      2371 allocation units available on disk.

Volume Serial Number is 3F2F-19DB

Format another (Y/N)?N

C>
```

Figure 3-2
Formatting a data disk with volume label

Windows 3.1

displayed at the top of the directory listing. Labeling a disk internally is a good practice. This will help you to identify a disk if the external label (the sticker) is lost.

The switches, or parameters, for the FORMAT command can be combined. Figure 3–3 illustrates one example. Insert a blank disk in drive A. At the C> prompt, type *FORMAT A:/S/V*. Follow the instructions at the prompt, and enter a volume label. This command creates a system disk with a volume label that can be used to boot the system.

3–3
LABEL COMMAND

If you forget to give a volume label to a disk when formatting, you can always add the volume label later with the LABEL command. This command also can be used to change an existing volume label.

Figure 3–4 illustrates this procedure. Insert the data disk with the CUSTOMERS volume label in drive A. At the C> prompt, type *LABEL A:* and press Enter. Enter *SUPPLIERS* as the volume label and press Enter. Now you have changed the volume label from CUSTOMERS to SUPPLIERS.

By using the VOL (volume) command, you can find out if a disk has a label or not. Just type *VOL* at the DOS prompt and press Enter.

Figure 3–3
Formatting a system disk with volume label

```
C>FORMAT A:/S/V
Insert new diskette for drive A:
and press ENTER when ready...

Checking existing disk format.
Saving UNFORMAT information.
Verifying 1.2M
Format complete.
System transferred

Volume label (11 characters, ENTER for none)? CUSTOMERS

  1213952 bytes total disk space
   119808 bytes used by system
  1094144 bytes available on disk

      512 bytes in each allocation unit.
     2137 allocation units available on disk.

Volume Serial Number is 371E-19DD

Format another (Y/N)?N

C>
```

Figure 3–4
Changing a volume label

```
C>LABEL A:
Volume in drive A is CUSTOMERS
Volume Serial Number is 371E-19DD
Volume label (11 characters, ENTER for none)? SUPPLIERS

C>
```

Chapter 3 Commonly Used DOS Commands

```
C>DISKCOPY A: A:
Insert SOURCE diskette in drive A:
Press any key to continue . . .
Copying 80 tracks
15 sectors per track, 2 side(s)
Insert TARGET diskette in drive A:
Press any key to continue . . .
Insert SOURCE diskette in drive A:
Press any key to continue . . .
Insert TARGET diskette in drive A:
Press any key to continue . . .
Insert SOURCE diskette in drive A:
Press any key to continue . . .
Insert TARGET diskette in drive A:
Press any key to continue . . .
Volume Serial Number is 1CC9-2C39
Copy another diskette (Y/N)? N
C>
```

Figure 3-5
DISKCOPY command

3-4 DISKCOPY COMMAND

The DISKCOPY command generates an exact duplicate of a disk. When you use the DISKCOPY command, the target disk does not need to be formatted because the DISKCOPY command formats while it is copying. Remember that only nonprotected disks can be copied. Protected disks are designed by the vendors to guard against illegal copying of their programs. Figure 3-5 illustrates the DISKCOPY command. If your computer has two external drives of the same size, insert the disk to be copied in drive A and a blank disk in drive B, type *DISKCOPY A: B:* and press Enter. Follow the prompts. When copying is complete, answer N to stop the DISKCOPY command. Now you have created an exact copy of the disk in drive A in drive B. If you have a computer with only one external drive, type *DISKCOPY A: A:* and press Enter. The computer reads the first disk; next you pull this disk out and insert the second disk is the same drive. So the one disk is functioning as both A and B. Be aware, however, that you may have to swap the disks several times before you are finished copying.

Whenever you are working with a DOS command that deals with two drives or two separate locations in one drive, the command always works on a from-to basis. The first drive or location is the source (from) and the second is the target (to).

Figure 3-6
DISKCOMP command

```
C>DISKCOMP A: A:

Insert FIRST diskette in drive A:

Press any key to continue . . .

Comparing 80 tracks
15 sectors per track, 2 side(s)

Insert SECOND diskette in drive A:

Press any key to continue . . .

Insert FIRST diskette in drive A:

Press any key to continue . . .

Insert SECOND diskette in drive A:

Press any key to continue . . .

Compare OK

Compare another diskette (Y/N) ?
```

3-5 DISKCOMP COMMAND

The DISKCOMP command is used to verify whether the copy generated by the DISKCOPY command is 100 percent correct. Figure 3-6 illustrates this process. If your computer has a hard disk (drive C) and two external drives (A and B) of the same size, follow these steps. At the C> prompt, insert the desired disk in drive A and the disk for comparison (the duplicate) in drive B, type *DISKCOMP A: B:,* and press Enter. Follow the instructions at the prompt. You will see the message

Compare OK

if your disks are identical. If your computer has only one drive, or its drives are not of the same size, you can use drive A for both drives. Type *DISKCOMP A: A:* and follow the prompts.

3-6 CHKDSK COMMAND

You use the CHKDSK command to determine the memory status of your disk or your computer. It tells you the total amount of disk space in bytes (free or unused), bytes on the disk, memory available on your PC, and the memory being used. Figure 3-7 illustrates this command. At the C> prompt insert the desired disk in drive A, and then type *CHKDSK A:*. Press Enter and you will see the information provided in Figure 3-7. We used a sample disk that includes SYS files from DOS 5.0.

The CHKDSK command can be used with the V and F parameters. The V parameter enables you to view the files and their paths on a given disk. Figure

```
C>CHKDSK A:

Volume SUPPLIERS    created 06-21-1992 6:23p
Volume Serial Number is 371E-19DD

   1213952 bytes total disk space
     71680 bytes in 2 hidden files
     48128 bytes in 1 user files
   1094144 bytes available on disk

       512 bytes in each allocation unit
      2371 total allocation units on disk
      2137 available allocation units on disk

    655360 total bytes memory
    585168 bytes free

C>
```

Figure 3–7
CHKDSK command

```
C>CHKDSK A:/V
Volume Serial Number is 1033-18EA
Directory A:\
A:\COUNTRY.SYS
A:\EGA.SYS
A:\KEYBOARD.SYS
A:\DISPLAY.SYS
A:\HIMEM.SYS
A:\ANSI.SYS
A:\RAMDRIVE.SYS
A:\SMARTDRV.SYS
A:\JACKSON.SYS
A:\PRINTER.SYS
A:\SSTOR.SYS
A:\MOUSE.SYS

   1213952 bytes total disk space
    204288 bytes in 12 user files
   1009664 bytes available on disk

       512 bytes in each allocation unit
      2371 total allocation units on disk
      1972 available allocation units on disk

    655360 total bytes memory
    585168 bytes free

C>
```

Figure 3–8
CHKDSK/V command

3–8 illustrates this command. At the C> prompt, we inserted the sample disk in drive A. We typed *CHKDSK A:/V* and pressed Enter.

Using CHKDSK with the F parameter enables you to correct errors in the directory or file allocation table on a given disk. If there is no error, the normal output is generated, which is similar to that of the CHKDSK command alone. Figure 3–9 illustrates this command. At the C> prompt, insert the desired disk in drive A, type *CHKDSK A:/F,* and press Enter. In drive A, we inserted the sample disk that included SYS files from DOS 5.0.

Figure 3-9
CHKDSK/F command

```
C>CHKDSK A:/F
Volume Serial Number is 1033-18EA

   1213952 bytes total disk space
    204288 bytes in 12 user files
   1009664 bytes available on disk

       512 bytes in each allocation unit
      2371 total allocation units on disk
      1972 available allocation units on disk

    655360 total bytes memory
    585168 bytes free

C>
```

Figure 3-10
SYS command

```
C>SYS A:
System transferred

C>
```

3-7
SYS COMMAND

The SYS command is used to copy the DOS hidden files from the DOS disk to another disk. To use this command, you must have formatted the desired disk using the FORMAT/B command. This disk will not be a self-booting disk until you transfer COMMAND.COM from the DOS disk. With a self-booting disk, you do not need the DOS disk to get your computer started. The self-booting disk does the job by itself. Figure 3-10 illustrates the procedure. Insert the disk that has been formatted with the FORMAT/B command in drive A. At the C> prompt, type *SYS A:* and press Enter.

If you list the directory of the disk in drive A with the DIR command, you will see nothing new, because only the hidden files are transferred. To verify the process, you can measure the space available on this disk by using the CHKDSK command before and after execution of the SYS command. You can tell that something, indeed, has been transferred; you can see it by using the CHKDSK/V command.

3-8
COPY COMMAND

The COPY command is used for copying one or several files from one disk to itself or to another disk. If you are making a duplicate copy of a file on the same disk, you must use a different file name for the target (duplicate) file, otherwise you will receive an error message. The COPY command, combined with wildcard characters, can be very powerful. Table 3-2 shows several versions of the COPY command. In these examples, the default drive is C. FILE1 is any valid file name and EXT is any valid file extension.

Figure 3-11 illustrates one example of the COPY command. Insert a formatted disk in drive A. At the C> prompt, type *COPY *.SYS A:* and press

Chapter 3 Commonly Used DOS Commands

Table 3-2
Various COPY commands

Command	Description
COPY FILE1.EXT B:	Copy FILE1.EXT from C to B
COPY B:FILE1.EXT	Copy FILE1.EXT from B to C
COPY *.COM B:	Copy all files with COM extension from C to B
COPY B:*.COM	Copy all files with COM extension from B to C
COPY *.* B:	Copy all files from C to B
COPY B:*.*	Copy all files from B to C
COPY FILE1.EXT File2.EXT	Copy a file from C to C with a different name
COPY B:FILE1.EXT B:File2.EXT	Copy a file from B to B with a different name
COPY FILE1.EXT + File2.EXT File3.EXT	Combine File1 and File2 and generate a third file (File3) in C (There must be one space between FILE2.EXT and FILE3.EXT)
COPY FILE1.EXT B:/V	Copy FILE1.EXT from C to B and verify the process

```
C>COPY *.SYS A:
COUNTRY.SYS
EGA.SYS
KEYBOARD.SYS
DISPLAY.SYS
HIMEM.SYS
ANSI.SYS
RAMDRIVE.SYS
SMARTDRV.SYS
DRIVER.SYS
PRINTER.SYS
SSTOR.SYS
MOUSE.SYS
     12 file(s) copied

C>
```

Figure 3-11
Example of COPY command

Enter. This command copies all SYS files from drive C to A. You can verify this by checking the directory of drive A with *DIR A:* command.

3-9 COPY VERSUS DISKCOPY

There are four major differences between the COPY *.* and DISKCOPY commands. First, the COPY *.* command can be used to duplicate a disk; however, the target disk must be formatted first. DISKCOPY formats while it is copying. Second, COPY *.* does not transfer the hidden files from the source disk to the target disk. If you want to maintain the information on the target disk, do not use the DISKCOPY command—this command erases the target disk. You must always use the COPY command instead. Third, COPY *.* copies files contiguously (files are stored in adjacent sectors), reorganizing the files and speeding up access of files. Fourth, when you use the COPY command, it is not necessary to have the DOS disk in one of your drives (COPY is an internal command). When using the DISKCOPY command, the DOS disk must be in one of your drives (DISKCOPY is an external command).

3-10
COMP COMMAND

The COMP command is used to verify whether a particular file has been copied correctly. The two files can be on one disk or on different disks. Figure 3-12 illustrates one example of this command. At the C> prompt, insert the sample disk in drive A. Suppose that we want to compare DRIVER.SYS on these two disks. At the C> prompt, type *COMP DRIVER.SYS* and press Enter. The computer asks you to enter the second file name. Type *A:DRIVER.SYS* and press Enter. (In DOS 5.0, press Enter twice to bypass the Option choice.) DOS responds

```
Files compare OK
```

Remember, you always must use the driver identification if the two files are not on the same disk.

3-11
RENAME COMMAND

You use the RENAME command to change the name of a file or several files. Figure 3-13 shows an example of this command. At the C> prompt, insert the sample disk in drive A. Suppose that you want to change DRIVER.SYS to JACKSON.SYS in drive A. At the C> prompt, type *RENAME A: DRIVER.SYS JACKSON.SYS* and press Enter. You can check your work by looking at the directory for the A drive. The RENAME command can be used with wildcard characters, which means you can rename several files at once. For example, RENAME *.COM *.XYZ renames all COM files to XYZ files in your default drive.

Figure 3-12
Example of COMP command

```
C>COMP DRIVER.SYS
Name of second file to compare: A:DRIVER.SYS
Option :
Comparing DRIVER.SYS and A:DRIVER.SYS...
Files compare OK

Compare more files (Y/N) ? N

C>
```

Figure 3-13
Example of RENAME command

```
A>RENAME DRIVER.SYS JACKSON.SYS

A>
```

3-12 DELETE AND ERASE COMMANDS

You can use either the DELETE (DEL) or the ERASE command to erase one file or the entire disk. For example, to erase EDLIN.COM from drive A, type *DEL A:EDLIN.COM* at the C> prompt. To erase the entire disk in drive A, type *DEL A:*.** at the C> prompt. An alternative method of erasing is to use the ERASE A:EDLIN.COM or ERASE A:*.* commands. Be careful, however; these commands can be dangerous, especially when they are combined with wildcard characters.

3-13 ATTRIB COMMAND

The ATTRIB command protects a file from being deleted accidentally. This command can be very helpful to protect essential commands such as COMMAND.COM, without which you cannot boot the system. Figure 3-14 illustrates an example of this command. At the C> prompt, type *ATTRIB +R COMMAND.COM* and press Enter. This file is now a **read-only file.** If you try to delete it with either the ERASE or the DEL command, you will receive an Access Denied message.

If you would like to remove the read-only status from this file, type *ATTRIB -R* and the file name. Remember the ATTRIB command is available only in DOS versions 3 and above.

To make your entire disk a read-only disk, issue the command *ATTRIB +R *.** and press Enter.

```
C>ATTRIB +R COMMAND.COM
C>
```

Figure 3-14
Example of ATTRIB command

SUMMARY

This chapter reviewed commonly used DOS commands—FORMAT, DISKCOPY, CHKDSK, DISKCOMP, COMP, COPY, RENAME, DEL, ERASE, and ATTRIB. Understanding these commands makes it easier to work with DOS. In the next chapter, we talk about directories and subdirectories.

REVIEW QUESTIONS

*These questions are answered in Appendix A.

1. What version of the FORMAT command is the most commonly used?
*2. What version of the FORMAT command is used to make a disk self-booting?
3. What version of the FORMAT command is used to leave the correct space for system files?
4. What is a volume label? Why should you always use a volume label? How do you change an existing volume label?
*5. When do you use the DISKCOPY command? Do you need to format the target disk to use the DISKCOPY command?
6. When do you use the DISKCOMP command?
7. What are the applications of the CHKDSK command?

Windows 3.1

8. To find out how much space is available on your disk, what command should you use?
9. What are the two possible parameters that can be used with the CHKDSK command? What are the applications of each?
*10. What are the applications of the SYS command?
11. How do you verify whether a SYS command issued earlier has been successful?
12. What command do you use to transfer all the EXE files from drive C to a formatted disk in drive A?
*13. What command do you use to combine FILEA.ABC and FILEB.ABC into a third file called FILEC.ABC?
14. What version of the COPY command should you use to verify the COPY procedure?
15. What version of the COPY command should you use to copy the entire disk A to disk B without losing the existing contents of disk B?
*16. What are the differences between COPY *.* and DISKCOPY?
17. What are the applications of the COMP command? The RENAME command?
18. What version of the DEL command should you use to erase the entire disk in drive A?
19. What are the applications of the ATTRIB command?

HANDS-ON EXPERIENCE

1. This exercise assumes DOS is installed in your C drive. Insert a blank disk in drive A and do the following:
   a. Format the disk in drive A.
   b. Format the disk in drive A as a self-booting disk.
   c. Format the disk in drive A with 9 or 15 sectors per track.
   d. Format the disk in drive A with a volume label called TRY.
   e. Change the volume label from TRY to EXERCISE.
2. Using the DISKCOPY command, generate a duplicate of a sample disk in drive A. Using the DISKCOMP command, verify whether this is a correct copy. Using the CHKDSK command, find out how much unused space exists on your disk. Use the DEL *.* command to erase the entire disk in drive A.
3. Use the appropriate command to transfer DOS hidden files from drive C to A. Copy all COM files from C to A, and then erase the entire disk in drive A.
4. Copy the COMMAND.COM file from C to A. Now, by using the ATTRIB command, make this file a read-only file. How do you know a file is read-only? Remove the read-only status from the file.
5. Copy the COMMAND.COM file from drive C to A. Use the RENAME command to rename this file to TRY.ABC.
6. Select any two files from the DOS disk. By using the COPY command, combine these two files into a file called COMBINE.XYZ in drive A. Now copy this file to drive B or C by using the COPY/V command. Using the ERASE command, erase the file.

KEY TERMS

Formatting
Read-only file
Volume label

Chapter 3 Commonly Used DOS Commands

KEY COMMANDS

ATTRIB (external) DISKCOMP (external) LABEL (external)
CHKDSK (external) DISKCOPY (external) RENAME (internal)
COMP (internal) ERASE (internal) SYS (external)
COPY (internal) FORMAT (external) VOL (internal)
DELETE (DEL) (internal)

MISCONCEPTIONS AND SOLUTIONS

Misconception You are using command FORMAT A:/ and receive an Invalid Parameter message.

    Solution You must include either the V or S parameter when you use / with the FORMAT command.

Misconception You are working with the COPY command and receive the error message

```
FILE CANNOT BE COPIED TO ITSELF 0 FILE(S) COPIED.
```

    Solution You are either using the same name on the same disk or left out the drive identifier for the second file. Either use a different name for the second file or copy the same file with the same name to a different disk.

ARE YOU READY TO MOVE ON?

Multiple Choice

1. The command to format a self-booting disk with a volume label using drive A is
   a. FORMAT A:
   b. FORMAT B:
   c. FORMAT A:/V
   d. FORMAT B:/V
   e. FORMAT A:/S/V
2. To change the name (volume label) of a disk, the command to use is
   a. VOLUME
   b. LABEL
   c. NAME
   d. TYPE
   e. none of the above
3. The CHKDSK command tells you all of the following except
   a. the amount of memory available
   b. the amount of memory being used
   c. the version of DOS being used
   d. the amount of disk space available
   e. the amount of disk space used
4. The SYS command transfers the following file(s) to the disk:
   a. IBMBIO.COM
   b. IBMDOS.COM
   c. COMMAND.COM

d. both a and b

e. all of the above

5. The COPY command can do all of the following except
   a. format the disk
   b. copy from/to floppy disk and hard disk
   c. copy selected files
   d. verify that the files have been copied correctly
   e. copy more than one file at a time

6. An advantage of COPY over DISKCOPY is that the COPY command
   a. formats the disk
   b. copies protected files
   c. copies the hidden files
   d. maintains the files already on the target disk
   e. none of the above

7. To remove only the file TEST.MIS from the disk in the default drive, the command is
   a. DELETE TEST.MIS
   b. DELETE *.MIS
   c. DELETE TEST.*
   d. DELETE *.*
   e. REMOVE TEST.MIS

8. To generate a new file FILE3 by combining FILE1 and FILE2, the command is
   a. COPY FILE1, FILE2, FILE3
   b. COPY FILE1 + FILE2 FILE3
   c. COPY FILE1 AND FILE2 TO FILE3
   d. FILE1 + FILE2 = FILE3
   e. none of the above

9. Which of the following is/are *not* true about the DISKCOPY command?
   a. It formats the target disk.
   b. It is destructive.
   c. It cannot be used with a single disk drive.
   d. It cannot be used to copy to/from a hard disk.
   e. all of the above

10. Which command verifies that the file FILE1.EXT was copied correctly to drive B?
    a. DISKCOPY FILE1.EXT B:
    b. COPY FILE1.EXT B:
    c. VER FILE1.EXT B:
    d. CHECK FILE1.EXT B:
    e. COMP FILE1.EXT B:/V

True/False

1. Only floppy disks need to be formatted.
2. The target disk does not need to be formatted when using the DISKCOPY command.
3. DISKCOPY only works with a hard disk.
4. DISKCOPY automatically checks and verifies that it has copied correctly.

Chapter 3 Commonly Used DOS Commands

5. CHKDSK/V enables you to see the files and their paths on a disk, including the DOS hidden files.
6. Assuming that all disks are formatted and that there are no system files, DISKCOPY A: B: and COPY A:*.* B: copy the same files from A to B.
7. There is no command to verify that the command COPY FILE1.ABC B: has copied FILE1.ABC correctly.
8. You must change the file name if you want to make a copy of a file on the same disk.
9. DELETE is used to remove one or more files; ERASE is used only to clear the entire disk.
10. The ATTRIB command can be used to protect a file from being accidentally deleted.

ANSWERS

Multiple Choice	True/False
1. e	1. F
2. b	2. T
3. c	3. F
4. d	4. F
5. a	5. T
6. d	6. T
7. a	7. F
8. b	8. T
9. c	9. F
10. e	10. T

Directories and Subdirectories

4-1 Introduction
4-2 Defining a Directory
4-3 Important Commands for Directories
4-4 Example 1: Directory Creation
4-5 Example 2: Copying to Directories
4-6 Example 3: Copying from One Subdirectory to Another
4-7 Example 4: Removing a Directory
4-8 Hard Disk Management
4-9 Partitioning a Hard Disk
4-10 Preparing a Hard Disk
4-11 Backing Up a Hard Disk
4-12 Restoring a Crashed Hard Disk

4-1
INTRODUCTION

In this chapter we consider the process of establishing directories and subdirectories on a floppy or hard disk. Commands for creating a directory, changing a directory, and removing or erasing a directory are explained. The chapter concludes with information on hard disk management. This includes preparing a hard disk, backing it up, and restoring it in case of a crash. Directory operations enable you to manage your hard disk very effectively.

4-2
DEFINING A DIRECTORY

When you format a disk, DOS automatically creates a **directory** for you. This directory usually is called the **root directory.** Because of the advances in disk technology, more and more files can be stored on a disk. These files are stored based on the date that they were created. When the number of these files increases, it becomes extremely difficult to manage them properly. It becomes a time-consuming process to locate one file among several hundred. By using a directory, you can store all your graphics files in one location, and all your word processing files in another location, and so on.

There is a limit to the number of files that can be stored on a floppy or a hard disk. The root directory on a single-sided disk can hold up to 64 files; on a double-sided disk there can be up to 112 files. A high-density disk can hold up to 224 files, and a hard disk up to 512 files. To create a better mechanism for storing and maintaining files and to bypass these limitations, you can create subdirectories.

A **subdirectory** is basically an electronic folder that contains a listing of files that you have grouped together based on a given scheme. (Subdirectory names follow the same conventions as file names.)

Consider a file cabinet in your office. Suppose that you store all important sales documents in this file cabinet. One method of storage is to throw all the sales documents in the cabinet as they arrive. In this case, retrieving information is a very difficult task. Another method is to divide the file cabinet into three separate parts (three subdirectories) by using some kind of folders. You can then divide the folders into more logical parts (lower level subdirectories). After this segmentation, you can put each document into its proper folder. This method improves the retrieval time. Figure 4–1 illustrates this example.

The directory below the root directory is considered a subdirectory to the root directory. A directory immediately below a subdirectory is considered a subdirectory to that subdirectory. In Figure 4–1, the WEST, SOUTH, and EAST regions are subdirectories to the root directory. OREGON and CALIFORNIA are subdirectories to the WEST region. We can break this down further into SOUTHERN and NORTHERN California, and so on.

As another example, suppose that on your hard disk you create four subdirectories for WordPerfect, Lotus 1-2-3, dBASE, and Quattro. All your word processing documents will be saved under the WORDPERFECT directory, all your spreadsheets will be saved under the 1-2-3 directory, and so forth. Under 1-2-3, you may want to create two subdirectories, one for your graphics files and one for your database files. This can continue for several levels, based on your specific needs.

The root directory is always identified by a back slash (\). The current subdirectory is identified by a period (.) and the parent subdirectory (the directory immediately above the current directory) is identified by two periods (..).

Chapter 4 Directories and Subdirectories

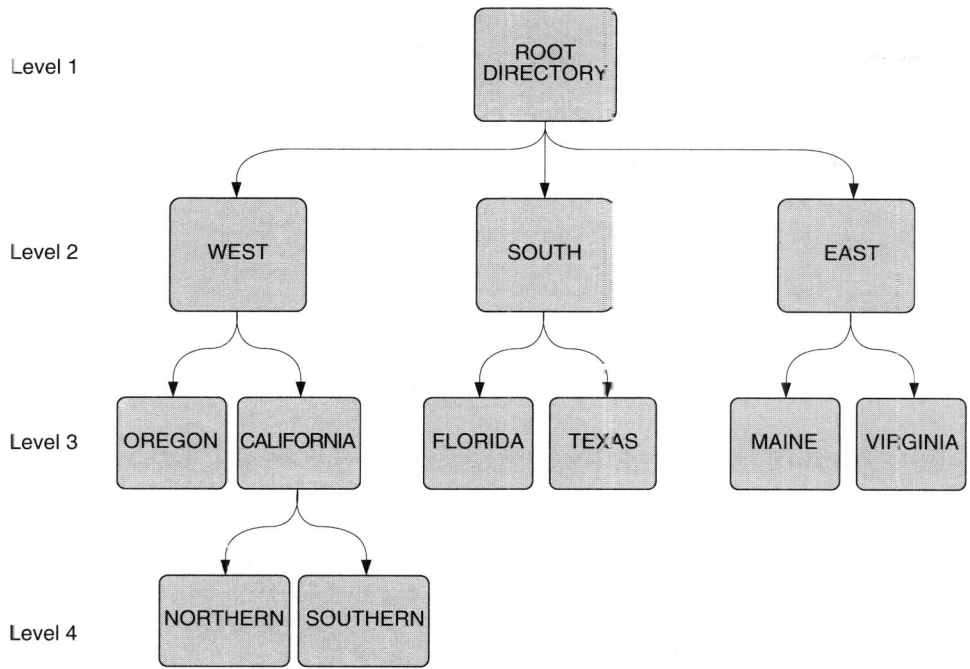

Figure 4-1
Example of directory structure

4-3 IMPORTANT COMMANDS FOR DIRECTORIES

To create a subdirectory, use the DOS command MKDIR (make directory), or MD. You must be in the directory immediately above the subdirectory you are creating.

To change to a subdirectory or make a subdirectory the current directory, use the CHDIR (change directory), or CD, command. The CD command uses several different parameters as shown in Table 4-1.

To remove a subdirectory, you first must erase all the files and subsequent subdirectories by using either the DEL or ERASE command. Then use the RMDIR (remove directory), or RD, command.

If you do not know in which directory you are working, use the PROMPT PG command to solve the problem. At the DOS prompt, type *PROMPT PG*. The default prompt changes to a prompt that identifies the current directory. For example, if you are working in the OREGON directory in drive A, your new prompt will read

A>OREGON>

Parameter	Function
CD.	Displays the current directory
CD..	Moves up one directory level
CD\	Moves up to the root directory from any directory level
CD..\..	Moves up two directory levels
CD\WEST\OREGON	OREGON becomes the current directory

Table 4-1
CD command parameters

To display the structure of your directory, use the TREE command. The command TREE/F displays each directory on your disk and the files stored within each directory.

Another powerful command that you can use with directories is the PATH command. This command establishes a search path. Suppose that you are working with a data disk in drive A. If you issue an external DOS command from drive A, you will receive an error message (because the DOS disk is in drive C). If you type *PATH C:* at the C> prompt, DOS searches the root directory on drive C for any commands that it cannot find in the current drive or directory (in our case drive A). You also can establish multiple search paths by using the PATH command and a semicolon (;). Suppose that you want to tell your computer to search for DOS commands in drive A and in a subdirectory on drive C called EXTERNAL. The following search path will do the job:

PATH A:\; C:\EXTERNAL

When you establish a search path, it remains in effect until you turn off your PC. To cancel a search path, type *PATH* and press Enter.

One very powerful command for working with directories is XCOPY. The XCOPY command enables you to copy all the directories and the files included within them from source drive/directory to the destination drive/directory. As an example, consider the disk in drive A which includes 205 files in Lotus, dBASE, and WordPerfect directories. To copy all these files and these directories from the A drive to the B drive the command is (default is C drive)

XCOPY A: *.* B:/S

The S parameter indicates that all subdirectories will be copied as well as the files. The S parameter copies all the subdirectories except the empty ones. The E parameter copies all the subdirectories including the empty ones. For the above example, the XCOPY command with the E parameter would be

XCOPY A: *.* B:/E

4-4

EXAMPLE 1: DIRECTORY CREATION

Start DOS and format a blank disk. Insert the formatted disk in drive A. At the C> prompt, type *PROMPT PG* and press Enter. From now on you will know which directory you are working with. Type *DIR A:* followed by Enter to see the contents of your disk before directory creation. In our case the disk is empty. Remember that DOS commands are not case sensitive.

Type *A:* followed by Enter. This changes the default from C> to A>. To create three directories named WEST, SOUTH, and EAST, type the following commands and press Enter after each:

MD WEST
MD SOUTH
MD EAST

Type *DIR* and press Enter. You will see the information presented in Figure 4-2. It shows there are three directories.

```
A>DIR

Volume in drive A is SUPPLIERS
Volume Serial Number is 371E-19DD
Directory of A:\

WEST          <DIR>      01-01-93    9:12p
SOUTH         <DIR>      01-01-93    9:12p
EAST          <DIR>      01-01-93    9:12p
       3 file(s)            0 bytes
                      1140736 bytes free

A>
```

Figure 4-2
Three subdirectories within the root directory

Type *CD\WEST* to make WEST the current directory. To create the subdirectories OREGON and CALIFORNIA, type the following commands and press Enter after each:

MD OREGON
MD CALIFORNIA

Next, type *CD* to return to the root directory and type *CD\SOUTH* to make SOUTH the current directory (remember to press Enter after each command). Create the subdirectories FLORIDA and TEXAS with the following commands (remember to press Enter after each one):

MD FLORIDA
MD TEXAS

Type *CD* to return to the root directory. Type *CD\EAST* to make EAST the current directory and enter the following:

MD MAINE
MD VIRGINIA

Type *CD* to go back to the root directory. Enter the command *CD\WEST\CALIFORNIA* to make CALIFORNIA the current directory. Next, type the following commands to create the NORTHERN and SOUTHERN subdirectories:

MD NORTHERN
MD SOUTHERN

You have now constructed the diagram presented in Figure 4-1. Type *CD* to return to the root directory. At the C> prompt, type *TREE A:*, and press Enter. You will see information similar to that shown in Figure 4-3.[1]

Copying to directories is similar to copying files. However, in a directory environment, you must provide a specific path for a given file.

4-5

EXAMPLE 2: COPYING TO DIRECTORIES

---

[1] In earlier versions of DOS, the branches of the tree are not shown graphically.

Figure 4-3
DOS-generated tree-structured directory

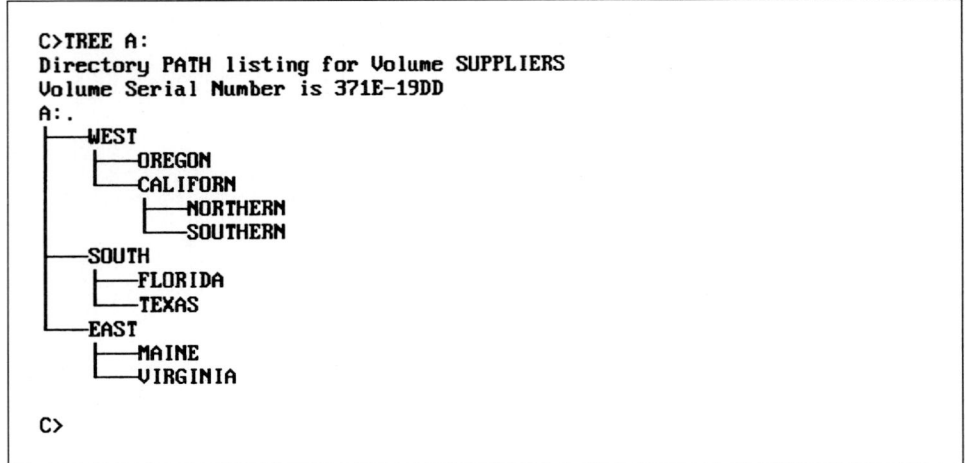

Start DOS and insert the disk you just created in drive A. Suppose that you want to copy all files with the COM extension from drive C (the DOS disk) to the WEST subdirectory. From the C> prompt, type

COPY *.COM A:\WEST

Now you can check the contents of WEST (by using the DIR command) to verify your work.

Suppose that you want to copy COMMAND.COM from drive C to subdirectory SOUTHERN. The command is

COPY COMMAND.COM A:\WEST\CALIFORNIA\SOUTHERN

If you check the contents of the SOUTHERN directory, you will see COMMAND.COM residing there.

4-6
EXAMPLE 3: COPYING FROM ONE SUBDIRECTORY TO ANOTHER

Suppose that you want to copy COMMAND.COM from the SOUTHERN subdirectory to the NORTHERN subdirectory. The command for this from the C> prompt is

COPY A:\WEST\CALIFORNIA\SOUTHERN\COMMAND.COM A:\WEST\CALIFORNIA\NORTHERN

Generate a directory listing of both the SOUTHERN and NORTHERN subdirectories. They should be identical.

4-7
EXAMPLE 4: REMOVING A DIRECTORY

You decide to remove both the SOUTHERN and NORTHERN subdirectories. Start DOS and insert the disk you have been working with in drive A. To remove a directory, first you must erase all the files and subsequent directories. At the C> prompt type the following:

Chapter 4 Directories and Subdirectories 65

```
DEL A:\WEST\CALIFORNIA\NORTHERN\COMMAND.COM
DEL A:\WEST\CALIFORNIA\SOUTHERN\COMMAND.COM
```

Now both the NORTHERN and SOUTHERN subdirectories are empty. Type *CD* and press Enter to return to the root directory. (You must be in either the root directory or in a directory one level above the subdirectory to be removed). Enter the following commands, remembering to press Enter after each line:

```
RD A:\WEST\CALIFORNIA\NORTHERN
RD A:\WEST\CALIFORNIA\SOUTHERN
```

4-8 HARD DISK MANAGEMENT

As a result of decreasing costs and advancements in hard disk technology, hard disks are becoming more popular among PC users. The major difference between a hard disk and a floppy disk is the massive storage space available on a hard disk. You can store all your application programs on a hard disk and relieve yourself of the pain of dealing with hundreds of floppy disks. It is also safer to store application programs on the hard disk. Damaging a floppy disk is more likely than damaging the hard disk.

Generally speaking, hard disks are more durable than floppy disks; however, hard disks are prone to crashing. A hard disk **crash** happens when the drive head comes in contact with the surface of the disk. Experts recommend that you use the programs SHIPDISK.COM or PARK.COM to park the drive head before turning off the system. These two utilities are not on the DOS disk, but you can get them from the vendors of your computer. To use these programs, insert the disk containing these commands in drive A. From the A> prompt, type the command *PARK.COM* or *SHIPDISK.COM* and follow the prompts.

To be able to work with a hard disk, you should be able to perform the following tasks:

- Partition the hard disk (using the FDISK command)
- Back it up (using the BACKUP command)
- Restore the files if the hard disk crashes (using the RESTORE command)

We discuss these commands in the next few pages. Remember that all the DOS commands you have learned so far except DISKCOPY and DISKCOMP work in a hard disk environment. These two commands do not work because there is a significant size difference between a floppy and a hard disk. Hard disk commands can be used with DOS 2.0 and above.

4-9 PARTITIONING A HARD DISK

A hard disk provides huge amounts of storage space compared with a floppy disk. To better manage this storage, you should **partition** the hard disk. Partitioning simply means dividing your hard disk into smaller chunks. You can partition a hard disk into separate drives, such as C, D, E, and so forth. You can install different operating systems besides DOS on your system. These may include UNIX, OS/2, or Windows. You may need to do this if you are using software packages that require operating systems other than DOS.

Figure 4–4
FDISK menu

```
                    MS-DOS Version 5.00
                    Fixed Disk Setup Program
              (C)Copyright Microsoft Corp. 1983 - 1991

                         FDISK Options

Current fixed disk drive: 1

Choose one of the following:

1. Create DOS partition or Logical DOS Drive
2. Set active partition
3. Delete partition or Logical DOS Drive
4. Display partition information


Enter choice: [1]




Press Esc to exit FDISK
```

In any event, partitioning helps you to better manage your hard disk. To use the FDISK program, at the C> prompt type *FDISK* and press Enter. You will see the screen shown in Figure 4–4. This is a menu-driven system—you can walk through it and select the options you need.

4–10
PREPARING A HARD DISK

Just like floppy disks, hard disks also need to be formatted. Remember, you format the hard disk only once. If you mistakenly format a hard disk that you are using, all the valuable information is lost permanently (you better have a backup!). To format your hard disk, put the disk that includes the FORMAT command in drive A. At the A> prompt, type *FORMAT C:/S/V*. The S parameter is used to transfer system files to the hard disk and to make it a self-booting system. The V parameter is used to provide a volume label for the hard disk.

4–11
BACKING UP A HARD DISK

Because your hard disk includes thousands of important files and data items, you should **back up** your hard disk periodically. You can back up a hard disk on floppies or you can use a tape backup system. The command for backing up a hard disk is BACKUP, and it can take several parameters, as shown in Table 4–2.

The following are some specific examples of the BACKUP command:

- C> BACKUP C :*.* A:/S
  Backs up the entire drive C to drive A.
- C> BACKUP C :*.* A:/S/M
  Backs up all the new files that have been modified since the last backup.

Chapter 4 Directories and Subdirectories

Table 4–2
BACKUP command parameters

Parameter	Function
/S	Backs up the entire disk (files and directories)
/M	Backs up files that have been modified since the last time that the BACKUP command was used
/A	Adds new backup files to an existing backup disk without erasing any of the current files
/D	Backs up files that have been modified on or after a given date. The format for the date is [month-day-year] ([01-25-93], for example).

Figure 4–5
BACKUP command

```
C>BACKUP C:\*.* A:/S

Insert backup diskette 01 in drive A:

WARNING! Files in the target drive
A:\ root directory will be erased
Press any key to continue . . .

*** Backing up files to drive A: ***
Diskette Number: 01
```

- C> BACKUP C :*.* A:/S/A/D 10/10/92
  Backs up all the files created since 10/10/92 and adds them to the disk in drive A without erasing any of the files in this drive.

  Figure 4–5 illustrates an example of the BACKUP command.

4–12 RESTORING A CRASHED HARD DISK

If your hard disk fails, it is not a difficult task to put it back to normal if you have a backup. To restore your disk, you must use the DOS RESTORE command. From the C> prompt, type

RESTORE A : C :*.* /S

Figure 4–6 illustrates a sample screen of the RESTORE command. This example assumes that your hard disk is technically sound and that the only problem is the data on it has been lost. If your hard disk has been damaged, you

Figure 4–6
Example of RESTORE command

```
C>RESTORE A: C:\*.*/S

Insert backup diskette 01 in drive A:
Press any key to continue . . .

*** Files were backed up 01-01-1993 ***

*** Restoring files from drive A: ***
Diskette: 01
```

Figure 4-7

Displaying a backup disk

```
C>DIR A:

 Volume in drive A is BACKUP   001
 Volume Serial Number is 1CC9-2C39
 Directory of A:\

BACKUP    001     1212928 01-01-93    9:36p
CONTROL   001         855 01-01-93    9:36p
        2 file(s)     1213783 bytes
                            0 bytes free

C>
```

must repair or replace it first, then use the RESTORE command to put all the data back on it.

If you have several disks and you want to discover whether a disk is a backup or an original, you can use the DIR command. If the disk is a backup, at the top of your directory you will see BACKUP @@@. Figure 4-7 illustrates this process. DOS 5.0 identifies the backup disk by its number, *not* the @@@ symbol. This is the case in Figure 4-7.

SUMMARY

This chapter reviewed directory and subdirectory operations. We discussed commands for directory creation, changing a directory, and removing a directory. We also discussed the TREE command for displaying the structure of a directory and the PROMPT command for customizing the DOS prompt in a tree-structured environment. The chapter concluded with valuable information on hard disk management.

REVIEW QUESTIONS

*These questions are answered in Appendix A.

1. What is a directory? A subdirectory?
2. Is there a limit on the number of directories on a disk (hard or floppy)?
*3. Why are subdirectories important, particularly in a hard disk environment?
4. What constitutes valid directory names?
5. How is the root directory identified?
6. What does a back slash (\) mean? A single period? Double periods?
7. What is the command to create a subdirectory? For changing directories? For removing directories?
*8. How do you move up one directory level? Two directory levels?
9. What command is used to display the structure of a directory?
10. What command is used to customize the DOS prompt in the subdirectory environment?
11. How do you copy a file from the root directory to a directory three levels down?
*12. How do you erase a directory?
13. Can a subdirectory that contains five files be removed? If yes, how? If no, why not?
14. What is hard disk management?
*15. How do you partition a hard disk?

Chapter 4 Directories and Subdirectories

16. How do you format a hard disk?
17. How do you back up a hard disk?
18. How do you restore a crashed hard disk?
19. What is the command for backing up all the files updated since January 15, 1992?
*20. What is the command for backing up the new files to a disk in drive A without losing the contents of the disk in drive A?

HANDS-ON EXPERIENCE

1. Put a formatted disk in drive A. Create three subdirectories (MARKETING, FINANCE, and PRODUCTION) in drive A. Under MARKETING, create two additional directories called DIVISION1 and DIVISION2. Copy all COM files from drive C to DIVISION1. Copy all SYS files from drive C to DIVISION2. Copy all files from DIVISION1 to MARKETING. Display the structure of your directory by using the TREE command.
2. Start DOS and insert a formatted disk in drive A. Next, do the following:
   a. Customize the DOS prompt by using PROMPT PG.
   b. Create subdirectories D1, D2, D3, and D4 on drive A.
   c. Under D1, create two subdirectories, E1 and E2.
   d. Under E1, create two subdirectories, F1 and F2.
   e. Copy all the COM files from drive C to F2.
   f. Remove F2.
   g. Make F1 the current directory.
   h. By using CD., display the current directory.
   i. By using CD.., move up one directory level.
   j. By using CD\, move up to the root directory.
3. Consult your DOS manual and walk through the FDISK command.
4. Get the BACKUP command started. Back up a hard disk to several floppy disks. How do you restore a hard disk?

KEY TERMS

Back up   Directory   Root directory
Crash   Partition   Subdirectory

KEY COMMANDS

BACKUP (external)   PARK.COM (external)   RMDIR (RD) (internal)
CHDIR (CD) (internal)   PATH (internal)   SHIPDISK.COM (external)
FDISK (external)   PROMPT PG (internal)   TREE (external)
MKDIR (MD) (internal)   RESTORE (external)   XCOPY (external)

MISCONCEPTIONS AND SOLUTIONS

Misconception You are working with subdirectories and receive an INVALID DIRECTORY error message.

Solution You have either misspelled the name of the directory or the directory does not exist. Issue the TREE command to see if such a directory exists.

Windows 3.1

Misconception   You are trying to remove a directory and receive a DIRECTORY NOT EMPTY error message.

> **Solution**   Your directory must be empty. Use the DEL or ERASE command to erase all the files; then you can remove the directory. The current directory must not be the directory you are attempting to delete. You must be either in the root directory or in a directory one level above the subdirectory you are trying to delete.

Misconception   You issue the TREE command and receive a BAD COMMAND error message.

> **Solution**   Remember, TREE is an external command. Either you must have DOS in the default drive or you must specify a path to reach DOS.

ARE YOU READY TO MOVE ON?

Multiple Choice

1. The main directory created on a newly formatted disk is called the
    a. subdirectory
    b. root directory
    c. primary directory
    d. file directory
    e. none of the above

2. In the file specification C:\SALES\CUSTOMERS\ABC\ORDER.JAN, ABC is a sub-directory of
    a. ROOT
    b. SALES
    c. CUSTOMERS
    d. ORDER.JAN
    e. none of the above

3. The command to create a subdirectory is
    a. MAKE
    b. CREATE
    c. RD
    d. MD
    e. RMDIR

4. To make another subdirectory the current directory, the command to use is
    a. CD
    b. RD
    c. MD
    d. GOTO
    e. none of the above

5. The command to allow DOS to display the current directory is
    a. DISPLAY PG
    b. SHOW PG
    c. SEE PG
    d. DIR PG
    e. PROMPT PG

Chapter 4 Directories and Subdirectories

6. Formatting the hard disk will
   a. divide the disk into sectors and tracks
   b. partition the disk into C:, D:, E:, and so forth
   c. erase all data
   d. both a and b
   e. both a and c
7. One of the best methods of protecting your data is to
   a. create subdirectories
   b. back up the disk
   c. run CHKDSK periodically
   d. run TREE/F periodically
   e. format the disk
8. If the disk you have is a backup, a directory listing will show
   a. THIS IS A BACKUP DISK
   b. BACKUP ***
   c. DOS BACKUP
   d. BACKUP @@@ or its number
   e. none of the above
9. If you want to place the files from a backup disk onto the hard disk, use the command
   a. RESTORE
   b. DUMP
   c. REPLACE
   d. BACKUP/R
   e. none of the above
10. Subdirectories are useful because they
    a. prevent loss of data from a head crash
    b. eliminate the need to back up the disk
    c. provide better file management and organization
    d. prevent unauthorized access
    e. all of the above

True/False

1. When you format a disk, DOS automatically creates the root directory for you.
2. There is no limit to the number of files that can be stored in the root directory.
3. Subdirectories are directories created below the root directory or existing subdirectories.
4. The root directory is always identified by two periods (..).
5. Removing a subdirectory with the RMDIR or RD command will erase all files in the subdirectory.
6. The PATH command enables DOS automatically to search various subdirectories for commands that it cannot find in the current directory.
7. Experts recommend that you use a utility to park the heads of a hard disk before turning off the computer.
8. All partitions of the hard disk must have the same operating system on them.
9. One cannot overemphasize the importance of maintaining a current backup of the hard disk.
10. BACKUP/M is used to back up the entire disk.

ANSWERS

Multiple Choice	True/False
1. b	1. T
2. c	2. F
3. d	3. T
4. a	4. F
5. e	5. F
6. e	6. T
7. b	7. T
8. d	8. F
9. a	9. T
10. c	10. F

Windows 3.1: An Overview

5–1   Introduction
5–2   Advantages of Windows
5–3   Understanding Windows Terminology
5–4   Getting In and Getting Out of Windows
5–5   Using a Mouse in the Windows Environment
5–6   Using the Keyboard in a Windows Environment
5–7   Running Windows in Different Modes
5–8   Getting Help
      5–8–1   Help Facility
      5–8–2   Help on a Specific Topic
      5–8–3   Tutorial Facility
5–9   Different Parts of a Windows Screen
5–10 Upgrading to Windows 3.1

5-1
INTRODUCTION

We begin this chapter by discussing some of the unique advantages of Windows as a graphical-based environment compared with a character-based environment such as DOS. Then we focus on the procedures for getting in and out of Windows and for using a mouse and the keyboard in the Windows environment. Running Windows in different modes is also considered in this chapter, as are the help and tutorial facilities. The chapter describes the different parts of a Windows screen and concludes with some highlights on upgrading to Windows 3.1 from 3.0.

5-2
ADVANTAGES OF WINDOWS

Windows 3.1 is an operating system based on a **graphical user interface (GUI)** environment (pronounced "gooey") that runs "on top" of DOS. This means your computer must first have DOS installed to be able to run Windows. The graphical environment presents several unique advantages not found in the DOS character-based environment. Let us consider some of these advantages:

- Windows is easier to use than DOS. With Windows you do not need to memorize the strict DOS command syntax. Instead, you can perform all DOS functions, and more through a series of pull-down menus. Pull-down menus open a series of options from which a user can choose.
- All Windows applications share the same principles. When you learn one Windows application, you can easily transfer some or all of what you have learned to other applications.
- Windows applications allow you to work with a mouse, the keyboard, or shortcut keys. All of these options enable you to become more efficient in using Windows programs.
- Windows presents a **multitasking** environment, which means that you can run more than one program at the same time. Imagine that you are using WordPerfect to type a report and you decide that you need a spreadsheet created in Lotus 1-2-3. If you are using Windows, you can easily switch to Lotus 1-2-3 and incorporate the desired spreadsheet into your report. You can even integrate a graph into the report. Or maybe you decide that you need a telephone number from your online telephone directory. You can easily run your telephone directory software, access the correct phone number, then exit the directory software—all without ever leaving WordPerfect.
- Windows applications and DOS applications can run simultaneously. You can even run multiple DOS programs and multiple Windows programs at the same time if your computer has enough memory and adequate processing speed.
- You can link several files together using Windows. As a result, if you change data in one file, the same data in the linked files will be changed automatically.
- Better memory management is possible with Windows. You are not restricted by the traditional 640K DOS memory barrier; Windows can use main memories well above the conventional memory barrier. Windows also makes your hard disk an extension of your RAM. If a program does not fit into your RAM, it will simply spill over to your hard disk.
- Accessory programs are available in the Windows package. Windows comes with a group of accessories that are readily available at no additional charge.

Chapter 5 Windows 3.1: An Overview

Ease of Use
Shared principles among Windows applications
Use of mouse, keyboard, and shortcut keys
Multitasking
Ability to run Windows and DOS applications at the same time
Ability to link files together
Better memory management
Inclusion of several accessories in the same package

Table 5-1
Unique advantages of windows

These accessories include Windows Write, a word processor; Windows Paintbrush, a drawing program; Windows Terminal, a communications program; and Windows Print Manager, a program that allows you to work and print at the same time. Many more useful programs such as Calculator, Calendar, Notepad, Cardfile, and Clock are part of Windows. We will discuss these accessories in subsequent chapters.

The unique advantages of Windows are summarized in Table 5-1.

5-3 UNDERSTANDING WINDOWS TERMINOLOGY

Windows, similar to other software, has its own terminology. Some of the most important terms are desktop, icon, mouse, window, and dialog box.

Think of **Desktop** the way you think of the surface of a desk. All your work in Windows takes place on the desktop. When you start Windows, you start at the desktop. You can do a number of tasks from the desktop; among the most common tasks are these: (1) fast switching from one application to another; (2) changing icon spacing (i.e., changing the distance between icons on the screen), rearranging the placement of icons, deleting unwanted icons, and so forth; (3) displaying documents, and (4) changing colors.

An **Icon** is a graphic representation of an application or a document. You can move the mouse pointer to the desired icon and double-click the left button of the mouse to start the application or open a document.

The **mouse** will be explained in detail in section 5-5. It is the main interface between you, Windows, and Windows applications. Although you can use the keyboard or shortcut keys, the mouse is the most efficient way to execute most Windows tasks.

A **window** is similar to a screen. It displays different parts and different settings of an application at any given time.

A **dialog box** is a window (square box) that includes options which appear when a command needs additional information before it can be executed.

5-4 GETTING IN AND GETTING OUT OF WINDOWS

Windows must be installed on a hard disk; it will not run on a floppy disk system. After you install Windows, switch to the drive and directory that contain your Windows files by using the DOS CD command (i.e., CD WINDOWS); then type *WIN* and press Enter. If you are working in a computer lab, Windows may be one of your applications. If this is the case, just press the application number or the character representing the application. In any event, you will be presented with a screen similar to the one shown in Figure 5–1—the Program Manager window (discussed in detail in Chapter 9) with the Main group window open. Your screen might be different because of the specific configuration of your system.

There are three methods you can use to get out of Windows.

1. Move the mouse pointer to the File option at the upper left of the screen and click the left button of the mouse. You will be presented with a screen similar to the one shown in Figure 5–2. Move the mouse pointer to the Exit Windows option and click the left button.
2. Move the mouse pointer to the control-menu box (the small square) at the far upper left of the screen and *double-click* the left button of the mouse. (See Figures 5–1 and 5–17 to locate the control-menu box.)
3. Move the mouse pointer to the control-menu box and click the left button of the mouse. You will be presented with a screen similar to the one shown in Figure 5–3. Move the mouse pointer to the Close option and click the left button.

Regardless of which of the three methods you use, you will be presented with a screen similar to the one shown in Figure 5–4. You can click on the **OK** option to leave Windows. If you click on the **Cancel** option, you are indicating that you have changed your mind and wish to stay in Windows. When you exit Windows, you exit either to DOS or your starting menu, depending on how you started Windows in the first place.

Figure 5–1
Windows starting screen: Program Manager window and Main group window

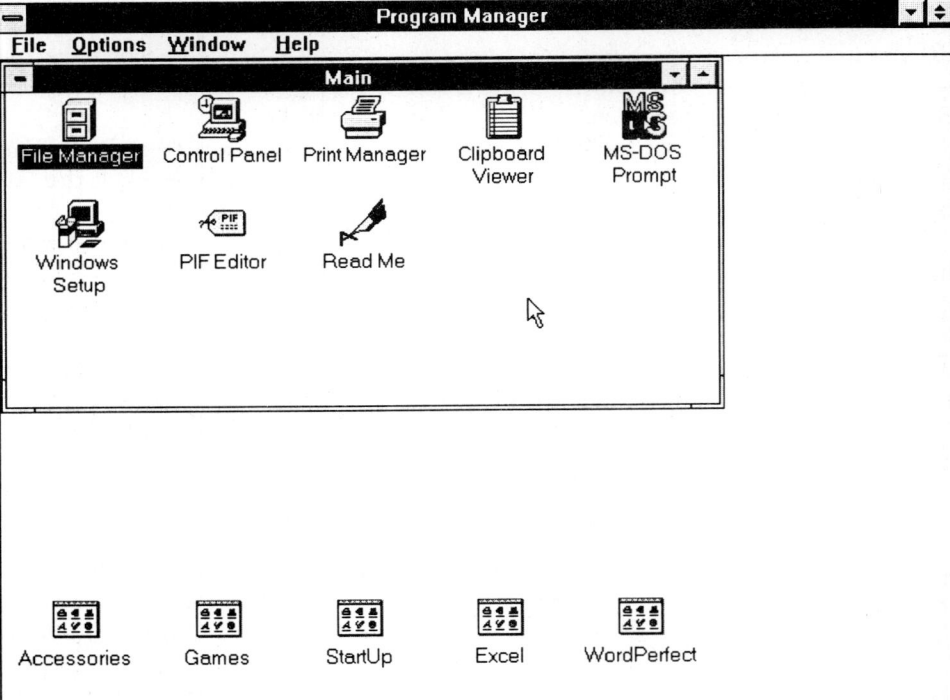

Chapter 5 Windows 3.1: An Overview

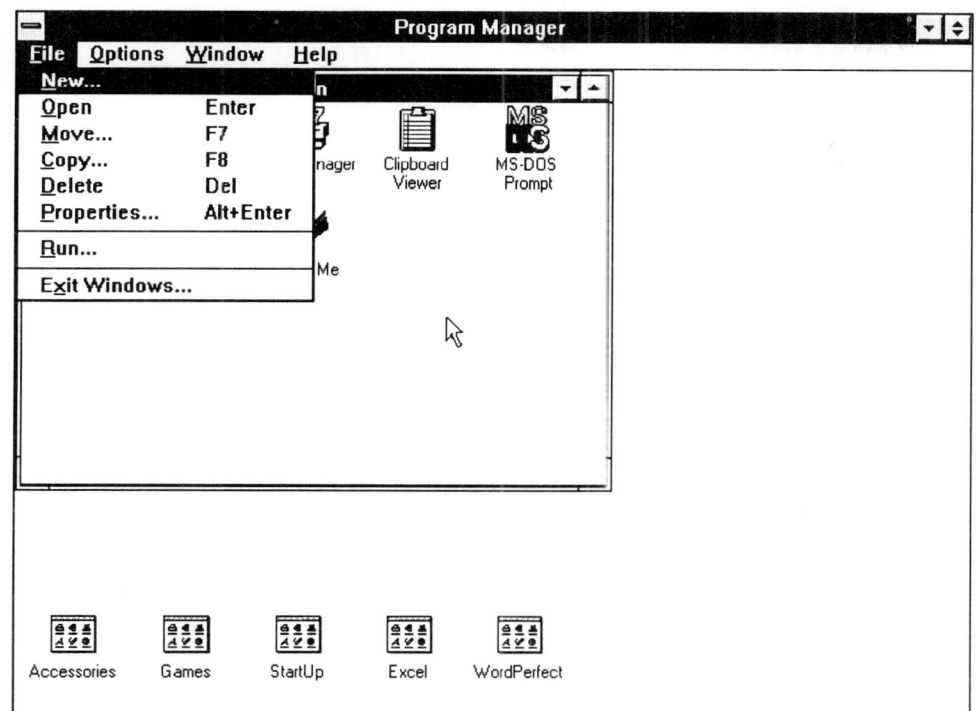

Figure 5–2
File pull-down menu

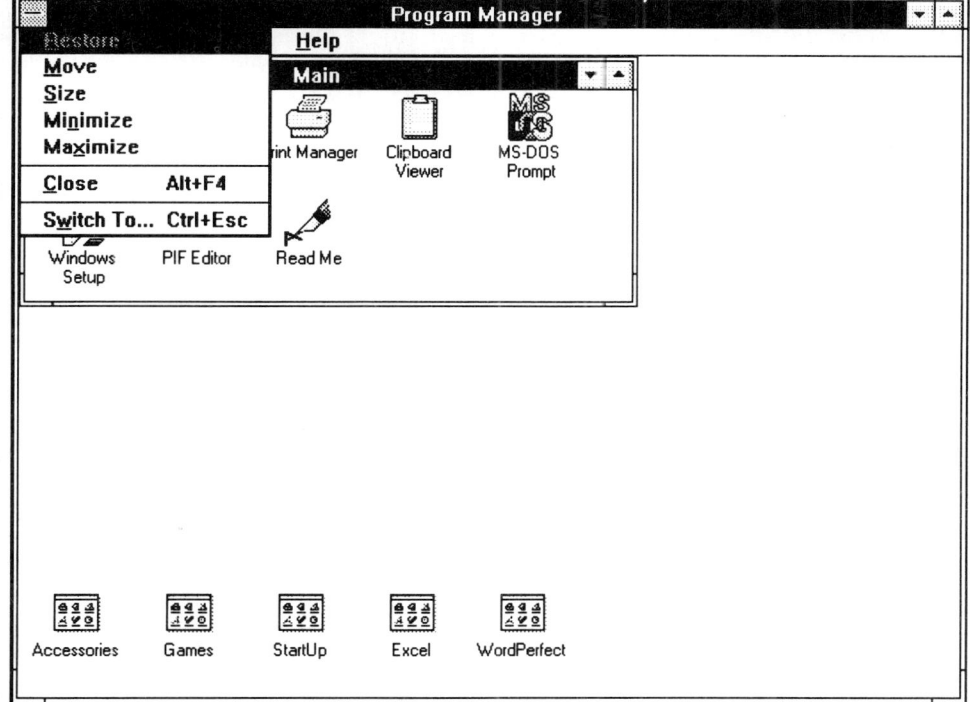

Figure 5–3
Control-menu box options

Figure 5-4
Windows exit dialog box

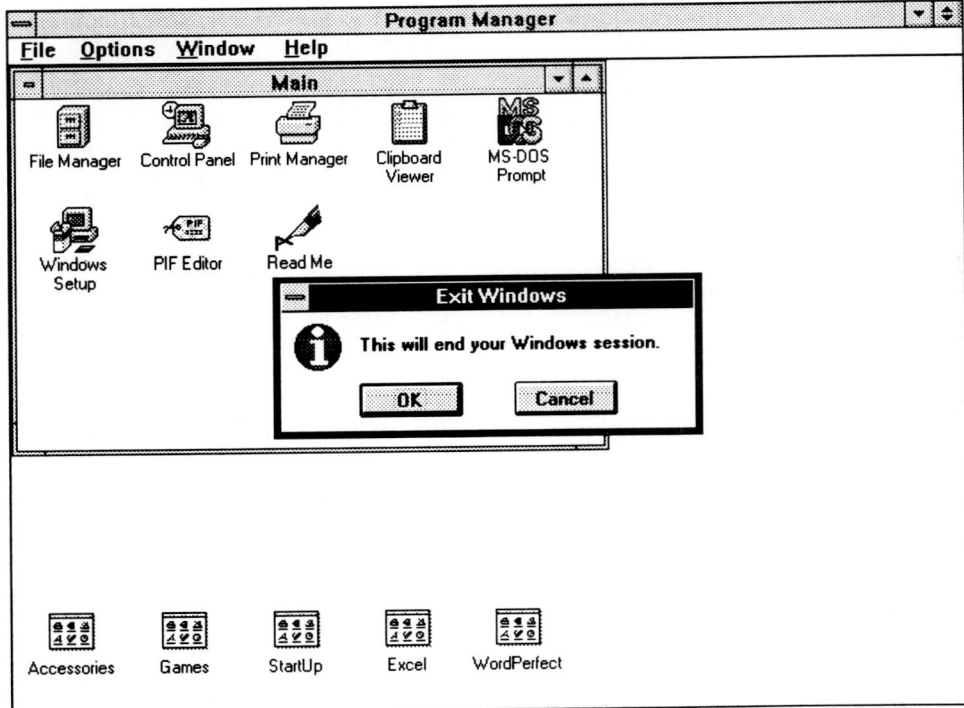

5-5
USING A MOUSE IN THE WINDOWS ENVIRONMENT

Windows offers the user three interface options: keyboard, mouse, and shortcut keys. Most users agree that a mouse is preferable to a keyboard in graphical environments such as Windows because of its speed, accuracy, ease of use, and other special functions that it can provide. Using a mouse, you can easily select pull-down menu options, quickly execute application programs, move and/or resize Windows groups, relocate icons to new locations on the screen, and much more. You will learn how to perform these tasks in the following paragraphs.

If you are right handed, hold the mouse in your right hand and place the mouse on the right side of the keyboard; if you are left handed, hold the mouse in your left hand and place it on the left side. Place the mouse on a flat surface (preferably on the mouse pad) and rest your hand on top of it. Place your thumb on one side of the mouse and the two fingers opposite it on the other side. This will leave your index finger and middle finger positioned over the mouse buttons. Lightly rest your fingers on these buttons. To see how the mouse works, move the mouse in a circular motion and look on the screen for the **mouse pointer.** You will see that it is also moving in a circular pattern, matching the movements of the mouse on your desk. If you move the mouse to the left, the mouse pointer moves to the left side of the screen; if you move the mouse away from you, the mouse pointer moves to the top of the screen; and so on.

Now let's try selecting some menu items using the mouse. Move the mouse so that the mouse pointer is pointing to the File option at the upper left of the screen; then click the left button of the mouse. If you do this correctly, the File pull-down menu will be displayed (see Figure 5-2). Move the mouse pointer to the Window option and click the left button again to display the Window pull-down menu (Figure 5-5). (The contents of this menu in your system might be different from that shown in Figure 5-5.) Notice that positioning the mouse

Chapter 5 Windows 3.1: An Overview

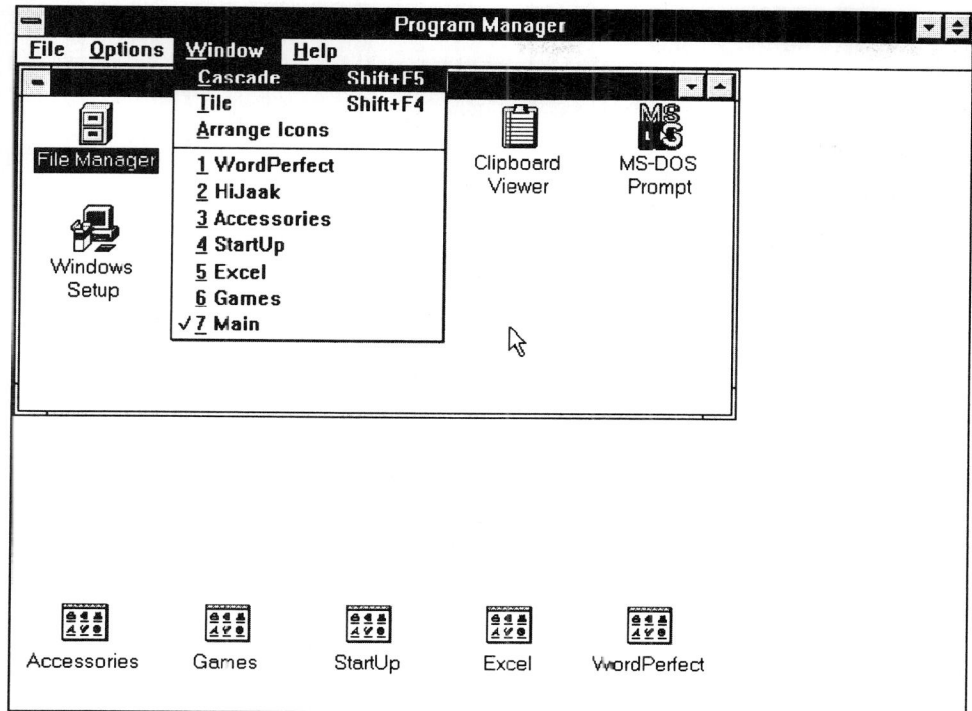

Figure 5-5
Window pull-down menu

pointer and clicking the left button of the mouse selects the desired menu item automatically. For now, move the mouse pointer back to the middle of the screen and click the left button to "deselect" any currently highlighted menu items.

Rapid double-clicking of the left button of the mouse while pointing the mouse pointer onto an icon automatically executes the application that the icon represents. To see how this works, move your mouse pointer to the Accessories icon and double-click the left button. This automatically opens the Accessories window; see Figure 5-6. Now you can double-click on any of the accessories to open them. If you do not have accessories on your desktop, try double-clicking with another icon. Close the Accessories window by double-clicking the control-menu box (at the upper left of the Accessories window).

Let's try another example. Move the mouse pointer to the MS-DOS Prompt icon in the Main group; then double-click the left button of the mouse. Windows responds by displaying a DOS prompt. At this point you can execute any of the DOS commands introduced in previous chapters. Type the command *EXIT* and press Enter to return to the Windows Program Manager screen.

You can move windows, group icons, application icons, and so forth to other locations on the screen by means of a method called **click and drag**. To try this, point the mouse pointer onto the title bar of the Main group window. (See Figure 5-17 for the location of the title bar.) Click the left button of the mouse; then while holding the button down, drag the mouse pointer to a new location on the screen. Notice that an outline form of the Main group moves with the mouse pointer. When you release the left button, your window will be relocated to the position of the mouse pointer when you released the left button.

Let's try changing the size of the Main group window. Slowly move the mouse pointer to the right edge of the Main group window. Notice that at a certain position over the edge of the window, the mouse pointer becomes a

Figure 5–6
Applications in the Accessories group

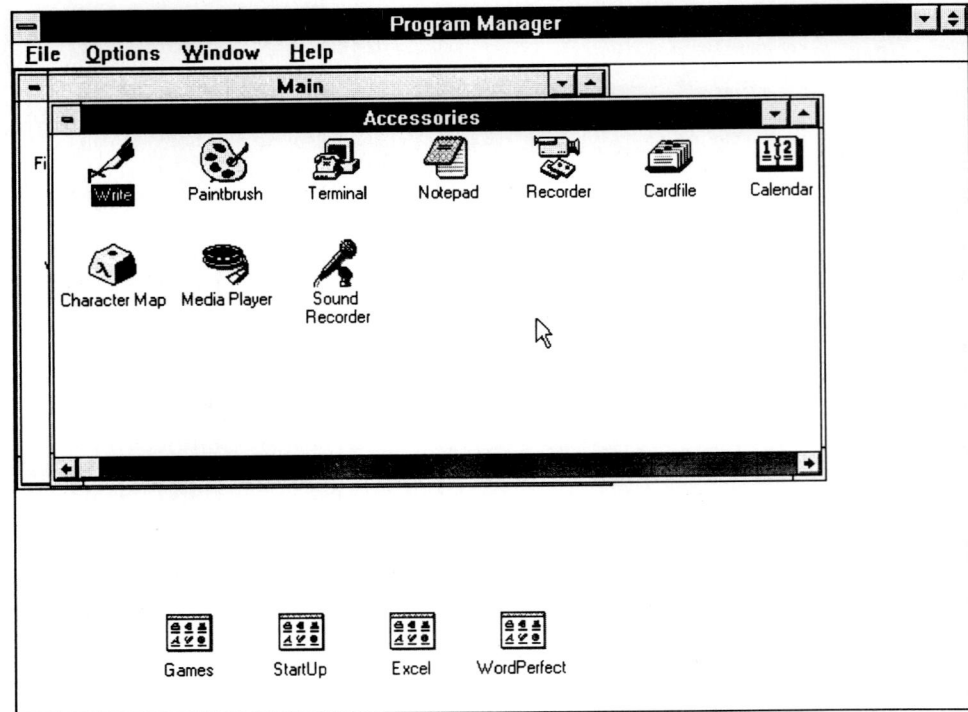

double-pointing arrow. When you see this, click and drag the left button of the mouse a small distance to the right. Again, notice the outline form; when you release the mouse button, your window will conform to the specified size. If you change your mind before releasing the left button, press the Esc key.

As a final example of moving screen items to new locations, move the mouse pointer onto the MS-DOS Prompt icon inside the Main group window. Click and drag the icon to a new location inside of the window; then release the left button of the mouse. Your icon will obediently follow your command to position itself in a new location. For now, drag the icon back into its previous position in the group window. Important tasks performed by the mouse are summarized in Table 5–2.

Table 5–2
Important tasks performed by the mouse

Task	How to Do It
Selecting from a menu	Move the mouse pointer to the menu option and click the left button of the mouse.
Executing a program or application	Move the mouse pointer to the desired icon and double-click the left button of the mouse.
Moving group or application icons	Position the mouse pointer onto the icon then click the left button of the mouse and drag.
Changing a window size	Point to any edge of the desired window, click the left button of the mouse, and drag.
Moving group or application windows	Point to the desired title bar, click the left button of the mouse, and drag.

Chapter 5 Windows 3.1: An Overview

5-6 USING THE KEYBOARD IN A WINDOWS ENVIRONMENT

Windows and Windows programs can be used with the keyboard in addition to the mouse. Keyboards have been around for years, so people are more familiar with them than with the mouse. Figure 5-7 illustrates the IBM PC XT keyboard and Figure 5-8 shows the IBM Enhanced keyboard.

You can use all of the following areas of a keyboard when working with Windows:

- The typing keys located in the center of the keyboard. These keys are similar to those on a typewriter.
- The numeric and cursor-movement keys located on the right side of the keyboard. Numeric keys are used to enter numbers; cursor-movement keys are used to move the cursor around. Enhanced keyboards have a dedicated cursor-movement pad, which can be used for any cursor movement. If you press the Num Lock key (on the IBM enhanced keyboard), the numeric pad serves as a 10-key machine.
- The function keys (F1 through F12) across the top of the enhanced keyboard or (F1 through F10) on the left side of standard keyboards. All these keys perform different functions depending on the application program you are using.

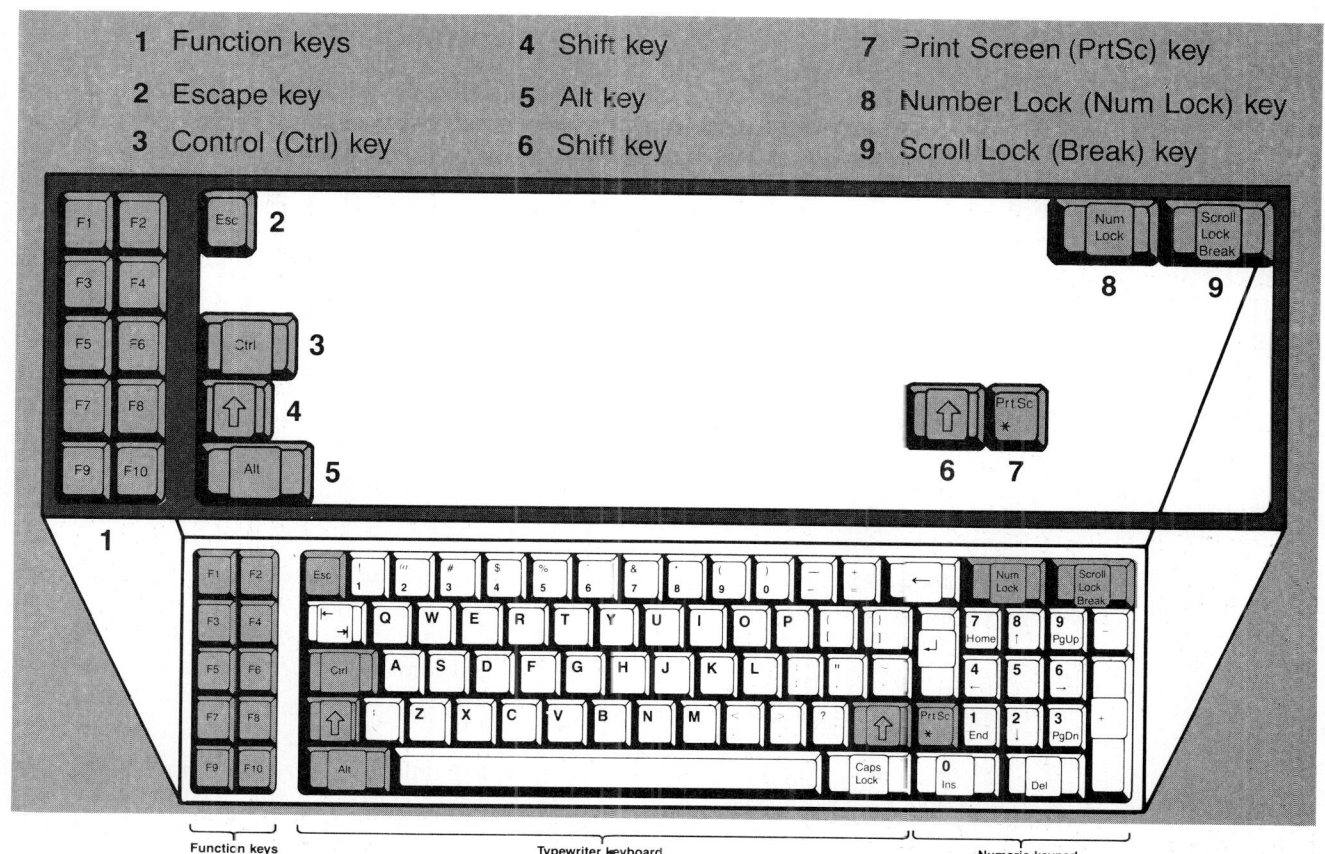

Figure 5-7
IBM XT keyboard (courtesy of International Business Machines Corp.)

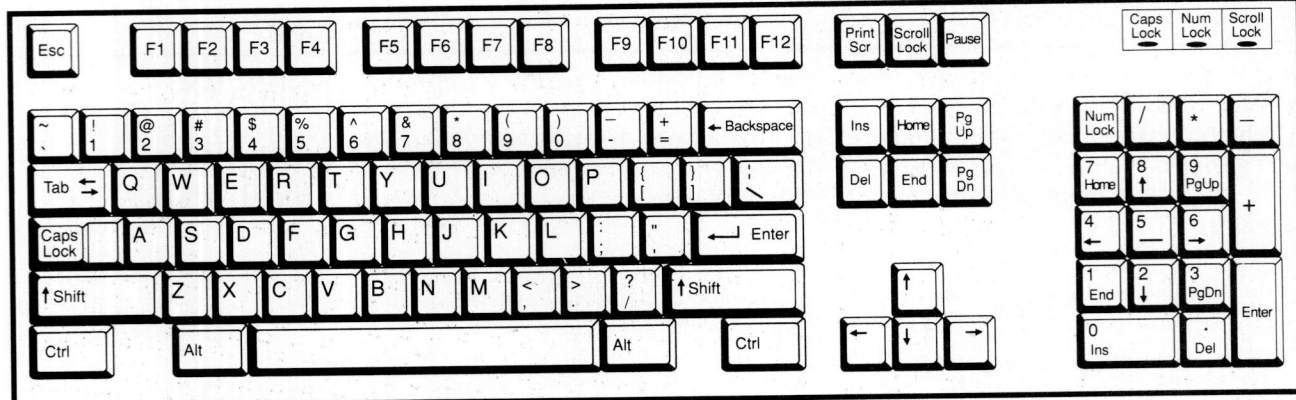

Figure 5-8
IBM enhanced keyboard (courtesy of International Business Machines Corp.)

Windows and Windows applications commands can also be executed through the use of key combinations, or shortcut keys. The key-combination method always involves using one or more of the following special keys—Shift, Alt, or Ctrl—combined with another key. These keys are called shortcut keys because they simplify the number of functions that your keyboard can perform. For example, Alt-F invokes the File menu. To use a key combination, you must first press either the Shift, Alt, or Ctrl key and hold it down while pressing the second key. For reasons of simplicity, however, we focus on the mouse in this book. Only some of the powerful key combinations will be mentioned.

5-7 RUNNING WINDOWS IN DIFFERENT MODES

Windows 3.1 can run in two different modes: **Standard mode** or **Enhanced mode.** Standard mode is used for 80286-based computers or 80386- and 80486-based computers with less than 2 MB of RAM. The 386 Enhanced mode is used for 80386- and 80486-based computers with more then 2 MB of RAM.

During the installation process, Windows automatically selects the mode that fits the computer's configuration. To determine the mode in which your computer is operating, from the Program Manager menu (see Figure 5-1) select the Help option; then select About Program Manager. For example, Figure 5-9 indicates that the Windows used in this book is operating in 386 Enhanced mode.

You also can decide to start your Windows in a certain mode. To do this, change to the drive and directory that contain your Windows files; then follow one of these steps:

- Type *WIN/S* (press Enter) to start in Standard mode.
- Type *WIN/3* (press Enter) to start in 386 Enhanced mode.

Remember that Enhanced mode is available only if you are running Windows on a 386- or 486-based computer with at least 2 MB of RAM (higher memory is recommended).

The Standard mode provides access to extended memory and enables the user to switch between applications, including those not specifically designed to run with Windows. The 386 Enhanced mode provides access to the virtual

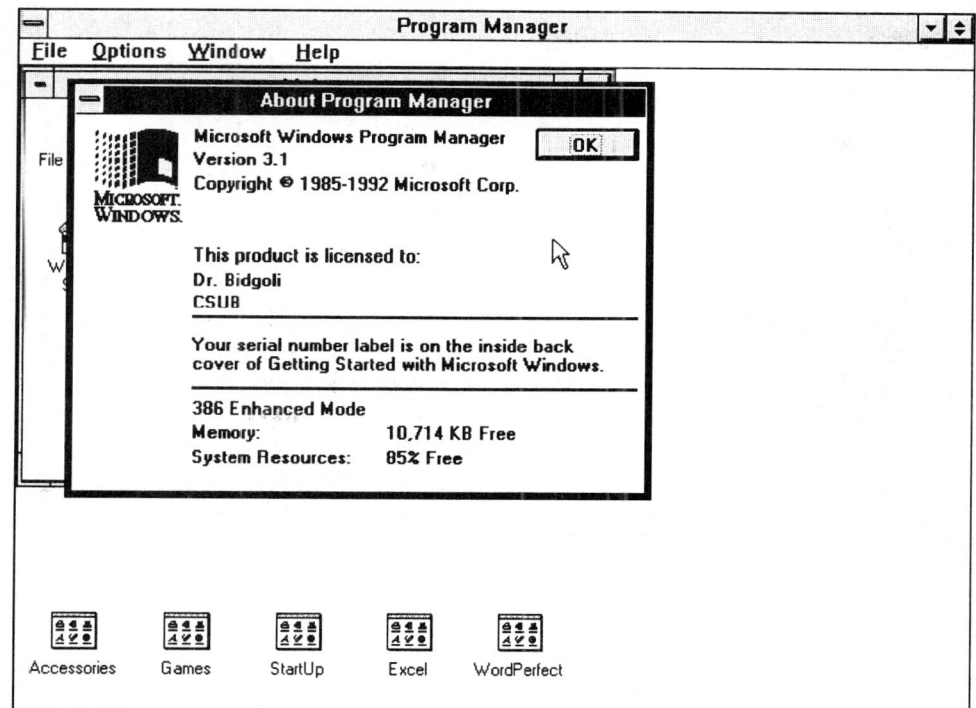

Figure 5-9
Finding the mode in which the computer is operating

memory capabilities of 386 and 486 processors. In this mode, applications have access to more memory than is physically available on a system, and you can still switch between applications. In theory, virtual memory means there is no limit on the amount of memory of the system.

5-8 GETTING HELP

5-8-1 Help Facility

As you can see in Figure 5-1, one of the options in the Program Manager menu is Help. If you move the mouse pointer to the Help option and click the left button of the mouse, you will see a screen similar to the one presented in Figure 5-10. Now you can move the mouse pointer to any of these options and click the left button to execute the desired option. For example, if you click the left button while on the Contents option, you will see a screen similar to Figure 5-11. You can click the left button while on any of these underlined items to receive help on the topic.

The part of this screen under Commands will always tell you about the choices in a particular menu bar. For example, to receive help on File, move the mouse pointer to File Menu Commands and click the left button of the mouse. You will be presented with a screen similar to Figure 5-12. To get out of this help screen, click the left button anywhere outside of this window on the desktop. As usual, you can also double-click the left button on the control-menu box at the upper left of the Help window.

Figure 5-10
Starting screen of the Help option

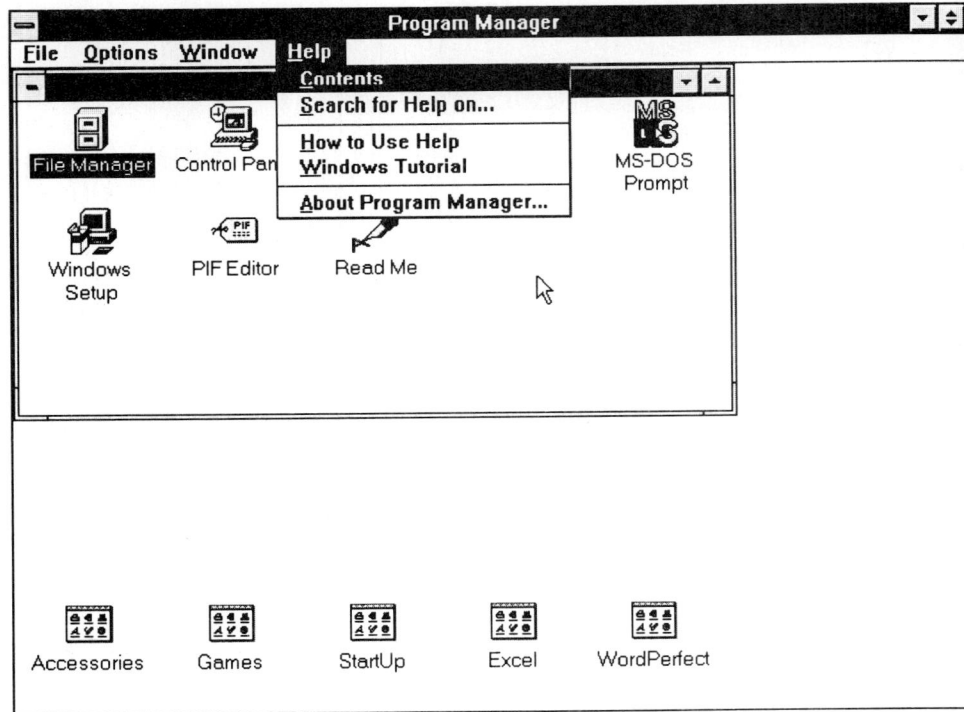

Figure 5-11
Information under the Contents option of the Help menu

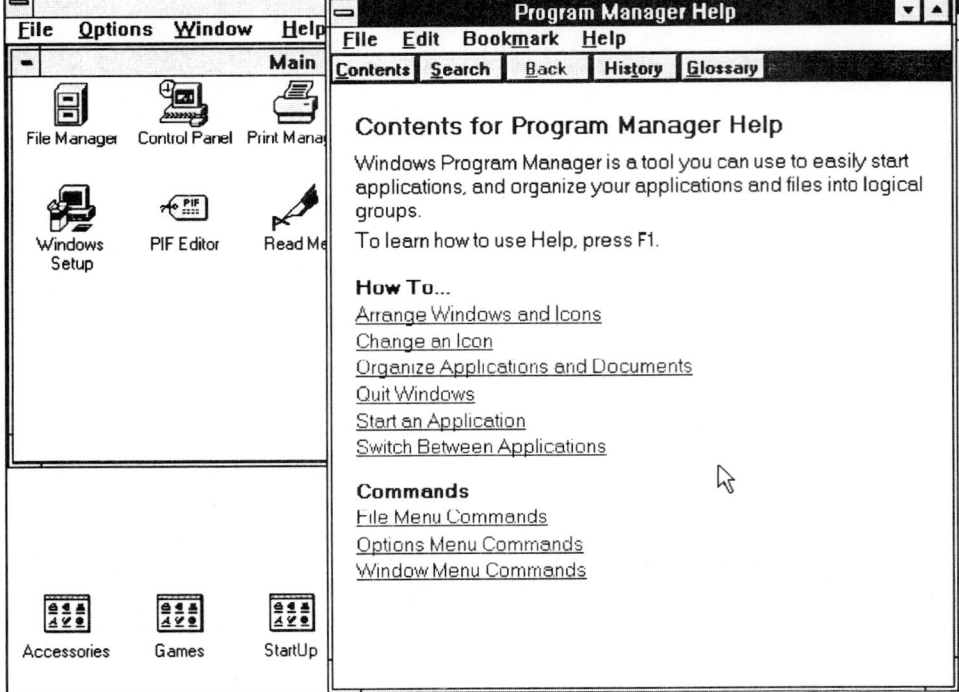

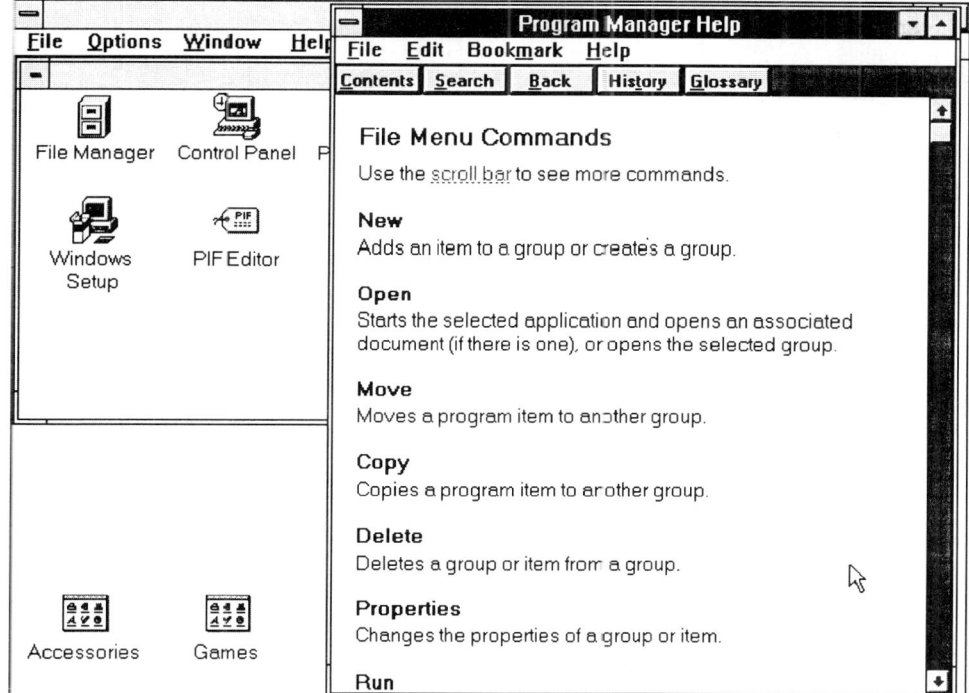

Figure 5-12
Online help on File menu commands

Help on a Specific Topic 5-8-2

Online help in Windows allows you to search for help on a specific topic. As you can see in Figure 5-11, one of the options on the top of the screen is Search. If you click the left button while here, you will be presented with a screen similar to the one in Figure 5-13. To receive help on a particular topic, follow these steps:

1. Type a word from the list provided in the text box. You can also point the mouse pointer to one of the words, such as "applications, starting," and then click the left button. To see all the words available, click the left button while on the down-arrow icon in the lower right corner of this window.
2. Click left while on Show Topics option. All the related topics will be displayed in the Select a topic box; see Figure 5-14.
3. In the Select a topic box, click the left button while on the desired topic. We selected Starting an Application by Using MS-DOS Prompt; then we clicked left on Go To. As you can see in Figure 5-15, the requested help on the desired topic is displayed.

A summary of other Help options shown in Figure 5-11 is provided in Table 5-3.
    A summary of the menu bar commands shown in Figure 5-11 is presented in Table 5-4.

Tutorial Facility 5-8-3

If you select the Windows Tutorial option from the Help pull-down menu (see Figure 5-10), you will be presented with a screen similar to Figure 5-16. This

Figure 5-13
Help search screen

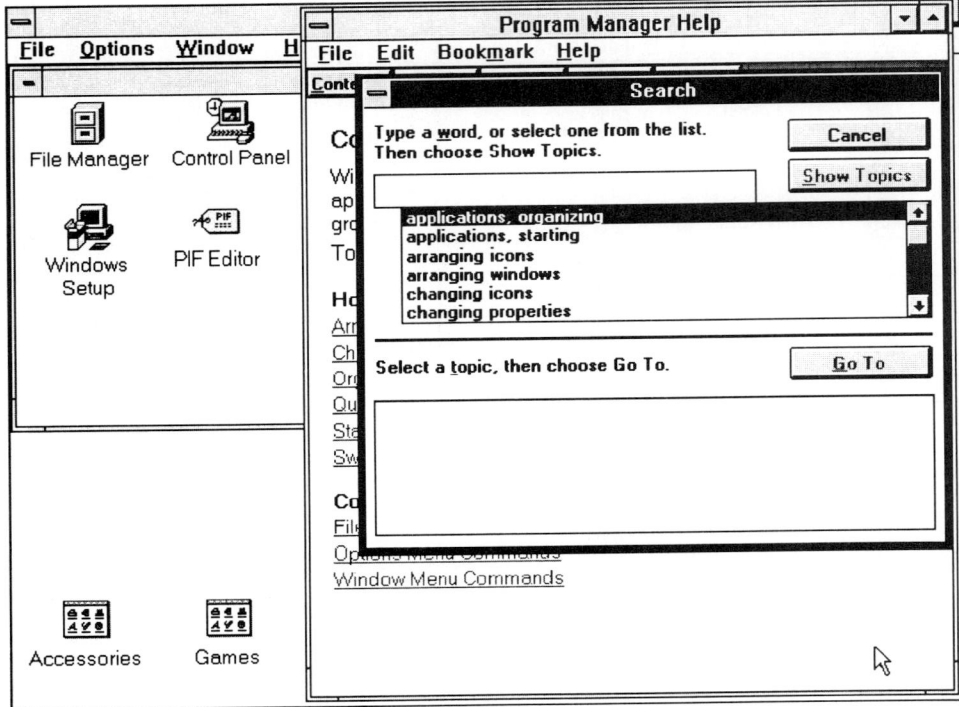

Figure 5-14
Contents of the Select a topic box after selecting the Show Topics option

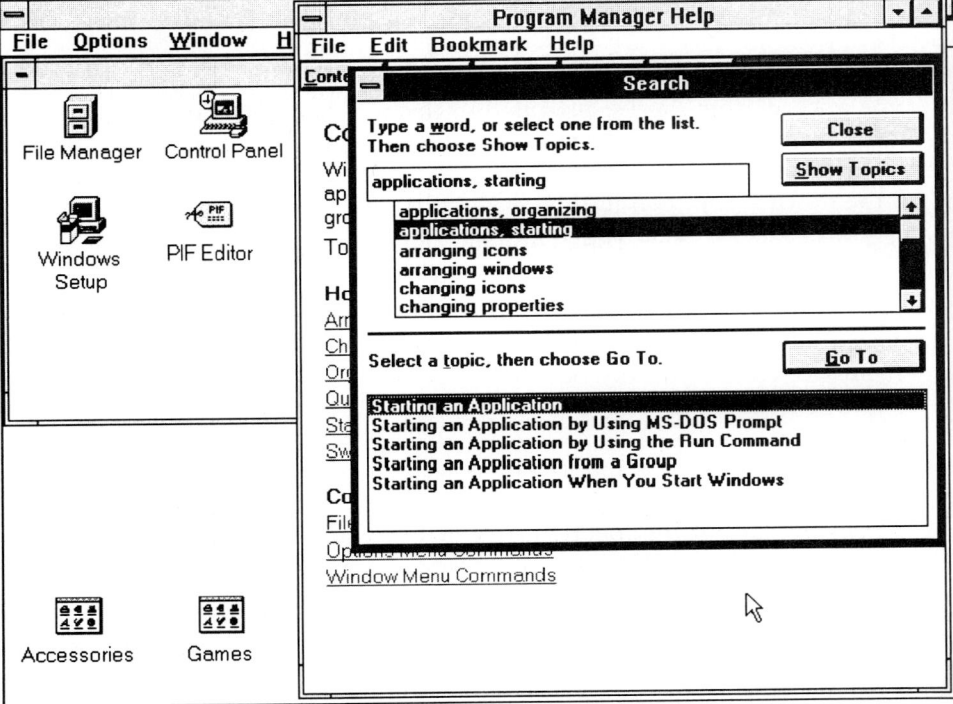

Chapter 5 Windows 3.1: An Overview

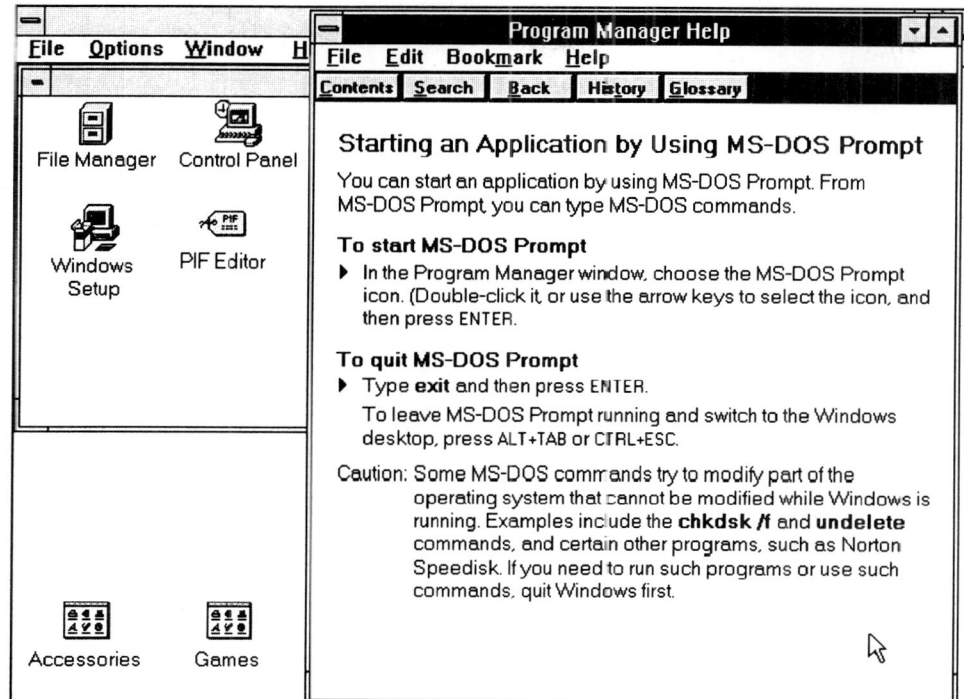

Figure 5-15
Help displayed on a specific topic

Option	Function
Contents	Displays the contents of the program's help file. Select one of the listed subjects to jump to that subject.
Back	Displays the most recent help subject that you reviewed. You can continue selecting the back option until you get to the contents screen.
History	Displays the last 40 help subjects that you recently reviewed in the current Windows session. To return to a specific subject, double-click it.
Glossary	Displays an alphabetized list of terms used in the online help

Table 5-3
Help options in the help screen

Command	Function
File	Is used to open a help file, print a help topic, or review the print setup
Edit	Is used to copy a help topic to the clipboard or to annotate (attach your own note) to the currently displayed help topic. Clipboard is a temporary holding area that will be explained in detail in Chapter 9.
Bookmark	Is used to mark help locations for easy reference
Help	Is used to find out how to open Windows Help and about the active application (copyright, version, name)

Table 5-4
Summary of the menu bar commands in the help screen

Figure 5-16
Starting screen of the Windows tutorial

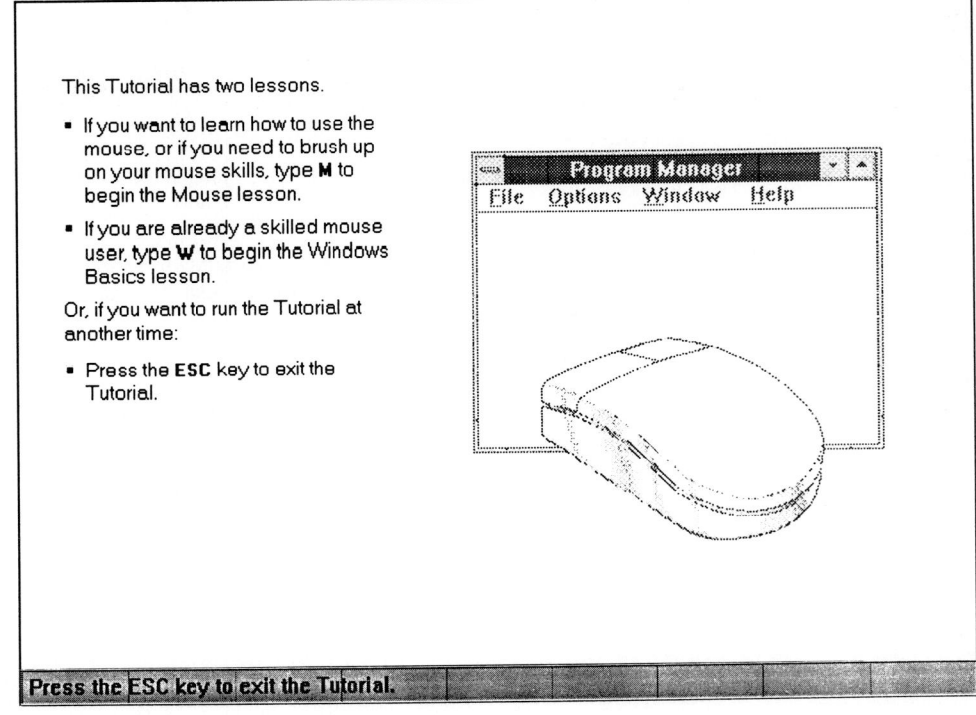

online tutorial provides an overview of Windows and mouse operations. If you have not used a mouse before, this tutorial is very helpful for learning Windows principles as well as mouse operations.

5-9
DIFFERENT PARTS OF A WINDOWS SCREEN

Most of the Windows screens include the elements illustrated in Figure 5-17. Refer to the figure as you read the following explanations of each element:

- The window title is usually the name of the application, name of a document, or name of a file. In Figure 5-1, the window title is Program Manager. In Figure 5-17 the title is Notepad-[Untitled]—because no document has been opened yet. If you open a document called TEST, then the title would be Notepad-[TEST].

- The control-menu box appears at the upper left of each window. By using control-menu commands, you can resize, move, maximize, minimize, and close windows and switch to other applications. If you use a mouse, you can perform all of the tasks just mentioned by clicking and dragging. If you double-click the left button of the mouse while on this box, the application will be closed.

- Insertion point indicates the current position of the cursor at any given time in your document. Text and graphs will be inserted at this point.

- The menu bar lists the available menu options. For example, in Figure 5-1 the menu bar includes File, Options, Window, and Help. In Figure 5-17 the menu bar includes File, Edit, Search, and Help.

- The minimize button reduces the window to an icon.

Chapter 5   Windows 3.1: An Overview

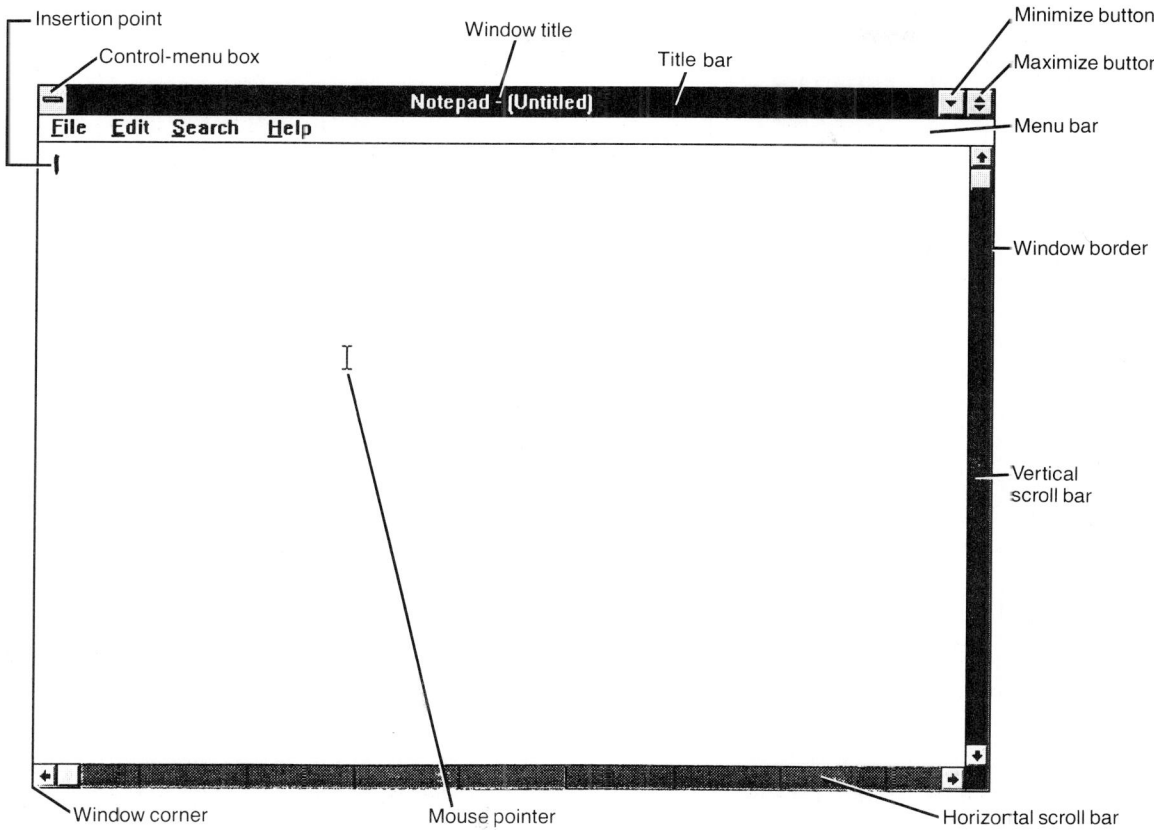

Figure 5-17
Windows screen elements

- The maximize button enlarges the active application window so that it fills the entire desktop. After you enlarge a window, the maximize button is replaced by the restore button (two small triangles on top of each other). You can click the restore button to return a window to its previous size.
- The window border is the outside edge of a window. You can lengthen or shorten the border on each side of a window by clicking the left button of the mouse while on the border then dragging to a new location.
- The vertical and horizontal scroll bars are used to view parts of a document that do not fit into the current screen.
- The mouse pointer is a small arrow that moves on the screen corresponding to the movement of the mouse on the desktop. The mouse pointer changes to a double-pointed arrow when the mouse pointer is moved to the edge of a window.
- The window corner can be used to shorten or lengthen two adjoining sides of a window border at the same time.

Compared with Windows 3.0, Windows 3.1 has a number of improvements. It also includes a series of new features not available in earlier versions; these features are listed in Table 5-5.

5-10
UPGRADING TO WINDOWS 3.1

Table 5-5
New features and improvements in Windows 3.1

TrueType fonts
Object Linking and Embedding
New File Manager
Drag and drop
Online tutorial
Printing enhancements
Multimedia

The **TrueType fonts** feature provides a full set of type fonts with enough variety to meet diverse printing needs. (A type font is a specific typeface in a specific size and style.) TrueType fonts are scalable; therefore, you can choose the exact font size you need for your documents.

The **object linking and embedding** feature enables you to transfer and share information among a number of applications. For example, suppose you are working on a report in WordPerfect in which you have embedded (inserted) a spreadsheet analysis created in Microsoft Excel. To make changes to the spreadsheet analysis, select the spreadsheet by double-clicking on it while in your WordPerfect document. Excel will be loaded automatically, whereupon you can make all your changes, save it, and return to your report in WordPerfect. You don't have to remember where the analysis is: Windows finds it for you.

By means of object linking, you can use the same information (object) in a number of documents. An object can be a drawing, a document, or even a sound file. You create the object and then connect (link) it to as many documents as you so desire. We will discuss this feature in more detail in Chapter 13.

Those of you who have used earlier versions of Windows will notice that the File Manager has a new look: a split window with a directory listing on the left and the contents of the "open" directory on the right. File Manager will be described in detail in Chapter 11.

The **drag and drop** feature makes it easier to print, copy, or move a file in the File Manager. For example, you can print a file by dragging its file icon from File Manager and dropping it onto the minimized Print Manager window. This can be done easily using the mouse.

As previously introduced in this chapter, Windows 3.1 offers an online tutorial in which you can practice working with a mouse and performing basic tasks.

Printing enhancements such as installing printers and connecting to network printers are now easier to handle. You can perform these tasks by using either Windows Print Manager or Windows Control Panel.

Finally, new **multimedia** features enable applications to use multimedia devices so that different types of media—sound, graphics, animation, and video—can be added to files and documents.

SUMMARY

This chapter described the unique advantages of the Windows environment. In addition, basic topics such as getting in and getting out of Windows, understanding commonly used terms, using a mouse and the keyboard in a Windows environment, and running Windows in different modes were discussed. The help and tutorial facilities of Windows were highlighted. The chapter explained different parts of a Windows screen and concluded by listing the new and improved features of Windows 3.1.

Chapter 5 Windows 3.1: An Overview

REVIEW QUESTIONS

*These questions are answered in Appendix A.
1. What are three of the unique advantages of Windows compared with DOS?
2. What is multitasking?
*3. What is memory management? Why and how does Windows better use a computer's memory.
4. What are some of the accessories of Windows 3.1?
5. How do you get Windows started?
*6. How do you exit Windows?
7. What is the desktop? What is an icon?
8. What are some of the advantages of a mouse compared with a keyboard?
9. What are some of the applications of the mouse in a Windows environment?
10. How do you invoke a Windows menu option using a mouse?
11. What are shortcut keys?
*12. Which special keys are used for key combinations?
13. What are the two modes in which Windows 3.1 can operate?
14. How do you start Windows in a specific mode?
15. How do you determine the mode in which your computer is operating?
*16. How do you invoke the help facility of Windows?
17. How do you start the Windows tutorial?
18. What options are included in the Help pull-down menu?
19. What options are included in the Windows tutorial opening screen?
*20. What are some of the components of a Windows screen?
21. What is the insertion point?
22. What is the application of the minimize button?
23. What is the mouse pointer?
24. How do you move the mouse pointer around?
25. How do you enlarge a window to fill the entire screen? How do you return the enlarged window to its original size?
26. What are some of the highlights or improvements of Windows 3.1 compared with 3.0?

HANDS-ON EXPERIENCE

1. Start Windows. Use the mouse to invoke the File pull-down menu; select Exit and then OK to leave Windows.
2. Start Windows again. This time exit Windows by means of the keyboard. To do this, first press Alt-F to access the File pull-down menu; then move the cursor to Exit Windows and press the Enter key twice.
3. Using the mouse, select one at a time the File, Options, Window, and Help menus from inside the Program Manager. What is available under each option?
4. By double-clicking the left button of the mouse, open the Accessories icon. What is available in this group?
5. By using the Help and About Program Manager options, find out the mode in which Windows is operating.
6. Invoke the Windows tutorial program and spend one hour with it. What is available?
7. Use the Search option to display help about changing icons.
8. Use the Glossary option in the Help menu to display the first 20 items in the list.

Windows 3.1

9. By using the Print option from the File menu in the Program Manager Help window, print the contents screen.
10. Use the mouse to enlarge the Main group window. Then return it to its previous size.
11. Double-click on the MS-DOS Prompt icon. At the DOS prompt, by using the DIR command, generate a listing of the current directory. Type *EXIT* and press ENTER to return to Windows.

KEY TERMS

Click and drag	Graphical user interface (GUI)	Object Linking and Embedding
Desktop	Icon	Online tutorial
Dialog box	Multimedia	Standard mode
Drag and drop	Multitasking	TrueType fonts
Enhanced mode	Mouse	Window
File Manager	Mouse pointer	

KEY COMMANDS

Commands for Program Manager (see Figure 5–1)

WIN/3 (from DOS—to start Windows in 386 Enhanced mode)

WIN/S (from DOS—to start Windows in Standard mode)

MISCONCEPTIONS AND SOLUTIONS

Misconception Press the ALT key to activate the menu and move the cursor to an option to execute the option, but this is time consuming.

> **Solution** If a name in the menu bar has an underlined letter, you can press Alt to activate the menu bar and open the desired menu; then type the letter that is underlined. For example, to exit Windows from the File Manager press Alt-F; then press X. An even faster method is to click the left button of the mouse while on the desired menu item.

Misconception Performing search operations in the Help menu by typing the entire word in the Search For box is time consuming.

> **Solution** The help facility matches characters you type as closely as possible with the available key words. Just type the closest word or a part of the word that comes to mind.

ARE YOU READY TO MOVE ON?

Multiple Choice

1. The following statements are all true about Windows except
   a. it will run without DOS being in your computer
   b. it is a graphical environment
   c. it is a multitasking environment
   d. it is easier to operate than DOS
   e. all are true
2. The following statements are all true about Windows except
   a. you can run Windows and DOS applications at the same time
   b. you can link several programs together

Chapter 5 Windows 3.1: An Overview

    c. Windows provides better memory management

    d. all are true

    e. only a and b are true

3. The following items are all included in the accessories group of Windows 3.1 except

    a. File Transfer

    b. Write

    c. Paintbrush

    d. Terminal

    e. Print Manager

4. To start Windows, first change to the drive and directory that contain your Windows files then, before pressing Enter, type

    a. *FILE*

    b. *RUN*

    c. *WIN*

    d. *TEST*

    e. *GO*

5. All the following tasks can be performed from the Windows desktop except

    a. fast application switching

    b. icon spacing changes

    c. displaying your document

    d. changing colors

    e. all are possible

6. The following are all possible applications of a mouse except

    a. invoking a menu

    b. exiting from Windows

    c. deselecting a menu

    d. all are possible

    e. only a and c are possible

7. If you are using a keyboard in the Windows environment, which of the following is *not* true?

    a. You can use the middle part of the keyboard.

    b. You cannot use the function keys.

    c. You can use the key combinations.

    d. You can use the numeric keypad.

    e. These are all correct.

8. Which of the following statements about running Windows is incorrect?

    a. It runs in Standard mode on all computers.

    b. It runs in 386 Enhanced mode on all computers.

    c. It runs in Standard mode on 286 or higher microprocessors.

    d. It runs in 386 Enhanced mode on any 386 computer with at least 2 MB of RAM.

    e. These are all correct.

9. To start the help facility of Windows,

    a. type *Help* at the DOS prompt and press Enter

    b. select the Help option from any Windows application menu

    c. type *Tutor* at the C> prompt and press Enter

    d. select Help from the File menu

    e. none of the above

10. The following are all parts of a Windows screen except
    a. window title
    b. control-menu box
    c. maximize icon
    d. title bar
    e. DOS prompt

True/False

1. The minimize button is used to reduce the window to an icon.
2. The window border is the outside edge of a window.
3. The vertical and horizontal scroll bars are used to view only the first five lines of a window.
4. The mouse pointer indicates the present position of the pointer.
5. The multimedia feature is not available in Windows 3.1.
6. Windows applications do not all follow the same principles.
7. Windows presents a multitasking environment.
8. Windows cannot be used to link several programs together.
9. Paintbrush is one of the accessories of Windows 3.1.
10. Application switching is not possible from the Windows desktop.

ANSWERS

Multiple Choice	True/False
1. a	1. T
2. d	2. T
3. a	3. F
4. c	4. T
5. e	5. F
6. d	6. F
7. b	7. T
8. b	8. F
9. b	9. T
10. e	10. F

Windows Paintbrush

6–1	Introduction
6–2	What Is Paintbrush?
6–3	Getting In and Getting Out of Paintbrush
6–4	The Paintbrush Screen
6–5	Drawing a Simple Illustration
6–6	Selecting Foreground and Background Colors and Line Width
6–7	Working with the Toolbox
6–8	Undoing Your Last Change
6–9	Entering Text into Drawings
6–10	Printing Drawings
6–11	Working with Cutout Tools
6–12	Using the Toolbox for Drawing Lines and Shapes
	6–12–1 Straight Lines
	6–12–2 Curved Lines
	6–12–3 Boxes
	6–12–4 Circles and Ellipses
	6–12–5 Polygons and the Filled Polygons
	6–12–6 Airbrush
6–13	Paintbrush Menus
	6–13–1 File Menu
	6–13–2 Edit Menu
	6–13–3 View Menu
	6–13–4 Text Menu
	6–13–5 Pick Menu
	6–13–6 Options and Help Menus

6-1
INTRODUCTION

This chapter concentrates on Paintbrush as an accessory of Windows 3.1 that is easy and fun to use. After you learn how to get in and out of Paintbrush, you will see how the mouse functions in the Paintbrush environment. The chapter provides an overview of selecting color, line width, and tools. It also introduces the essential steps for entering text into a drawing and for printing a drawing. The process of working with a portion of a drawing, called the cutout, is explained. Several of the tools provided by Paintbrush are illustrated and Paintbrush menus are highlighted.

6-2
WHAT IS PAINTBRUSH?

Paintbrush is a powerful illustration tool that allows you to draw a variety of charts and graphs, thereby significantly improving the appearance of a report. When you draw an illustration using Paintbrush, you can save it for future use, you can edit it, you can cut and paste it, you can even export it to other programs such as Microsoft Word (a powerful word processor), Windows Write, and so forth. Paintbrush is both easy and fun to use. You do not need to be an artist—anybody can draw with Paintbrush.

6-3
GETTING IN AND GETTING OUT OF PAINTBRUSH

To start Paintbrush, double-click on the Accessories icon. Then double-click again on the Paintbrush icon. If the Accessories window is already displayed, just double-click on the Paintbrush icon in the Accessories window. Click left on the maximize icon at the upper right of the screen to let Paintbrush fill the entire screen. At this point, you will be presented with a screen similar to the one shown in Figure 6–1.

Figure 6–1
Starting screen of Paintbrush

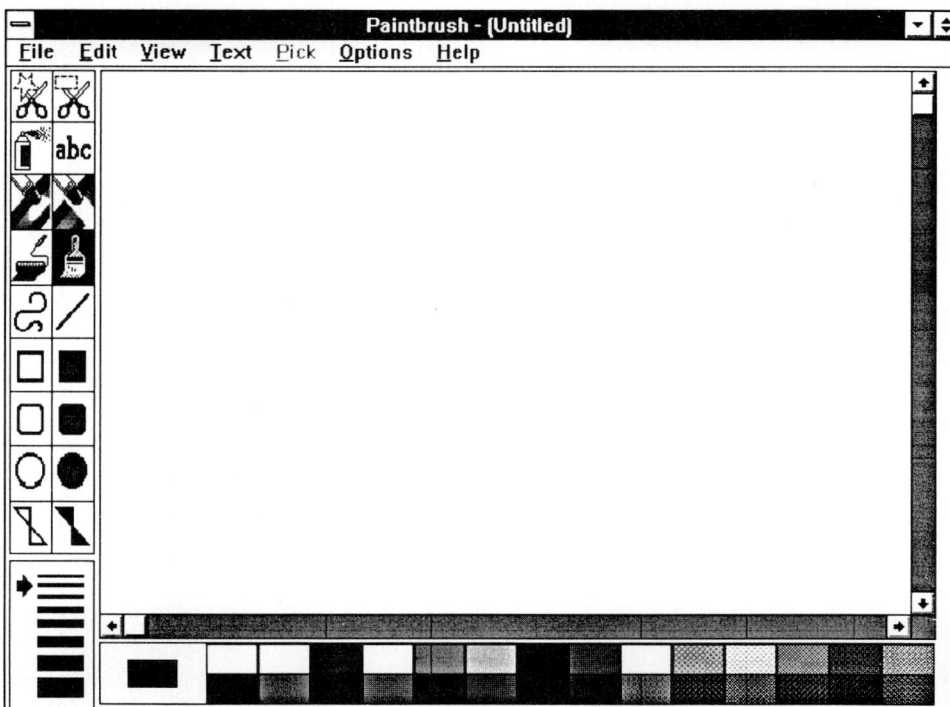

Chapter 6 Windows Paintbrush

To exit Paintbrush, as usual you can double-click on the control-menu box at the upper left of the screen. You can also select the File menu and then Exit.

6-4 THE PAINTBRUSH SCREEN

Figure 6-2 illustrates the several distinct areas in the Paintbrush screen:

- The title bar indicates the name of the program, which is Paintbrush, and a specific name—at the present time it is "Untitled." As soon as you save an illustration, the word "Untitled" will be changed to the name of the illustration.
- The menu bar displays the main menu of the Paintbrush. It includes the File, Edit, View, Text, Pick, Options, and Help options.
- The center part of the screen is the drawing area. You will draw your charts and illustrations here.
- The **toolbox** on the left side of the screen displays all the tools from which you can choose. These tools, as you will see later in this chapter, allow you to draw a variety of illustrations, type text, and erase the typed text.
- The **linesize box** allows you to select a line with different widths. When you select one of these widths, your tools use that line thickness.
- The **palette,** which includes the colors and patterns for the background and foreground, enables you to generate pleasant-looking charts in different colors.

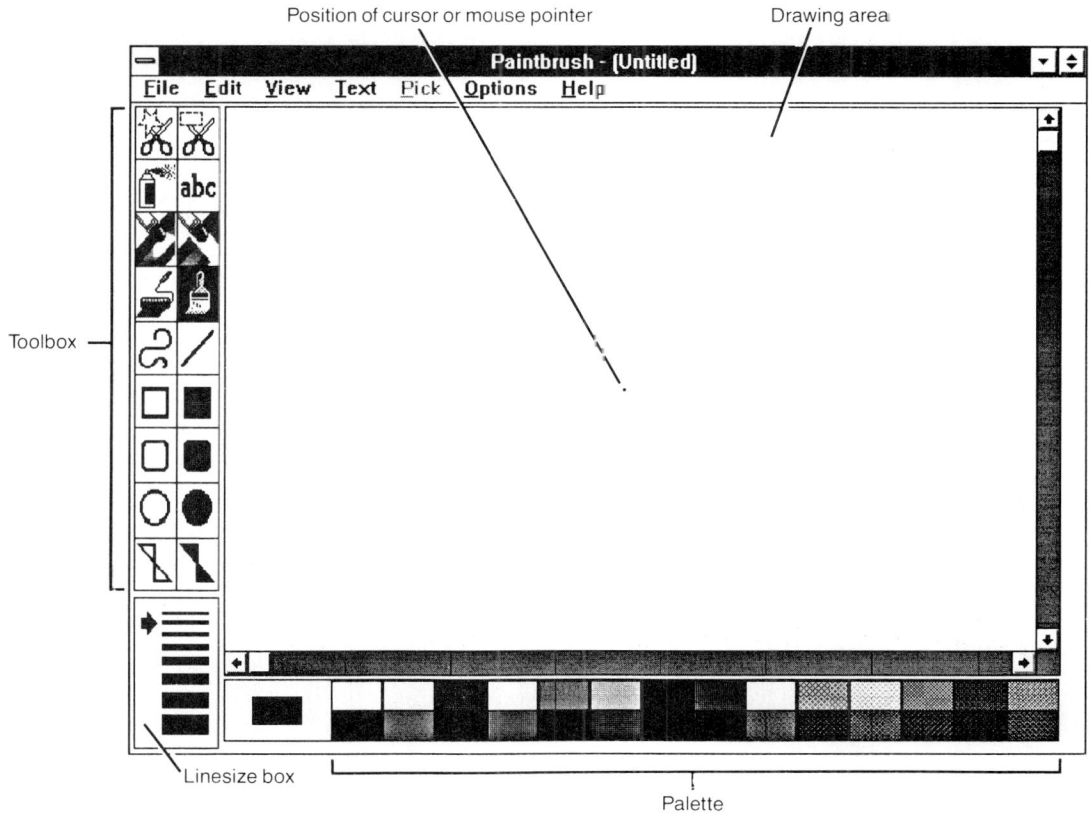

Figure 6-2
Ingredients of the Paintbrush screen

- The position of the cursor or the mouse pointer indicates the location where you can start drawing your illustrations.

Paintbrush is the only Windows application discussed in this book that uses both the left and right buttons of the mouse. If a specific button is not specified, assume the left button. You can move around in a large drawing area by means of the scroll bars. Simply click on one of these bars.

6-5
DRAWING A SIMPLE ILLUSTRATION

Before we get into the details of the Paintbrush program, let us draw a simple illustration of a circle and a solid square. Follow these steps:

1. Move the mouse pointer to the thickest line in the linesize box and click the left button of the mouse. From now on all your tools will be using this thickness.
2. Move the mouse pointer to any colors in the palette that you like and click the left button. We selected red. As soon as you do this, the selected color will be displayed in the foreground indicator. The background is white by default.
3. Move the mouse pointer to the hollow circle (the eighth tool in the left column) in the toolbox and click the left button. Now this tool is highlighted to indicate that it has been selected.
4. Move the cursor anywhere in the drawing area. While you are pressing the left button of the mouse, drag the mouse pointer to the right, then down, and release it. As soon as you release the mouse button, the circle will be drawn.
5. Move the mouse pointer to the solid square (the sixth tool in the right column) in the toolbox and click the left button. Now this tool is highlighted because it has been selected.
6. Move the mouse pointer anywhere in the drawing area and click the left button. While you are pressing the left button, drag the mouse in any direction and release it. Your work should be something similar to the illustration in Figure 6-3. The sizes of the solid square and the circle depend on how far you dragged the mouse pointer. They can be smaller or larger than the ones presented here. Later in this chapter, you will learn the technique for redoing or erasing these illustrations.

6-6
SELECTING FOREGROUND AND BACKGROUND COLORS AND LINE WIDTH

When you start Paintbrush, the **foreground color** is black and the **background color** is white; see Figure 6-4.

To select a different background color, click the *right button* of the mouse on the desired color. As soon as you do this, the background color will be changed to the selected color. To see your new background color, you must invoke the File menu and select the New option.

To select a different foreground color, click the left button on the desired color in the palette.

Chapter 6 Windows Paintbrush

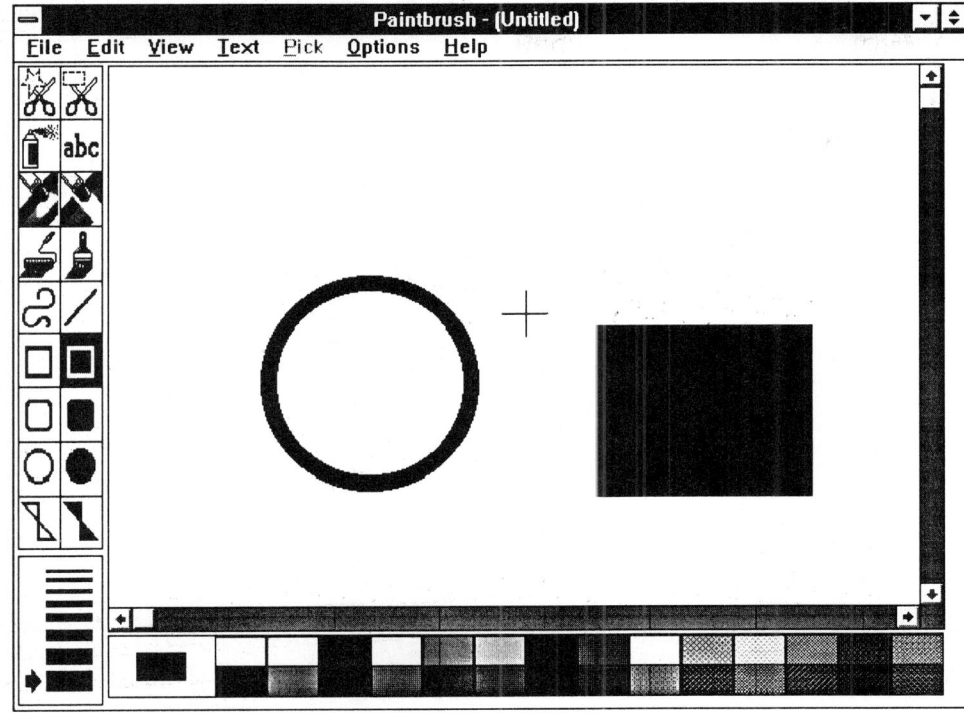

Figure 6-3
Circle and solid square drawn using Paintbrush

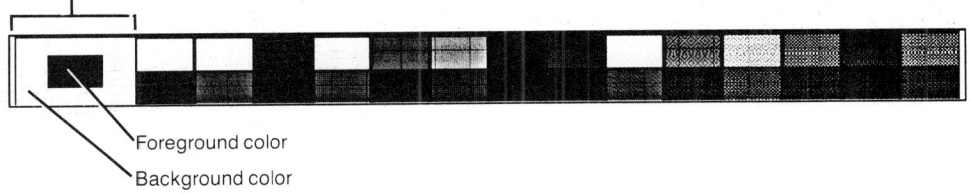

Figure 6-4
Paintbrush palette

At the lower left of the Paintbrush screen, notice the linesize box again. These lines are used for drawing lines or drawing the width of the border around an object. To select a line width, just click the left button on the particular line.

6-7
WORKING WITH THE TOOLBOX

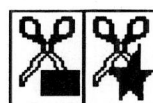

The Paintbrush toolbox includes 18 tools from which you can choose (Figure 6-5). These tools help draw various shapes, erase them, and insert text into your drawings.

The scissors and pick tools are used to select an object or a portion of an object and to copy or paste it to another area of the screen. You can define a free-form **cutout** with the scissors tool or a rectangular cutout with the pick tool. You can manipulate the selected graph (also called a cutout) by using the Pick menu.

Figure 6–5
Paintbrush toolbox

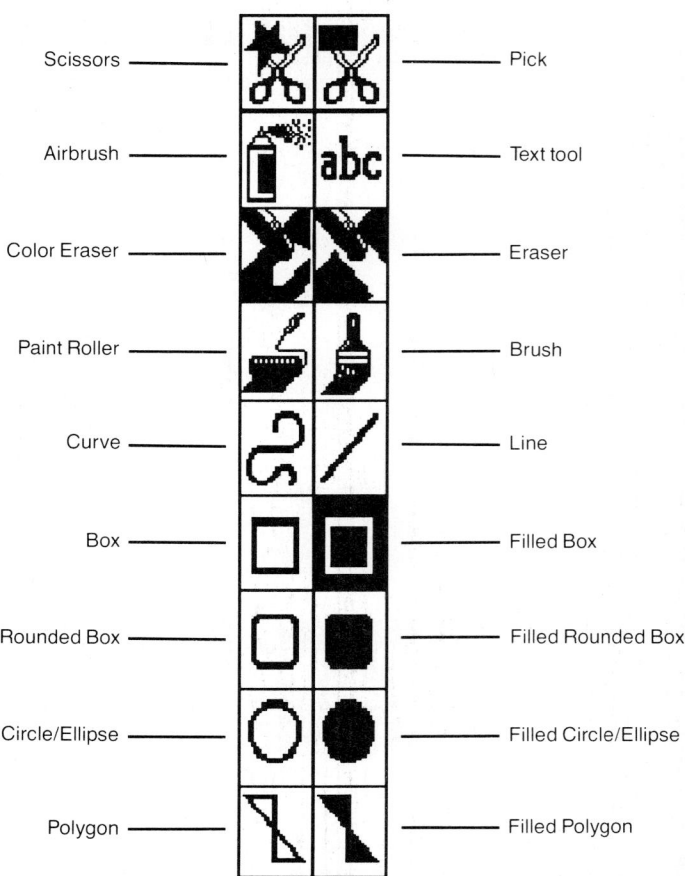

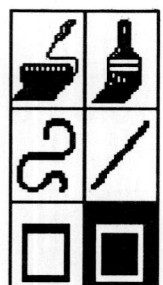

The airbrush tool spray paints. The text tool allows you to enter text into your drawings. After entering text, you can use the Text menu to change the appearance of your text.

The color eraser and eraser tools allow you to change or erase a color. You can use the color eraser in two ways to change colors in another part of your drawing: (1) dragging the color eraser cursor over an area of a drawing changes the selected foreground color under the cursor to the selected background color; and (2) double-clicking the left mouse button on the color eraser tool changes every occurrence of the selected foreground color in the drawing area to the selected background color. The eraser changes all the foreground color that it touches to the selected background color.

The paint roller and brush tools are used for painting. The paint roller fills an object with a particular color. Before you use any of these tools, you can select the line width and the desired background and foreground colors from the palette. The brush tool paints a line of color. You can select a variety of brush shapes by choosing Options Brush Shapes and clicking the left mouse button on the desired shape.

The curve and line tools allow you to draw curved and straight lines, respectively.

The box and filled box tools draw a square hollow box and a square filled box, respectively.

Chapter 6 Windows Paintbrush

The rounded box and filled rounded box tools draw rounded hollow and rounded filled boxes.

The circle/ellipse and filled circle/ellipse tools are used to draw circles and ellipses or filled circles and ellipses.

The polygon and filled polygon tools are used to draw multisided objects with straight sides. In all of these situations, you should select the line width and the desired color from the palette first before selecting the desired tool from the toolbox.

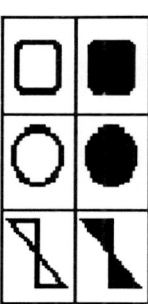

6-8 UNDOING YOUR LAST CHANGE

If you make a change to your drawings and you are not satisfied with the change, you can undo your change by selecting the Undo option from the Edit menu, or you can press Ctrl-Z for a shortcut. The Backspace key will also erase your last change; follow these steps:

1. Press the Backspace key. As soon as you do this, the cursor changes into a square with an X inside.
2. Press the left button of the mouse and drag the mouse cursor over the parts of the object that you want to delete. When you are finished, release the mouse button.

These techniques erase only your last action. To completely erase a screen, you should invoke the File menu and select the New option and respond No to the confirmation dialog box.

6-9 ENTERING TEXT INTO DRAWINGS

Typing text in Paintbrush is similar to typing text in Windows Write (discussed in the next chapter), except that word wrap does not take place in Paintbrush. Also, the cursor does not realign itself with previously typed text if you switch to a different tool and later switch back to the text tool. Despite these limitations, the text tool feature can make your charts more meaningful.

In Figure 6-6, we typed a line of text inside a rectangle. To type the text, follow these steps:

1. Move the mouse cursor to the text tool in the toolbox and click the left button of the mouse.
2. Move the mouse cursor to the desired location and click left. Now you will see a blinking cursor.
3. Start typing. Type *THIS IS A SAMPLE TEXT*. If you want to type another line, press Enter and type your new line(s).

The format and appearance of this text is in the default format. However, you can invoke the Text menu and select any of the available formatting

Figure 6-6
Simple drawing with sample text

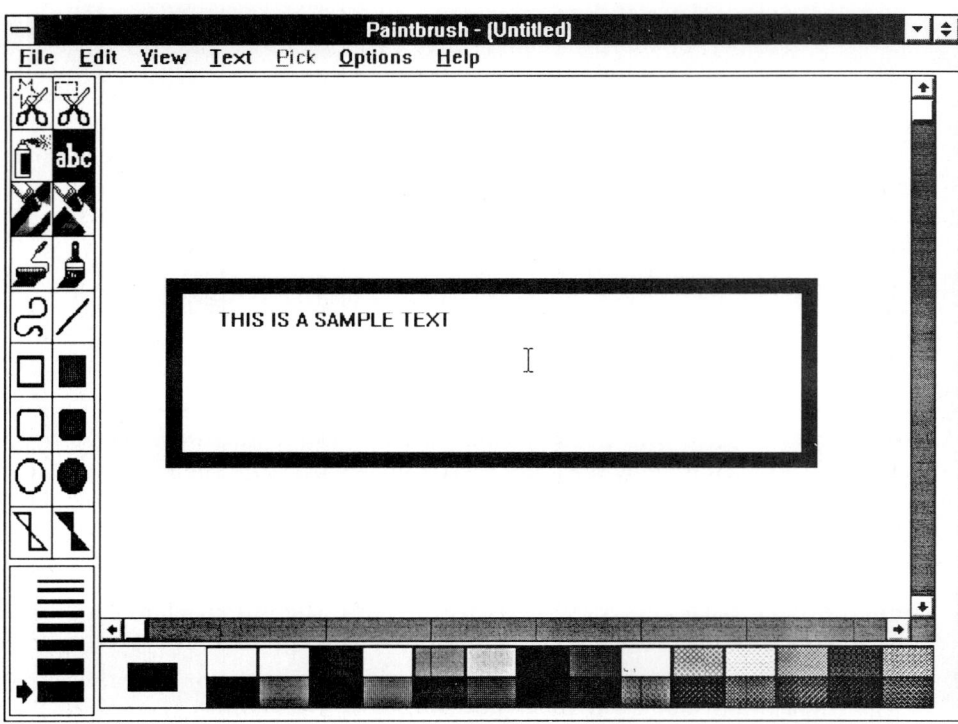

features such as bold, italic, underline, outline, or shadow and then type your text. You can also select a different font from the Text menu.

6-10
PRINTING DRAWINGS

To print a drawing, invoke the File menu and select the Print command. You will be presented with a screen similar to the one in Figure 6-7. As you can see in this figure, the default is the Whole drawing. The quality of the print is set to Proof (the default); you can change it to Draft if you so desire. If you are satisfied with the setting, click left on OK. In a few seconds your drawing will be printed. The Draft option produces an unenhanced copy of your drawing by means of the fastest speed of your printer. The Proof option produces a copy of your drawing that makes use of as many of your printer's advanced features as possible.

As you can see in Fgure 6-7, one of the options in the dialog box is Partial. To print a portion of your drawing, follow these steps:

1. From the File menu select Print.
2. In the Print dialog box, click on the Partial option.
3. Click on OK. Paintbrush adjusts the size of the drawing area so that the entire illustration is displayed on the screen.
4. Move the cursor to the starting area for printing; then press and hold down the left button of the mouse. Drag the cursor until the entire section you want to print is covered.

Chapter 6 Windows Paintbrush

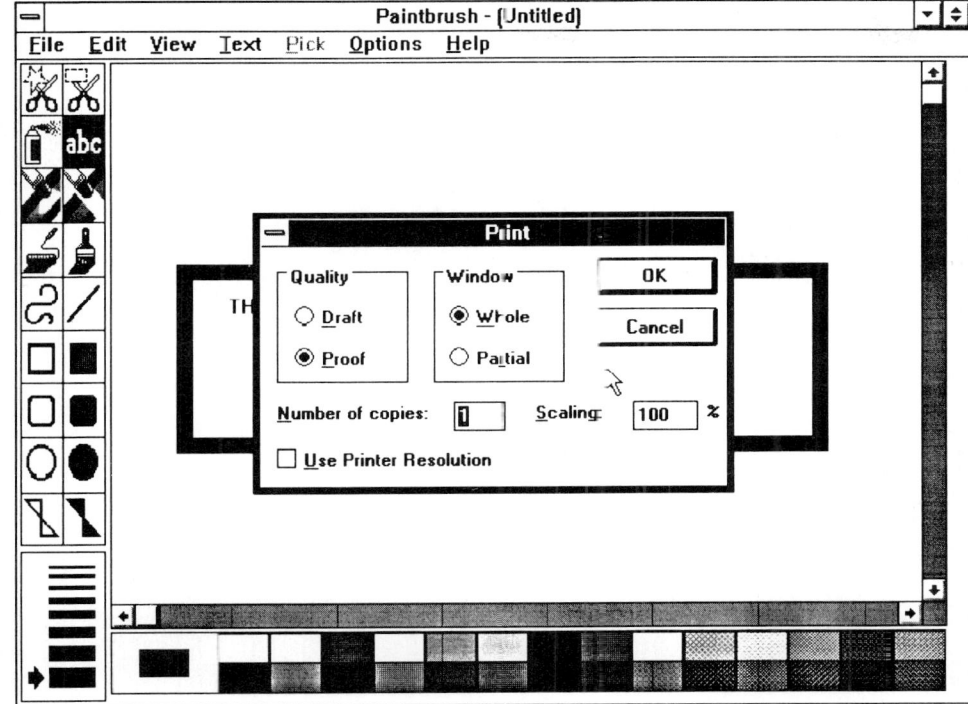

Figure 6–7
Print dialog box

5. Release the left button. In a few seconds your partial illustration will be printed.

6–11 WORKING WITH CUTOUT TOOLS

The scissors tool (top left tool in the toolbox) and the pick tool (the top right tool in the toolbox) can be used to cut and paste a portion of your drawing. You can define a free-form cutout (with scissors) or a rectangular cutout (with pick). To define a free-form cutout, follow these steps:

1. Select the scissors tool then move the cursor to the drawing area.
2. Move the mouse pointer to the desired location and while you are holding down the left button of the mouse, draw a circle around the part of the drawing.
3. After circling the desired area, release the mouse button. If you make a mistake, click anywhere on the screen to start over.

To define a rectangular cutout, select the pick tool. The rest of the steps are the same. Figure 6–8 shows a free-form cutout and Figure 6–9 shows a rectangular cutout.

After defining a cutout, you can use commands from the Edit menu to cut, copy, and paste the cutout. You can also copy it (save it) into a file for future use by selecting the Edit and Copy To menu choices. Commands from the Pick menu allow you to manipulate the cutout—flip it horizontally or vertically, inverse it, shrink it, enlarge it, or tilt it.

Figure 6-8
Example of a free-form cutout

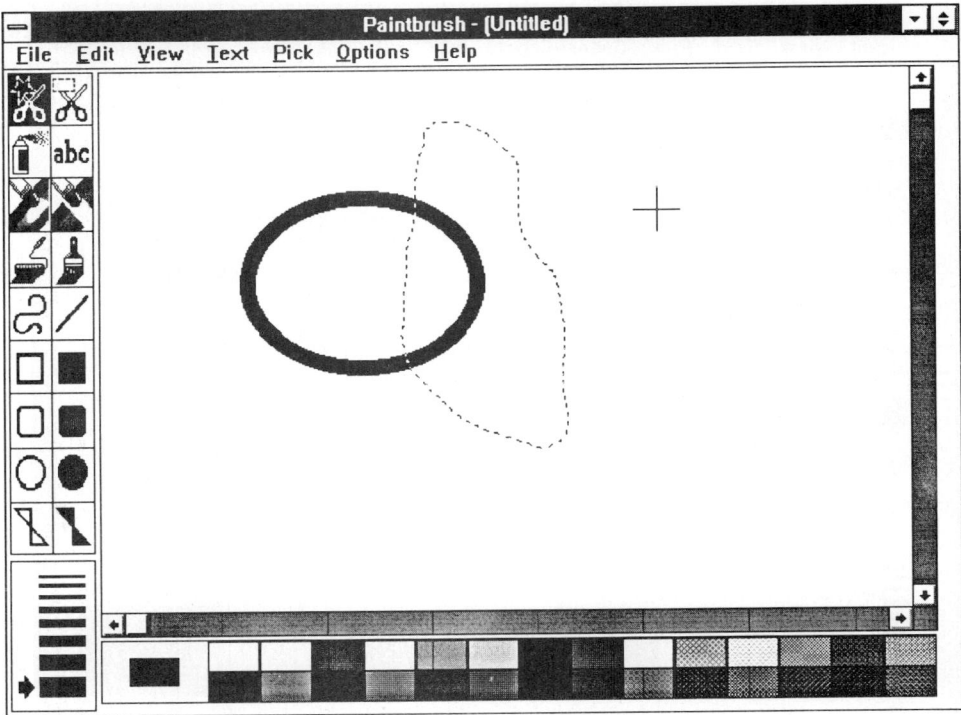

Figure 6-9
Example of a rectangular cutout

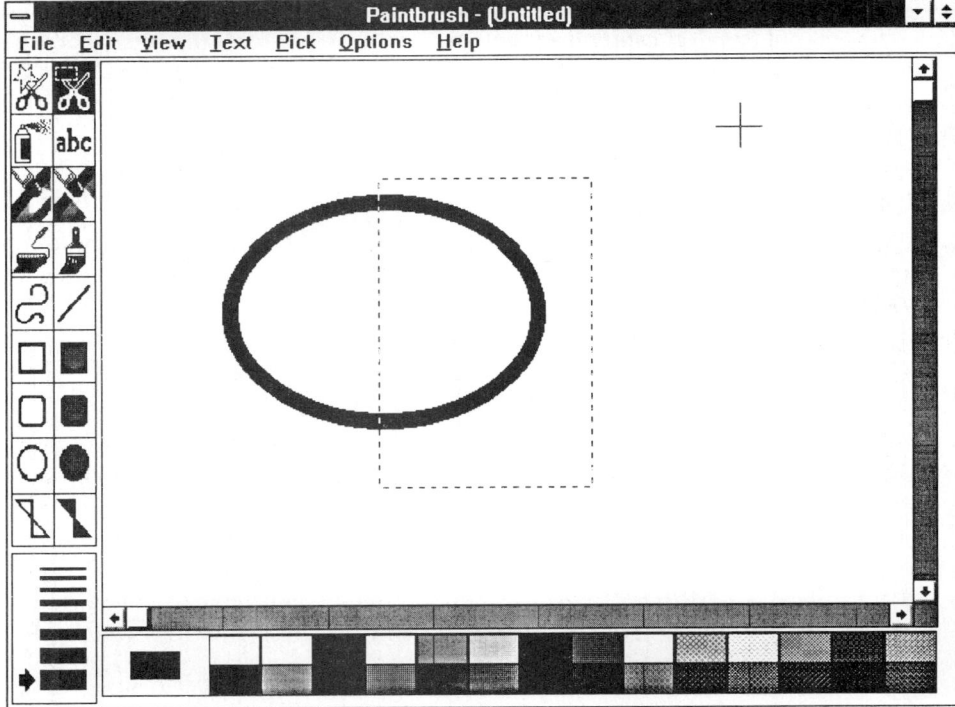

Chapter 6 Windows Paintbrush

6–12 USING THE TOOLBOX FOR DRAWING LINES AND SHAPES

As you can see in Figure 6–5, the Paintbrush toolbox includes eight shapes and two lines. The shape tools are filled and unfilled boxes, circles, and ellipses. The two lines are the curve and the straight lines. To use these tools for drawing, follow these steps:

1. Select a line width.
2. Select a tool.
3. Select a foreground color.
4. Select a background color.
5. Position the pointer in your desired location in the drawing area.
6. Draw the line or the shape.

Filled shapes are filled with the selected foreground color and bordered with the selected background color. If you do not want the border, select a white background color.

All your drawings will be done using the left button of the mouse. The right button is for selecting the background color. You can also use the right button to erase a line (straight or curve) as it is being drawn before releasing the left button.

Straight Lines

6–12–1

Figure 6–10 shows some examples of straight lines. To draw a perfectly horizontal or vertical line, press and hold down the Shift key while you drag the mouse pointer. To draw lines, follow these steps:

1. Select a foreground color.
2. Select a line width.

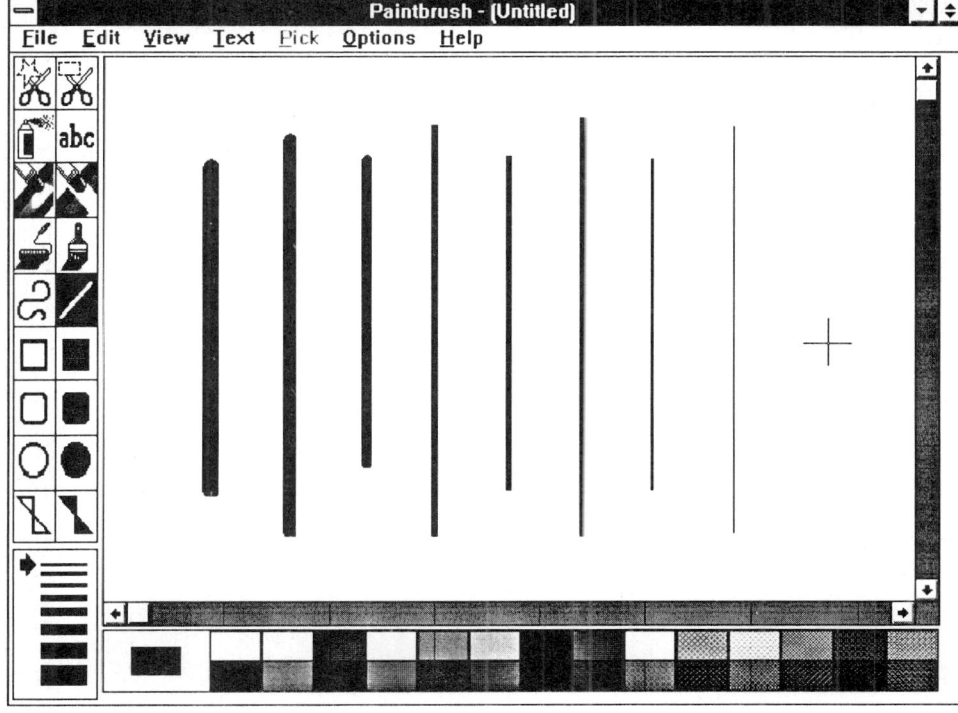

Figure 6–10
Examples of straight lines

3. Select the line tool from the toolbox.
4. Move the pointer to the drawing area.
5. Press the left button of the mouse and drag it. When you are satisfied with the line, release the button. As mentioned earlier, before releasing the left button, you can press the right button to erase the line.

6-12-2 Curved Lines

To draw a curved line, select the curve tool and follow the five steps in section 6-12-1 for drawing a straight line. After drawing the line, click and drag the mouse pointer away from the line in any direction. Release the mouse button; then click and drag in another direction to add more curves to the line. Figure 6-11 shows some examples.

6-12-3 Boxes

Paintbrush supports four different boxes: filled and unfilled squared-corner boxes and filled and unfilled rounded-corner boxes. To draw a box, follow these steps:

1. Select a foreground color.
2. For drawing a filled box, select a background color for the border. If you do not want to see the border, make the foreground and background colors the same.
3. Select a line width.
4. Select the desired box from the toolbox.

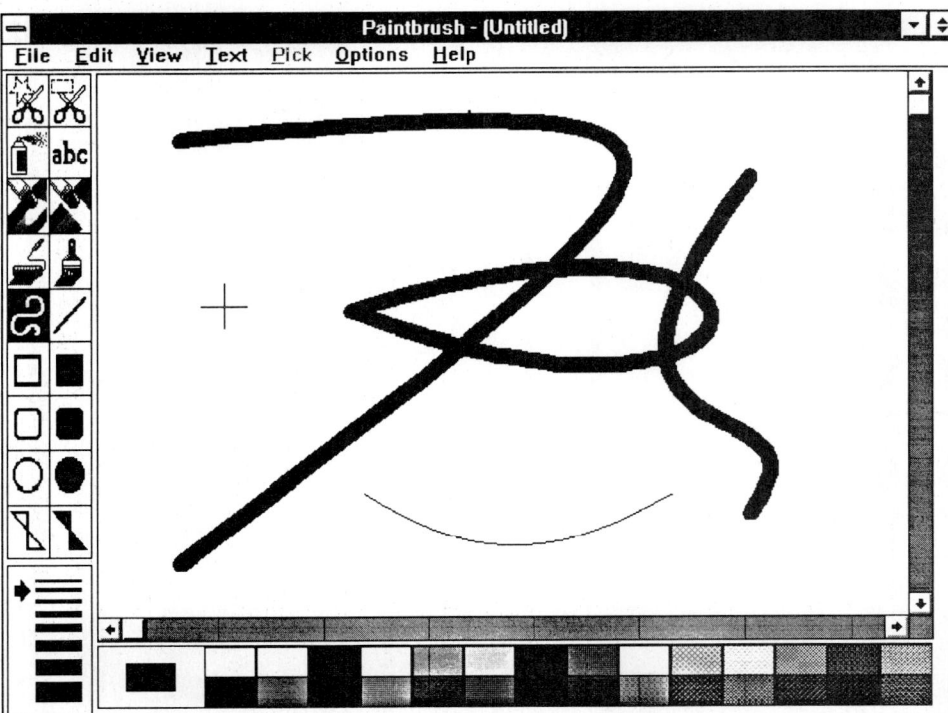

Figure 6-11
Examples of curved lines

5. Move the mouse pointer to the drawing area and click the left button to establish one corner of the box. Drag the mouse pointer to an opposite corner.
6. When you are satisfied with your drawing, release the left button. As with drawing lines, you can erase the box by clicking the right button of the mouse before releasing the left button. To draw perfect boxes, press and hold down the Shift key while you are dragging the mouse pointer. See Figure 6-12 for some examples.

Circles and Ellipses

6-12-4

To draw circles and ellipses or filled circles and ellipses, basically follow the steps outlined for drawing boxes. To draw a perfect circle or filled circle, press and hold down the Shift key as you drag the mouse pointer. Figure 6-13 shows some examples.

Polygons and Filled Polygons

6-12-5

To draw a polygon or a filled polygon, follow these steps:

1. Select a foreground color.
2. Select a background color for a filled polygon to distinguish the border. If you do not want a border, select similar foreground and background colors.
3. Select the line width.
4. Select the desired polygon from the toolbox.
5. Move the mouse pointer to the desired location in the drawing area and drag it.

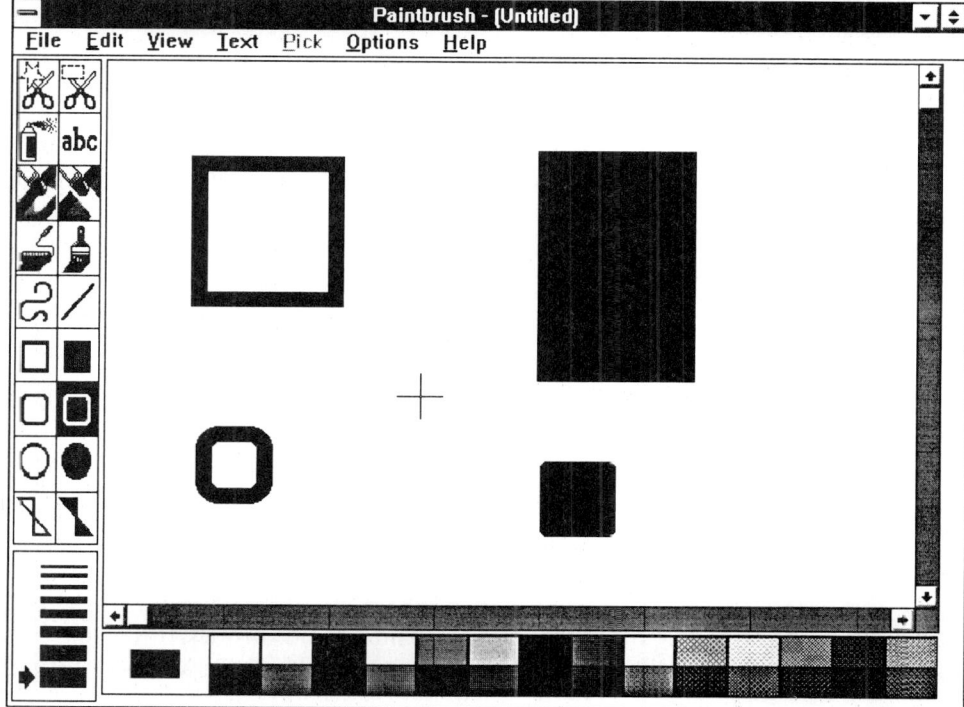

Figure 6-12
Examples of boxes

Figure 6-13
Examples of circles and ellipses

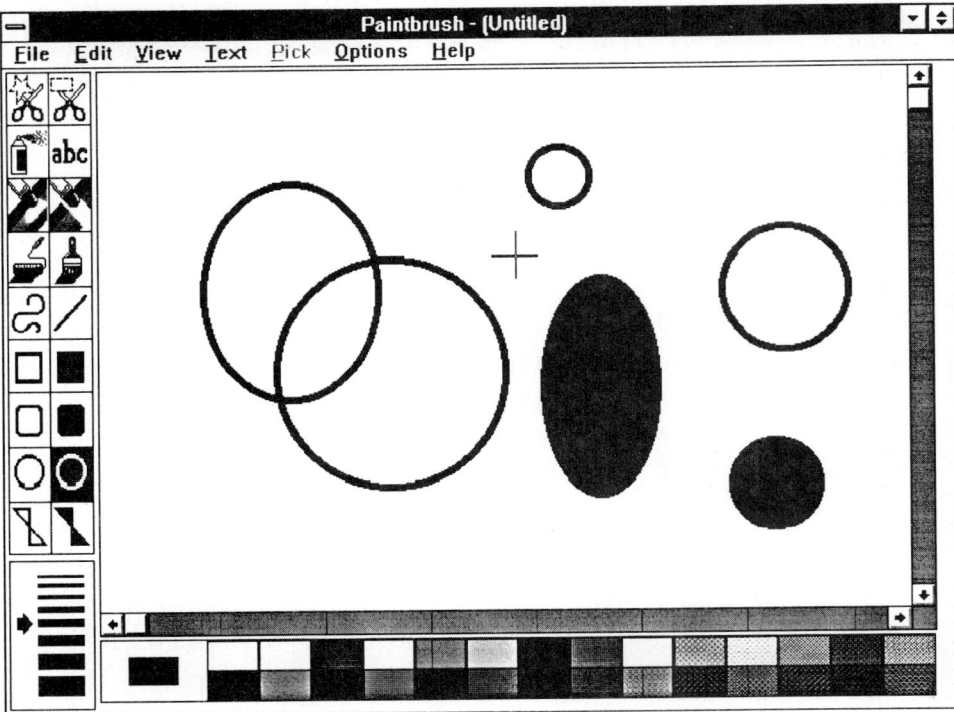

6. When you decide that you have established the first side of the polygon, release the left button of the mouse.
7. Continue adding sides until you are ready to add the last side.
8. To add the last side, double-click the left button. To draw a perfectly horizontal or vertical line, press and hold down the Shift key as you drag the mouse pointer. Figure 6-14 shows some examples.

6-12-6 Airbrush

The airbrush tool is useful for free-form drawing. The steps for using the airbrush are similar to those for drawing a line. Just select the airbrush tool from the toolbox and follow the steps outlined for drawing a line. Figure 6-15 shows examples drawn by means of the airbrush.

6-13 PAINTBRUSH MENUS

As you have probably noticed in the Paintbrush illustrations, there are seven options available in the main menu. Each option is briefly explained next.

6-13-1 File Menu

Figure 6-16 shows that the File option includes eight choices. The New option allows you to start a new drawing. When you select this option, Paintbrush asks you if you want to save your changes. The New option erases your current screen and starts a new drawing. The Open option allows you to open a file that was saved previously. You can retrieve a previously saved file for editing or printing.

The Save option, also accessed by Ctrl-S, saves a file under its current name. The Save As option saves a file under a new name.

Chapter 6 Windows Paintbrush

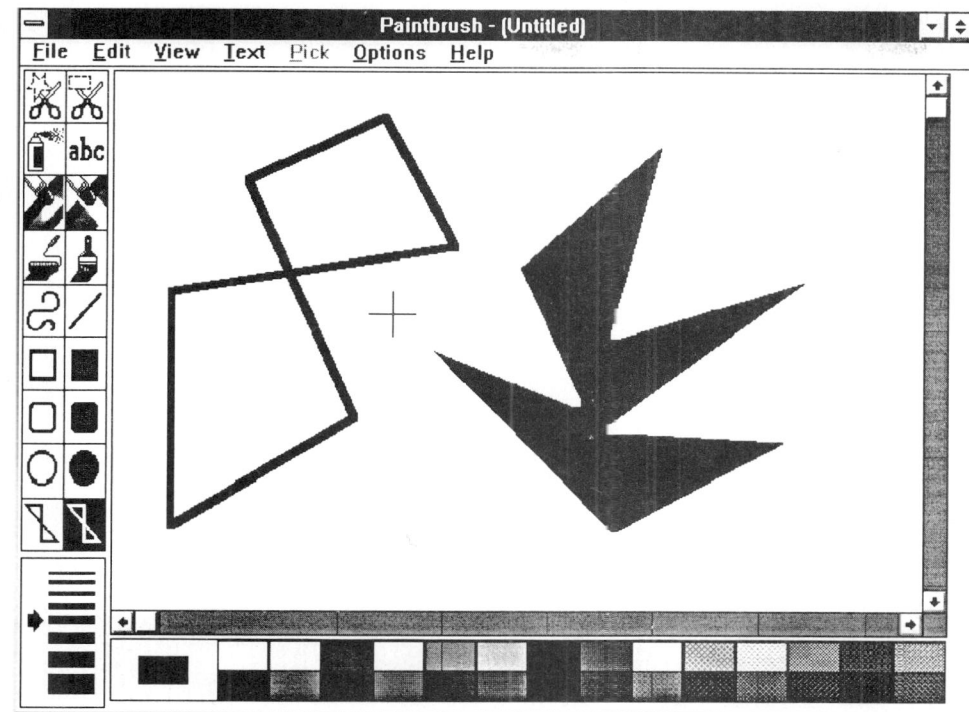

Figure 6–14
Examples of polygons

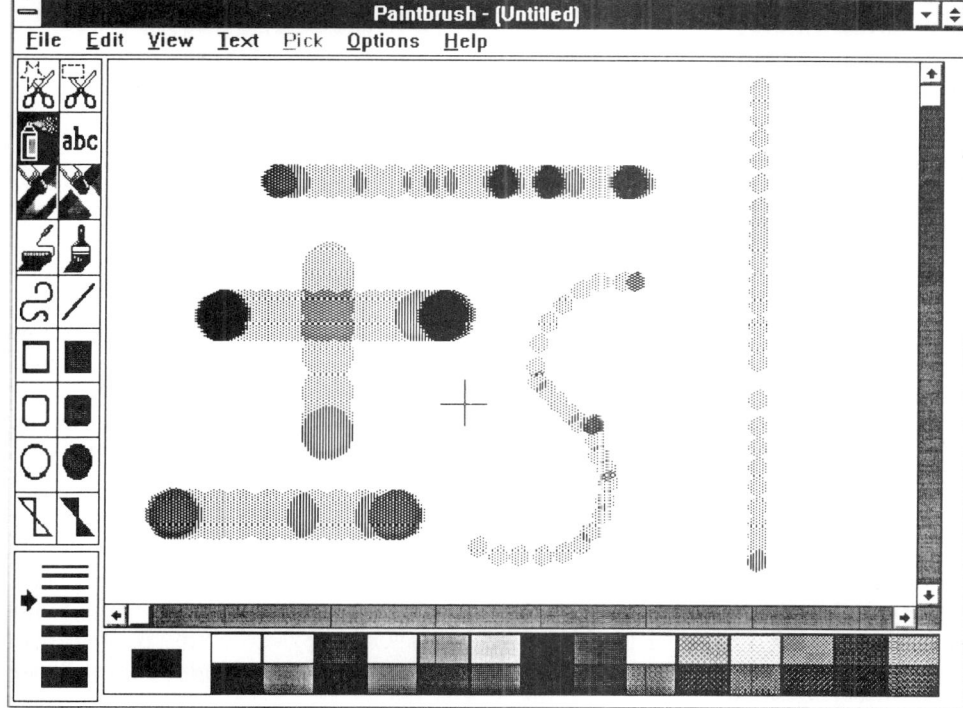

Figure 6–15
Examples of airbrush

Figure 6-16
Paintbrush File menu

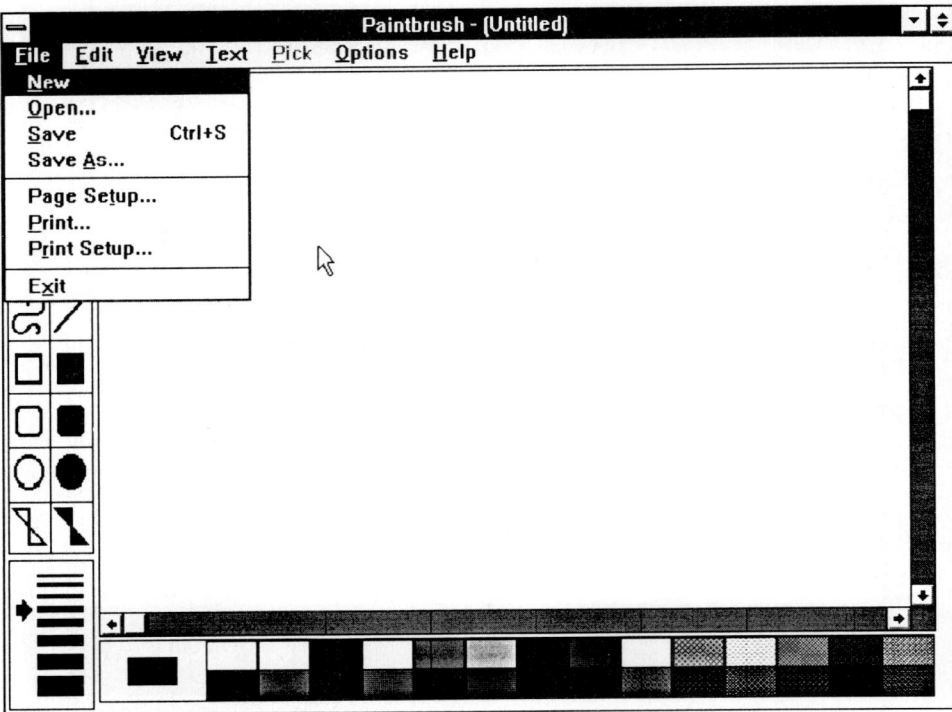

The Page Setup option gives you the current setup of your page. In the Page Setup dialog box, you can insert changes. For example, you can include a header or a footer, or you can change the top, bottom, left, or right margins. After specifying the desired setup, click left on OK. In most cases the default page setup should work just fine.

The Print option allows you to print your drawing using a printer. The Print Setup displays the setup of your printer. Invoke the Print Setup dialog box to make any changes.

Finally, the Exit option allows you to exit Paintbrush.

6-13-2 Edit Menu

As Figure 6-17 illustrates, the options in the Edit menu allow you to perform various editing tasks. You can reverse your last action by using the Undo (Ctrl-Z) command. You can cut a portion of your drawing by using the Cut (Ctrl-X) command. To copy a portion of your drawing use the Copy (Ctrl-C) command. The copy will go to the Clipboard (a temporary holding area) and you can use it later. By means of the Paste (Ctrl-V) command, you can paste the previously removed drawing to another place. The Copy To command allows you to save a portion of a drawing to a file for future use. Finally, by using the Paste From command, you can import a drawing or a portion of a drawing from a disk file and paste it into your current drawing.

6-13-3 View Menu

Figure 6-18 shows the options in the View menu. You can view a drawing better by means of the Zoom In (Ctrl-N) and Zoom Out (Ctrl-O) commands. If you create a drawing that is larger than the drawing area and the entire screen, use

Chapter 6 Windows Paintbrush

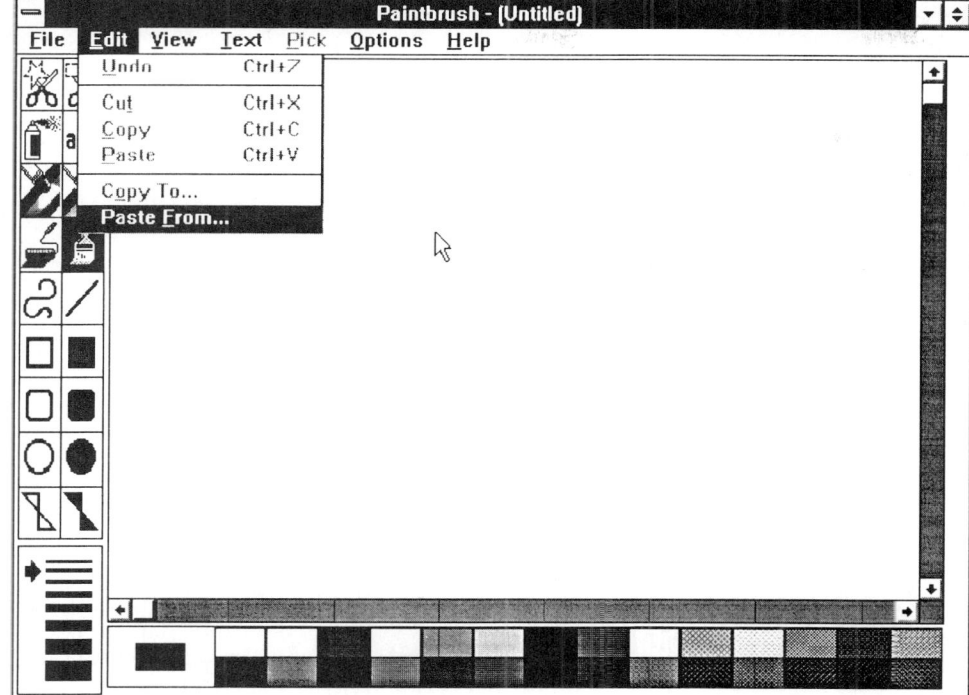

Figure 6–17
Paintbrush Edit menu

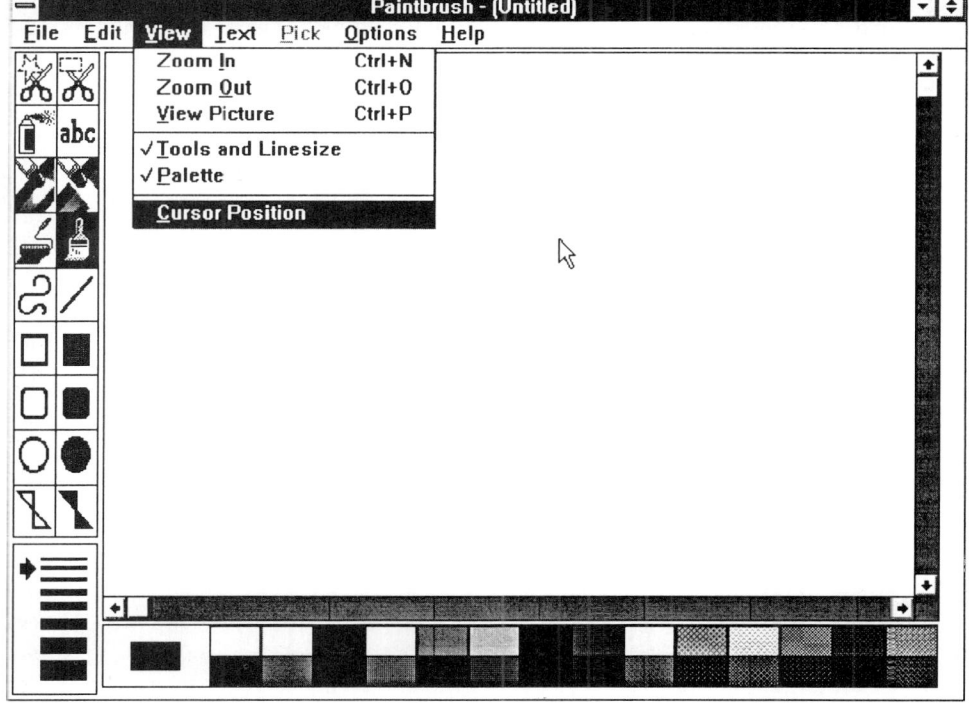

Figure 6–18
Paintbrush View menu

the Zoom Out command (or press Ctrl-O). To cancel the Zoom Out command, use the Zoom In command (or press Esc). The View Picture (Ctrl-P) option removes everything from the screen except your drawing. To return the screen to normal, just click the left button of the mouse. Click on the Tools and Linesize to remove these elements from the screen. Click on Palette to remove it from the screen. The Cursor Position option displays a small display box at the upper right of the screen that keeps track of the cursor's position by points.

6-13-4 Text Menu

As Figure 6–19 shows, the options in this menu can enhance the text of your drawing. You can select bold, italic, underline, outline, and shadow from this menu. You can also invoke various fonts available on your system.

6-13-5 Pick Menu

The Pick menu is displayed if you have used either the scissors or pick tools from the toolbox. By means of the options in the Pick menu, you can manipulate a cutout; see Figure 6–20.

6-13-6 Options and Help Menus

The selections in the Options menu are used mostly for color manipulation (Figure 6–21). Select Image Attributes, for example, to convert your drawing screen into black and white. You can save your current colors by selecting the Save Colors option.

The Help menu includes the general help facility for Windows and specific topics for Paintbrush.

Figure 6–19
Paintbrush Text menu

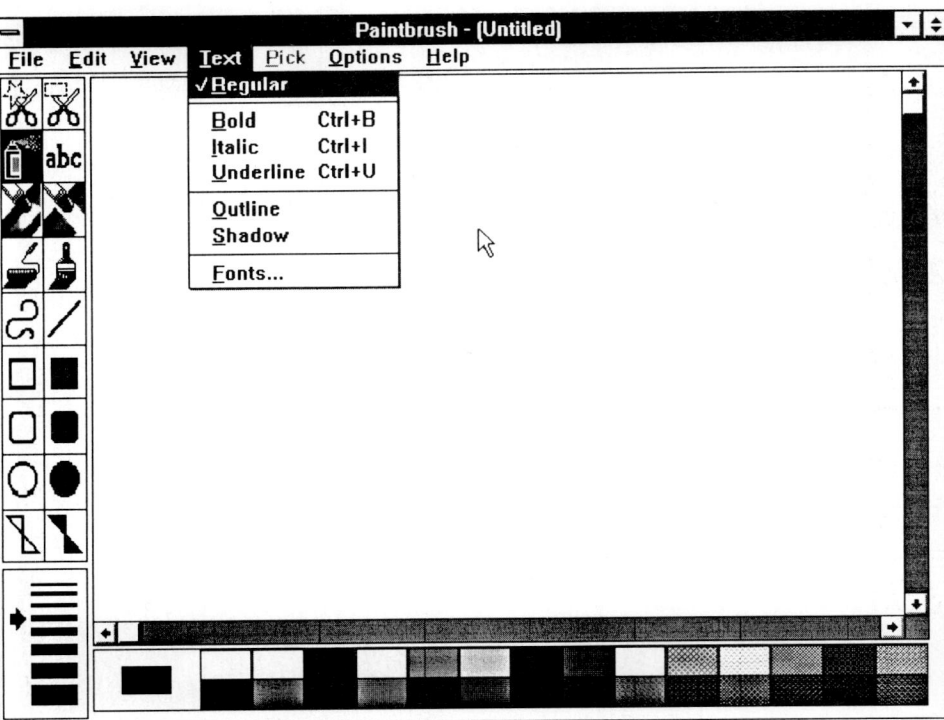

Chapter 6 Windows Paintbrush

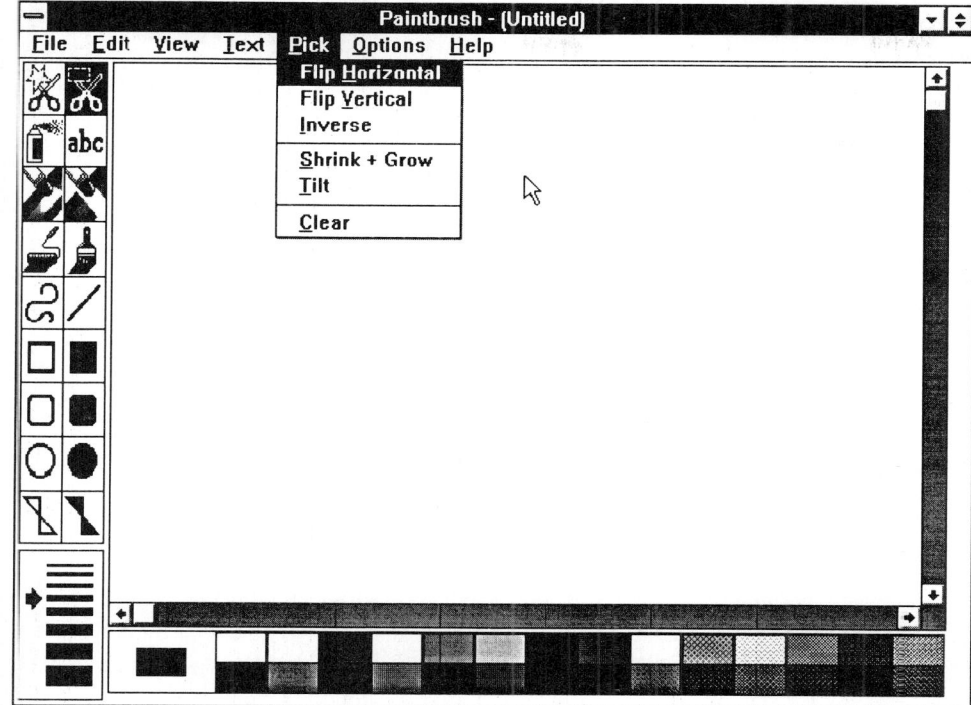

Figure 6-20
Paintbrush Pick menu

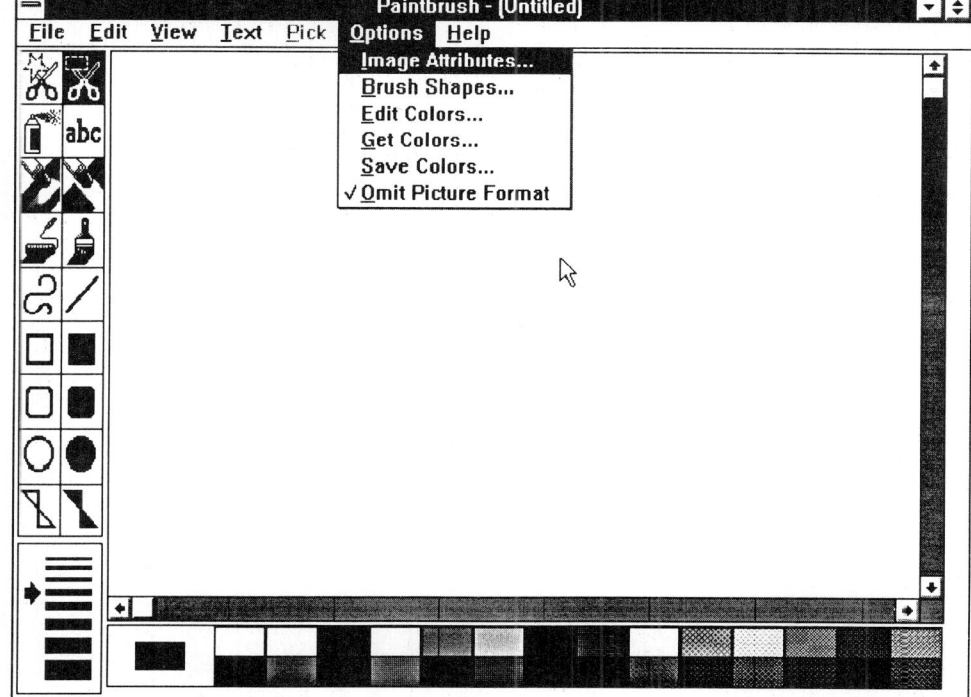

Figure 6-21
Paintbrush Options menu

Windows 3.1

SUMMARY

Paintbrush is one of the powerful accessories available in Windows 3.1. After explaining the process of getting in and out of Paintbrush, the chapter described the Paintbrush screen, including how the mouse functions in the drawing area. It also introduced the steps for drawing lines and shapes, entering text into a drawing, and printing a drawing. Several illustrations of lines and shapes generated by Paintbrush were presented. The chapter concluded with an overview of Paintbrush menus.

REVIEW QUESTIONS

*These questions are answered in Appendix A.

1. What is Paintbrush? What can Paintbrush do for you?
2. How do you start Paintbrush? How do you exit from it?
3. What are some of the distinct areas on the Paintbrush screen?
4. What is the palette?
*5. What is the toolbox? How many tools are available in the toolbox?
6. In how many ways can you use the color eraser tool?
7. How do you move the cursor to different areas of the drawing screen?
*8. What is the purpose of the right button of the mouse?
9. What are the six steps for drawing a shape?
10. How do you select the foreground color? How do you select the background color?
*11. How do you convert a drawing area to black and white?
12. How do you change the line width?
13. What are the applications of the scissors tool?
14. What are the applications of the pick tool?
15. How do you erase a portion of the screen? How do you erase the entire screen?
*16. How do you undo your most recent change?
17. How do you enter text into a drawing?
18. Can you enhance the text that you have entered into a drawing? If yes, how?
19. How do you print a drawing? Can you generate more than one copy of a drawing?
*20. How do you print a portion of a drawing?
21. What are cutouts? How do you manipulate a cutout?
22. How do you generate a perfect square?
23. How many different types of boxes can be generated using Paintbrush? How many different types of lines can be generated?
*24. How do you save a drawing?
25. What are the applications of the New command in the File menu?
26. What is the difference between the Save and Save As commands?
27. What are some of the editing features of Paintbrush?
28. How do you remove the palette, toolbox, and linesize box from the drawing screen?
29. What are the applications of the pick menu?

HANDS-ON EXPERIENCE

1. Get Paintbrush started and do the following:
   a. Draw a straight line. Clear the screen.
   b. Draw a curved line. Clear the screen.

Chapter 6 Windows Paintbrush

    c. Draw a perfect square. Clear the screen.

    d. Draw a perfect filled square. Clear the screen.

2. Experiment with the foreground and background colors. How do you change the foreground color from red to black?
3. By selecting all the different line widths, draw eight different squares. What are the differences in the appearance of these squares?
4. Draw a rectangle by using the pick tool from the toolbox. Divide it into two and manipulate this cutout by means of the options in the Pick menu.
5. Use the airbrush tool to write your name. Then use the Undo command from the Edit menu to erase it. Press Ctrl-Z to undo the Undo command.
6. Draw a circle and enter the following text in the circle: *THIS IS A TEST!*
7. Use the Print command from the File menu to generate two copies of the drawing in question 6.

KEY TERMS

Background color
Cutout
Foreground color
Linesize box
Palette
Toolbox

KEY COMMANDS

Ctrl-Z (to undo your last action)
Edit (to invoke the Edit menu)
File (to invoke the File menu)
Pick (to invoke the Pick menu)
Options (to invoke the Options menu)
Text (to invoke the Text menu)
View (to invoke the View menu)

MISCONCEPTIONS AND SOLUTIONS

Misconception There are several methods by which you can start a new Paintbrush drawing. The File New option is one of these methods, but it is time consuming.

    Solution A much faster method is to double-click on the eraser tool in the toolbox, or move the cursor to the eraser tool and press F9-Ins.

Misconception You can change from color to black-and-white patterns by selecting Options and Image Attribute and clicking on black and white. However, once you have begun a drawing in color or in black and white, you must stay with that selection.

    Solution Always change color at the beginning of your drawing session.

Misconception One way to open Brush Shapes is to invoke the Options menu and select the Brush Shapes option. Now you can select a desired shape by clicking on it. This procedure is time consuming.

    Solution A faster method is to double-click on the brush tool in the toolbox. You can also move the cursor to the brush tool in the Toolbox and press the F9-Ins keys.

Misconception You used the paint roller tool with a full-size drawing and the paint leaked.

    Solution The Zoom In (Ctrl-N) option from the View menu is useful for patching areas where the paint has leaked through.

ARE YOU READY TO MOVE ON?

Multiple Choice

1. Using Paintbrush, you can
   a. draw a line
   b. save a line for future use
   c. edit a line
   d. print a line
   e. do all of the above

2. All of the following are included in the Paintbrush screen except
   a. title bar
   b. menu bar
   c. drawing area
   d. toolbox
   e. they all are included

3. How many tools does the toolbox include?
   a. 18
   b. 17
   c. 16
   d. 15
   e. 14

4. Where on the screen is the palette located?
   a. bottom
   b. right
   c. left
   d. center
   e. top

5. To move the cursor to one of the areas of the Paintbrush screen, you must first move the mouse pointer then
   a. double-click the right button of the mouse
   b. click the right button of the mouse
   c. double-click the left button of the mouse
   d. click the left button of the mouse
   e. none of the above

6. The equivalent of the undo command is
   a. Ctrl-A
   b. Ctrl-Z
   c. Shift-Z
   d. Ctrl-B
   e. Ctrl-D

7. To change your Palette to black and white, you must select the Image Attributes option from the
   a. File menu
   b. Options menu
   c. View menu
   d. Edit menu
   e. Text menu

8. All of the following tools are used for painting except
   a. airbrush
   b. brush
   c. scissors
   d. paint roller
   e. they all are
9. To draw a perfect shape, while you are dragging the mouse during drawing, you must press the
   a. PgUp key
   b. PgDn key
   c. Ctrl key
   d. Shift key
   e. Alt key
10. To undo your last change, select the Undo command from the
    a. File menu
    b. View menu
    c. Edit menu
    d. Options menu
    e. Text menu

TRUE/FALSE

1. Paintbrush allows you to enter text into a drawing.
2. Entered text can be enhanced.
3. The Print command allows you to generate only one copy of a drawing.
4. You cannot perform a partial print using Paintbrush.
5. To create a cutout, you can only use the scissors tool.
6. To define a rectangular cutout, you should use the pick tool.
7. After defining a cutout you can edit it.
8. The brush tool can only have one shape.
9. The New option is under the Edit menu.
10. The shortcut key for undo is Ctrl-D.

ANSWERS

Multiple Choice	True/False
1. e	1. T
2. e	2. T
3. a	3. F
4. a	4. F
5. d	5. F
6. b	6. T
7. b	7. T
8. c	8. F
9. d	9. F
10. c	10. F

Windows Write

7-1	Introduction
7-2	Starting Windows Write
7-3	Your First Electronic Document
7-4	Saving a Document
7-5	Retrieving a Saved Document
7-6	Moving Around in a Document
	7-6-1 Using the Keyboard
	7-6-2 Using the Mouse
7-7	Inserting and Deleting Text
7-8	Printing Text
7-9	Selecting Text
7-10	Find and Replace Operations
7-11	Cut and Paste Operations
7-12	Moving Text
7-13	Undoing Your Last Action
7-14	Line Spacing
7-15	Enhancing Text
7-16	Inserting Page Breaks

7-1
INTRODUCTION

In this chapter we focus on Windows Write as a word processing program. After explaining the process of getting in and getting out of Write, the chapter describes how to create an electronic document and how to save it on disk. Moving around in the document by means of the keyboard and the mouse is highlighted. The chapter shows you how to insert and delete text, how to print text using a printer, and how to apply cut and paste and find and replace operations. It concludes with discussions of some of the enhancing features of Write and insertion of page breaks.

7-2
STARTING WINDOWS WRITE

Windows Write offers many features not found on a typewriter. With Write you can create a document, edit it, cut and paste, save it onto a disk, and print it using a printer. If you have Write, you do not need correction fluid to erase unwanted text! Everything is done electronically with a high degree of efficiency and effectiveness. Throughout this chapter, you will learn many powerful features of Write.

Start Windows and double-click left on the Accessories icon. You will see a screen similar to the one shown in Figure 7-1. Find Windows Write with the other accessory programs.

To start the Write program, double-click on its icon. Click left on the maximize button in the upper right corner of the Write window to enlarge the window so that it fills the entire display area. You will be presented with a screen similar to the one in Figure 7-2. As soon as you do this, the Write window occupies the entire screen and the maximize button is changed to a restore button (shown by two small triangles). If you click on the restore button, your

Figure 7-1
Accessories window

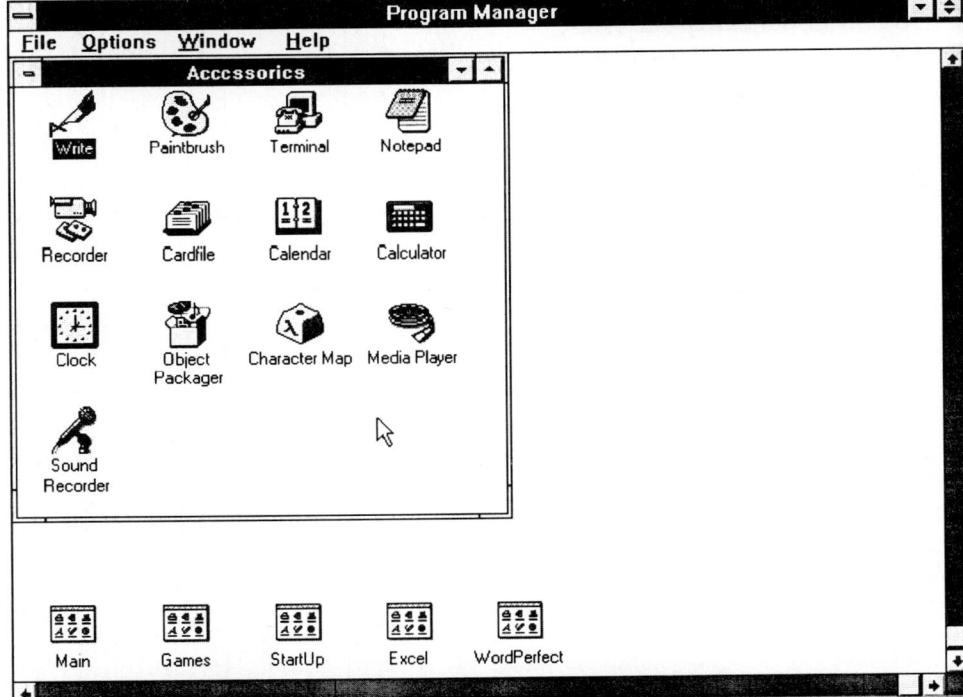

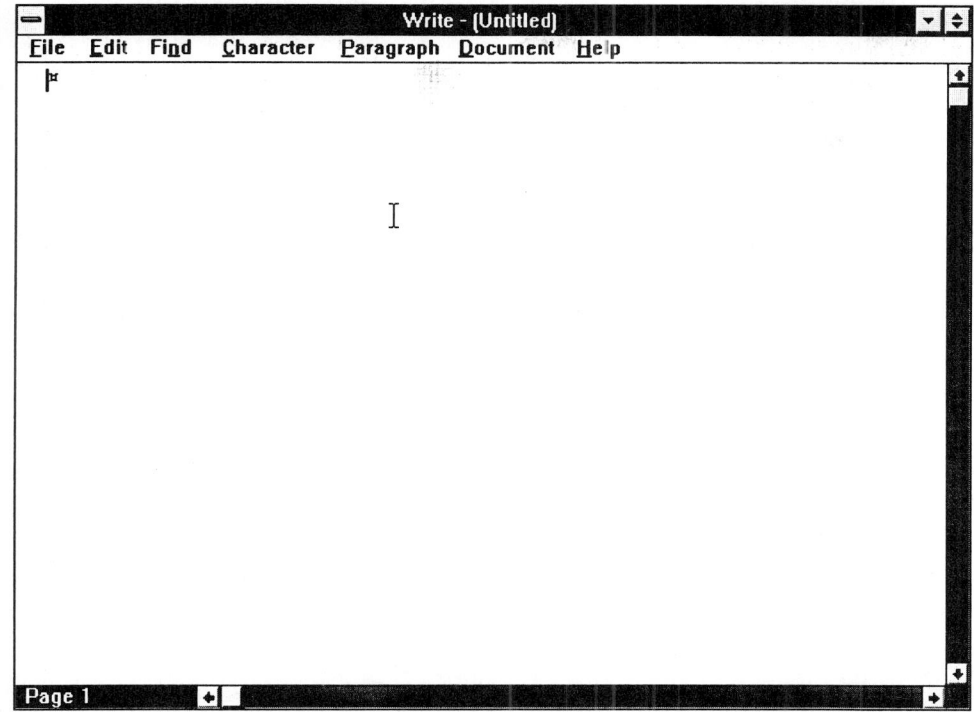

Figure 7-2
Starting screen of Windows Write

screen will return to its previous size. A title bar across the top displays the name of the program (Write) and the name of the document (Untitled, until you save a document). There is a menu bar below the title. The vertical scroll bar is on the right edge of the screen. You can click the upward or downward arrow in the vertical scroll bar to view your text (if your text is longer than one screen). At the bottom of the screen notice the horizontal scroll bar; this allows you to scroll left and right within your document.

At the upper left of Figure 7-2, you can see the insertion point and the end mark, which marks the end of your document. At the upper right, notice the minimize and maximize buttons. At the lower left, the page status tells you that you are in Page 1. This will change when you complete one page of typing. Remember that a page is not a screen; a page is the amount of text that will fit on a sheet of a paper.

7-3 YOUR FIRST ELECTRONIC DOCUMENT

In the blank screen presented in Figure 7-2, type the following:

> Using Windows Write you can perform various word processing tasks. Cutting and pasting will become a simple task. When you make mistakes do not panic!

Your screen should be similar to the one presented in Figure 7-3. When you type do not press the Enter key. Write automatically performs word wrap and moves to the next line. Just keep typing until you are done. For now, do not be concerned about any mistakes; you will learn how to correct mistakes later.

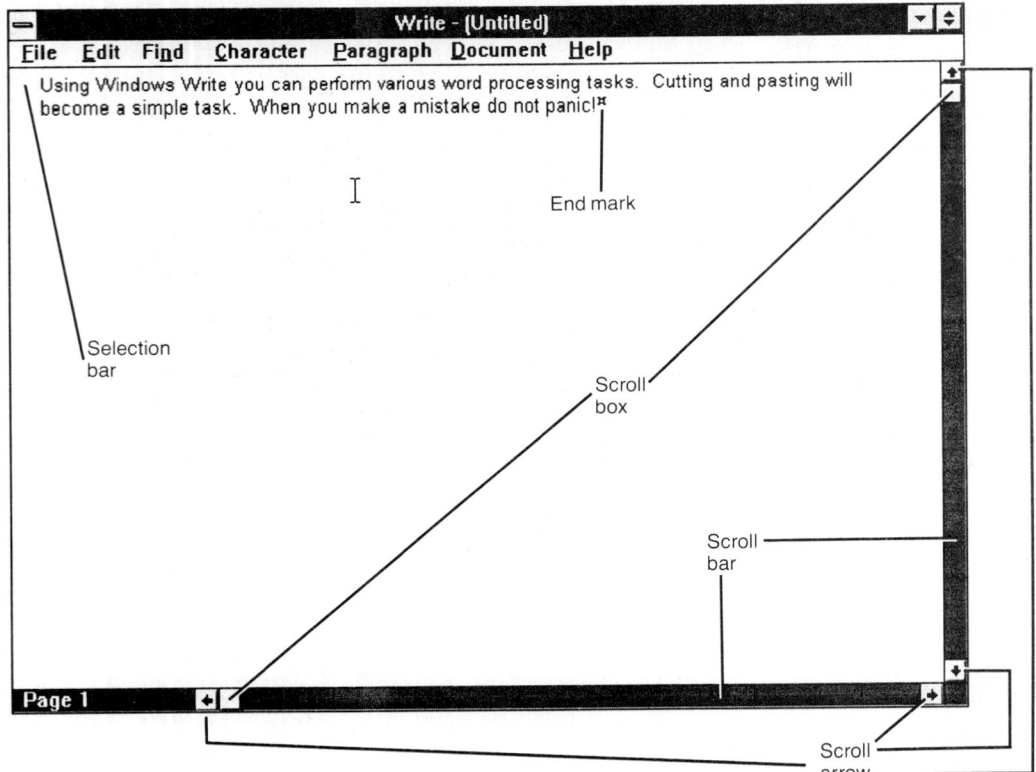

Figure 7-3
Your first document

Notice that the end mark always remains at the end of your typed text. When you start typing, the end mark moves accordingly.

7-4
SAVING A DOCUMENT

While you are typing, your document stays in RAM. If there is a power failure, your document will be lost. To avoid this problem, it is a good practice to save your document onto a disk every 10 minutes or so.

To save your document, you first must select a name of up to eight characters. You can use digits and some of the special characters such as the underscore. Try to select names that have some meaning. For example, TRIP, SALARY, and HOUSE are all meaningful names. Write assigns the WRI extension to a file name automatically. When you are ready to save the document, click on the File option. You will be presented with a screen similar to Figure 7-4. Click left on the Save As option from this menu. You will be presented with a screen similar to the one shown in Figure 7-5. Follow these steps:

1. From the Drives list, select a drive if you want to save your file to a drive other than the current drive. To do this, click left anywhere in the Drives box. All the available drives in your computer will be displayed. Click left on the desired drive.

2. From the Directories list, select a directory if you want to save your file in a directory other than the current one displayed in the Directories box. In

Chapter 7 Windows Write

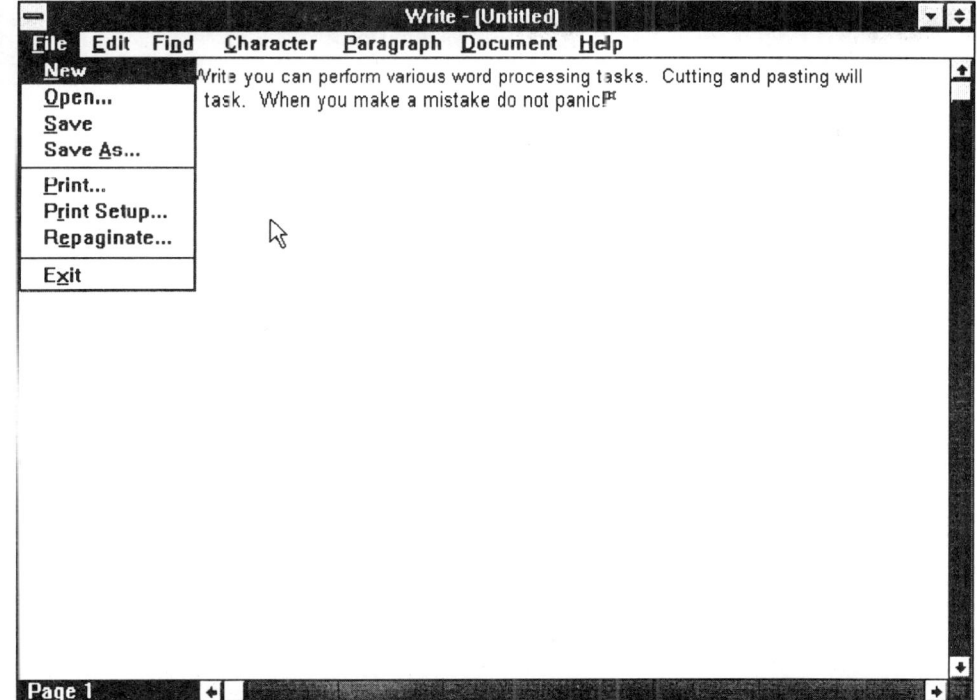

Figure 7-4
File pull-down menu

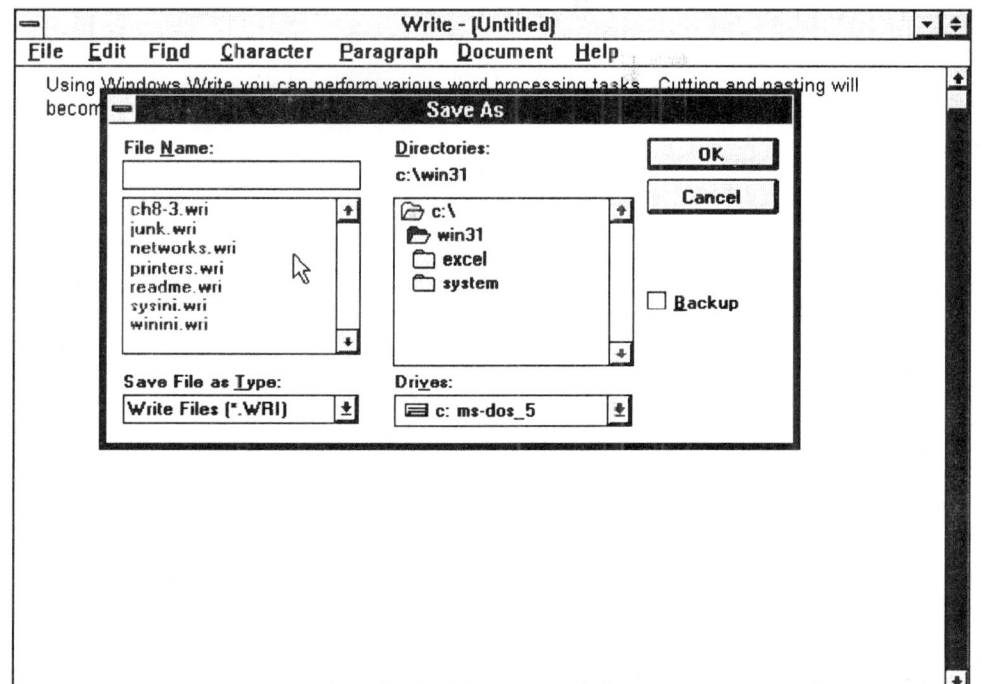

Figure 7-5
Save as dialog box

Figure 7–5 the current directory is win31. Again, you can scroll through all the available directories and select the desired one.

3. If necessary, click left in the File Name box, then type a name of up to eight characters.
4. If you want to save your file in a format other than the Write format, select the format you want from the Save File as Type list. This option is helpful if you want to use a file with other software.
5. Press Enter or click left on OK. We saved this sample file in drive C under the name CH7-3 in the win31 directory. If you decide not to save your file, click left on Cancel.

As you can see in Figure 7–5, on the right side of the Save As dialog box there is a Backup option. Selecting this option allows you to make an automatic backup of your file. The file will be saved under the same name as your original file but with the BKP extension.

As soon as you save your document, the word "Untitled" at the top of the screen changes to the name under which you saved the file.

If you make any changes to this file, you have two options to save it again. You can use the Save option from the File menu to save the file under its present name, or you can use the Save As option to save the file under a new name. If you use the Save option, the new file will replace the old one regardless of any differences in size. If the file has not been saved before, both the Save and Save As command will display the Save As dialog box.

7–5
RETRIEVING A SAVED DOCUMENT

In many cases you may want to retrieve a saved document. For example, you may want to edit the document or add more text to it. If you are already working with a document, and the document has not been saved, Write asks you if you want to save the current document before opening another document. Your options are Yes, No, or Cancel. Selecting Yes allows you to save the current document before opening another one. Selecting No opens a new document without saving the current one. Selecting Cancel cancels the retrieve operation and allows you to stay with the current document. To retrieve the document that you saved earlier in this chapter (Ch7-3), follow these steps:

1. Select the File menu, then select Open. You will be presented with a screen similar to the one in Figure 7–6. The Open dialog box is similar to the Save As dialog box.
2. Select the drive from the Drives box (if you saved your file in a drive other than the default drive).
3. Select the directory from the Directories box (if you saved your file in a directory other than the default directory).
4. From the List Files of Type box, select the type of the file if it is not a Write format.
5. In the File Name box select the file that you want or type the name of the file and press Enter. If the file name is displayed in the File Name box, just double-click on the name. As soon as you do this, the file will be retrieved and displayed on the screen. Notice that the name of the file will be displayed in the title bar.

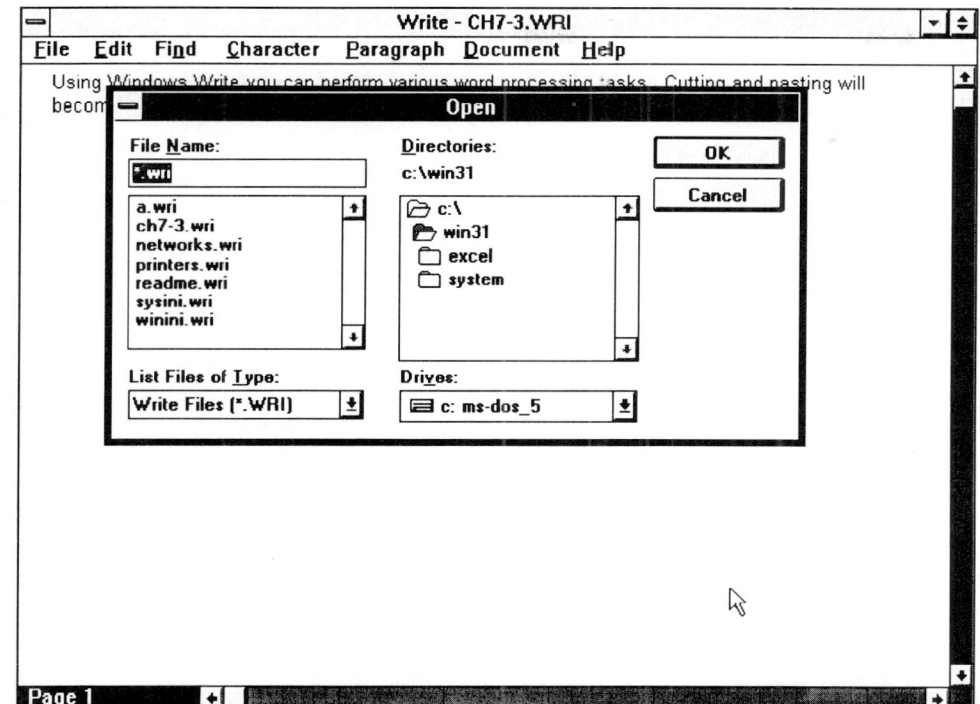

Figure 7-6
Open dialog box

7-6
MOVING AROUND IN A DOCUMENT

Using the Keyboard

7-6-1

You can use the right-, left-, up-, and down-arrow keys to move the cursor by one character to the right, left, up, or down, respectively. You can also press the space bar to move the insertion point to the right. When you press the Enter key, you move to the next line. In addition to these keys, Write uses some special keys for moving the insertion point around. Table 7–1 provides a summary of these keys.

Note that the number 5 in a keystroke combination (Table 7–1) must be pressed from the numeric keypad (on the right side of the keyboard). To do this, disable the Num Lock key first; then press and hold down the 5 key while pressing the other key.

Using the Mouse

7-6-2

One of the applications of the mouse is for moving the insertion point. Let us say you want to add more text to the end of the second line of your document. To do this follow these steps:

1. Move the mouse pointer to the end of the sentence in the second line.
2. Click the left button of the mouse. As soon as you do this, the insertion point moves to the I-beam's position. Whenever you position the mouse pointer over an area of text that can be edited, the pointer appears as an **I-beam.** The

Table 7-1
Cursor-movement keys in Windows Write

Keystroke(s)	Moves to
5- →	Next sentence
5- ←	Previous sentence
5- ↑	Previous paragraph
5- ↓	Next paragraph
5- PgDn	Next page
5- PgUp	Previous page
Ctrl- →	Next word
Ctrl- ←	Previous word
Ctrl- Home	Beginning of the document
Ctrl- End	End of the document
Ctrl- PgDn	Bottom of the window
Ctrl- PgUp	Top of the window
End	End of a line
Home	Beginning of a line
PgDn	Next screen down
PgUp	Next screen up

capital "I" indicates that you can edit this text as necessary (refer to Figure 7–2). Now you can start typing the next text.

You can also use the mouse to scroll the screen in any direction: up, down, right, or left. To do this, position the mouse pointer on one of the scroll bar arrows and click the left button of the mouse. If you click left and hold down any of the scroll bar arrows, you will scroll continuously. You also can drag the scroll box within the scroll bars to move to a different location in your document.

Remember, scrolling and moving are not the same. First you must scroll to the desired section of the document; then click the left button of the mouse to move the insertion point to the desired location.

7-7
INSERTING AND DELETING TEXT

To insert text into a document, move the insertion point to the desired location and start typing. The new text is inserted at the position of the insertion point and the existing text is moved to the right. If any unwanted characters appear in your document, you can erase them by using the Backspace or the Del (Delete) keys after moving the insertion point to those characters within the document.

7-8
PRINTING TEXT

To print your text in Write, invoke the File pull-down menu and select Print. You will be presented with a screen similar to the one in Figure 7–7. If the default setup is acceptable, just click left on OK and your document will be printed. Notice that the default print range is All, meaning that your entire document will be printed. Alternatively, you can click left on Pages and specify the desired beginning and ending page numbers for printing. You can specify the number of copies to print by typing the number in the Copies box. The default is one copy. Collate your copies by clicking left on the Collate Copies box.

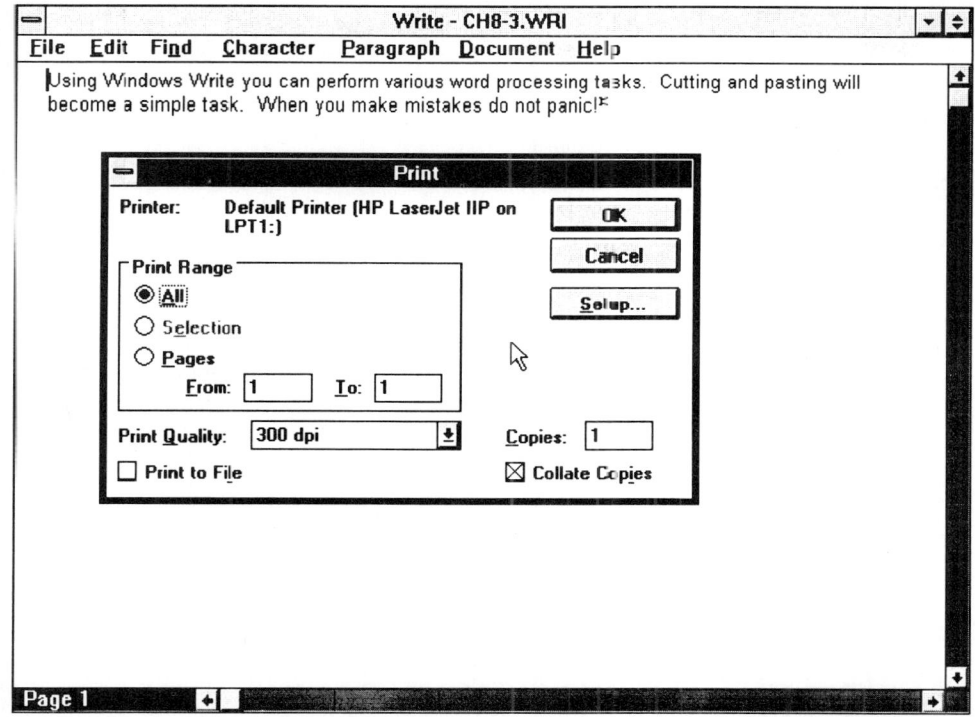

Figure 7-7
Print dialog box

Write also allows you to select the print quality. For some laser printers, the default is draft— 75 dpi. DPI stands for dots per inch. The higher this number, the higher the quality of the printout. If you click left on the down arrow next to the Print Quality option, you will see the high (300 dpi) and medium (150 dpi) print quality settings as well. Write also allows you to print to a file for future printing.

7-9 SELECTING TEXT

To perform editing tasks, you first must select the text to be edited. In some other word processing software, the process of **selecting text** is called blocking or highlighting the text. The simplest method for selecting text is to move the mouse I-beam to the desired character and then click the left button of the mouse. As soon as you do this, the insertion point is moved to the mouse I-beam location. Now you can click left and drag the mouse in any direction that you like. While you are dragging the mouse, your text will be highlighted. Table 7-2 summarizes other techniques for selecting text.

To deselect the selected text, click left anywhere in your document. (If you are using the keyboard, press any of the arrow keys.)

7-10 FIND AND REPLACE OPERATIONS

One of the most interesting features of word processing programs is the capability of finding a text string and then replacing it with a new text string—a **find and replace** operation. Write allows you to search for a text string up to 255 characters in length and change all occurrences or certain occurrences of the text string with a new text string.

Table 7-2
Techniques for selecting text using a mouse

To Select	Technique Used
One word	Double-click left on the word
Several words	Click left on the first word then drag the mouse pointer in the desired direction
One line	Click left on the selection bar (this is the space to the left of the text—see Figure 7-3)
One paragraph	Double-click left on the selection bar to the left of the paragraph
Entire text	Press and hold down the Ctrl key; then click left on the selection bar
Text between two distant points	Move the insertion point to the beginning point, click left, move to the second point, press and hold down the shift key, and click left again

Let's say in our sample document, you want to find every occurrence of the word "Write." Follow these steps:

1. Activate the Find menu. You will see a screen similar to the one in Figure 7-8.
2. Select the Find option from this menu. You will be presented with a screen similar to the one in Figure 7-9.
3. In the Find What box type *Write*. Click left on Match Case if case (uppercase or lowercase) is important to you. If so, remember that WRITE and write are considered different.
4. Click left on the Find Next option, and the word "Write" will be highlighted in the document.

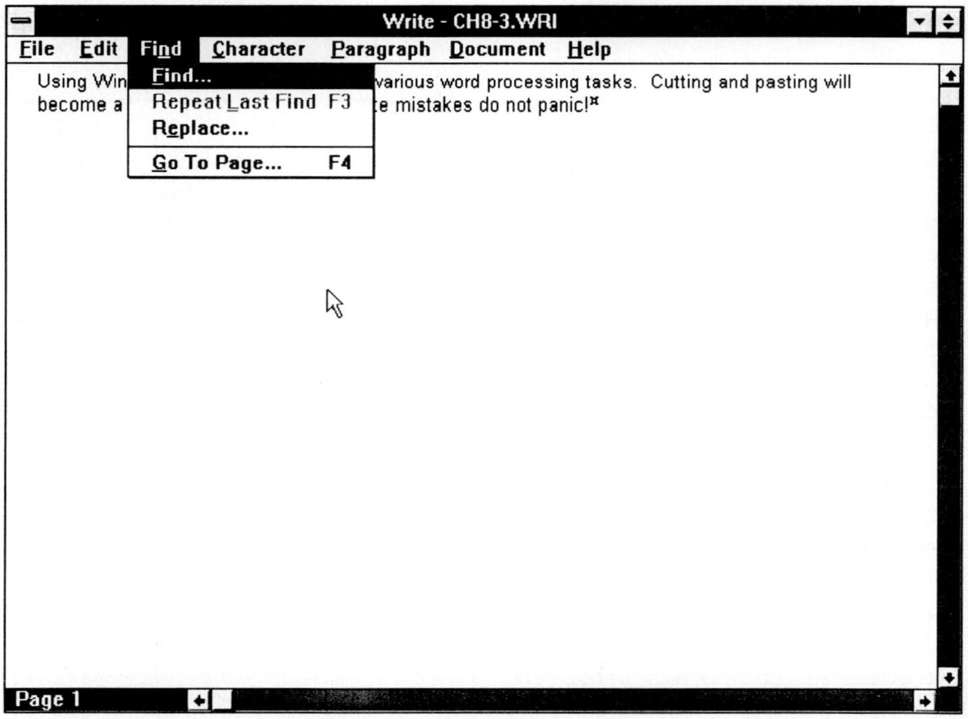

Figure 7-8
Find pull-down menu

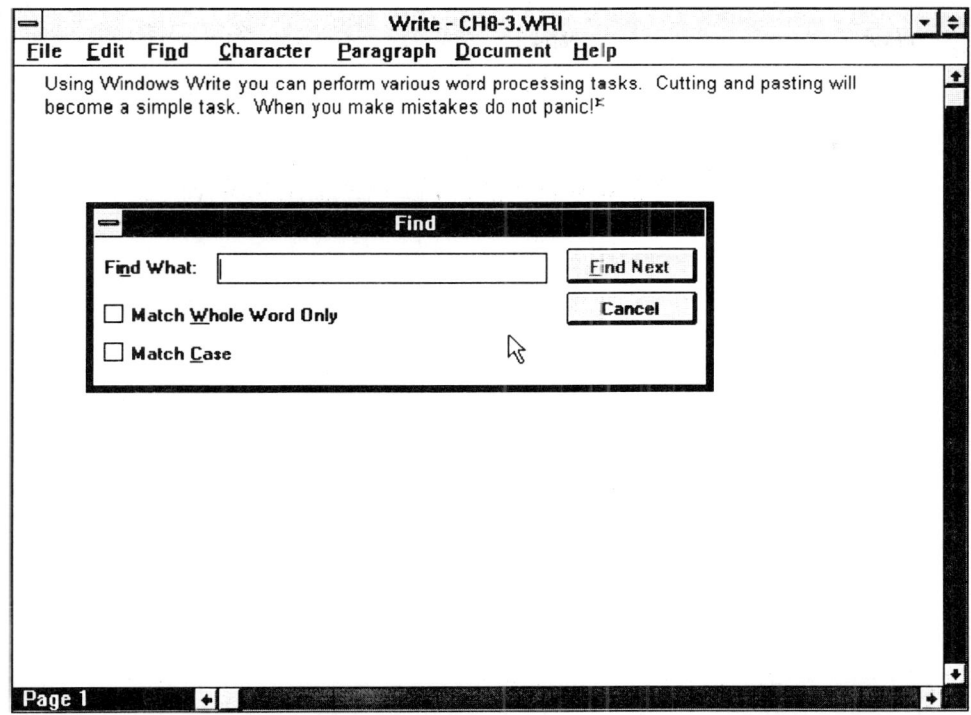

Figure 7-9
Find dialog box

To perform find and replace operations, follow these steps:

1. Invoke the Find menu.
2. Select the Replace option. At this time the Replace dialog box will be displayed; see Figure 7-10. Notice that the word "Write" is still in the Find What box.
3. Click left in the Replace With box. Then type *Word*.
4. Click left on the Replace option. As soon as you do this, "Write" is replaced with "Word." To replace all occurrences of Write with Word, click on the Replace All option. (This option will be displayed as soon as you type the text in the Replace With box.)

7-11 CUT AND PASTE OPERATIONS

Similar to other word processing programs, Write allows you to **cut and paste,** that is, to cut a portion of your text and paste it somewhere else—cut it permanently or just copy a portion of the text and paste it somewhere else. When you copy, basically you are duplicating a portion of your text. When you use the Copy command, the copied text is stored temporarily in the **Clipboard,** a temporary holding area that is shared by all Windows components. All these operations are done through the Edit menu.

To copy text, follow these steps:

1. Select the text that you want to copy.
2. Select the **Edit** menu. You will see a screen similar to the one in Figure 7-11. Select the Copy command (use Ctrl-C for a shortcut).

Figure 7-10
Replace dialog box

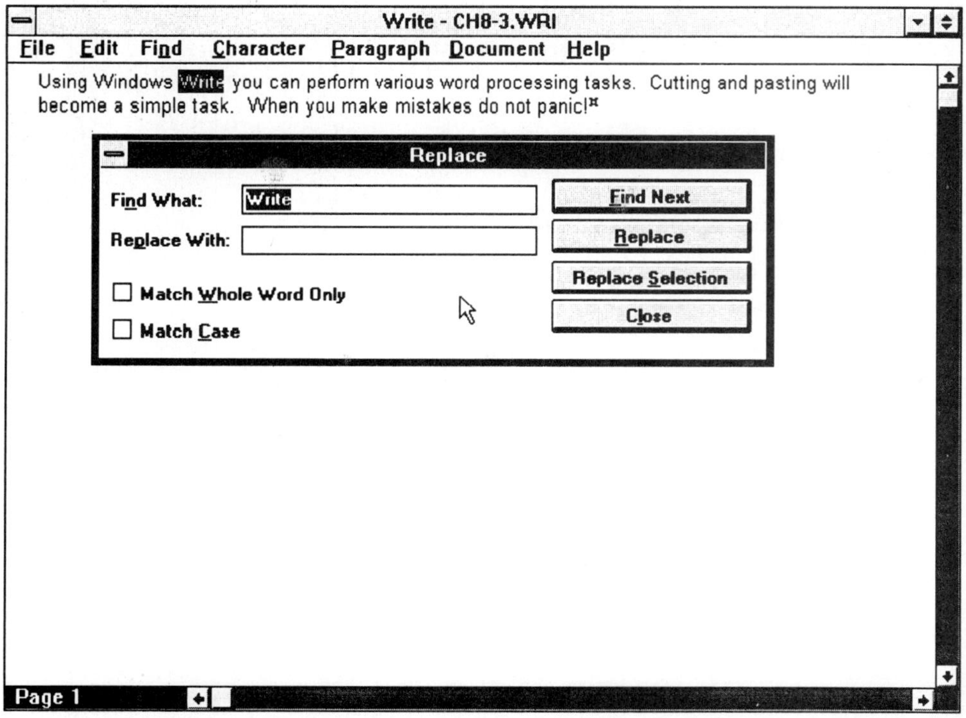

Figure 7-11
Edit pull-down menu

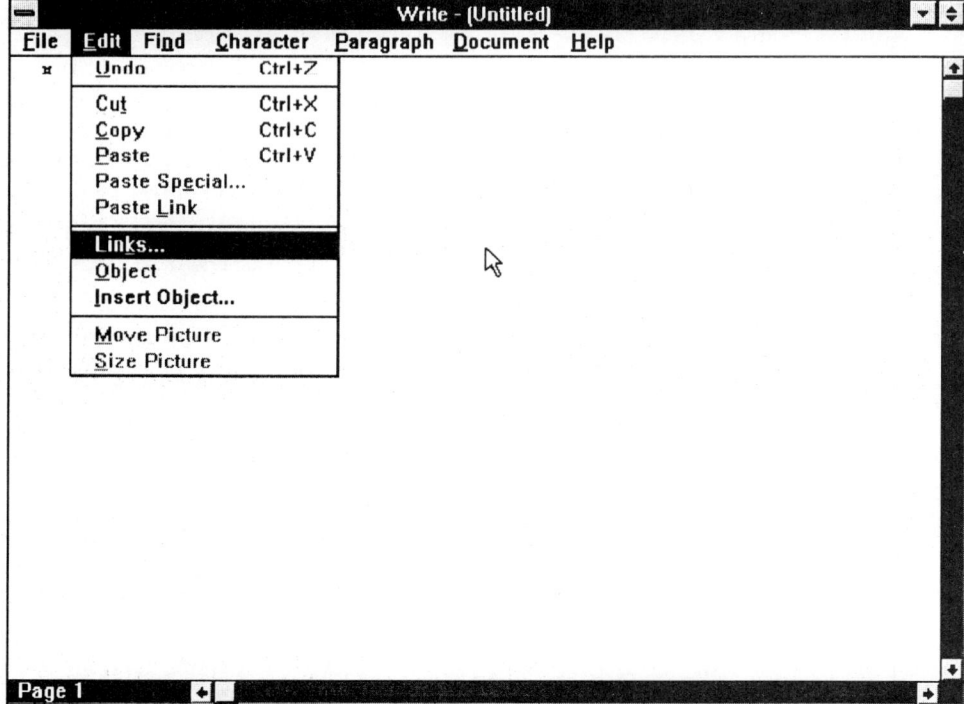

3. Move the insertion point to the desired location.
4. Select the **Edit** menu; then select **Paste.** Your selected text will be pasted back into the document at this position. (You can also use **Ctrl-V** for a shortcut.)

You can copy the contents of the Clipboard as many times as you wish in different places within your document. The contents of the Clipboard is replaced by the next cut or copy operation, or it is erased when you exit Windows.

7-12 MOVING TEXT

To move a portion of your text from one location to another location, follow these steps:

1. Select the text that you want to move.
2. Select the Edit menu (see Figure 7–11); then select the Cut command (use the **Ctrl-X** keystroke combination for a shortcut.) As soon as you select the Cut command, your highlighted text is moved to the Clipboard *and* it is removed from its present position. The remaining text is closed up.
3. Move the insertion point to the desired new location.
4. Select the Edit menu; then select the Paste command to finalize the operation.

7-13 UNDOING YOUR LAST ACTION

If you have edited your text (e.g., by erasing, moving, or formatting) and you change your mind, you can reverse your last action. To do so, follow these steps:

1. Select the Edit menu.
2. Select the Undo command. As soon as you do this, your text will return to its previous form. For example, the deleted text will be restored. The shortcut key for the Undo feature is Ctrl-Z.

7-14 LINE SPACING

By default, Write prints your text in single-space format. You can change this format to double-space or a space-and-a-half format. To change line spacing to your desired format, follow these steps:

1. Select the text for which you want to change the line spacing.
2. Select the Paragraph menu. You will be presented with a screen similar to the one shown in Figure 7–12. As you can see, the default Single Space is indicated by the check mark.
3. Select one of the three options: Single Space, $1\frac{1}{2}$ Space, or Double Space.

As soon as you make your choice, the selected text will conform accordingly.

Figure 7-12
Paragraph pull-down menu

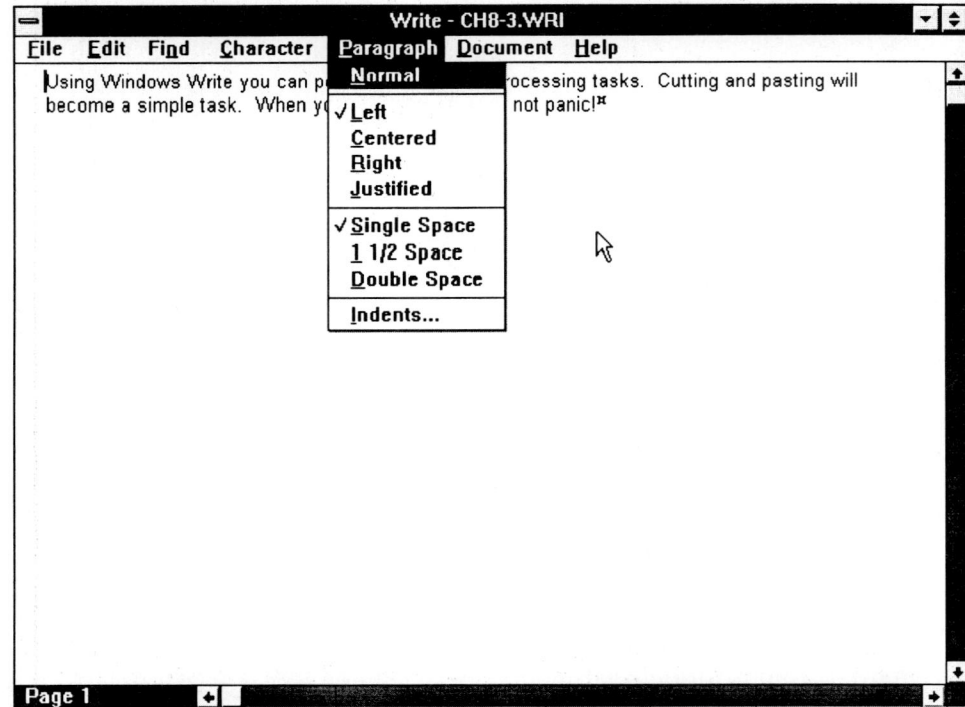

7-15
ENHANCING TEXT

Write provides a variety of options for **enhancing** the appearance of your document. By means of these enhancing features, you can make your document more readable. All the enhancing features are found in the Character pull-down menu; see Figure 7-13.

To enhance existing text (text that has already been typed), you must first select it. Then apply the enhancing feature to it. You can also enhance text as you type it by first choosing the desired enhancement, then typing the text. To turn the enhancement feature off, you must select it again or select the Regular option (F5) from the Character menu. The Regular option deselects all active enhancements.

As Figure 7-13 indicates, the Write enhancement features include Bold (Ctrl-B), Italic (Ctrl-I), Underline (Ctrl-U), Superscript, Subscript, Reduce Font and Enlarge Font, and Fonts.

Several enhancement features can be applied to the same text. For example, you may want to make your text both bold and italic. To do this, first select your text, then select the Bold command, and then, without deselecting the text, select the Italic command.

Let us look at an example. In the sample document presented in Figure 7-3, assume that you want to make the first line bold and the second line italic. Follow these steps:

1. Select the first line.
2. Select the Character menu.
3. Select the Bold command.
4. Select the second line.
5. Select the Character menu.
6. Select the Italic command.

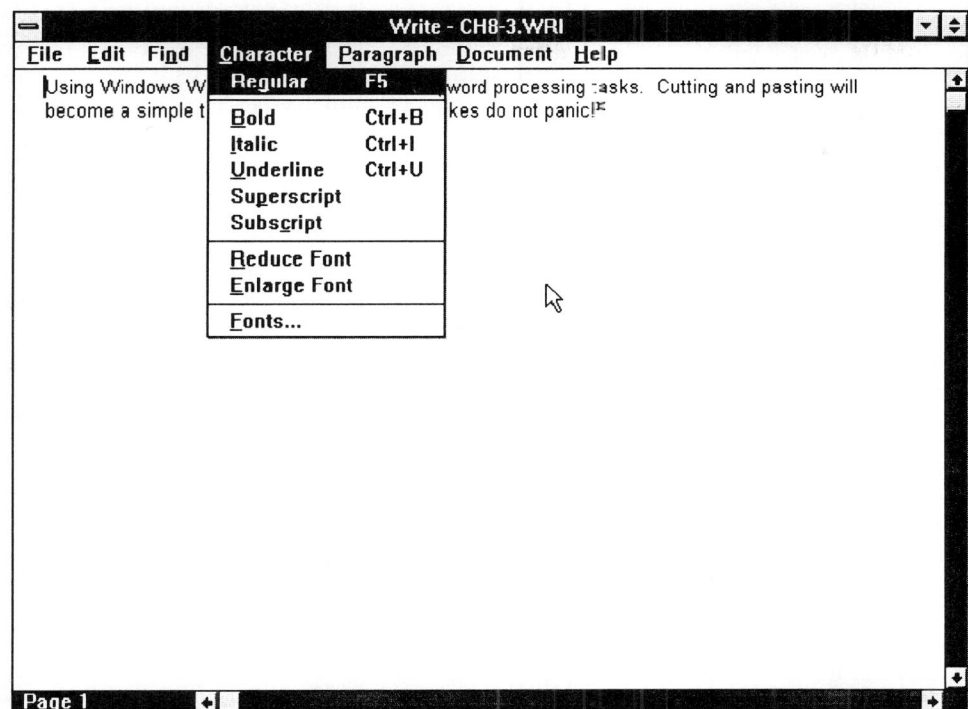

Figure 7-13
Character pull-down menu

If you print this document, you will see one similar to Figure 7-14.
To return the text to its original setting, follow these steps:

1. Select the desired text.
2. Select the Character menu.
3. Select the Regular command to remove all the enhancements. (You can also press the F5 key as a shortcut.)

You can also select the enhancing feature for the second time in order to remove it from your text. For example, if your text is italic, select italic again to remove this enhancement. Make sure that you are removing the enhancement from the correct text; otherwise, you may apply the enhancement instead of removing it.
The Character menu allows you to reduce or enlarge your text. Each time that you enlarge the text, it is changed to the next font size. A **font** is a specific **typeface** in a specific size and style. When you reduce a font, it gets smaller; for example, it goes from 36 point to 24 point, or from 24 point to 14 point, and so forth. A point is $\frac{1}{72}$ of an inch; for example, 36 point is half of an inch. To apply these two features to your text, follow these steps:

1. Select the desired text.
2. Select the Character menu.
3. To reduce, select Reduce Font option. To enlarge, select the Enlarge Font option.

> **Using Windows Write you can perform various word processing tasks. Cutting and pasting will** become a simple task. When you make mistakes do not panic!

Figure 7-14
Sample document printed with bold and italic

7-16
INSERTING PAGE BREAKS

Write automatically inserts **page breaks** into a document as soon as it reaches the end of a page. However, in some cases you may want to insert a page break sooner than its normal place. To do this, you have a couple of options available to you. Your first option is to insert manual page breaks. To do so, follow these steps:

1. Position the insertion point where you want to begin a new page.
2. Press Ctrl-Enter. This is sometimes called a hard page break.

To remove a manual page break, follow these steps:

1. Position the insertion point at the left end of the line below the page break.
2. Press the Backspace key.

A soft, or an automatic, page break appears as a double arrow in the left margin. A manual, or hard, page break appears as a heavy dotted line. See Figure 7–15.

The second option for entering a page break is to repaginate a document. To do so, follow these steps:

1. Select the File menu.
2. Select the Repaginate option. You will be presented with a screen similar to the one in Figure 7–16.
3. Select the Confirm Page Breaks option if you want to confirm each page break or to move the suggested page breaks.
4. Select OK. The Repaginating Document dialog box appears (Figure 7–17). Suggested page breaks appear as a double arrow in the left margin.

Figure 7–15
Example of a manual and an automatic page break

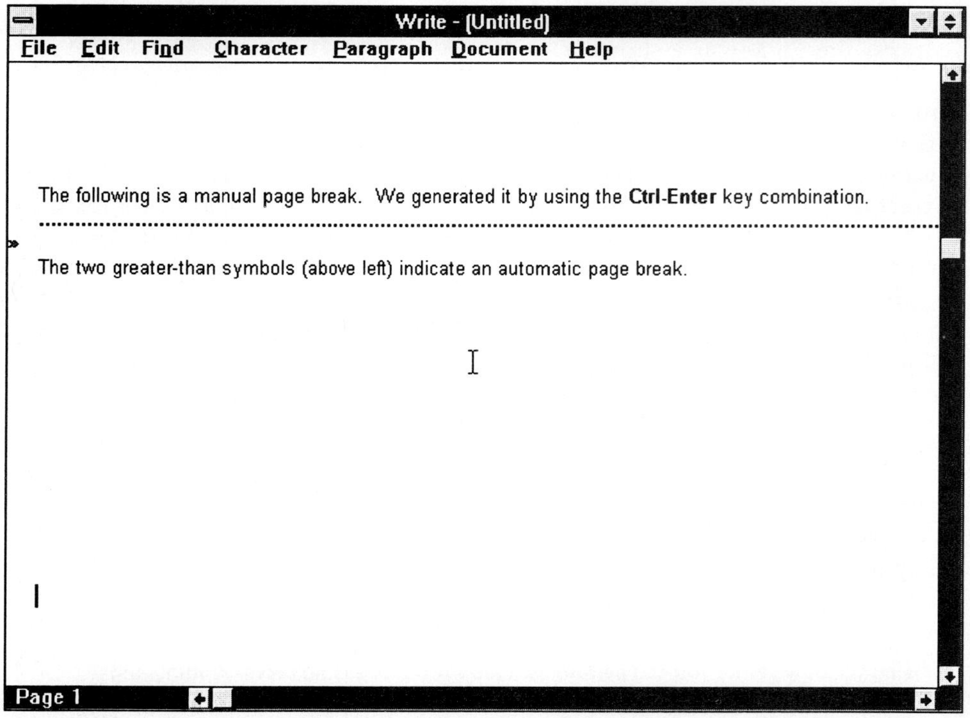

Chapter 7 Windows Write

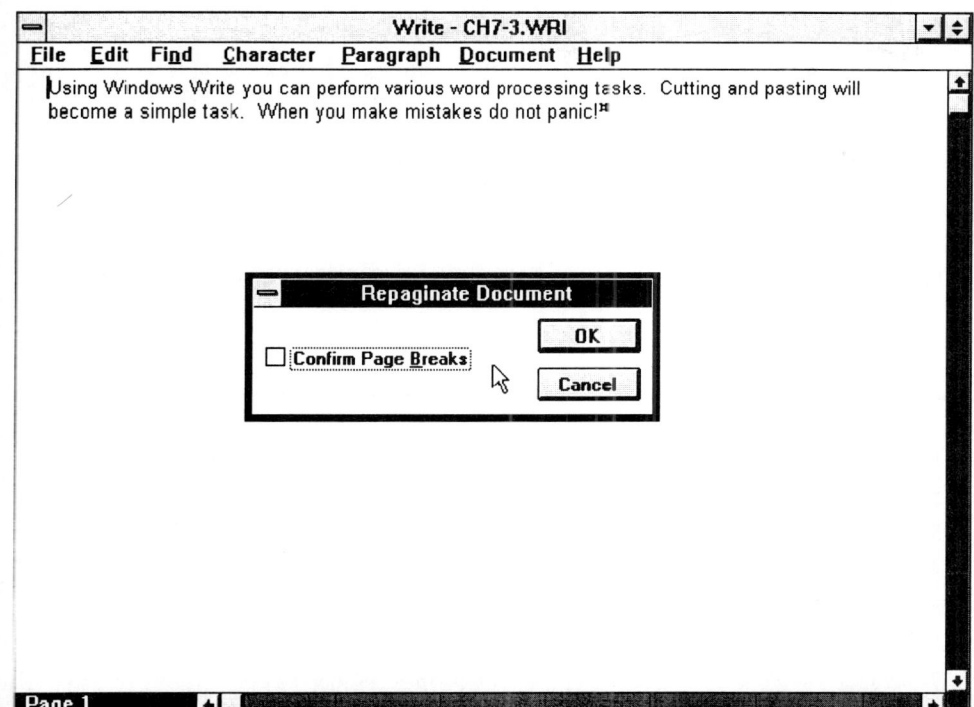

Figure 7-16
Repaginate dialog box

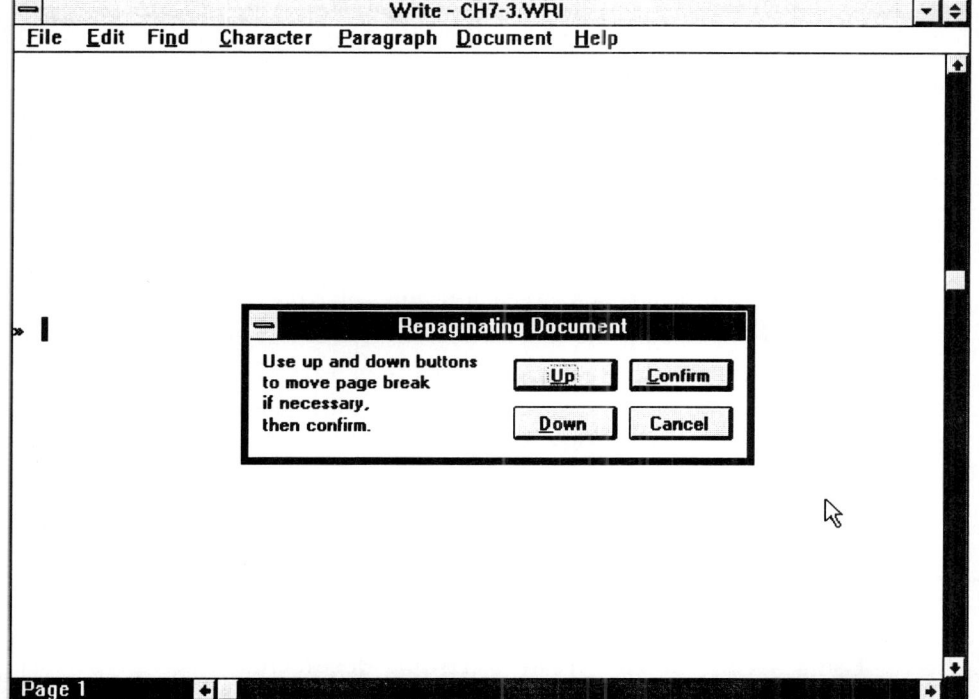

Figure 7-17
Repaginating document dialog box

5. Choose the Up or Down boxes to move the suggested page breaks up or down.
6. Select Confirm to finalize the process.

SUMMARY

This chapter provided an overview of Windows Write as a powerful word processing program. The processes of starting Write, creating a document, saving a document onto a disk, and moving around in a document were discussed. Find and replace, cut and paste, line spacing, and enhancing text were among the operations explained. The chapter concluded with instructions for inserting page breaks into a document.

REVIEW QUESTIONS

*These questions are answered in Appendix A.
1. What are some of the features of Windows Write as a word processing program?
2. How do you start Write? How do you exit from it?
*3. What is the difference between the Save and Save As commands?
4. What file extension does Write attach to a file name?
5. What is the file extension when you use the Backup option?
6. How do you open a saved document?
*7. Does Write allow you to generate a file that is compatible with other software? If yes, how?
8. What are some of the keys used for moving the insertion point?
9. How do you move the insertion point using the mouse?
10. How do you delete unwanted text? How do you insert text into a document?
11. How do you print a Write document?
*12. Using Write, can you generate several copies of a document?
13. How do you select (highlight or block) text?
14. What are some of the techniques available for text selection?
15. How do you find and then replace a word with another word?
16. Does Write support the Match Case option?
*17. What is the difference between copying and moving text?
18. Can you paste the copied text more than once?
19. What is the Clipboard?
20. How do you undo the last change to your document? What can be undone?
21. How do you change the line spacing of text?
22. What are some of the text enhancement features of Write?
23. Can you apply more than one enhancement feature to a given text area?
*24. How do you remove an enhancement option from text?
25. How do you reduce the size of text? How do you enlarge it?
26. How do you insert page breaks?
27. What is the difference between automatic and manual page breaks?

HANDS-ON EXPERIENCE

1. Start Write and type the following text:

   Using Write you can create electronic documents. You can perform various editing tasks. After your document is typed, you can save it onto

Chapter 7 Windows Write

a disk. You can enhance the text by applying several enhancement features available in Write.

    a. Save this document under the name SAMPLE in drive A.
    b. Generate a backup of this document.
    c. Exit Write.
    d. Start Write again and retrieve SAMPLE.
    e. Press Ctrl-End and add the following sentence to the bottom of your text:

       Compared with a typewriter a word processor such as Write presents numerous advantages.

    f. Move this last sentence to the beginning of your text.
    g. Copy this sentence (the one that you just moved) to the end of your text.
    h. By using the Save As command, save this new document under the filename SAMPLE1 in drive A.
    i. Exit Write.

2. Start Write again and do the following:
    a. Retrieve SAMPLE1.
    b. Print it.
    c. Make the first sentence bold.
    d. Make the second sentence italic.
    e. Make the last line enlarged.
    f. Print your document.

3. Using both the keyboard and the mouse, practice with all the arrow-movement keys. What are the advantages of a mouse over the keyboard for moving around in a document?

4. Using the SAMPLE1 file, do the following:
    a. Replace "Write" with "Word."
    b. Save the file under the same file name in drive A.
    c. Double space the text.
    d. Insert the following text right after "electronic document":

       Using electronic documents makes it easier to edit text.

KEY TERMS

Clipboard	Find and replace	Page break
Cut and paste	Font	Selecting text
Enhancing text	I-beam	Typeface

KEY COMMANDS

Ctrl-B (to make text bold)	F3 (to repeat the last find)	File (to invoke the File menu)
Ctrl-C (to copy text)	Character (to invoke the Character menu)	Paragraph (to invoke the Paragraph menu)
Ctrl-I (to make text italic)	Edit (to invoke the Edit menu)	
Ctrl-U (to underline)		
Ctrl-V (to paste text)		
Ctrl-X (to cut text)		

MISCONCEPTIONS AND SOLUTIONS

Misconception You try to move the insertion point by using Tab key, the space bar, or the Backspace key. The Tab key and the space bar add blank space to your document; the Backspace key erases the character to the left of the insertion point.

Solution Use one of the arrow keys instead.

Misconception You want to transfer a Write document to another Windows program that does not accept WRI format. You might think that you have to retype the entire document.

Solution Use the Windows Clipboard. Your document will be transferable to any Windows program. (We will discuss the Clipboard further in Chapter 9.)

ARE YOU READY TO MOVE ON?

1. Which one of the following is *not* true about Write. Using Write you can
   a. create an electronic document
   b. boldface your text
   c. italicize your text
   d. enlarge your text
   e. They are all correct

2. The Write main menu includes all of the following options except
   a. Edit
   b. Find
   c. Italic
   d. File
   e. Help

3. When you save a Write file, what extension does Write automatically attach to it?
   a. WRI
   b. WP
   c. WK1
   d. BAK
   e. none of the above

4. What is the maximum number of characters a Write file name can be?
   a. 8
   b. 6
   c. 4
   d. 12
   e. none of the above

5. To retrieve a saved file, what command must you select from the File menu?
   a. New
   b. Save
   c. Save As
   d. Open
   e. Exit

6. If you are using the keyboard, you can press Ctrl-→ to move to the
   a. preview word
   b. next word
   c. next paragraph

Chapter 7 Windows Write 139

    d. next page

    e. none of the above

7. Press 5-← to move to the

    a. previous page

    b. previous sentence

    c. next page

    d. next paragraph

    e. none of the above

8. To delete an unwanted character, use

    a. the Backspace key

    b. the Del key

    c. either a or b

    d. the down-arrow key

    e. the up-arrow key

9. The Print menu allows you to

    a. print all of your document

    b. print only the first 10 pages if you so desire

    c. print more than one copy

    d. do a, b, and c

    e. do only a and b

10. To select text you can

    a. select a word

    b. select several words

    c. select one line

    d. select one paragraph

    e. do all of the above

True/False

1. By means of the Find menu, you can specify the case of your text.
2. Write allows you to search for a text string of up to 355 characters in length.
3. The shortcut for Copy is Ctrl-C.
4. The shortcut for Paste is Ctrl-P.
5. The Clipboard remembers your text that has been cut or copied, even after you turn the computer off.
6. You can undo your last change in Write.
7. Line spacing is single space by default.
8. Bold and italic are two examples of write enhancement features.
9. After applying an enhancement feature to a text, you cannot remove it.
10. You cannot reduce or enlarge text using Write.

ANSWERS

Multiple Choice
1. e
2. c
3. a
4. a
5. d
6. b
7. b
8. c
9. d
10. e

True/False
1. T
2. F
3. T
4. F
5. F
6. T
7. T
8. T
9. F
10. F

Windows Basic Operations

8–1   Introduction
8–2   Menu Conventions
8–3   Opening the Control Menu
        8–3–1   For an Application Window or Icon
        8–3–2   For a Document Window
        8–3–3   For a Dialog Box
8–4   Control-Menu Commands
8–5   Moving a Window
8–6   Moving an Icon
8–7   Modifying the Size of a Window
8–8   Reducing a Window to an Icon
8–9   Enlarging a Window
8–10   Restoring an Icon to a Window
8–11   Navigating Through Screens Using Scroll Bars
8–12   Closing a Window
8–13   Different Parts of a Window
8–14   The Task List

8-1
INTRODUCTION

This chapter is an overview of the basics of Windows operations. It introduces the Windows menu conventions and the process of opening the control menu for an application window, a document window, and a dialog box. We discuss the commands in the control menu and how to move windows and icons. Instructions for reducing, enlarging, and closing windows are provided. In conclusion, we look at the different parts of a window and the Task List feature for arranging icons and windows.

8-2
MENU CONVENTIONS

To be able to use Windows menus effectively, you need to understand the **menu conventions** that are part of Windows. Table 8–1 summarizes these conventions. In Figure 8–1 note the key combinations—one of the conventions. To generate this figure, we opened the Write application from the Accessories group and clicked left on the Character option. In Figure 8–2 note the check marks and ellipsis (. . .). To generate this screen, we clicked left on the Paragraph option in the Write menu. When you select an option with ellipsis, you are presented with a dialog box. Figure 8–3 was generated by selecting Indents . . . from the Paragraph menu shown in Figure 8–2.

8-3
OPENING THE CONTROL MENU

8-3-1 For an Application Window or Icon

The control-menu box contains a small rectangle and is located at the upper left of a window or a dialog box. To open the **control menu,** click the left button of the mouse while on the control-menu box. If the desired window is hidden (i.e., not displayed on the screen), press Alt-Esc repeatedly to navigate through the open windows of the application until you reach the desired one; then click left on the control-menu box. To open the control menu of a group icon, click left on the icon. For example, click left on the Accessories icon to open its control menu. In any event, you will see a screen similar to the one presented in

Table 8–1
Windows menu conventions

Convention	Meaning
Triangle (▲) next to an option	When you select this option, a cascading menu is displayed from which you can choose options.
Check mark (√) next to an option	This means the option is in effect. Click left on the option to remove the effect.
Ellipsis (. . .) after an option	When you choose this option, a dialog box is displayed.
Key combination next to an option	This is a shortcut for that particular option. This key combination can be used instead of accessing the option through the menu.
Dimmed command	This command or option cannot be used because its use would not be appropriate at this time. For example, you may need to select another item before using this command.

Chapter 8 Windows Basic Operations

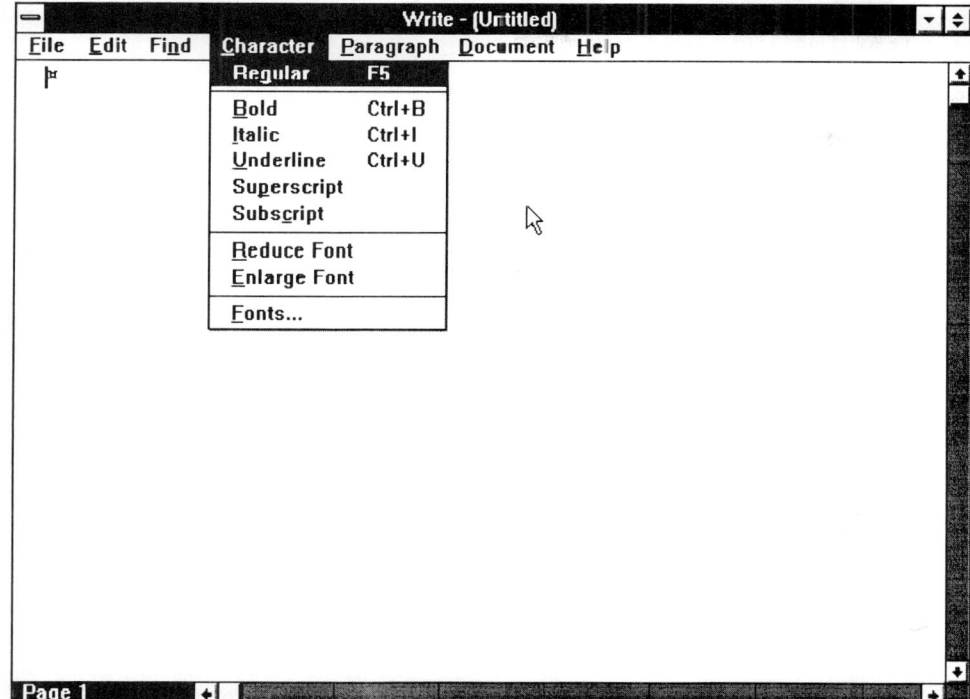

Figure 8-1
Screen with key combinations

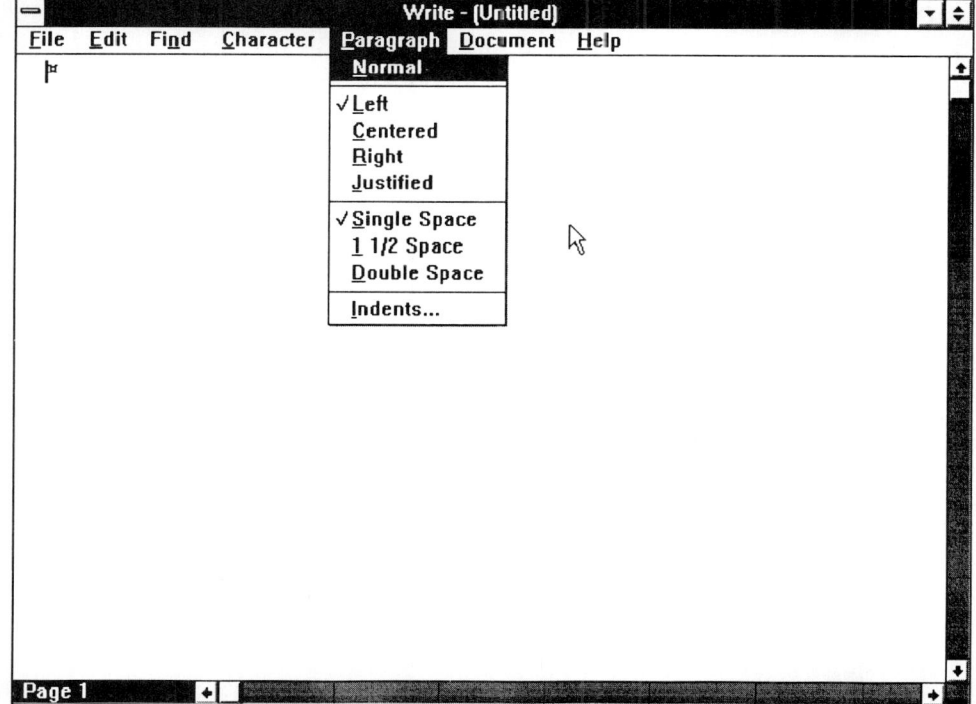

Figure 8-2
Menu with ellipsis

Figure 8-3
Dialog box

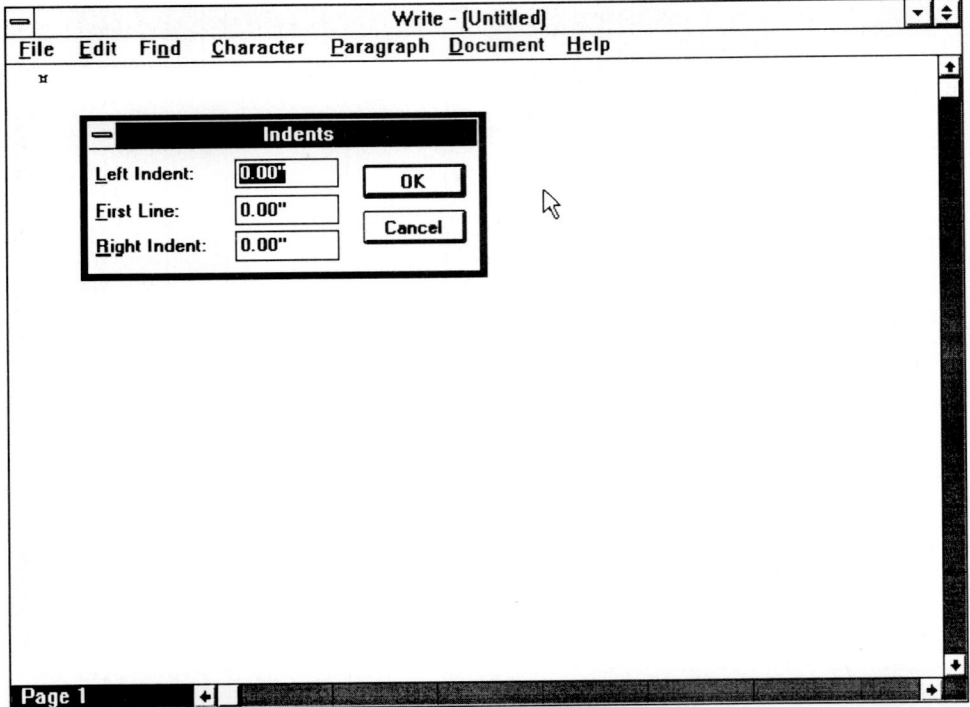

Figure 8-4. This figure was generated by clicking left on the control-menu box in a Write window.

8-3-2 For a Document Window

Using the mouse, click left on the control-menu box in a **document window.** You will be presented with a screen similar to the one in Figure 8-5. A document window is a window within an application window, for example, a window within WordPerfect (Figure 8-5). There can be more than one document window open at a time. Figure 8-5 was generated by clicking left on the control-menu box of a document in WordPerfect for Windows. As you can see, the options in this figure differ somewhat from those in Figure 8-4.

8-3-3 For a Dialog Box

To open the control menu of a dialog box, click left on the control-menu icon at the upper left of the dialog box (Figure 8-6). We opened Write, selected the Paragraph option, and then selected Indents (see Figure 8-3). Then we clicked left on the control-menu box to generate Figure 8-6. To close the control menu without choosing a menu item, click the left button of the mouse.

8-4 CONTROL-MENU COMMANDS

Table 8-2 summarizes the control-menu commands. Some applications do not have all of these commands. For example, refer to Figures 8-4 and 8-5; these figures do not include all the commands outlined in Table 8-2.

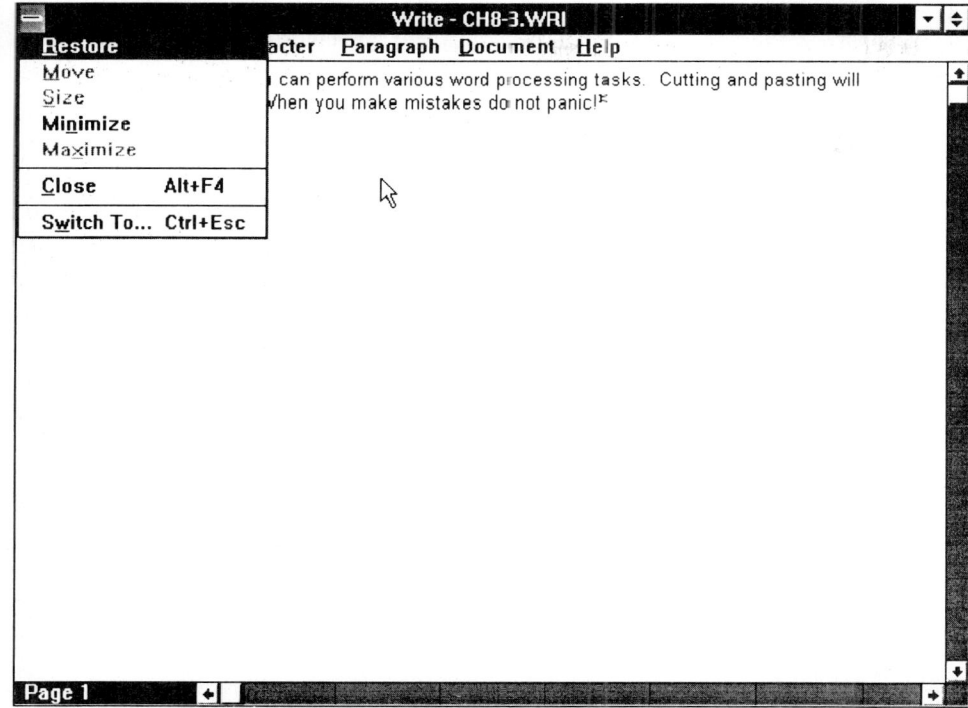

Figure 8–4
Control menu options

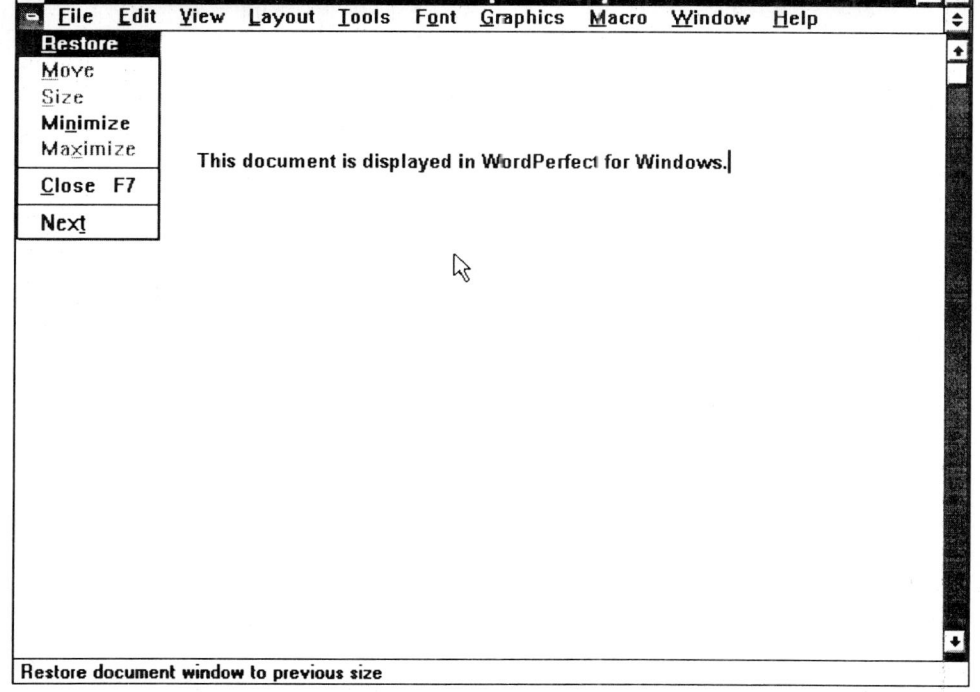

Figure 8–5
Opening the control menu for a document window

Figure 8-6
Opening the control menu for a dialog box

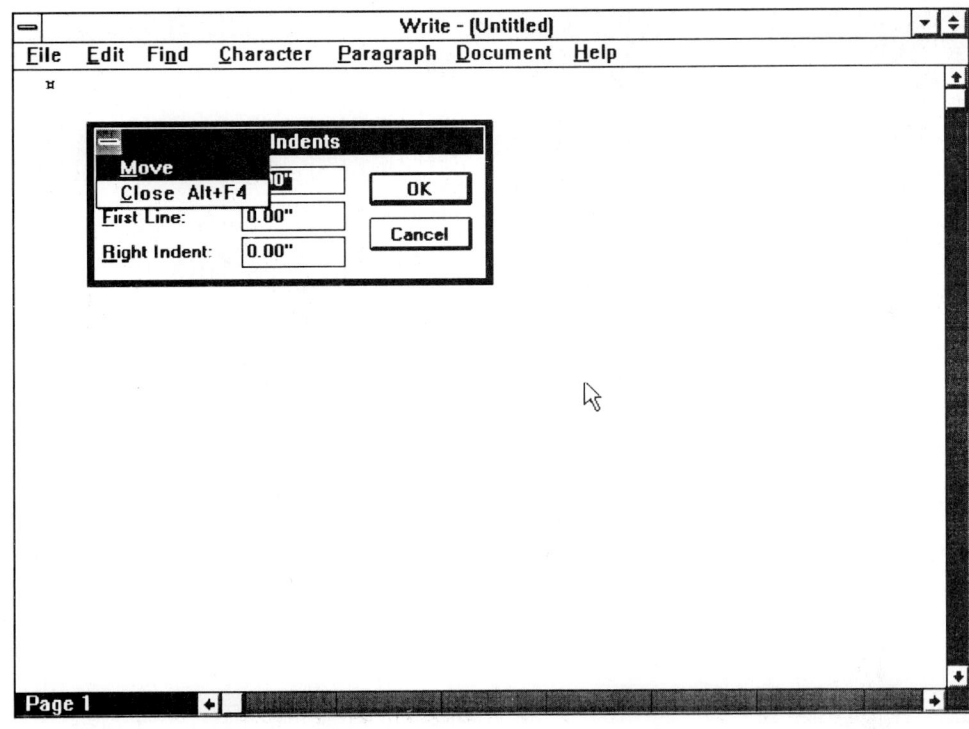

Table 8-2
Control-menu commands

Command	Function
Close (Alt-F4)	Closes a window or a dialog box. You can also use this command to quit an application from an application window.
Edit	Displays a cascading menu with additional commands.
Maximize	Enlarges a window to its maximum size.
Minimize	Reduces a window to an icon.
Move	Uses the keyboard to move a window to another location.
Next	Switches between open document windows and icons. This feature is available for document windows only. (See Figure 8-5.)
Restore	Restores the window to its former size after you have enlarged it (by using the Maximize command) or reduced it to an icon (by using the Minimize command).
Size	Uses the keyboard to change the size of a window.
Switch To (Ctrl-Esc)	Opens the Task List, a feature that enables you to switch between active applications. The Task List also arranges windows and icons on the desktop. See Figure 8-7. (We discuss the Task List in detail later in the chapter.)

8-5
MOVING A WINDOW

To move a window from one location to another using the mouse, follow these steps:

1. Click left and drag the title bar of the window to the new location. To do this, position the mouse pointer anywhere in the title bar; then press and hold down the left button of the mouse and drag the mouse pointer.

Chapter 8 Windows Basic Operations

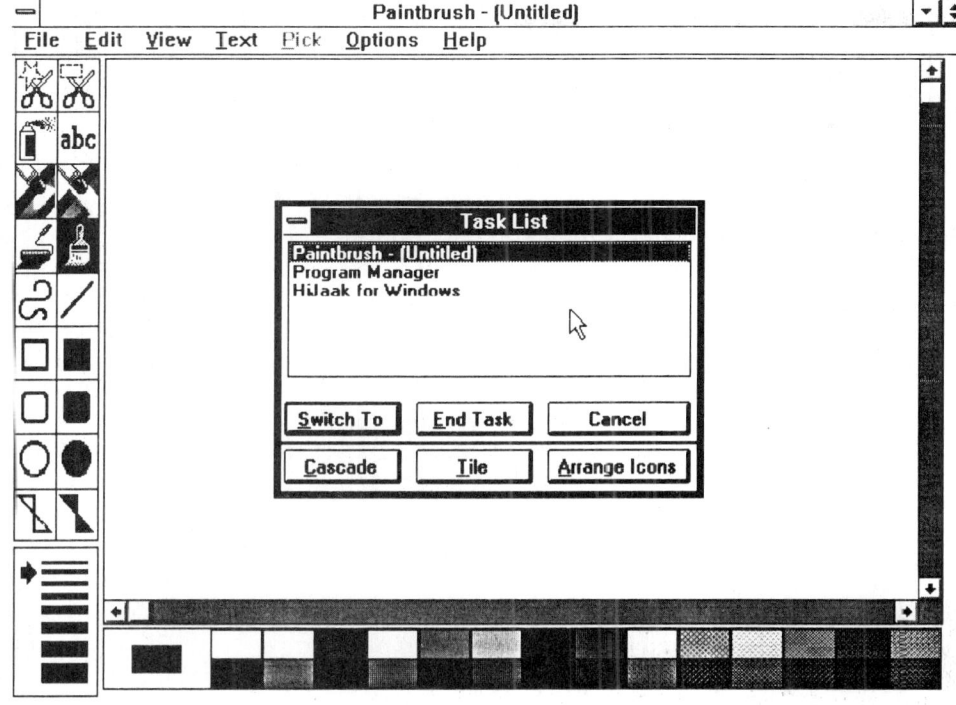

Figure 8-7
Task List dialog box

2. When you are satisfied with the new location, release the mouse button. To cancel the move operation, press the Esc key before you release the mouse button.

8-6
MOVING AN ICON

Any application or document icon can be moved into any other group window on the desktop. You might want to move your commonly used icons into a window that is always open. However, application and document icons cannot be moved into another application window. For example, the Write icon cannot be moved into the Paintbrush window.

To move an icon, use the mouse and follow these steps:

1. Position the mouse pointer on the desired icon; then click left and drag the icon to the desired location.
2. Release the mouse button. If you change your mind, drag the icon back to its previous location.

8-7
MODIFYING THE SIZE OF A WINDOW

To reduce or enlarge the size of a window, use the mouse and follow these steps:

1. Select the desired window by clicking left anywhere inside of the window.
2. Position the mouse pointer on one of the four window corners or one of the four window borders. At this time, the mouse pointer changes to a double-pointed arrow.
3. Click left and drag the corner or border until you are satisfied with the new size; then release the mouse button. To cancel the modification, before you release

the mouse button press the Esc key. If you drag a border, the window size changes only on the side of the border that you drag. If you drag a corner, the two adjoining sides that form the corner are moved at the same time.

8-8
REDUCING A WINDOW TO AN ICON

After you have used an application you may want to reduce the window for this application to an icon so that you save space on your desktop. When you do this, the application is still running, but is displayed as an icon and not as a window. To open the application again, press the Alt-Esc key to display all the active application icons, then double-click left on its icon.

To reduce a window to an icon, Click left on the minimize button (the downward-pointing triangle button at the upper right of the window).

To open this window again, double-click left on its icon, or select the Restore option from the desired control menu.

8-9
ENLARGING A WINDOW

A window can be enlarged to fill a larger portion of the desktop. To do so, Click left on the maximize button (the upward-pointing arrow at the upper right of the window).

At this point, the window is enlarged to its maximum size, and the maximize button is replaced by the restore button. The restore button is represented by two small triangles on top of each other. If you click left on the triangles, the window will return to its previous size.

8-10
RESTORING AN ICON TO A WINDOW

To restore an icon to a window, select the Restore option from the control menu of the icon to be restored. To restore a window to its original size using the mouse, click the restore icon at the upper right of the window, or select the Restore option from the control menu.

8-11
NAVIGATING THROUGH SCREENS USING SCROLL BARS

Some windows and dialog boxes include scroll bars that you can use to view information that is not displayed on the current screen. Figure 8-8 illustrates vertical and horizontal scroll bars.

To scroll throughout a screen using the mouse, position the mouse pointer in the vertical or horizontal scroll bar then click the left button of the mouse.

The scroll bars can be used to move to different positions within a document. For example, you may click left on the up arrow at the top of the vertical scroll bar to move up or on the down arrow at the bottom of the vertical scroll bar to move down within the document. Likewise, you can click left on the left arrow at the left side of the horizontal scroll bar to move left and on the right arrow at the right side of the horizontal scroll bar to move right.

Chapter 8 Windows Basic Operations

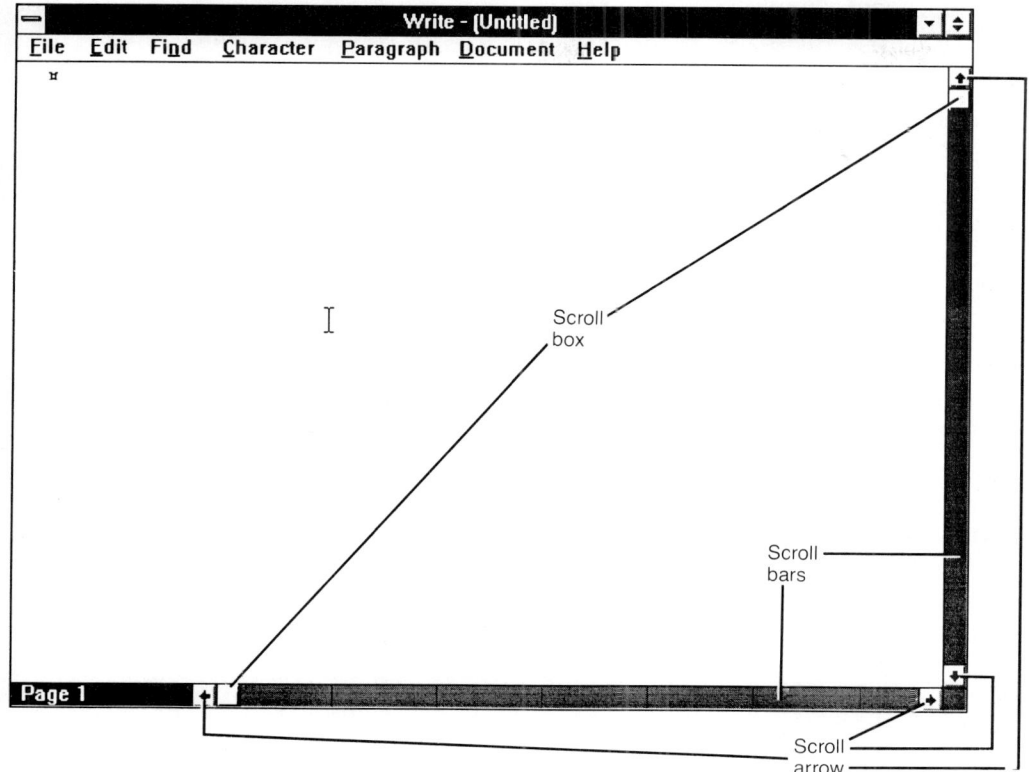

Figure 8-8
Screen with scroll bars

The scroll boxes within the scroll bars indicate your approximate position within the document. Bigger vertical movements can be made by clicking left anywhere in the vertical scroll bar (away from the scroll box), and bigger horizontal movements can be made by clicking left anywhere in the horizontal scroll bar (away from the scroll box). Table 8-3 presents other techniques of using the scroll bars.

Scroll bar	Result
Click on the up or down scroll arrow once	Moves one line (or some small distance) up or down
Click on the left or right scroll arrow once	Moves a small distance left or right
Click on the scroll bar above or below the scroll box on the vertical scroll bars or to the left or right of the scroll box on the horizontal scroll bar	Moves one screen up, down, left, or right
Position the mouse pointer on the scroll box within the scroll bar and drag it	Moves to any point
Position the mouse pointer on one of the scroll arrows and hold the left button of the mouse down	Scrolls continuously

Table 8-3
Techniques for moving using the scroll bars and the mouse

Windows 3.1

Table 8-4
Techniques for moving around using the keyboard

Press	Result
↑ (up arrow) or ↓ (down arrow)	Moves one line up or down
PgUp or PgDn	Moves one screen up or down
Ctrl-PgUp or Ctrl-PgDn	Moves one screen left or right
Ctrl-Home	Moves to the beginning of the document
Ctrl-End	Moves to the end of the document
End	Moves to the end of a line
Home	Moves to the beginning of a line

To use the keyboard to move around, disable the Num Lock key (not necessary in enhanced keyboards) and use one of the arrow keys. Table 8-4 summarizes techniques for scrolling with the keyboard.

8-12 CLOSING A WINDOW

To close a document or an application, close its window. To do this, select the File menu and the **Exit** option. You can also select Close from the control menu or double-click the control-menu box of the window you wish to close.

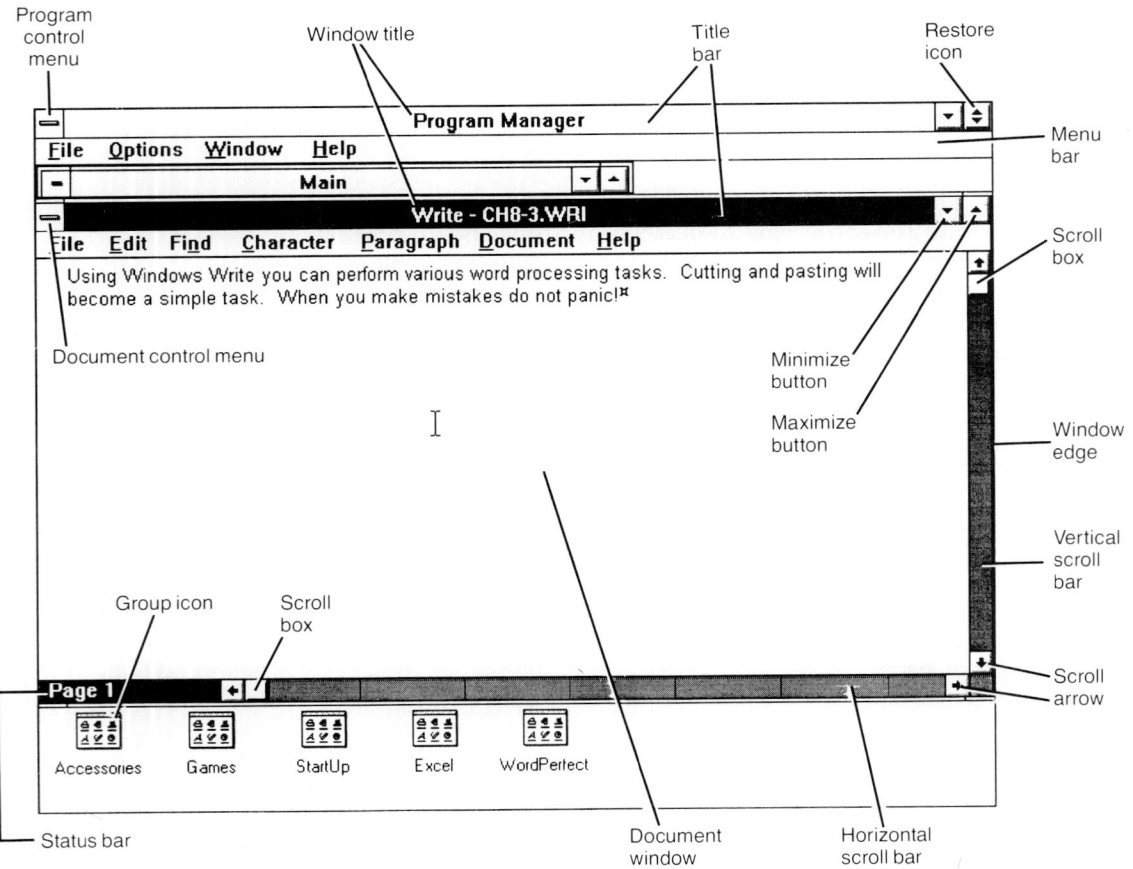

Figure 8-9
Sample window from Windows Write

Chapter 8   Windows Basic Operations   151

8-13 DIFFERENT PARTS OF A WINDOW

To become efficient using Windows, become comfortable with the different parts of a window. Figure 8–9 illustrates a window from Windows Write (one of the accessories of Windows 3.1 discussed in Chapter 7). Table 8–5 explains important parts of this window, which are similar to the parts of other windows.

8-14 THE TASK LIST

The **Task List** is a feature of Windows that allows you to switch between active programs and applications. You might, for example, switch back and forth between a word processing program and a spreadsheet. Display the Task List by pressing Ctrl-Esc. You can also click left on the control-menu box and select the Switch To option. You will be presented with a screen similar to the one shown in Figure 8–10.

The Task List allows you to do the tasks highlighted in Table 8–6.

Table 8-5 Different parts of a window running an application

Window Part	Description
Title bar	Bar that displays the name of the application and/or the document or both. Figure 8-9 shows that we are using a document named CH8-3 and that we are using the Windows Write application.
Menu bar	Bar that displays the pull-down menu options available. In Figure 8-9 the menu bar includes seven options: File, Edit, Find, Character, Paragraph, Document, and Help.
Status bar	Bar that displays document status; for example, we are in Page 1 of our document in Figure 8-9.
Maximize button	Button that increases a window to full screen size
Minimize button	Button that decreases an application window to an icon at the bottom of the screen
Document control menu	Menu that controls a document window's size and location. This menu box is located at the upper left of the document window.
Program control menu	Menu that controls a program window's size and location relative to other program windows. This menu box is located at the upper left of the program window.
Document window	Window within the program window. Contains the document that you are working with.
Program icon	A program or application window reduced to an icon. The File Manager and Paintbrush icons are examples of program icons. (There is no program icon in Figure 8-9. To see some, open the Accessories icon by double-clicking left on it.)
Window edge	An edge of a window that you can move to resize the window
Group icon	Any group window reduced to an icon. In Figure 8-9, notice Accessories, Games, StartUp, Excel, and WordPerfect group icons.

Figure 8−10
Task List menu

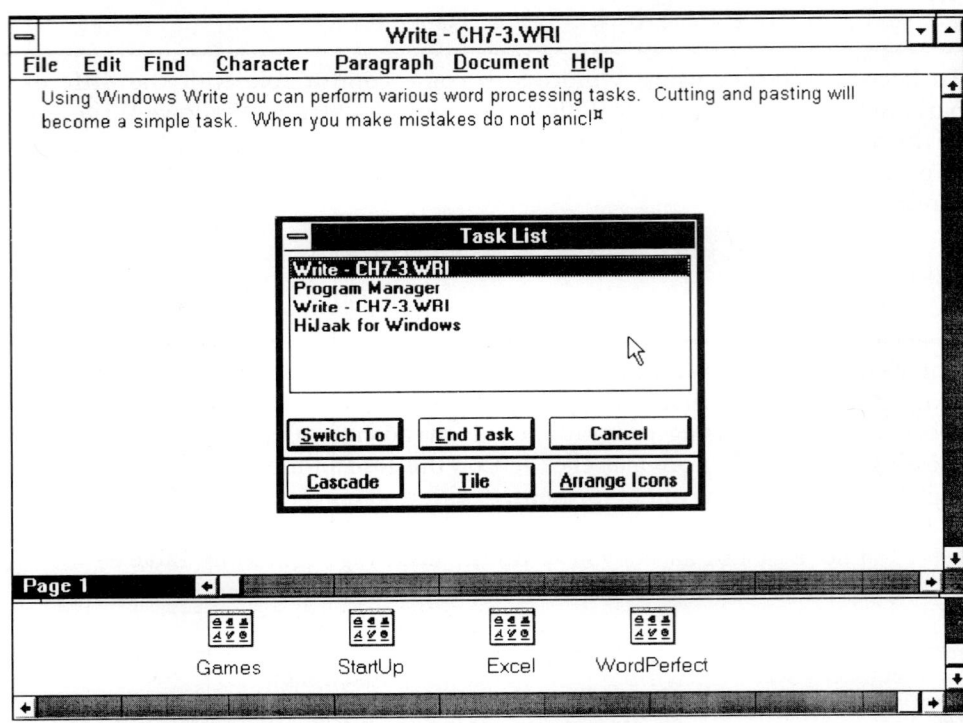

Table 8−6
Task List options

Option	Function
Switch To	Displays the window of the selected program in the Task List. In Figure 8−10 the selected program is Write-CH7-3.WRI. You can highlight an option and press Enter or double-click the option. You can also highlight the option then click left on Switch To.
End Task	Closes the highlighted program in the Task List. If the application contains work in progress that has not been saved, Windows will display a dialog box prompting you to take one of the following actions: Yes, No, or Cancel. If you select Yes and your document has not been saved, you will be presented with a Save As dialog box. Alternatively, if the file already has a name, your work will be saved under its present name. Selecting No will terminate the application without saving the work in progress, and selecting Cancel will not terminate the application. Therefore, you can highlight any application in the Task List and click left on the End Task button to terminate that application.
Cancel	Cancels the Task List. You can also press the Esc key.
Cascade	Arranges open windows in an overlapping cascade from top left to bottom right
Tile	Arranges all open windows to fill the screen with equal-sized or nearly equal-sized windows
Arrange Icons	Arranges all active minimized program icons along the bottom of the screen

SUMMARY

In this chapter we concentrated on the basics of Windows operations. We discussed opening and closing the control menu, using commands in the control menu, and moving windows and icons. The chapter also explained the processes of changing the size of windows and navigating through screens by means of scroll bars. The chapter concluded with an overview of the different parts of a window and functions of the Task List.

Chapter 8 Windows Basic Operations 153

REVIEW QUESTIONS

*These questions are answered in Appendix A.
  1. What are some of the conventions used in Windows menus?
  2. What does a check mark mean in a menu? How do you remove it?
 *3. What are key combinations and how are they used?
  4. How do you open a control menu in an application window using a mouse?
  5. How do you open a document window using a mouse?
 *6. How do you open the control menu for a dialog box using a mouse?
  7. What are some of the control-menu commands?
  8. What are the applications of the Minimize and Maximize commands?
 *9. For what purpose do you use the Move command from the control menu?
 10. What does the Switch To command do?
 11. How do you move a window around?
 12. If you are using the mouse and you decide not to finalize the move process, what should you do?
 13. How do you move an icon around?
*14. How do you modify the size of a window using the mouse?
 15. How do you reduce a window to an icon? How do you enlarge an icon to a window?
 16. How do you move forward through a screen using the vertical scroll bar?
*17. How do you move to any location using the scroll bar and the mouse?
 18. How do you move within a screen?
 19. How do you close a window?
 20. What are some of the parts of a typical window?
 21. Where is the title bar located? Where are the maximize and minimize buttons located?
*22. What is the Task List?
 23. How do you invoke the Task List?

HANDS-ON EXPERIENCE

1. By going through different Windows menus, do the following:
   a. Locate a menu with a triangle next to an option. What does this mean?
   b. Locate a menu with a check mark. Remove the check mark. Put it back.
   c. Locate a menu option with ellipsis. Select this menu option (you should see a dialog box).
   d. Locate a menu option with a key combination. Now use the key combination to execute the option.
2. Open the control menu for an application window and do the following:
   a. Close it by clicking on the Close option.
   b. Open it again and this time press Alt-F4 (Close). What happens? Select the Cancel option to stay in Windows (do not exit).
   c. Click on the maximize button. What is the effect?
   d. Click on the restore button (you should be back to your previous status).
3. Practice with all the commands in the control menu. What are the applications of these commands?
4. Select a window of your choice then move it to a different location. Now move it back to its previous location.

5. Repeat question 4 with an icon.
6. Select a window of your choice and reduce its size to half. Restore it to its original size.
7. Open the Write application and type one page of text; then do the following:
   a. Move up one screen.
   b. Move down one screen.
   c. Move left one screen.
   d. Move right one screen.
   e. Invoke continuous scrolling.
8. Invoke a window of your choice and locate the parts listed in Table 8–5. Do all windows include all these parts?
9. Open the Accessories window and do the following:
   a. Double-click on the Write icon to open it. Then reduce it back to an icon.
   b. Double-click on the Paintbrush icon to open it. Then reduce it back to an icon.
   c. Press Ctrl-Esc to invoke the Task List. Now you should see Write and Paintbrush among your active tasks.
   d. Click left on Paintbrush; then click left on Switch To. As you can see, you can easily move among active applications.
   e. Switch back to Write.

KEY TERMS

Application window
Control menu
Document window
Menu convention
Task List

KEY COMMANDS

Alt (to close a menu without choosing an option)

Control-menu commands (see Table 8–2)

Ctrl-Esc (to invoke the Task List)

Techniques for moving around (see Tables 8–3 and 8–4)

MISCONCEPTIONS AND SOLUTIONS

Misconception Sometimes you see more than one control-menu box. This is confusing.

  Solution The control-menu box at the far upper left of the screen controls the application (e.g., WordPerfect). The others control the windows inside the application window (e.g., a document in WordPerfect). The extreme upper left control menu is usually for the Program Manager.

Misconception To maximize a window, you click on the maximize button, but this is time consuming.

  Solution You can also maximize a Window by double-clicking on its title bar. To restore an application window to its previous size, double-click on the title bar again.

Misconception Working with several windows becomes confusing because one Window blocks others.

  Solution Use any of the following methods to display other windows: (1) Select the restore button to return the enlarged window to its previous size. (2) Select

Chapter 8 Windows Basic Operations

the Minimize option from the control menu to reduce the enlarged window to an icon. (3) Click left on the control-menu icon; then select Switch To and the desired program window from the Task List. (4) Click left on the Window option; then select the Tile option to tell Windows to display all open windows on the screen in a side-by-side format. (5) Click left on the Window option; then select the Cascade option to tell Windows to display all open windows on the screen in a stacked format.

Multiple Choice

ARE YOU READY TO MOVE ON?

1. A triangle next to an option means that if you select this option
   a. a cascading menu will be displayed
   b. the option is in effect
   c. a dialog box will be displayed
   d. a key combination will be displayed
   e. none of the above

2. A check mark next to an option means
   a. if you select this option a dialog box will be displayed
   b. this command is in effect
   c. this command cannot be selected
   d. this command does not have a key combination for a shortcut
   e. none of the above

3. To open the control menu in an application window
   a. click left on the upper left of the window
   b. press the space bar
   c. do both a and b
   d. press the Alt key twice
   e. none of the above

4. To display the names of all the active application windows, press
   a. Ctrl-Tab
   b. Alt-Tab
   c. Ctrl-Esc
   d. Alt then the space bar
   e. none of the above

5. The following are included in the majority of the control menus except
   a. Restore
   b. Move
   c. Maximize
   d. Minimize
   e. Open

6. The Switch To command in the control menu
   a. opens the Task List
   b. opens the control menu
   c. opens a dialog box

    d. Opens the File menu

    e. Opens the Edit menu

7. When you are moving a window around, before you finalize the move operation you can change your mind by pressing the

    a. Alt key

    b. Ctrl key

    c. Space bar

    d. Esc key

    e. none of the above

8. When you enlarge a window by clicking on the icon at the upper right, the maximize button is replaced by

    a. the minimize icon

    b. the restore icon

    c. the edit icon

    d. the Task List

    e. none of the above

9. A window can be enlarged to fill a larger portion of the screen by

    a. clicking on the Size command

    b. clicking on the Minimize command

    c. clicking on the Restore command

    d. clicking on the Maximize button

    e. none of the above

10. All of the following are parts of a window except the

    a. title bar

    b. menu bar

    c. minimize button

    d. maximize button

    e. they all are

True/False

1. The Switch To command is one of the options in the Task List menu.
2. The Tile option is *not* included in the Task List menu.
3. The Task List feature allows you to arrange active minimized application windows.
4. When you see ellipsis after an option, this means that if you choose this option a dialog box will be displayed.
5. You cannot remove the check mark from an option.
6. The Ctrl-Esc key combination displays the Task List.
7. To switch from one program to another, highlight the desired program in the Task List and click on Switch To.
8. The Move command is *not* included in the control menu.
9. The Restore command is *not* included in the Control Menu.
10. The Switch To option opens the file menu.

Chapter 8 Windows Basic Operations

Multiple Choice	True/False	ANSWERS
1. a	1. T	
2. b	2. F	
3. a	3. T	
4. c	4. T	
5. e	5. F	
6. a	6. T	
7. d	7. T	
8. b	8. F	
9. d	9. F	
10. e	10. F	

Working with Applications and Documents

9–1 Introduction
9–2 The Program Manager
    9–2–1 What Is the Program Manager?
    9–2–2 Parts of the Program Manager Window
9–3 Starting Applications
    9–3–1 From the Program Manager
    9–3–2 From the File Manager
    9–3–3 By Using the Run Command
    9–3–4 By Using the MS-DOS Prompt
9–4 Running Two or More Applications at the Same Time
9–5 Switching Between Applications
9–6 Selecting Text
9–7 The Clipboard
    9–7–1 Moving or Copying Information to the Clipboard
    9–7–2 Transferring Information from the Clipboard
    9–7–3 Working with the Clipboard Viewer
    9–7–4 Saving the Contents of the Clipboard to a File
    9–7–5 Retrieving a Clipboard File
    9–7–6 Clearing the Contents of the Clipboard
9–8 Quitting an Application
9–9 Working with Documents
    9–9–1 Opening Files
    9–9–2 Saving Files
    9–9–3 Switching Between Documents
    9–9–4 Working with Text
    9–9–5 Moving Around in Text
    9–9–6 Correcting Mistakes

9-1
INTRODUCTION

This chapter starts with an overview of the Program Manager—different parts of its screen and instructions for starting applications from it. The chapter then explains how to switch between two or more applications. After we discuss the operations performed with the Clipboard, we concentrate on various operations performed with files and documents. The processes of opening, saving, editing, and moving around in a document are explained. The materials presented in this chapter should significantly simplify your work with applications using Windows.

9-2
THE PROGRAM MANAGER

9-2-1
What is the Program Manager?

As soon as you start Windows, you start the Program Manager. Program Manager is always running during a Windows session. As you will see later in this chapter, you can perform a variety of tasks using the Program Manager. Among them are starting Windows and other (non-Windows) applications. When you run other applications, the Program Manager runs in the background.

If you run other applications, new windows containing the applications are displayed on the screen. These application windows may partially overlap or completely cover up other windows. The window on the very top is in the "foreground"; the windows that it is covering up are in the "background." In any event, Program Manager is always active, even though you may not see it.

The first time you start Windows, the Program Manager opens on your desktop with the Main group window open inside the Program Manager window (Figure 9–1). This is true, however, only if no changes have been made to the program by any user.

In our system, the Accessories group, Games group, StartUp group, Excel group, and Wordperfect group are all represented as group icons along the lower border of the Program Manager window (see Figure 9–1). Your screen might be different from what is presented in Figure 9–1 because windows can be configured in various ways by the user, and your system may display different applications depending on the software that you have installed.

9-2-2
Parts of the Program Manager Window

As you can see in Figure 9–2, Program Manager window has several parts:

- A **group window** is a separate window inside of the Program Manager window. In Figure 9–2, the Main group window is displayed; it includes icons that start different applications. From this window you can start applications such as File Manager, Control Panel, and so forth by double-clicking on their icons. Group windows are affected by these commands from the Program Manager menu bar: File, Options, Window, and Help.
- Program-item icons are displayed inside a group window and represent applications, documents, accessories, and so forth. You can select program-item icons to start particular applications. For example in Figure 9–2, double-click on the File Manager icon to start the File Manager.

Chapter 9 Working with Applications and Documents

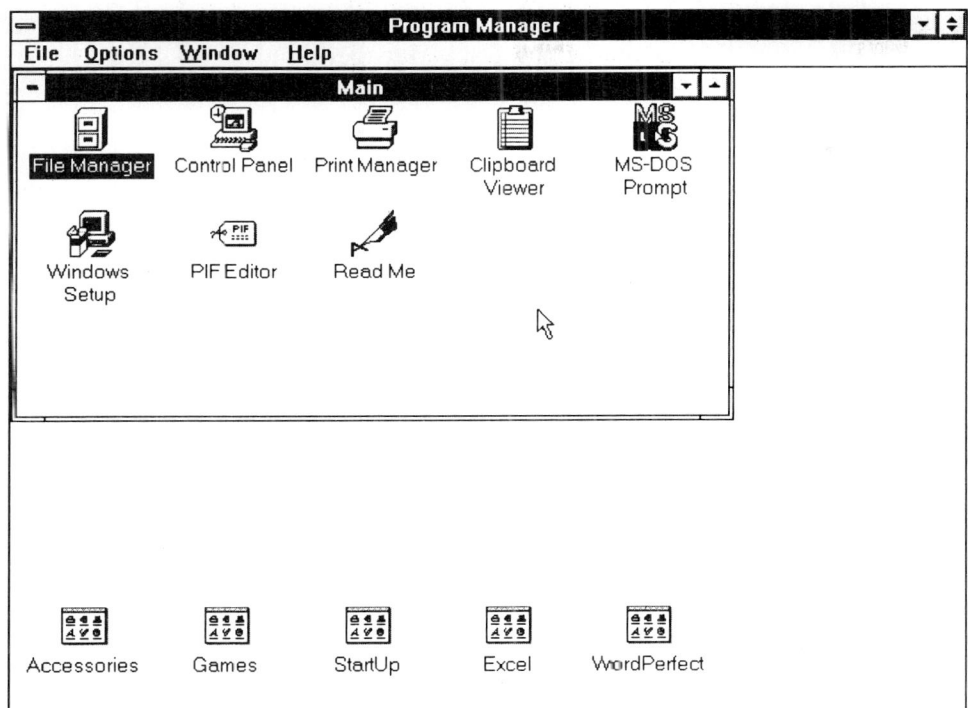

Figure 9-1
Program Manager window

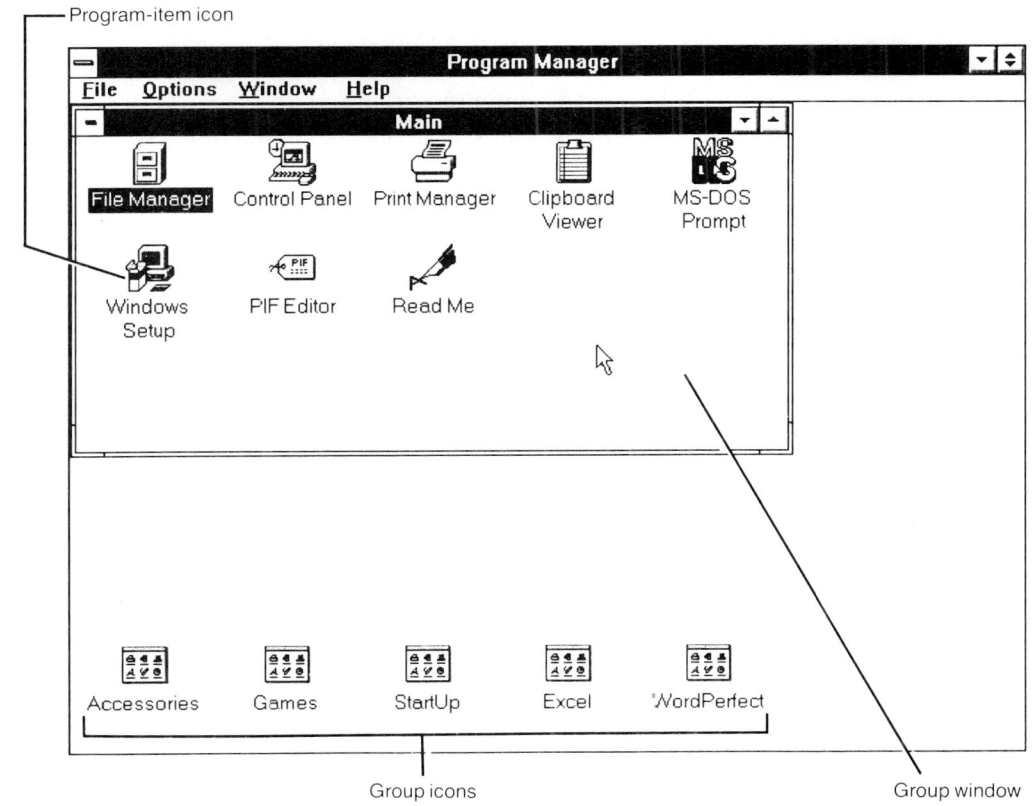

Figure 9-2
Parts of the Program Manager window

- A **group icon** is a minimized group window. These icons are usually displayed along the lower border of the Program Manager window. In Figure 9–2, notice the five group icons.

9–3 STARTING APPLICATIONS

9–3–1 From the Program Manager

To start an application from the Program Manager using the mouse, follow these steps:

1. Open the Program Manager (if it is not already open).
2. Open the group window (if it is not already open) that includes the desired application by double-clicking on the group icon (e.g., open the Accessories group window).
3. Double-click on the icon for the desired application (e.g., the Write icon).

9–3–2 From the File Manager

An application can also be started from the **File Manager** by selecting its program file from a directory window. A directory window is a File Manager window that displays the directory structure of your disk and the files and directories on the disk. File Manager includes a series of programs that help organize files and directories. (File Manager is discussed thoroughly in Chapter 11.) The program file must have an .EXE, .COM, .BAT, or .PIF extension.

To start an application using the File Manager, follow these steps:

1. Double-click on the File Manager icon within the Main group window.
2. Select the correct drive (e.g., drive C).
3. Click on the correct directory (e.g., WP51 for WordPerfect).
4. Double-click on the program name (e.g., WP.EXE).

If your desired directory and/or your desired program is not displayed on the screen, click on the arrow keys on the scroll bars to locate the desired file name; then double-click on the file name to run the application.

9–3–3 By Using the Run Command

Any application (Windows or non-Windows) that has not been added to a group window can be started by means of the Run command. Such applications are on your disk, but they do not have an icon representing them in the Program Manager. You have already seen that to run an application that has an associated icon in the Program Manager, you simply double-click on the icon. To run applications without the icons by selecting the Run command from the File menu, follow these steps:

1. From the File menu in the Program Manager, select Run. You will see a screen similar to the one in Figure 9–3.

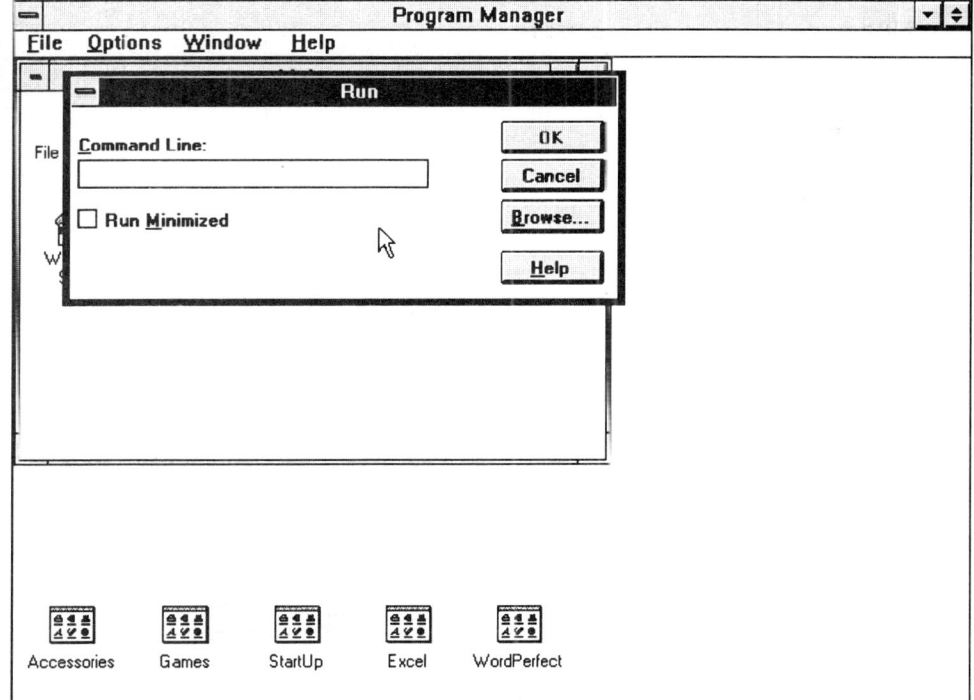

Figure 9-3
Run dialog box

2. Type in the program file name and its extension with its complete path. A program file is an executable file that starts an application or program. Each program file has a .BAT, .COM, .EXE, or .PIF file name extension. For example, to start Lotus 1-2-3, which is residing in the Lotus subdirectory in drive C, type *C:\LOTUS\123.EXE* in the Command Line box. You can select the Browse command (Figure 9-4) to display a listing of all the program files from which you can select. When the desired program file name is displayed, click left on it.

3. If you want the application to be reduced to an icon as soon as it starts, click on the Run Minimized box (see Figure 9-3). The advantage of doing this is simple. Let's say you plan to use several applications during your normal work session within Windows. However, you do not know which one you will use first. Running the applications minimized places their icons at the bottom of the desktop, which allows you immediate access to the application icons at the time you need them.

4. Click on OK or press Enter.

By Using the MS-DOS Prompt

9-3-4

You can also start applications from the MS-DOS prompt. To do so, follow these steps:

1. Open the Main group window from the Program Manager.
2. Double-click on the MS-DOS Prompt icon.

Now you can type any command that starts your application; for example, type *DBASE* to start dBASE III Plus or IV or type *WP* to start WordPerfect.

Figure 9-4
Run dialog box with Browse option opened

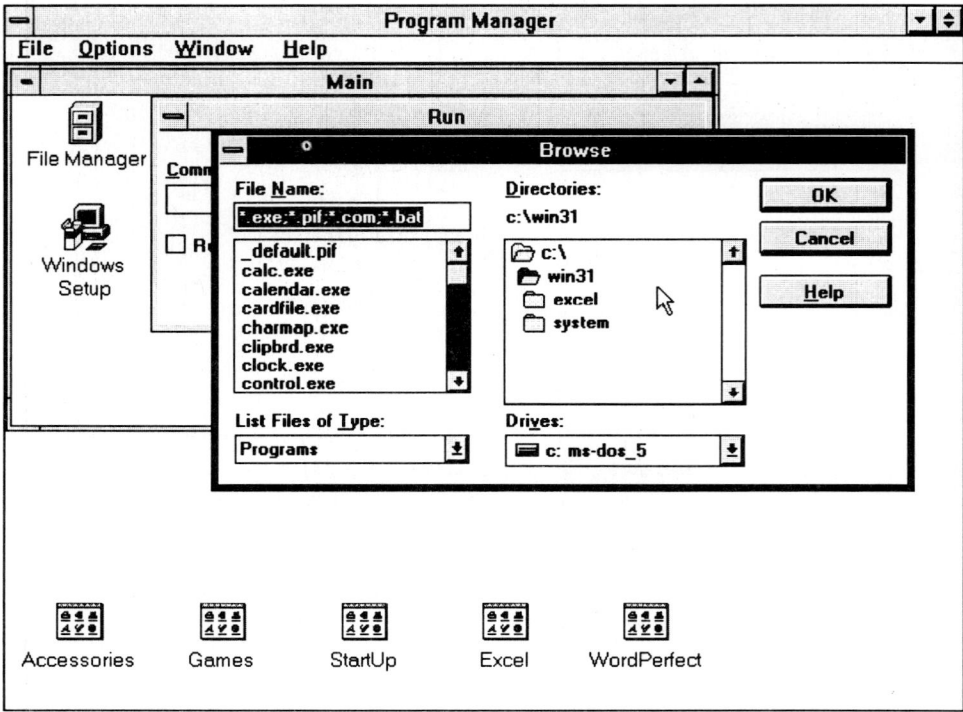

To exit the MS-DOS prompt and return to Windows, at the MS-DOS prompt type *EXIT* and press *Enter*.

9-4
RUNNING TWO OR MORE APPLICATIONS AT THE SAME TIME

Windows allows you to run more than one application at the same time, provided that you have enough memory. When you run several applications at the same time, however, the processing speed may be reduced. This is true because your system resources are being divided among several tasks. Faster processors such as the 486 and possibly the 586 minimize the problem.

Start the applications in the desired sequence using one of the methods that were just described. For example, double-click on the Accessories icon to open the Accessories window; then double-click on the Write icon to open the Write window. Click left on the minimize button at the upper right of the Write window screen. Double-click on the Paintbrush icon and click left on its minimize button. At this point, you are running both Write and Paintbrush as icons. To verify your work, press Ctrl-Esc to display the Task List. You will see that both Write and Paintbrush are among your active tasks (applications). Double-click left on any of the applications in the Task List to redisplay that application window.

9-5
SWITCHING BETWEEN APPLICATIONS

When you are running more than one application at a time, the window that you are currently working in is called the active window. The active window appears in the foreground. It might overlap or completely cover other application win-

Chapter 9 Working with Applications and Documents

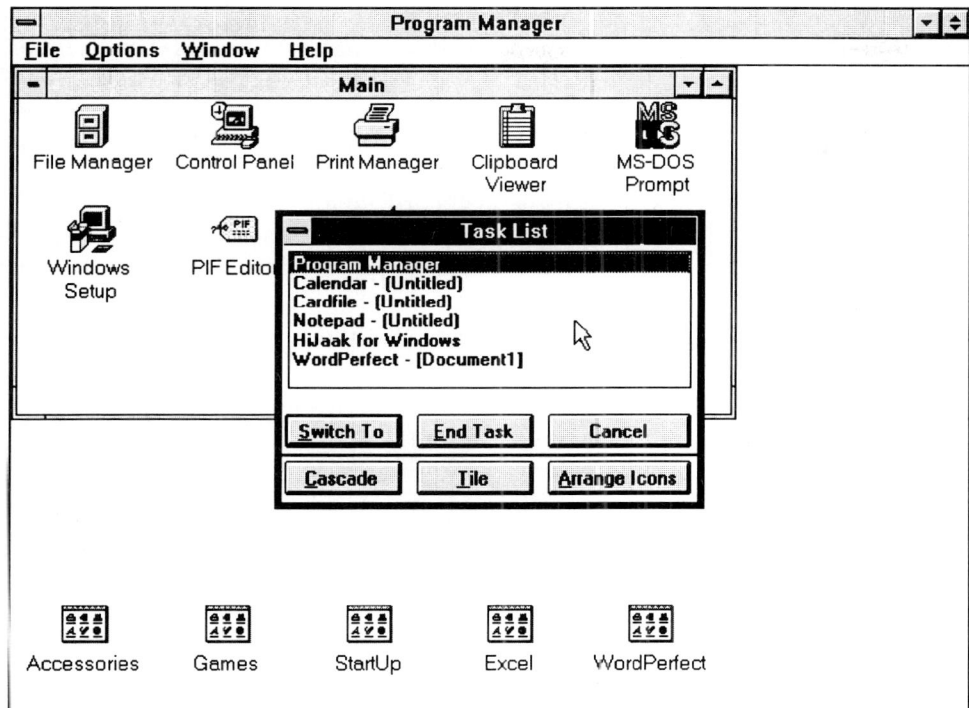

Figure 9-5
Task List dialog box

dows that are also running. To make another window active, you must select its window.

To switch between applications you can do any one of the following:

1. If the application is visible, click anywhere in the application's window. If the application is running as an icon, click left on its icon; then click left on Restore or just double-click on the icon.
2. Press Ctrl-Esc to display the Task List. You will be presented with a screen similar to the one in Figure 9-5. In the Task List window double-click on the name of the desired application, or highlight the name of the desired application and select Switch To from the options available in the Task List dialog box.

To return to the application that you last used, press Alt-Tab.

9-6
SELECTING TEXT

Selecting text allows you to perform editing commands on a block of text rather than on a single character. First you select (highlight or block) text; then you choose commands such as Cut, Copy, Bold, and so forth from the Edit menu of the application software.

To select text by means of the mouse, follow these steps:

1. Position the mouse pointer on the desired character, then click left and drag the insertion point to the end of the desired text.
2. Release the mouse button.

You can also click on the beginning of the desired text, move to (without dragging) the end of the block, then Shift-Click to highlight the text between the first point and the last point. To cancel the selection, click again anywhere in the document. Some applications (such as WordPerfect for Windows) allow you to select a word by double-clicking on it, a sentence by triple-clicking, the entire paragraph by quadruple-clicking, and so on.

To select text by means of the keyboard, follow these steps:

1. Use the arrow keys to move the insertion point to the beginning of the desired text.
2. Press and hold down the Shift key; then use the arrow keys to move the insertion point to the end of the desired text.
3. Release the Shift key. To cancel the selection, press an arrow key.

9-7 THE CLIPBOARD

Windows Clipboard serves as a temporary location for storing information. You can copy or move information from one application to the Clipboard; then you can copy (paste) the contents of the Clipboard to another application. The information that you copy to the Clipboard stays there until you clear the contents of the Clipboard or copy other information to it.

The Clipboard can also serve as a buffer for exchanging information among several applications. When you exit Windows or turn your computer off, the contents of the Clipboard is erased.

9-7-1 Moving or Copying Information to the Clipboard

When you are using a Windows application, you can easily **move text** or **copy text** to the Clipboard. You can also move or copy an image to the Clipboard. To copy or move information to the Clipboard, follow these steps:

1. Highlight or select the text or the information that you want to move or copy. Remember, you can copy or move text, graphics, or both. In most applications, clicking left anywhere on a graph will select it for moving or copying.
2. From the application's Edit menu (e.g., the Edit menu of Lotus 1-2-3 for Windows), select Cut or Copy. Cut removes the selected text or image from its current position. Copy only takes a snapshot and the existing information remains intact.

To copy the contents of an entire screen to the Clipboard, display the desired screen and press the Print Screen key or Shift-Prtsc or Alt-Prtsc. This process puts a snapshot (also called a bitmap) of the screen onto the Clipboard.

9-7-2 Transferring Information from the Clipboard

To transfer the contents of the Clipboard to another Windows application, follow these steps:

1. Start the desired application.
2. Position the insertion point at the place that you want the information from the Clipboard to appear.
3. From the application's Edit menu, select Paste.

Chapter 9 Working with Applications and Documents

Working with the Clipboard Viewer   9-7-3

By means of **Clipboard Viewer,** you can view, save, retrieve, and delete the contents of the Clipboard. To view the contents of the Clipboard, follow these steps:

1. Switch to the Program Manager (if you are not already there).
2. Open the Main group window (if it is not already an open window).
3. Double-click on the Clipboard Viewer icon. Click left on the maximize button to let Clipboard fill the entire screen. You will see a screen similar to the one shown in Figure 9-6. The sample text was copied to the Clipboard from the Write application.

You can view the information in the Clipboard in any of the formats that were supplied by the original application. To view a format from the Display menu, select the desired format; for example, choose Text. The Auto option displays the Clipboard contents in the format that it had when it was placed on the Clipboard. The other options are different formats supported by Windows. To return to the previous format that was displayed, from the Display menu, select Auto.

Saving the Contents of the Clipboard to a File   9-7-4

The contents of the Clipboard can be saved in a file for future use. To do so, follow these steps:

1. From the File menu in the Clipboard Viewer, select Save As. The Save As dialog box appears; see Figure 9-7.

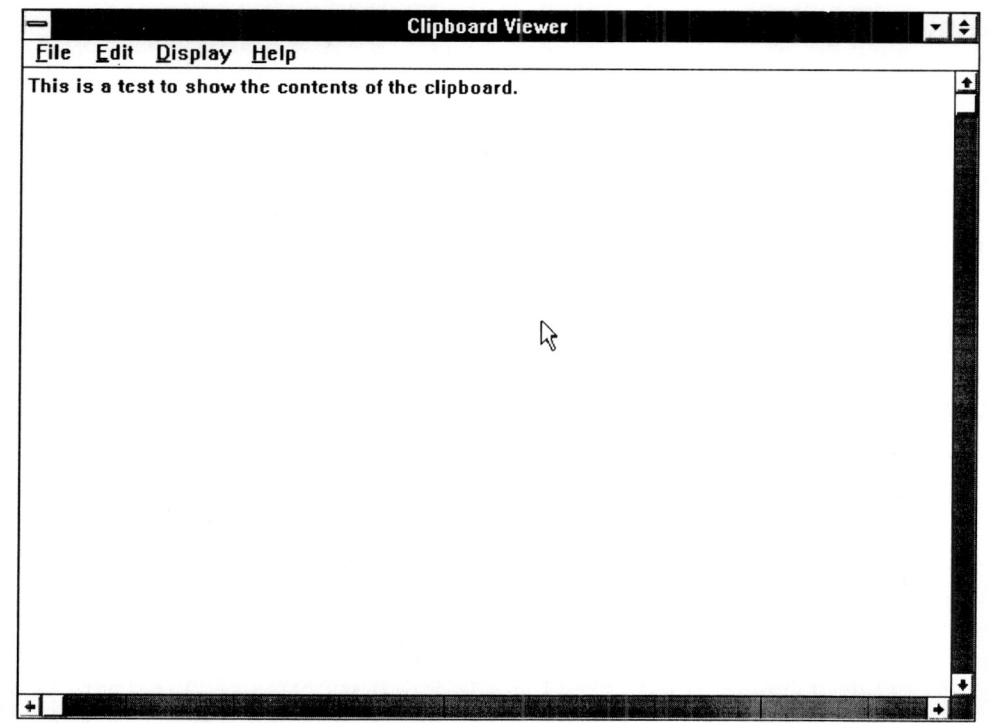

Figure 9-6
Clipboard Viewer menu

Figure 9-7
Save As dialog box of the Clipboard Viewer

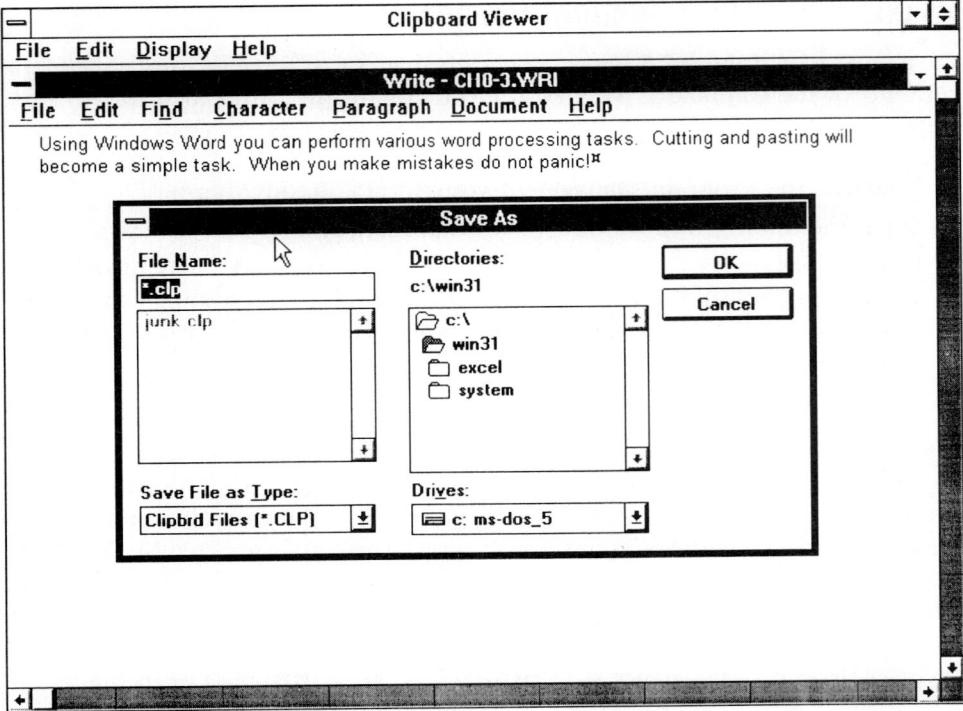

2. Type in a name up to eight characters. You must specify the complete path if you are saving to a directory and drive different from the default ones. The Clipboard automatically attaches a CLP extension to the file name.
3. Select OK to finalize the save procedure.

9-7-5 Retrieving a Clipboard File

To retrieve a Clipboard file, follow these steps:

1. Select Open from the File menu in the Clipboard Viewer. The Open dialog box appears; see Figure 9-8.
2. Select the .CLP file that you want to retrieve.
3. Select OK.

9-7-6 Clearing the Contents of the Clipboard

To clear the contents of Clipboard, follow these steps:

1. Select Edit from the Clipboard Viewer menu.
2. Select Delete. You will be prompted with the Clear Clipboard dialog box displaying Yes and No options. Selecting Yes will erase the contents; selecting No will not erase the contents of the Clipboard.

When you are in Clipboard Viewer, simply pressing the Del (Delete) key will also clear the contents of the Clipboard. Clearing the contents of the Clipboard frees up some of your computer resources. Remember, however, that placing new

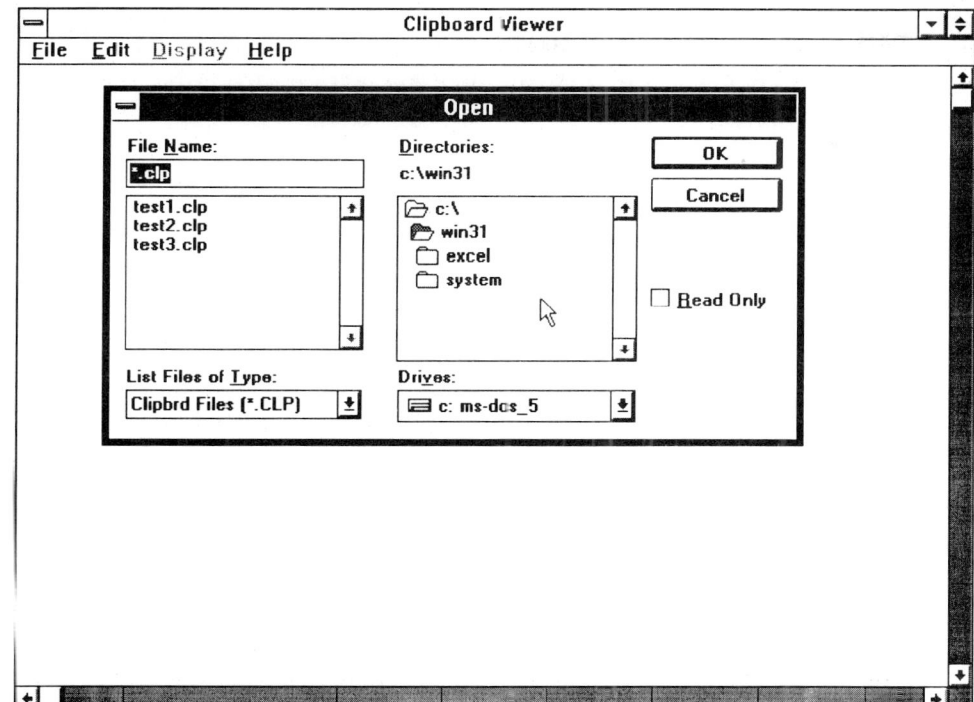

Figure 9-8
Open dialog box of the Clipboard Viewer

contents into the Clipboard automatically erases the old contents regardless of any differences in size.

9-8 QUITTING AN APPLICATION

When you are done working with an application, you should exit from it. There are a number of ways that you can do this. Use one of the following methods to exit a Windows application:

- From the application's File menu, select Exit.
- Or select Close from the Control menu.
- Or double-click on the control-menu box.
- Or press Alt-F4.

To quit a non-Windows application, use the application's Exit or Quit command. To return to Windows from the DOS prompt, type *Exit* and press Enter.

9-9 WORKING WITH DOCUMENTS

Basic file operations such as opening, saving, and editing are common to most Windows applications. Let us briefly discuss these common operations.

9-9-1 Opening Files

To open a file or document that has already been saved, follow these steps:

1. From the application's File menu, select Open. You will be presented with a dialog box similar to the one in Figure 9-8.

2. Select the correct drive from the Drives box. If the correct drive is not displayed, click left on the down arrow in the box. The available drives in your computer will be displayed; you can then click left on the desired one.
3. Select the correct directory from the Directories box.
4. In the List Files of Type box, select the type of file for which you are searching.
5. Double-click on the file name, or highlight the file and click left on OK. After highlighting the file name, you can also press Enter to open the file.

9-9-2 Saving Files

Most Windows programs include two commands for saving files: Save and Save As. When you select Save or Save As and if your file has not been saved before, you will be presented with the Save As dialog box. Refer to Figure 9-7.

If your file has already been saved, the Save command will save it again under its present name without presenting a dialog box. Use the Save command if you want to save a file under its present name. For example, if you have added to an existing file, you can save the new version of the file under its current name by selecting the Save option.

Use the Save As command if you want to save your file under a name different from its current name.

In any event, to save a new file follow these steps:

1. From the application's File menu select Save As or Save. You will be presented with the Save As dialog box (see Figure 9-7).
2. Select the drive and directory that you want to save your file to if you are saving in a drive and directory other than the default one.
3. Type in a name containing up to eight characters in the File Name box.
4. Select OK.

9-9-3 Switching Between Documents

Some applications allow you to open more than one document at a time. Each document is opened in its own window within the application. If you have more than one document window open, you can switch between them using one of the following methods:

- Click anywhere in the document window to which you want to switch.
- Or open the application's Window menu and select the desired document.

To navigate through all your open documents, press the Ctrl-F6 or Ctrl-Tab keys repeatedly until the document that you want is displayed. You can also use the Next command from the control menu to display your next document.

9-9-4 Working with Text

Working with text is basically the same in the majority of Windows programs. To type text, just start typing. When you run out of space on a line, the insertion point automatically moves to the next line. To terminate a line before its normal

Table 9-1
Moving around in documents

Key	To Move To
↑ (up arrow)	Previous line
↓ (down arrow)	Next line
→ (right arrow)	Right character
← (left arrow)	Left character
PgUp	Previous screen
PgDn	Next screen
End	End of the line
Home	Beginning of the line
Ctrl-→	Next word
Ctrl-←	Previous word
Ctrl-End	End of the document
Ctrl-Home	Beginning of the document

Table 9-2
Keys for correcting typing mistakes

Key	Function
Del (Delete)	Deletes the highlighted text or the character to the right of the insertion point
Backspace	Deletes the highlighted text or the character to the left of the insertion point
Ins (Insert)	Inserts characters at the insertion point. If you disable the Ins (Insert) key, then you are in typeover mode. In this mode, a new character replaces the old one.

termination, press Enter. To move the insertion point to the right, press the space bar once.

To type text in an existing document, move the insertion point to the desired location and start typing. The existing text is moved to the right. To get rid of unwanted characters, position the insertion point near the characters you wish to remove, then press the Del or the Backspace key.

Moving Around in Text 9-9-5

Most Windows programs use the keys outlined in Table 9-1 for moving around in documents. They also allow use of the mouse and scroll bar arrows for rapid cursor movements. Some programs contain key information with their documentation. DOS programs running in Windows use their normal keys for cursor movement and editing.

Correcting Mistakes 9-9-6

When you are typing text, do not worry if you make mistakes. You can use the keys outlined in Table 9-2 to correct your typing mistakes.

SUMMARY

This chapter described the Program Manager as one of the key components of the Windows program. It explained the process of starting an application using the Program Manager in several different ways. Next, various operations performed with the Clipboard were discussed. In the last part of the chapter, we concentrated on files and documents—opening, saving, and editing a document created in the Windows environment.

REVIEW QUESTIONS

*These questions are answered in Appendix A.

1. What is the Program Manager?
2. What are the different parts of the Program Manager screen?
3. How do you start an application from the Program Manager?
*4. How do you start an application from the File Manager?
5. What is a group icon?
6. What is a group window?
*7. What is a program file? What are some of the typical extensions for program files?
8. How do you use the Run command to start an application?
9. Usually, in which menu is the Run command located?
10. What is the MS-DOS Prompt?
11. How do you display the MS-DOS Prompt?
*12. How do you get back to Windows from the MS-DOS Prompt?
13. What are some of the problems you may encounter when you run several applications at the same time?
14. How do you switch between two applications?
15. What is the Clipboard? What are some of the uses of the Clipboard?
*16. How do you copy information onto the Clipboard?
17. Can you transfer a snapshot of your current screen onto the Clipboard? If yes, how?
18 How is information transferred from the Clipboard to another application?
19. What is the Clipboard Viewer?
20. What are the options in the Clipboard Viewer?
21 How do you save the contents of the Clipboard for future use?
*22. When you save the contents of the Clipboard, what is the file extension generated by the Clipboard?
23. How do you clear the contents of the Clipboard?
24. If you do not clear the contents of the Clipboard, when will it be cleared anyway?
*25. How do you quit an application?
26. How do you open a document?
27. How do you save a file?
28. How do you switch between documents?
29. How do you create text? How do you correct your mistakes?
*30. How do you move around in a document?
31. How do you select text? What are some of the applications of selecting text?

HANDS-ON EXPERIENCE

1. Start the Program Manager. What are some of the parts of the Program Manager? What are the menu options of the Program Manager? What is available under each menu option?

Chapter 9 Working with Applications and Documents

2. Select an application of your choice, for example, WordPerfect, and do the following:
   a. Start the application from the Program Manager. Quit it.
   b. Start the application from the File Manager. Quit it.
   c. Start the application by using the Run command. Quit it.
   d. Start the application from the MS-DOS Prompt. Quit it.
   Which method is easier for starting an application? Discuss.
3. Select two applications of your choice and start each one of them. How do you switch between these two applications?
4. Select an application of your choice and start it, for example, Microsoft Excel; do the following:
   a. Copy any screen from the application to the Clipboard.
   b. Start another application such as Windows Write and paste the contents of the Clipboard to this application.
   c. What are the menu options of the Clipboard Viewer?
   d. Clear the contents of the Clipboard.
   e. Copy a snapshot of the current screen to the Clipboard.
   f. Save the contents of the Clipboard to a file called TEST. What file extension is attached to this file?
5. Using a Windows application of your choice, do the following:
   a. Type these lines:

      Typing text in Windows programs is an easy job. You just type and continue typing. To skip a line, you must press Enter.

   b. Save this text under the file name TEST1 in your default drive and directory.
   c. Insert the words *or editing* before the word "text."
   d. Using Save As, save this file under the name TEST2.
   e. Exit the application.
   f. Start the application again and open TEST2.
   g. Exit the application again.

KEY TERMS

Clipboard Viewer
Copying text
File Manager
Group icon
Group window
Moving text
Program Manager
Selecting text

KEY COMMANDS

Alt-F4 (to quit an application)
Alt-Tab (to switch to another application)
Ctrl-Esc (to display the Task List)
Ctrl-Tab or Ctrl-F6 (to navigate through all the open documents)
Cursor-movement keys (see Table 9–1)
Editing keys (see Table 9–2)
File (to activate the File menu)
Options (to activate the Options menu)
Window (to activate the Window menu)

MISCONCEPTIONS AND SOLUTIONS

Misconception Using the keyboard, you try to drag Program Manager icons, but your attempts are not successful.

  Solution Dragging Program Manager icons can only be done by means of a mouse. There is no keyboard equivalent.

Misconception The Clipboard already contains information, so you are prompted to clear it. But if you select Yes, you lose the existing contents of the Clipboard.

  Solution If you need this information, select No; then use the Save As command from the Clipboard Viewer File menu to save the contents to a file for future use.

ARE YOU READY TO MOVE ON?

Multiple Choice

1. Which of the following statements about the Program Manager is correct?
    a. It starts as soon as you start Windows.
    b. Its menu bar includes four main menu options.
    c. It includes a group window.
    d. They are all correct.
    e. Only a and b are correct.

2. Which of the following is *not* included in the Program Manager window?
    a. group window
    b. program-item icons
    c. group icon
    d. all are included
    e. only a and b

3. You can start an application by using any of the following methods except
    a. typing its file extension in the Program Manager window
    b. from the Program Manager
    c. from the File Manager
    d. from the MS-DOS Prompt
    e. using the Run command

4. To display the Task List, press
    a. Alt-Tab
    b. Alt-Esc
    c. Ctrl-Esc
    d. Shift-Esc
    e. none of the above

5. To start an application from the File Manager you must select the program file. The program file can have any of the following extensions except
    a. .EXE
    b. .COM
    c. .BAT
    d. .PIF
    e. .WK1

6. To exit from the MS-DOS Prompt, before pressing Enter type
    a. *Quit*
    b. *Exit*

Chapter 9 Working with Applications and Documents 175

    c. *End*

    d. *Control*

    e. *Return*

7. How do you switch from one application to another?
   a. click anywhere in the application's window
   b. use the Task List
   c. do either a or b
   d. use the Accessories menu
   e. do a, b, and d

8. Which of the following options is *not* included in the Task List dialog box?
   a. Switch To
   b. Save To
   c. End Task
   d. Cascade
   e. Tile

9. Using the Clipboard you can
   a. transfer information between two applications
   b. save the contents of the Clipboard for future use
   c. both a and b
   d. keep its contents (without saving) even if you turn the computer off
   e. do none of the above

10. What file extension does Clipboard attach to a file when it saves a file?
    a. CLP
    b. WK1
    c. BAK
    d. EXE
    e. COM

True/False

1. When using the Clipboard, you can return to the previous format by selecting Auto from the Display menu.
2. The contents of the Clipboard cannot be saved for future use.
3. The Clipboard allows you to create a snapshot of the screen.
4. To quit an application you can press Alt-F4.
5. You cannot quit an application by selecting Exit from the File menu.
6. Windows allows you to do basic file operations such as saving, editing, and retrieving.
7. To navigate through all open applications one by one, you cannot use the Task list.
8. The arrow keys can be used to move around in a document.
9. You cannot select a graph for further operations.
10. When you select text, there is no way to deselect it.

ANSWERS

Multiple Choice	True/False
1. d	1. T
2. d	2. F
3. a	3. T
4. c	4. T
5. e	5. F
6. b	6. T
7. c	7. F
8. b	8. T
9. c	9. F
10. a	10. F

Customizing Your Windows Environment

10-1 Introduction
10-2 Working with Groups
    10-2-1 Opening a Group Window
    10-2-2 Reducing a Group Window to an Icon
    10-2-3 Rearranging Group Windows
    10-2-4 Organizing Group Icons
    10-2-5 Organizing Program-Item Icons
    10-2-6 Creating New Groups
    10-2-7 Deleting a Group
    10-2-8 Changing the Description of a Group
10-3 Working with Program Items
    10-3-1 Creating a Program Item
    10-3-2 Creating a Program Item for a Document
    10-3-3 Deleting a Program Item from a Group
    10-3-4 Copying Program Items from One Group to Another
    10-3-5 Moving a Program Item to Another Group
    10-3-6 Changing an Icon
10-4 Starting an Application When you Start Windows
10-5 The Control Panel
    10-5-1 Starting the Control Panel
    10-5-2 Displaying Custom Wallpaper
    10-5-3 Using a Screen Saver
    10-5-4 Installing and Configuring a Printer

10-1
INTRODUCTION

This chapter introduces several features of Windows that allow customization of Windows operations. We begin with the process of working with group windows—organizing windows and icons, creating a new group, deleting an unwanted group, and so on. Next we discuss creating program items, deleting a program item from a group, and moving and copying program items from one group to another. After the chapter shows you how to start an application when you start Windows, it introduces the Control Panel as an application for changing the appearance of the Windows environment. Three of the common applications of the Control Panel are highlighted: displaying Custom Wallpaper, using a Screen Saver, and installing and configuring a printer.

10-2
WORKING WITH GROUPS

A group contains **program-item icons** that represent applications, accessories, or documents. To start an application from a group, you have to select its icon. As you can see in Figure 10–1, Windows includes several predefined groups:

1. The Main group in the Main Window consists of system applications:
   a. File Manager manages files and disk drives.
   b. Control panel allows you to modify the configuration of Windows and your system.
   c. Print Manager allows you to install and configure printers.
   d. Clipboard Viewer allows you to view, edit, and save the contents of the Clipboard.
   e. MS-DOS Prompt allows you to temporarily exit to the DOS prompt.

Figure 10–1
Example of groups

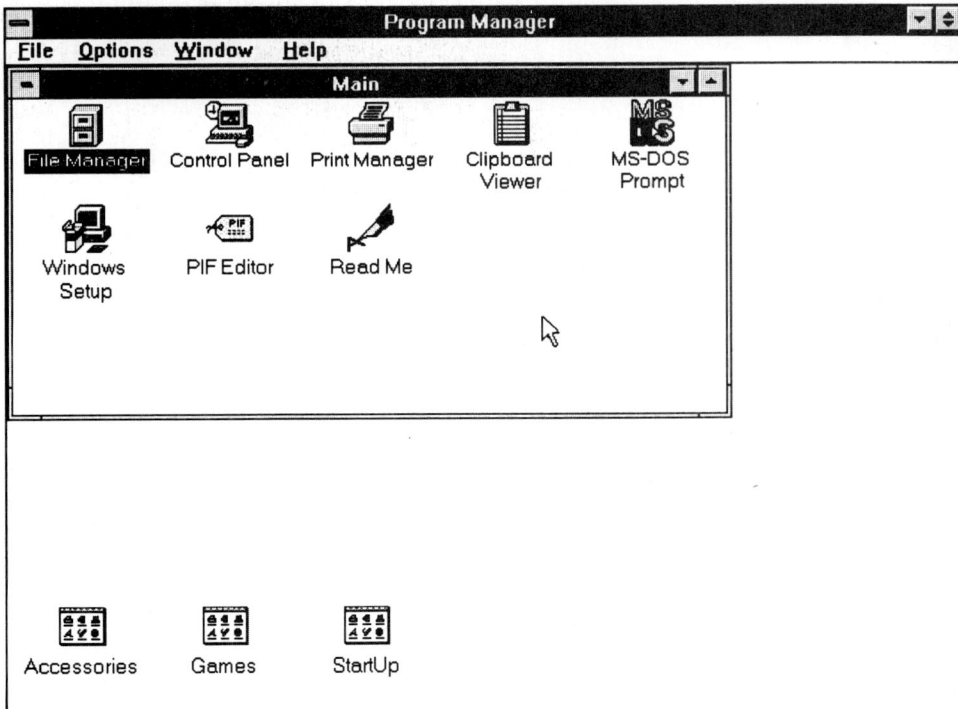

Chapter 10 Customizing Your Windows Environment

  f. Windows Setup displays the basic hardware configuration of the system.

  g. PIF Editor edits program information files.

  h. Read Me includes basic information about Windows.

2. The Accessories group includes several interesting applications such as Write for word processing, Paintbrush for painting, and Terminal for communications.
3. The Games group includes games that you can use to learn the basics of Windows or to just have fun.
4. The StartUp group contains applications that start when you start Windows. You can place any program-item icon in this group. The group is empty until you place program-item icons in it.
5. The Applications group contains applications found on your hard disk during the setup process. If you select Custom Setup during Windows installation and select not to have Windows set up applications from your hard disk, your Program Manager window will not contain an application group. This is the case in Figure 10-1.

Opening a Group Window   10-2-1

To start an application, you must first open its group window and select the appropriate program-item icon. Double-click on the group icon to open a group window. For example, to open the Accessories group window, double-click on its icon in the lower left of the screen presented in Figure 10-1.

Reducing a Group Window to an Icon   10-2-2

If you want to clear the desktop of a group window, you can reduce the group window to an icon.

   To reduce a group window to an icon, do one of the following:

- Click left on the minimize button.
- Double-click on the control-menu box for the group.
- Select the Close option from the control menu for the group.

Rearranging Group Windows   10-2-3

When you open several group windows, you may not be able to see all of them. Use the Cascade and Tile commands from the Window menu to rearrange all group windows so that at least a portion of each is visible.

   Cascade resizes and layers the open group windows within the Program Manager workspace so that you can see the title bar and one side of each window. In Figure 10-2 the Cascade command was used to organize the open Main, Accessories, Games, and StartUp group windows. To generate this screen, double-click on these four group icons—one at a time; then click left on Window and Cascade.

   Tile resizes and arranges the open windows side by side in the Program Manager desktop. To activate any of these windows, click left anywhere in the

Figure 10-2
Example of the Cascade command

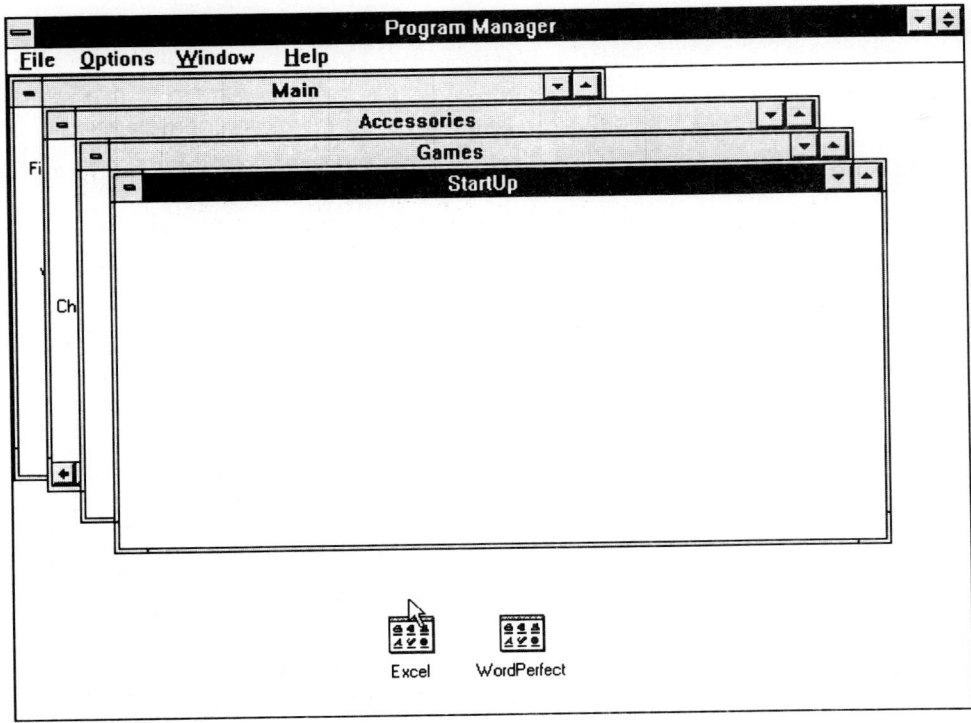

desired window. In Figure 10-3 the Tile command was used to organize the open Main, Accessories, Games, and StartUp groups. If all the program-item icons do not fit in the available space in each group, scroll bars appear automatically. By clicking on these scroll bars, you can view the rest of the program-item icons.

The keyboard shortcuts are Shift-F5 for Cascade and Shift-F4 for Tile.

10-2-4 Organizing Group Icons

A group icon can be moved within the Program Manager workspace by dragging it with the mouse or by using the Move command from the control menu for the group. You can also move program-item icons between group windows or onto group icons. To organize group icons, follow these steps:

1. Minimize each group window to an icon.
2. From the Window menu, select Arrange Icons. The group icons will be distributed evenly along the lower edge of the Program Manager window.

10-2-5 Organizing Program-Item Icons

To organize program-item icons, follow these steps:

1. Make sure the group window that includes the desired program-item icons is not minimized. If it is, double-click on it.
2. Choose the group window that includes the desired program-item icons.

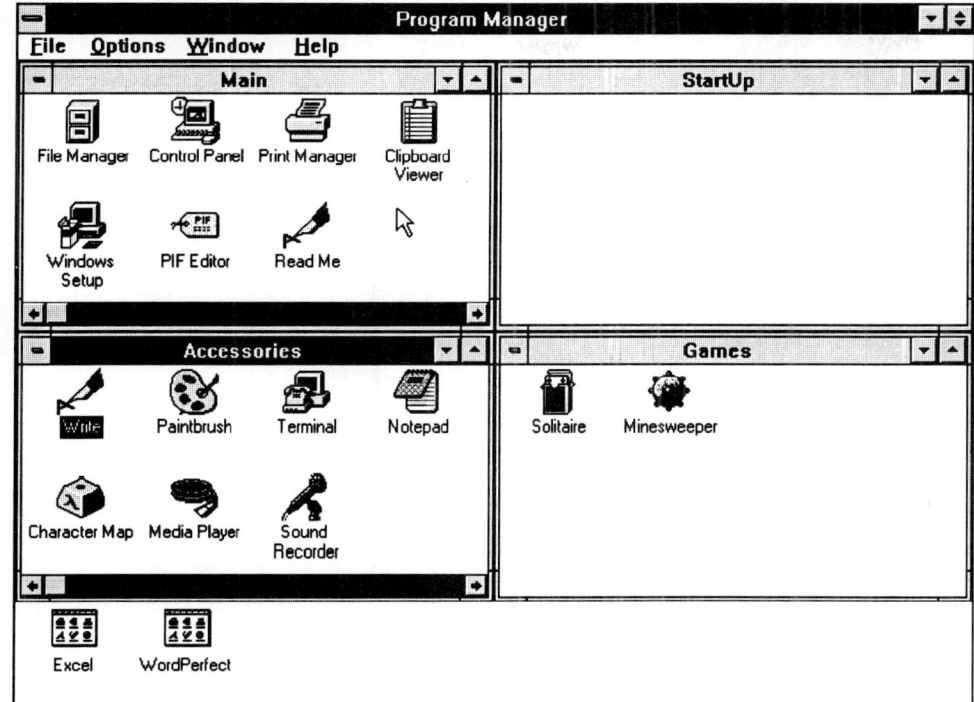

Figure 10-3
Example of the Tile command

3. From the Window menu, select Arrange Icons. This will distribute the program-item icons evenly within the selected group window. Distribution is according to the setting specified in the Icons menu box of the Desktop dialog box from within the Control Panel, see Figure 10-9.

You can instruct Windows to automatically organize your icons by selecting Auto Arrange from the Options menu. Remember, a check mark beside the command means that it is in effect. For example, if the Auto Arrange option is in effect and you drag one of the program-item icons to a different location, as soon as you release the mouse button the icon will automatically go back to its previous location.

Creating New Groups

10-2-6

To further customize your Windows operations, you can add one or several new groups to the Program Manager. These groups may include specific application(s). To create a new group, follow these steps:

1. From the File menu of the Program Manager menu, select New. You will be presented with a screen similar to the one in Figure 10-4.
2. Select the Program Group option; then select OK. You will be presented with a screen similar to the one in Figure 10-5.
3. In the Description box type in a description for the group that you want to create. This description will appear in the title bar of the group window and

Figure 10-4
New Program Object dialog box

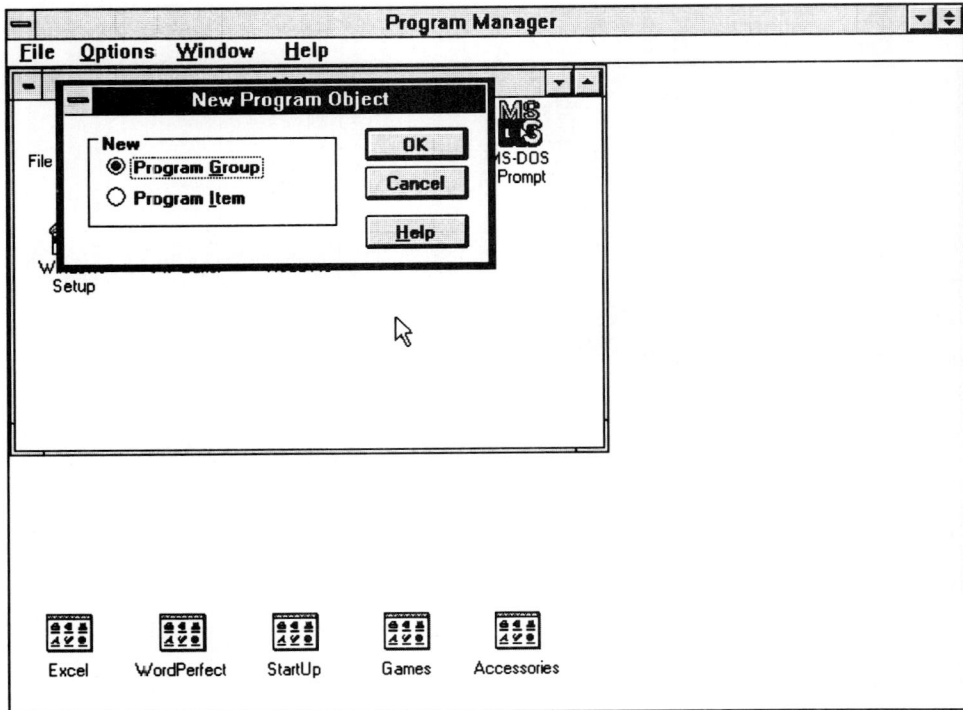

Figure 10-5
Program Group Properties dialog box

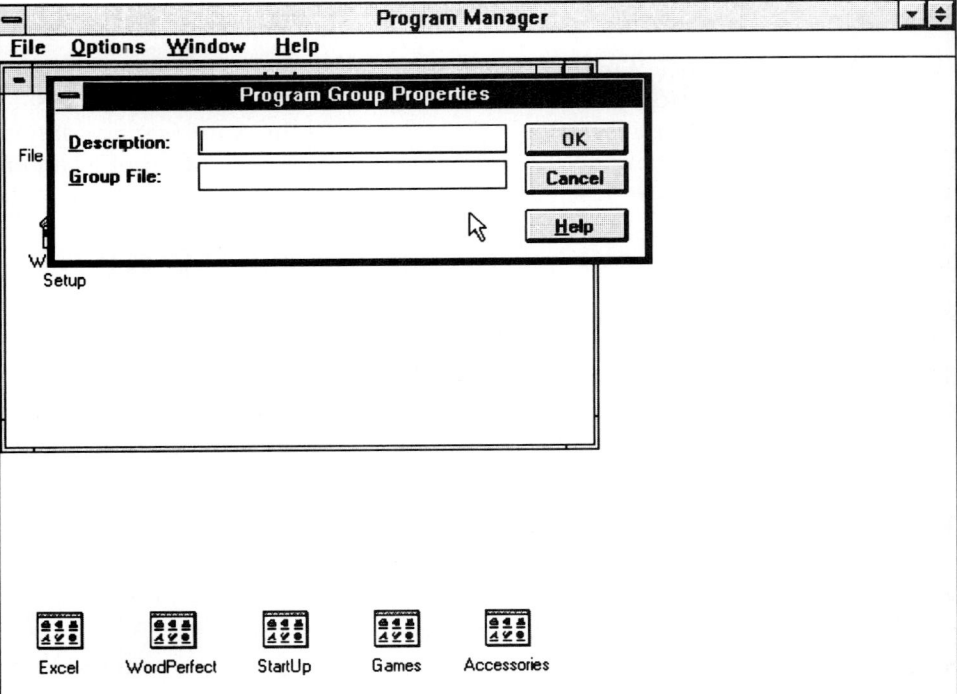

below the group icon when the group is minimized. Group descriptions can be up to 30 character in length. The description that you supply should be meaningful to the applications that it contains. For example, if you are creating a group for WordPerfect, the group description should be WordPerfect.
4. Select the OK button. Program Manager creates a .GRP file for the new group; for this reason, you can leave the Group File box blank.

After creating a group, you can add program-item icons to it. This topic will be discussed in section 10–3–1.

Deleting a Group 10-2-7

If a group is no longer needed, it can be deleted from the desktop to keep the desktop clean. To delete a group, follow these steps:

1. If the group is not already reduced to an icon, click left on the minimize button to reduce it.
2. Left click on the icon for the group that you want to delete. This will open the group control menu; however, ignore this menu.
3. While the control menu is displayed, from the File menu of the Program Manager select Delete. The Delete dialog box will be displayed.
4. Select yes to finalize the delete operation.

At this time the Program Manager deletes the selected group and any program-item icons in it. Remember that all the data and program files related to the deleted group remain on your hard disk. You have to delete them separately by using the DOS DEL command (see instructions in the next chapter) or by using the File Manager. If the group does not contain any program-item icons, the group does not have to be minimized to be deleted. Simply select the group and press the Del key, followed by Enter, to delete an empty group.

Changing the Description of a Group 10-2-8

The description of a group appears on the title bar of an open group window and beneath the group icon when the group is minimized. This description can be changed if you so desire. To change a group description, follow these steps:

1. Reduce the desired group to an icon.
2. Click left on the icon for the desired group. The Control menu will be displayed, but ignore it.
3. From the File menu from the Program Manager, select Properties. You will see a screen similar to the one in Figure 10–5.
4. In the Description box, type a new description and select OK. Remember, the length is limited to 30 characters.

10-3

WORKING WITH PROGRAM ITEMS

10-3-1 Creating a Program Item

You can create your own program item and later access it just as you access other program items. When you create a program item for an application, you specify the item's properties. Properties include a description of the item, a command line that drives the application, a working directory where any files that the application creates are stored, and the icon that Windows uses to represent the application.

Program items are created by means of the Program Manager, the File Manager, or the Windows Setup program. The following list provides the instructions for creating a program item using the Program Manager.

1. Left click on the group icon to which you want to add an item.
2. From the File menu in the Program Manager, select New. The New Program Object dialog box will be displayed; refer to Figure 10-4.
3. From this dialog box, select the Program Item option and OK. The Program Item Properties dialog box will be displayed (Figure 10-6).
4. In the Description box, type a unique description. Unique means something that has not been used before. This description becomes the label that appears in the title bar of the application when it is running and under the icon of the minimized group window. The description is limited to 40 characters.
5. In the Command Line box, type the name of the program file with its extension (including its complete path). For example, type *C:\LOTUS\123.EXE*

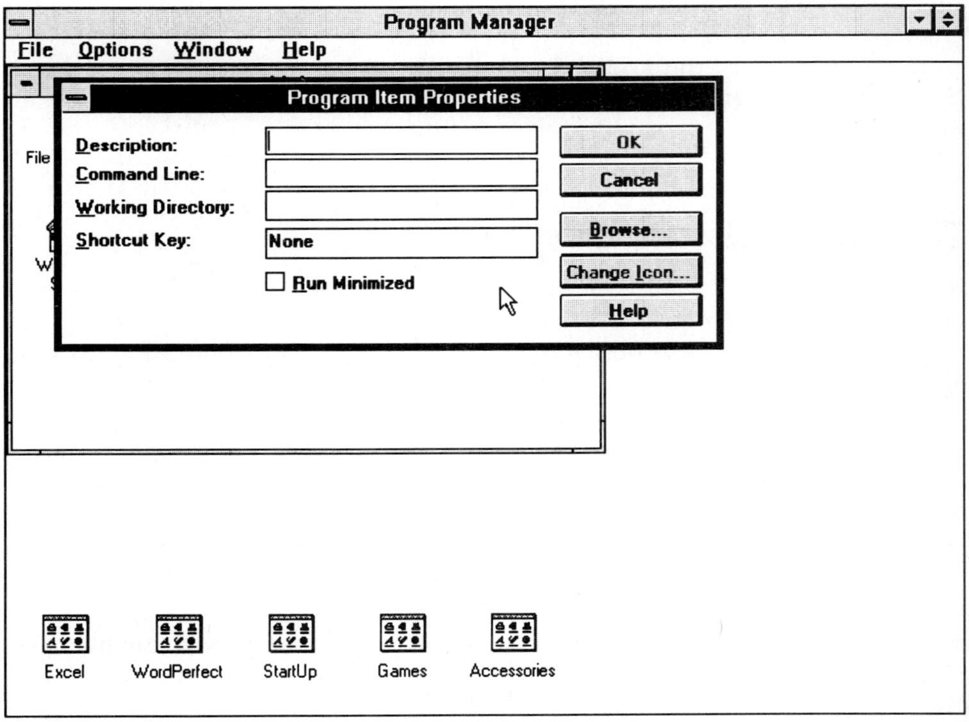

Figure 10-6
Program Item Properties dialog box

to specify Lotus 1-2-3 located in a directory named C:\LOTUS. If you do not know the program file name, use the Browse option (see Figure 10–6) to locate the desired program file name and click on OK.

6. In the Working Directory box, type the name of the directory where the new files created by this application will be stored. This directory will become the default directory for this application's data files.

7. In the Shortcut Key box type in a key combination as the shortcut. This combination can be used to switch to the application when it is running. Valid key combinations are Ctrl-Alt-Character (a character can be any letter, number, or special character), Ctrl-Shift-Character, Ctrl-Shift-Alt-Character, and Shift-Alt-Character. To specify a different combination of keys you must type the desired key combination. For example, press Ctrl, then press Shift, then press a character such as G. In this case, the shortcut key becomes Ctrl-Shift-G. To help you remember the shortcut keys that you have created, make them meaningful to the application. For example, you might choose Ctrl-Alt-C for Cardfile and Ctrl-Alt-N for Notepad.

8. If you want the application to run as an icon when it starts, click on the Run Minimized box (see Figure 10–6).

9. Select the Change Icon option to see the default icon for this program item (if there is one). To change the icon, choose the icon that you want to use and click on OK. If there is no default icon associated with the application that you are adding, Windows displays a message that no icons are available for the specified application. Click on OK. In this case, Windows will display the Change Icon dialog box, showing the icons available in the file called PROGMAN.EXE. You may scroll through the available icons to select an appropriate icon for the application that you are adding. If the icons available within PROGMAN.EXE are not acceptable, you may change the Change Icon file name from PROGMAN.EXE to MORICONS.DLL and click on OK. This file will display a variety of additional icons for your use.

10. If you are satisfied with your setup, select OK. The dialog box closes and the new program item icon appears in the group.

The limit on the number of program items in a group is 40.
    A simple way to create a program item icon is to use the File Manager, (discussed in Chapter 11). Simply drag the desired application icon (for example, Paradox) into any group or onto any group icon.

Creating a Program Item for a Document   10–3–2

At times it may be convenient to have an icon representing not only an application, but also a particular document created by that application. For example, let us say that you frequently work with a particular spreadsheet in Lotus 1-2-3. Double-clicking on this icon would run the Lotus 1-2-3 application with the spreadsheet already loaded and ready for editing.
    To create a program item for a document, follow the first five steps that were just described for creating a program item. Then after the program's file name in the Command Line box, press the space bar and type the name of the data file (including its complete path). For example, to specify a spreadsheet named FORECAST.WK1 located in the C:\WEST directory, type *C:\LOTUS\123.EXE*

C:\WEST\FORECAST.WK1. If the document is in the same directory as the application itself, you do not need to repeat the path. Complete the rest of the steps (6 through 10) as instructed in the previous section and click on OK.

10-3-3 Deleting a Program Item from a Group

If a program item is no longer needed, you can use the Program Manager to remove it from the group. When you remove a program item from a group, the application is not removed from the hard disk. You have to remove it from the hard disk by using the Delete command from the File Manager or from the DOS prompt. To delete a program item from a group, follow these steps:

1. If necessary, open the group window that includes the program item you want to delete by double-clicking on its icon.
2. Select the desired program-item icon by clicking on it.
3. From the File menu in Program Manager menu, select Delete, or just press the Del key. A confirmation message appears. Select the Yes option.

10-3-4 Copying Program Items from One Group to Another

To copy a program item from one group to another, complete these steps:

1. If you want to copy a program item to a specific location in the destination group window, you must open the group windows of both source and destination groups. If the location is not important, you can leave the destination group reduced to an icon.
2. Press and hold down the Ctrl key while you click the left button of the mouse and drag the program-item icon from its present position to its destination. Notice that the copying does not change the position of the icon in its present (source) group.
3. When the copied icon is on top of the destination group's icon or inside the destination group's window, release the mouse button and the Ctrl key. If the destination group is minimized, verify your work by opening the destination group window to make sure that the copied program-item icon is in this group window.

10-3-5 Moving a Program Item to Another Group

When you move a program-item icon, the icon is permanently moved from its present location. Moving is similar to cutting in a word processing program. Again, if you want to move a program-item icon to a specific location in the destination window, you must open the group windows of both source and destination groups. If the location is not important, you can leave the destination group reduced to an icon.

To move a program-item icon to another group, follow these steps:

1. If necessary, open the group window that includes the program-item icon that you want to move.
2. Click the left button of the mouse and drag the program-item icon to the destination group window or icon. Watch the mouse pointer—it becomes a replica of the program-item icon that you are moving.

Chapter 10 Customizing Your Windows Environment

3. When the program-item icon is inside the destination group's window or on top of the destination group's icon, release the mouse button.

Open the destination group window to verify your work if the group was minimized during the move operation.

Changing an Icon

10-3-6

When you add a new program-item icon to a group, the Program Manager scans the specified program-item file to see if it contains any icons. If any icons are found, one is selected automatically for you. If no icons are found, or if you wish to change the icon that was selected for you, you can click left on the Change Icon button in the Program Item Properties box (refer to Figure 10-6). Depending on the circumstances, one of the following situations will occur.

If your application contains one or more built-in icons, the Change Icon dialog box will be displayed; it will show the icon(s) that are available along with the application file name that contains the icon(s). If more than one icon is available for the application, you may select one of the others by scrolling through the available icons and double-clicking on the desired one. Alternatively, if only one icon is displayed, or if you are not satisfied with any of the icons that are available, you may select one of the many icons that are included with Windows. To do this, change the file name in the File Name box to PROGMAN.EXE; then press Enter. This file contains a variety of icons from which you can select. You can also change the file name to MORICONS.DLL to see an even larger collection of icons. See Figure 10-7 for an example of the icons available within MORICONS.DLL. At any rate, scroll through the available list of icons and make your selection by double-clicking on the desired one. You will be returned to the Program Item Properties dialog box, and the selected icon will be displayed. Click left on OK to finalize the process.

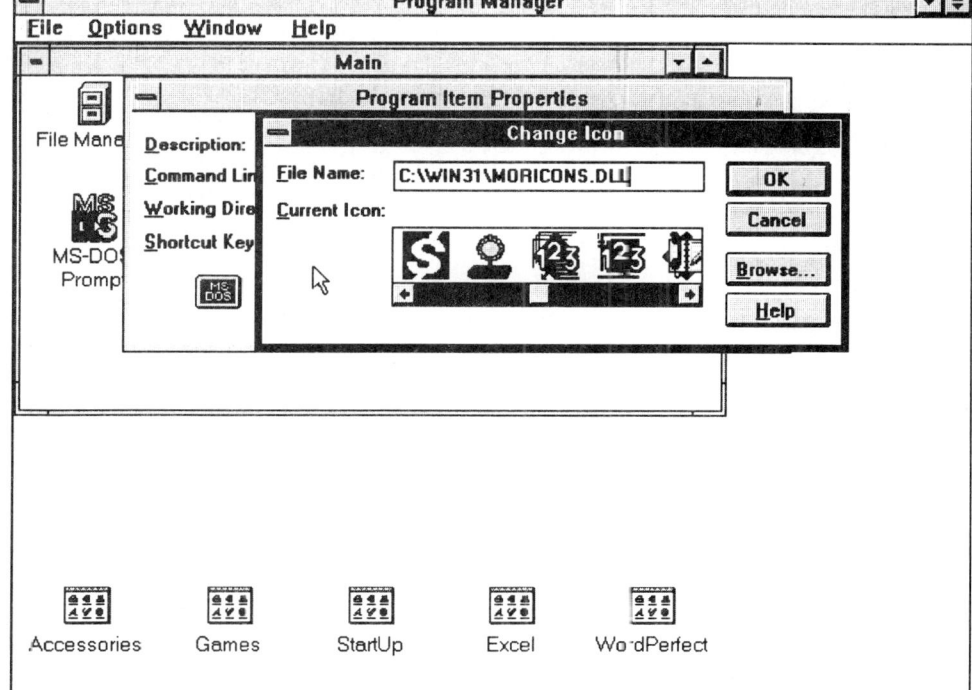

Figure 10-7
Some of the icons available within MORICONS.DLL file

If your application does not contain any built-in icons, the Program Manager will display the Change Icon dialog box. A message will tell you that no icons are available for the specified file and that you will have to make a selection from the icons included within PROGMAN.EXE. Click left on OK or press Enter to leave the message dialog box. Program Manager will redisplay the Change Icon dialog box, this time displaying the icons contained within the PROGMAN.EXE file. You may make your selection from these icons, or change the file name to MORICONS.DLL to view other icons as discussed before. Once you have made your selection by double-clicking on the desired icon, you will be returned to the Program Item Properties dialog box, and the selected icon will be displayed. Click left on OK to finalize the process.

10-4
STARTING AN APPLICATION WHEN YOU START WINDOWS

If you include a program-item icon for an application in the StartUp group, Windows starts the application automatically each time you start Windows. For example, if you want to start the Clipboard Viewer whenever you start Windows, move or copy the Clipboard Viewer icon from the Main group to the StartUp group. Program items in the StartUp group run in the order of their placement in the window, from left to right and from top to bottom.

You can also have Windows automatically reduce an application in the StartUp group (or any group for that matter) to an icon as soon as the application is executed. If you want several applications opened and immediately available for use upon startup, but are not sure which one(s) will be used first, open them as icons, thereby reducing screen clutter and providing a more organized screen. To do this, select the Run Minimized box when you are creating the program item, or use the Properties command in the File menu to specify the Run Minimized option for existing program items.

10-5
THE CONTROL PANEL

The **Control Panel** allows you to change the configuration of your system while you are using Windows. When you change options using the Control Panel, your changes are stored in the WIN.INI file so that they will be in effect the next time you start Windows. Some changes that you make with the Control Panel do not require that you restart Windows to effect the desired changes, whereas others might. For a description of the WIN.INI file, see Appendix A at the end of this book.

10-5-1
Starting the Control Panel

While in the Main group window, double-click on the Control Panel icon. You will be presented with a screen similar to the one in Figure 10-8. Your screen may differ from what is presented here because of what else is open on the desktop, what Windows settings are in effect, and the specific hardware configuration of your system. As you can see in Figure 10-8, there are 12 options available in the Control Panel dialog box in our system. Let us briefly explain these options:

Color	Used to change the color of the desktop and the majority of the desktop components
Fonts	Used to add or remove fonts
Ports	Used to set the communications options and other parameters for serial ports

Chapter 10 Customizing Your Windows Environment

Figure 10-8
Control Panel dialog box

Mouse	Used to customize the way you use this pointing device. You may adjust its speed and set any option specific to the type of the mouse in use.
Desktop	Used to change the appearance of your desktop, specify a Screen Saver (discussed later in this chapter), specify icon spacing and title wrapping, and set the cursor blink rate.
Keyboard	Used to adjust the keyboard repeat rate and delay
Printers	Used to install and configure printers. This may include paper size, orientation (portrait versus landscape) graphics resolution, and using Print Manager.
International	Used to specify international settings such as currency formats and date and time formats
Date/Time	Used to change computer date and time
386 Enhanced	Available only on systems that can run Windows in 386 enhanced mode. It specifies how applications running concurrently in 386 enhanced mode compete for use of peripheral devices and how much of the computer's resources are allocated to Windows applications running in the foreground and background.
Drivers	Used to install and configure drivers for optional devices such as sound cards and pen tablets

Sound   Assigns sounds to the computer and application events such as an appointment in the Calendar application (discussed in Chapter 12). This option can also be used to turn on or off the warning beep and system sounds.

10-5-2 Displaying Custom Wallpaper

One of the commonly used applications of the Control Panel is **Custom Wallpaper**. You can alter the appearance of your desktop by displaying a bitmap format graphic (any graphic file with a .BMP extension) as "Wallpaper" instead of the desktop color or pattern. To do this, follow these steps:

1. In the Control panel dialog box, double-click on the Desktop icon. The Desktop dialog box will be displayed; see Figure 10–9.
2. In the Wallpaper box, open the File box by clicking on the down-arrow scroll bar. A list of BMP files will be displayed.
3. Select a bitmap from this list. You can also type a name and a complete path for the bitmap without going through the list if the file is not in the Windows directory.
4. Choose either the Center or Tile option. The Center option positions the bitmap in the center of the desktop. The Tile option repeats the bitmap as many times as necessary to cover the desktop.
5. Select OK to finalize the process. If you want to remove a wallpaper from your system, in the File box select the None option at the top of the list of files; this is the default.

Figure 10–9
Desktop dialog box

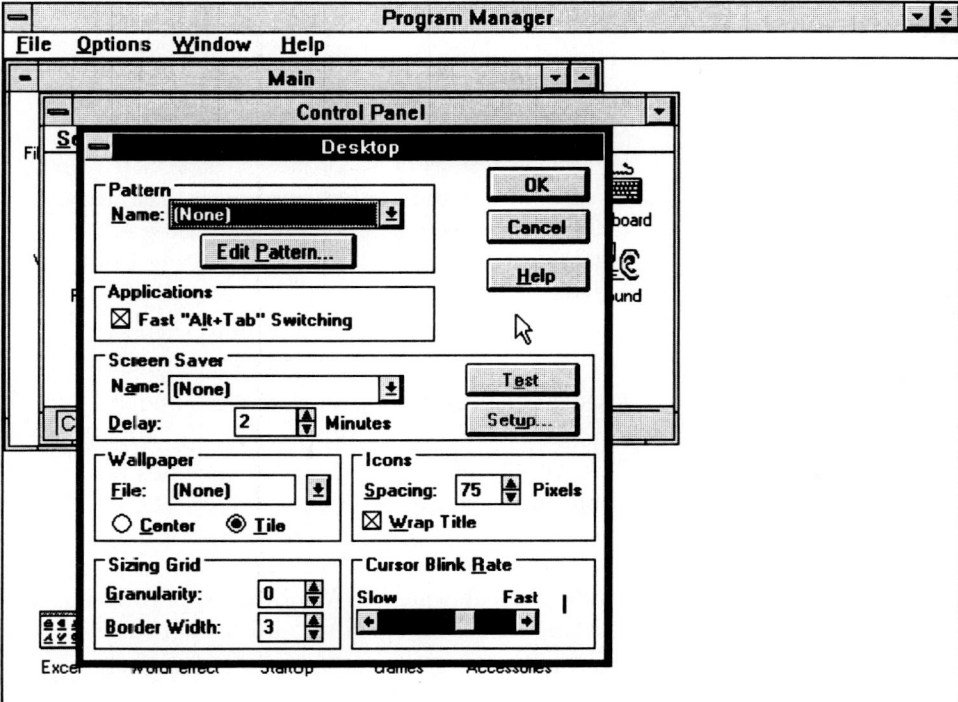

Using a Screen Saver

10-5-3

Another application of the Control Panel is **Screen Saver**. A Screen Saver is a moving pattern or bitmap that appears after you have *not* used your mouse or pressed a key on the keyboard for a specified amount of time. Screen Savers increase the life of your monitor; they also provide some security to your system. To use one of the several Screen Saver options provided by Windows, follow these steps:

1. In the Control Panel window, double-click the Desktop icon. You will see a screen similar to the one in Figure 10-9.
2. In the Screen Saver box, open the Name box by clicking the down-arrow scroll bar.
3. Select a Screen Saver from this list.
4. In the Delay box, click the up arrow to increase or the down arrow to decrease the number of minutes of keyboard and mouse inactivity that you want to elapse before the Screen Saver is activated. The default is 2 minutes.
5. Select OK to finalize the process.

To return to Windows when the Screen Saver is activated, either move the mouse or press any key.

After you select a Screen Saver, you can test it to see how it looks on your screen. To do this, in the Desktop dialog box click left on Test. The Screen Saver appears. If you do not like this one, you can select another.

Installing and Configuring a Printer

10-5-4

The Printers option from the Control Panel allows you to install a printer or change printer settings. To start the Printers option, double-click on the Printers icon in the Control Panel. You will see a screen similar to the one in Figure 10-10. Using this dialog box, you can remove a printer from your setup by using the Remove command, or you can add more printers to your setup by selecting the Add option. When you are done, select Close from the control menu. If you have not made any changes, exit the Printers dialog box by clicking left on Cancel. To get additional help, click left on Help.

This chapter focused on customizing the Windows environment. It explained how to open group windows, reduce them to icons, and arrange them in the workspace provided by the Program Manager. The chapter also described the processes of creating new groups and deleting unwanted groups as well as changing the description of a group, creating a program item, deleting a program item, and copying and moving a program item from one group to another. We also discussed the Control Panel and three of its commonly used applications: displaying Custom Wallpaper, using a Screen Saver, and installing and configuring a printer.

SUMMARY

---

*These questions are answered in Appendix A.

REVIEW QUESTIONS

1. What is usually included in a group window?
2. What are some of the groups included in Windows?

Figure 10-10
Printers dialog box

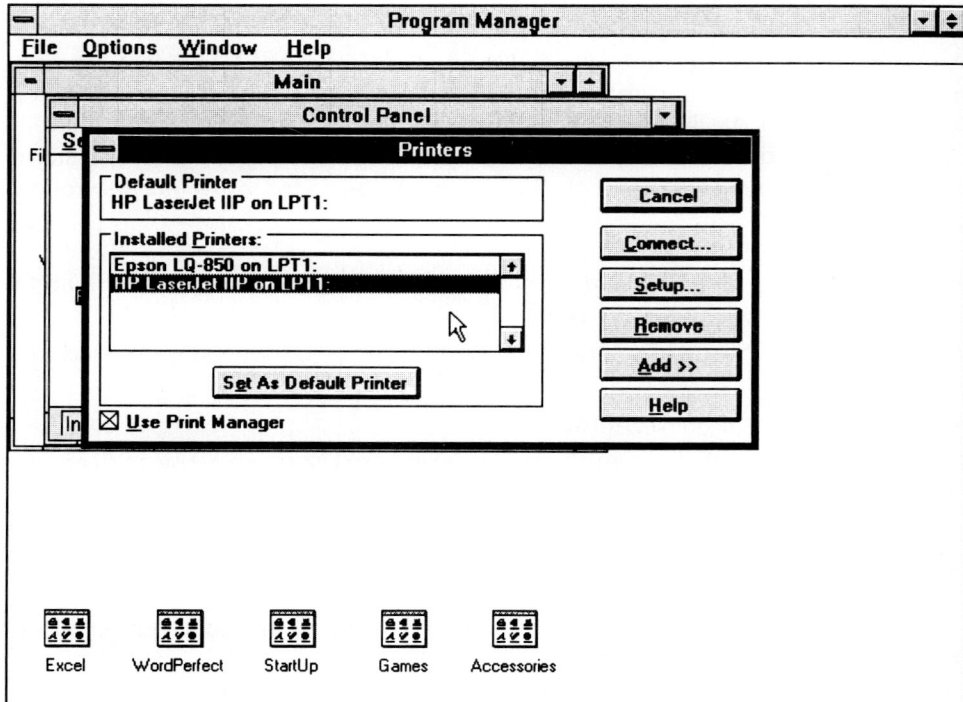

*3. How do you open a group window?
4. How do you reduce a group window to an icon?
5. How can you rearrange group windows?
6. What is the difference between the Cascade command and Tile command for rearranging group windows?
7. How do you organize group icons? How do you organize program-item icons?
*8. How do you create a new group?
9. What is the file extension created by Windows for a new group?
10. How do you delete an unwanted group?
11. What is the maximum length of a group description?
12. How do you change the description of a group?
13. How do you create a program item?
*14. How many different methods can be used for creating a program item?
15. When you create a program item, what do you usually type in the Command Line box?
16. What are some of the items included in the Program Item Properties dialog box?
17. What are the rules for creating a shortcut key when you create a program item? What is the limit on the number of program items in a group?
*18. Can you create a program item for a document?
19. How do you delete a program item from a group?
20. How do you copy a program item from one group to another?
21. When you copy a program item from one group to another, must you open the source and destination group windows? Discuss.
22. How do you move a program item from one group to another?
23. How do you change an icon?

Chapter 10 Customizing Your Windows Environment 193

*24. What should you do to start an application when you start Windows?
25. In what order are the applications in the StartUp group started?
26. Can you instruct Windows to automatically reduce an application in the StartUp group to an icon when the application is started? If yes, how?
27. What is the Control Panel? How do you start it?
28. What are some of the applications of the Control Panel?
29. Are the contents of the Control Panel the same for different computers and different Windows installations?
30. What is the application of the Drivers option in the Control Panel?
31. How do you display Custom Wallpaper?
*32. What are some of the Screen Saver options?
33. How do you test your Screen Saver to see how it looks?
34. How do you configure your printer using the Control Panel?

HANDS-ON EXPERIENCE

1. Start Windows and answer the following questions:
   a. What is included in the Main group window?
   b. Open the Accessories group window. What is included in this group?
   c. What is included in the Games group window?
   d. Reduce one of the open groups to an icon.
   e. Enlarge it back to a window.
2. Close all the open windows; then open four group windows of your choice and do the following:
   a. Arrange them using the Cascade command.
   b. Arrange them using the Tile command.
   c. What is the key combination for the Cascade command?
   d. What is the key combination for the Tile command?
3. Start Windows, if it is not already started, and do the following:
   a. Create a new group under the name TEST. Change the description to TEST1.
   b. Copy two program-item icons that you have in your Program Manager into this group (e.g., File Manager and Control Panel).
   c. Delete the two applications from this group.
   d. Delete the group itself.
4. Open two group windows of your choice and do the following:
   a. Copy one program item from the first group to the second group.
   b. Delete the copied program item from the second group window.
   c. Move one program item from the first group to the second group.
   d. Reverse part c.
   e. Change an icon of your choice to another icon. Change it back to the original icon.
   f. Include an application of your choice in the StartUp group. Exit Windows; then restart Windows. The application included in the StartUp group should start automatically.
5. Start the Control Panel and answer the following questions:
   a. What applications are included in your Control Panel window?
   b. Do you have all 12 applications introduced in this chapter?
   c. Using the Control Panel, select a Screen Saver for your computer.

Windows 3.1

   d. Change the appearance of your desktop by selecting a custom Wallpaper.
   e. Remove the Screen Saver created in part c.

KEY TERMS

Cascade
Control Panel
Custom Wallpaper
Program-item icon
Screen Saver
Tile

KEY COMMANDS

Shift-F4 (to invoke the Tile command)
Shift-F5 (to invoke the Cascade command)
File (to open the File menu)
Options (to open the Options menu)
Window (to open the Window menu)

MISCONCEPTIONS AND SOLUTIONS

Misconceptions You use an application frequently. Every time that you need this application you have to go through several steps to locate and run it.

   Solution It might be more convenient to add the application to a group in the Program Manager than to start it from the File Manager. You can also add it to the StartUp group; in this case, the application starts as soon as you start Windows.

Misconception You have selected a Custom Wallpaper and notice that some of your applications cannot run.

   Solution Windows uses more memory when displaying a Custom Wallpaper than when displaying a solid color or a pattern on the desktop. If you run out of memory, you must change to a color or pattern to free up some memory.

Misconception You have selected a Screen Saver and you notice that it does not appear on the screen.

   Solution If a non-Windows application is the active application, the Screen Saver does not appear on your screen, regardless of how the application was started.

ARE YOU READY TO MOVE ON?

Multiple Choice

1. Which of the following is *not* included among the Windows predefined groups?
   a. Main group
   b. Accessories group
   c. Games group
   d. StartUp group
   e. they are all included

2. By pressing one of the following key combinations, you can organize all the open Windows in a Tile format.
   a. Shift-F5
   b. Ctrl-Tab
   c. Shift-F4
   d. Ctrl-F10
   e. Ctrl-F9

Chapter 10 Customizing Your Windows Environment 195

3. To rearrange group windows, you can use
   a. the Cascade command
   b. the Tile command
   c. Shift-F5
   d. Shift-F4
   e. all of the above
4. To organize group icons, you have to
   a. select Arrange Icons from the Window menu
   b. select Arrange Icons from the File menu
   c. select Arrange Icons from the Options menu
   d. select Arrange Icons from the Help menu
   e. none of the above
5. When you are working with groups, you can do the following:
   a. create a new group
   b. delete an unwanted group
   c. rearrange the existing groups
   d. all of the above
   e. only a and c
6. To create a program item in a group, you have to
   a. select the desired group
   b. from the File menu select the New command
   c. from the New menu select the Program Item option
   d. do a, b, and c
   e. do only a and b
7. When you are creating a program item, in the command line you must type
   a. the program file and its extension
   b. the complete path
   c. both a and b
   d. only the program file followed by Enter
   e. only the file extension
8. Which one of the following is *not* a valid key combination?
   a. Alt-Alt-Shift
   b. Ctrl-Alt-Character
   c. Ctrl-Shift-Character
   d. Ctrl-Shift-Alt-Character
   e. Shift-Alt-Character
9. To delete a program item from a group after selecting the program item,
   a. select Erase from the File menu
   b. select Delete from the File menu
   c. select Copy from the File menu
   d. select Erase from the Options menu
   e. none of the above
10. To start an application when you start Windows, you must include the application icon in the
    a. Main group
    b. StartUp group

c. Accessories group
   d. Applications group
   e. Games group

True/False

1. The Control Panel can be used to visually change the appearance of your desktop.
2. The Ports option is *not* included as one of the applications in the Control Panel dialog box.
3. The Keyboard option in the Control Panel is used to adjust the mouse.
4. The limit for a program-item description is 40 characters.
5. Windows allows you to create a Custom Wallpaper.
6. Using the Control Panel, you can select one of the several Screen Savers available.
7. After selecting a Screen Saver, you cannot see how it looks until you reboot your computer.
8. You cannot configure your printer through the Control Panel; it must be done through DOS.
9. The Main group is one of the predefined groups in Windows.
10. Windows does *not* include a Games group.

ANSWERS

Multiple Choice
1. e
2. c
3. e
4. a
5. d
6. d
7. c
8. a
9. b
10. b

True/False
1. T
2. F
3. F
4. T
5. T
6. T
7. F
8. F
9. T
10. F

Managing Files and Floppy Disks Using the File Manager

11-1	Introduction
11-2	File Manager: Getting Started
11-3	What Is a Directory Window?
11-4	Selecting Files and Directories
11-4-1	Selecting Several Files or Directories That Are in Sequence
11-4-2	Selecting Several Files or Directories That Are out of Sequence
11-4-3	Deselecting Files or Directories
11-5	Changing Drives
11-6	Sorting the Contents of a Directory
11-7	Specifying the Type of File to Be Displayed
11-8	Naming a File or a Directory
11-9	Creating a Directory
11-10	Searching for a File or a Directory
11-11	Deleting a File or a Directory
11-12	Renaming a File or a Directory
11-13	Copying or Moving a File or Directory
11-14	Using Multiple Windows in File Manager
11-15	Associating Files with a Software Application
11-16	Printing a File
11-17	Formatting a Disk
11-18	Labeling a Disk
11-19	Copying a Disk
11-20	Creating a System Disk

11-1
INTRODUCTION

In this chapter we look at some of the important functions of the File Manager. The chapter shows how to get in and out of the File Manager and explains the processes of creating, selecting, changing, deleting, renaming, copying, and moving files and directories. It also describes the steps for sorting the contents of a directory window and the file association feature of Windows. Finally, the chapter illustrates the processes of formatting, labeling, and copying a disk and creating a system disk. As you will see, the File Manager simplifies the ordinary tasks of DOS introduced in Chapters 2 through 4 of this book.

11-2
FILE MANAGER: GETTING STARTED

Windows File Manager consists of several programs that help you to manage your files, directories, and disk drives effectively. The following tasks are some of those performed by the File Manager:

- Viewing files and directories
- Creating directories
- Removing directories
- Copying and moving files and directories
- Starting software applications
- Managing floppy disks

The functions of the File Manager are similar to the functions of DOS that were explained in Chapters 2 through 4. The major advantage of the File Manager over DOS is ease of use. The File Manager is easy to use because of the availability of pull-down menus and mouse support, which are not available for most DOS operations.

Remember that a file is a single document or a program stored on disk. Think of a directory as an electronic manila folder that stores several files. By means of directories, you can organize your files more effectively. (For a detailed discussion of directories, refer to Chapter 4.)

To start the File Manager, double-click on the File Manager icon in the Main group. Click on the maximize icon to enlarge the screen. You will be presented with a screen similar to the one in Figure 11–1. To leave the File Manager, select the Exit option from the File menu or you can double-click on the control-menu box.

11-3
WHAT IS A DIRECTORY WINDOW?

As you can see in Figure 11–1, when you start the File Manager, a **directory window** is displayed. On the left side of this figure, the tree structure (directory structure) of the current drive is displayed. On the right side, the names of all of the files contained within the current directory are displayed. When you select another directory, the information on the right side is changed accordingly to display the contents of the new directory.

The title bar displays the current directory path; in this case we are in the 123r23 directory. The root directory is identified by a back slash (e.g., \). Figure 11–2 illustrates all the parts of the directory window.

Chapter 11 Managing Files and Floppy Disks Using the File Manager

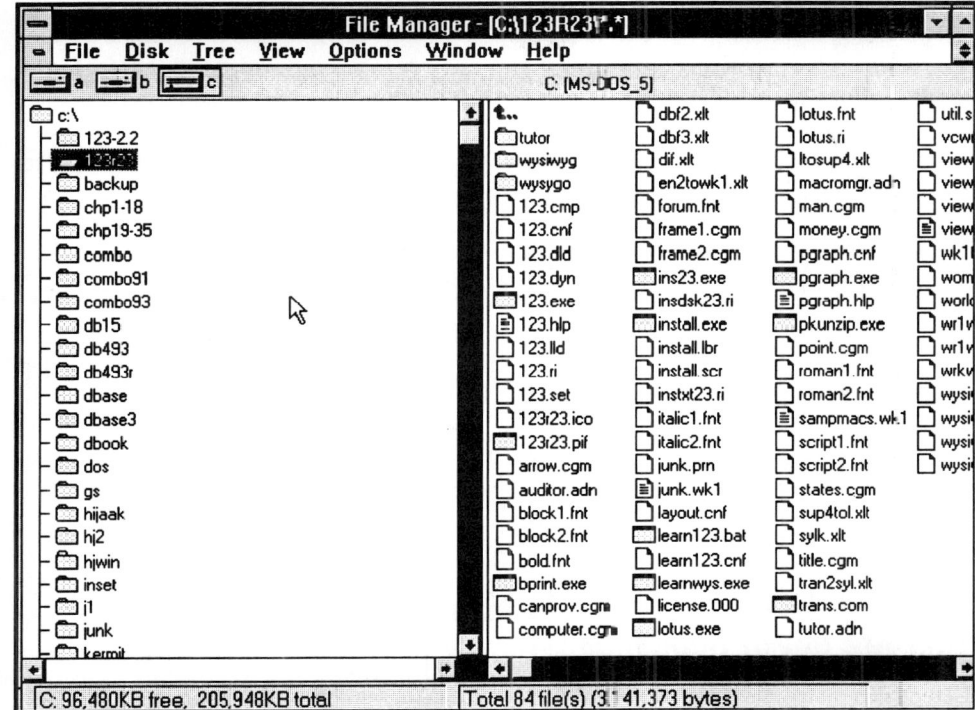

Figure 11–1
Starting screen of File Manager

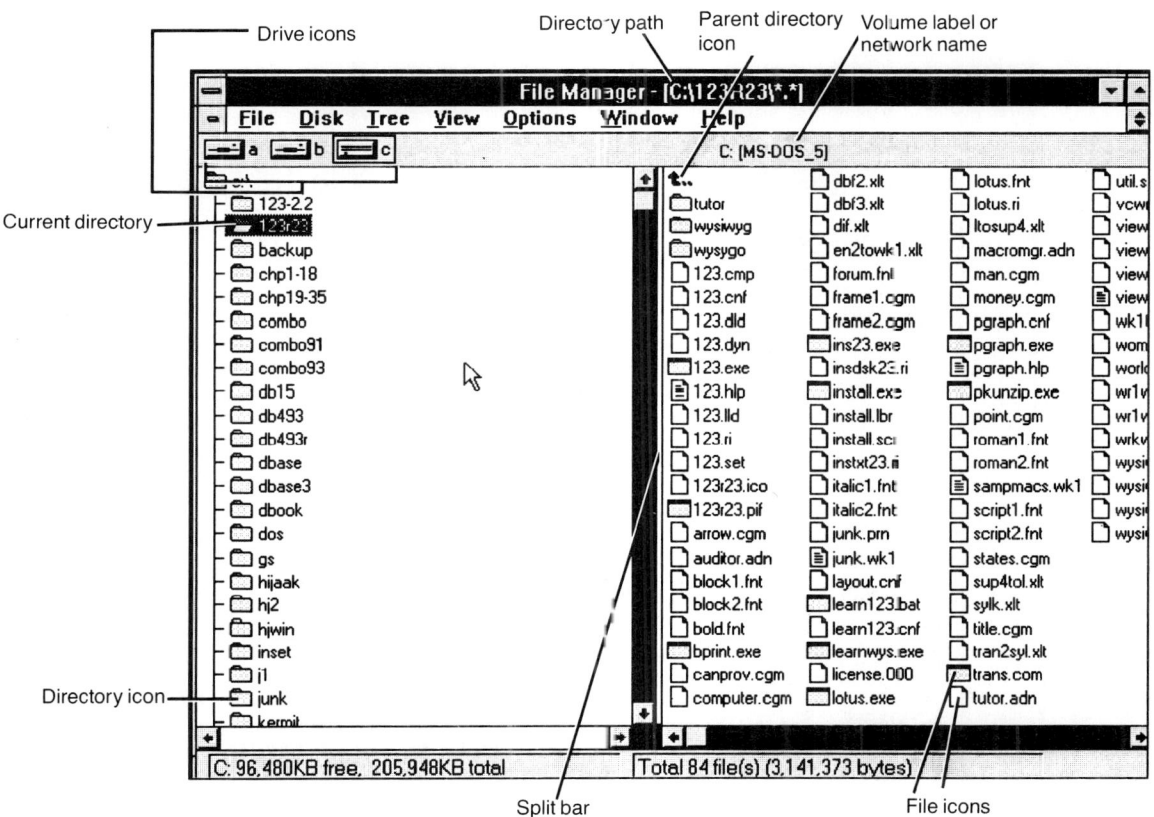

Figure 11–2
Parts of a directory window

11-4
SELECTING FILES OR DIRECTORIES

To select a file or a directory using the mouse, in the contents list click left on the file name or directory name that you want. As soon as a file or directory is selected, you can apply any of the File Manager commands to it. For example, you can copy it, move it, and so forth. When a file or directory is selected, its name and icon are highlighted in the directory window.

11-4-1 Selecting Several Files or Directories That Are in Sequence

Sometimes you may want to select several files or directories. For example, you may want to copy three files at once. Files can be in consecutive order or they can be scattered in several locations. If the files you want to select are in consecutive order, click left on the first file that you want to select; then press and hold down the Shift key while you click left on the last file in the group. In Figure 11-3 we used this method to select five files in the right side of the window. As you can see, all of the files are highlighted.

11-4-2 Selecting Several Files or Directories That Are out of Sequence

If the files or directories you want to select are *not* in consecutive order, press and hold down the Ctrl key while you click left on each item. Each selected item will be highlighted.

Figure 11-3
Five files highlighted

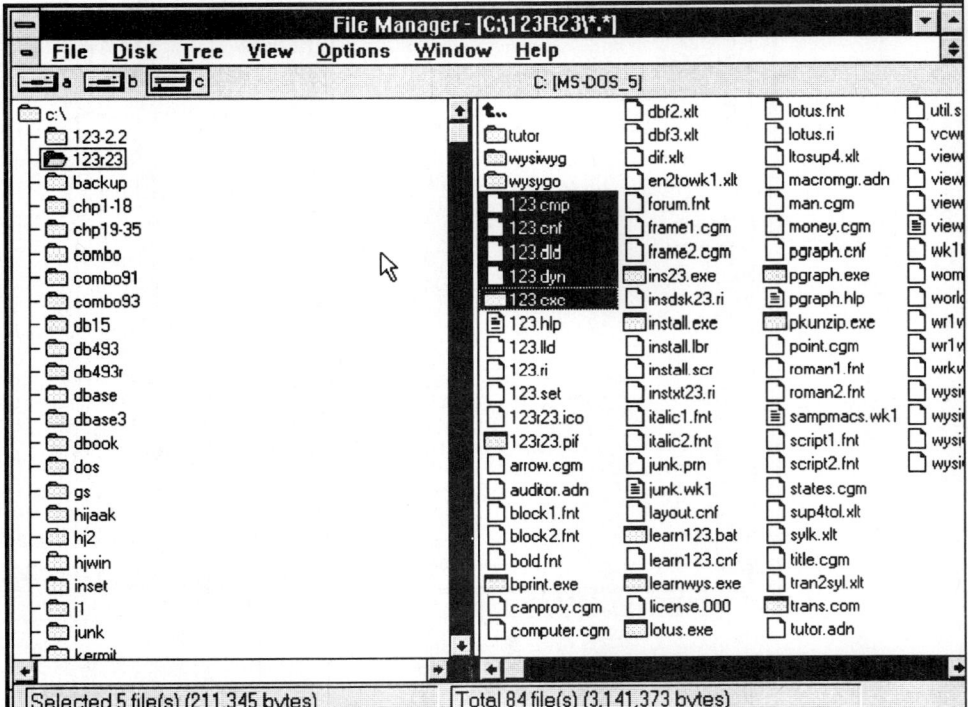

Chapter 11 Managing Files and Floppy Disks Using the File Manager

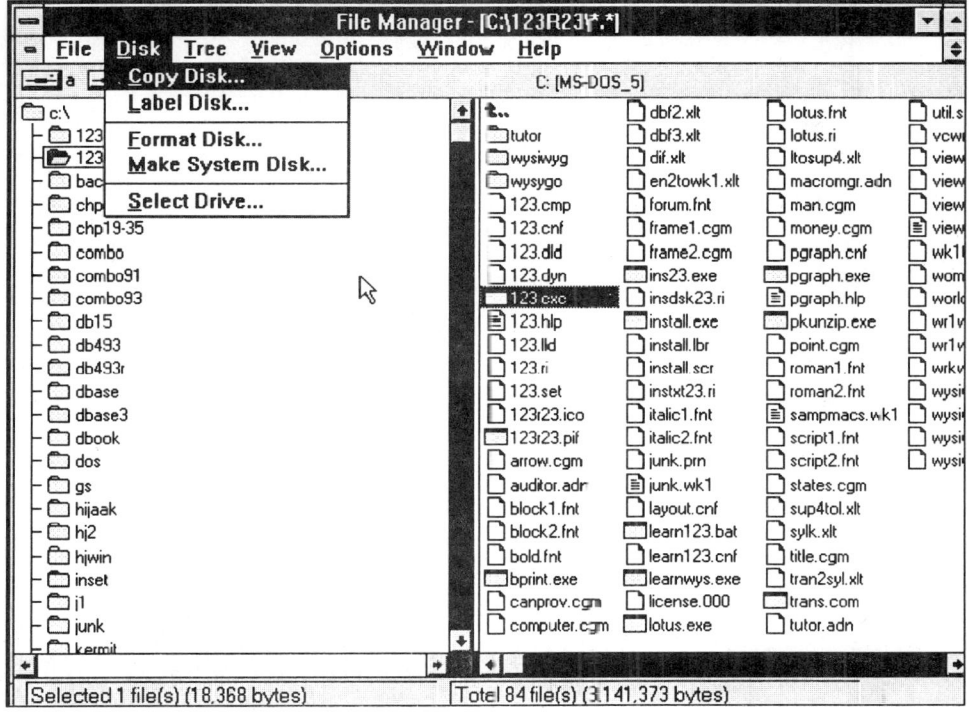

Figure 11-4
Disk menu

Deselecting Files or Directories

11-4-3

To deselect a file or directory without deselecting other files or directories, press and hold down the Ctrl key while you click left on the highlighted item. The highlight will disappear.

11-5 CHANGING DRIVES

The mouse allows you to change drives by selecting another drive icon in the drive bar. All you have to do is click left on the desired drive, for example, drive A. You can also change drives by choosing the Select Drive command from the Disk menu; see Figure 11-4.

11-6 SORTING THE CONTENTS OF A DIRECTORY

Sorted directories are easier to manage than those that are not. By default, Windows sorts the contents of a directory in alphabetical order; directories are listed first and file names follow. You can, however, change this order and sort files and directories by name, size, type, or the last date that they were modified.

    To see files and directories in alphabetical order, from the View menu (Figure 11-5), select Sort by Name.

    To sort files and directories by type, from the View menu select Sort by Type. When you select this option, directories and then files are listed alphabetically by extension. For example, files with the extension BAK appear before files with the extension COM.

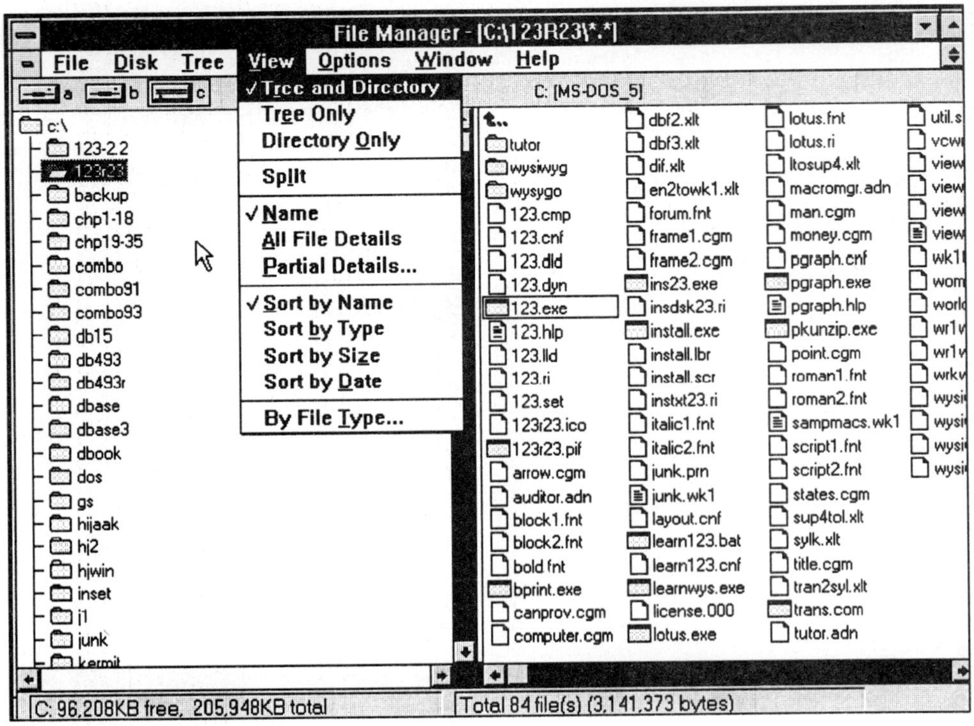

Figure 11-5
View menu

To sort files by size, from the View menu select Sort by Size. In this case, directories are listed first; then files are listed by size, from the largest file (in bytes) to the smallest file.

From the View menu select Sort by Date to sort files and directories by last modification date. Directories are listed first, sorted by date. Then files are listed by date, from the most recent to the least recent.

11-7
SPECIFYING THE TYPE OF FILE TO BE DISPLAYED

File Manager by default lists all the files in the current directory in the right side of the window. You can exercise full control over this display by selecting the type of file to be displayed. To specify which type of file to display in a directory window, follow these steps:

1. From the View menu, select the By File Type option. You will be presented with a screen similar to the one in Figure 11-6.

2. If you are interested in one particular type of file, you can use wildcards as explained in Chapter 2. For example, in the Name box type *.WK1; all your Lotus 1-2-3 spreadsheet files with this extension will be displayed. If you type *WK?, all your WK1, WK3, WKQ, WKE, and WKS files will be displayed.

3. Under File Type, you can select any of the four file types listed. Table 11-1 explains the choices.

4. If you want to display hidden and system files, select Show Hidden/System Files.

5. Select OK to finalize the process.

Chapter 11   Managing Files and Floppy Disks Using the File Manager

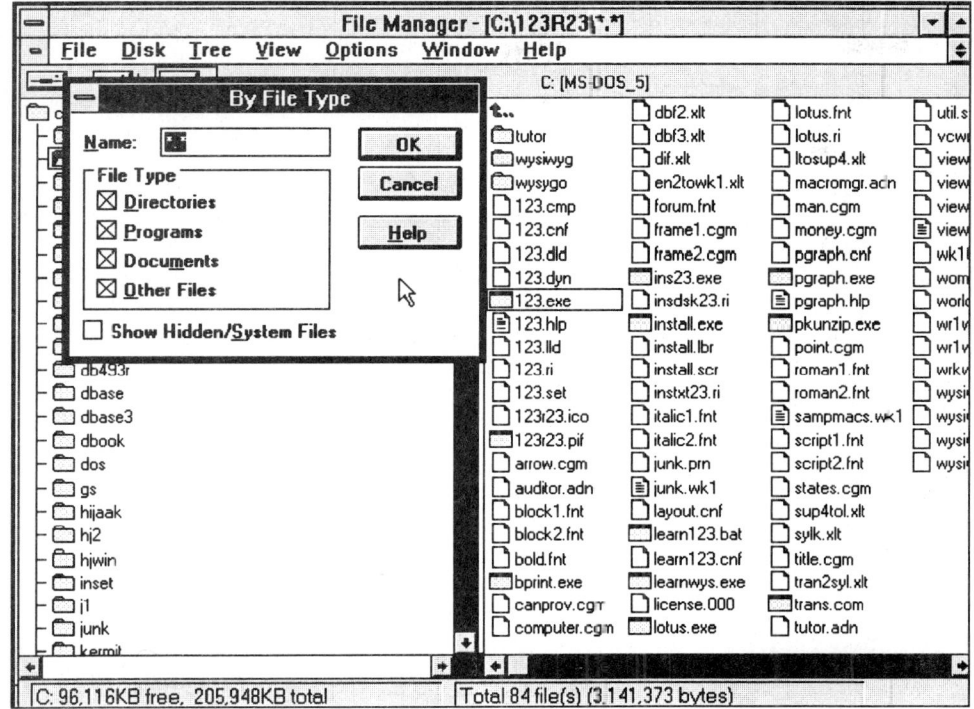

Figure 11-6
By File Type dialog box

Table 11-1
File types

You Select	Icon	Windows Displays
Directories	📁	The names of all the subdirectories in the current directory
Programs	▭	All the file names that have a .BAT, .COM, .EXE, or .PIF extension
Documents	📄	The names of graphics or text files associated with a software application
Other files	▯	File names that are not included in the three items above
Hidden/system files	▯!	The system BIOS (Basic Input Output System) files

By default, Windows displays all four types of files. To change what will be displayed, click left on any combination of the choices in the By File Type dialog box.

11-8
NAMING A FILE OR A DIRECTORY

To name a file or a directory, enter any name of up to eight characters. The name must start with either a letter or a number. Do not use a space in a directory or file name. Also, do not use the following names because they are reserved names that Windows uses: AUX, CON, COM1, COM2, COM3, COM4, LPT1, LPT2, LPT3, NUL, and PRN. Try to use names that have some meaning to you, for example, TAX, ACCOUNT, or PAYROLL.

Characters or numbers can be included in names; however, the following characters cannot be used: back slash (\), brackets ([]), colon (:), comma (,), equal sign (=), period (.), quotation mark ("), semicolon (;), forward slash (/), question mark (?), and vertical bar (|). Uppercase and lowercase characters are considered identical.

11-9
CREATING A DIRECTORY

A directory is similar to an electronic manila folder. After you create a directory, you can copy other files and directories into it. The use of directories simplifies file management by allowing a family of files to be included in one directory. For example, you can include all your spreadsheet files in one directory, all your word processing files in another directory, and so forth. To create a directory, follow these steps:

1. In the directory tree, select the directory in which you want to construct a new directory. For example, select WP51—the directory for WordPerfect. You can also create a brand new directory in the root directory of any of your drives. For example, to create a directory in drive A, click left on the icon for this drive and follow the rest of these steps.
2. From the File menu, select Create Directory. You will be presented with a screen similar to the one in Figure 11-7.
3. Type a name of up to eight characters.
4. Select OK to finalize the directory creation process.

Now you can copy any files and/or directories into the directory you created.

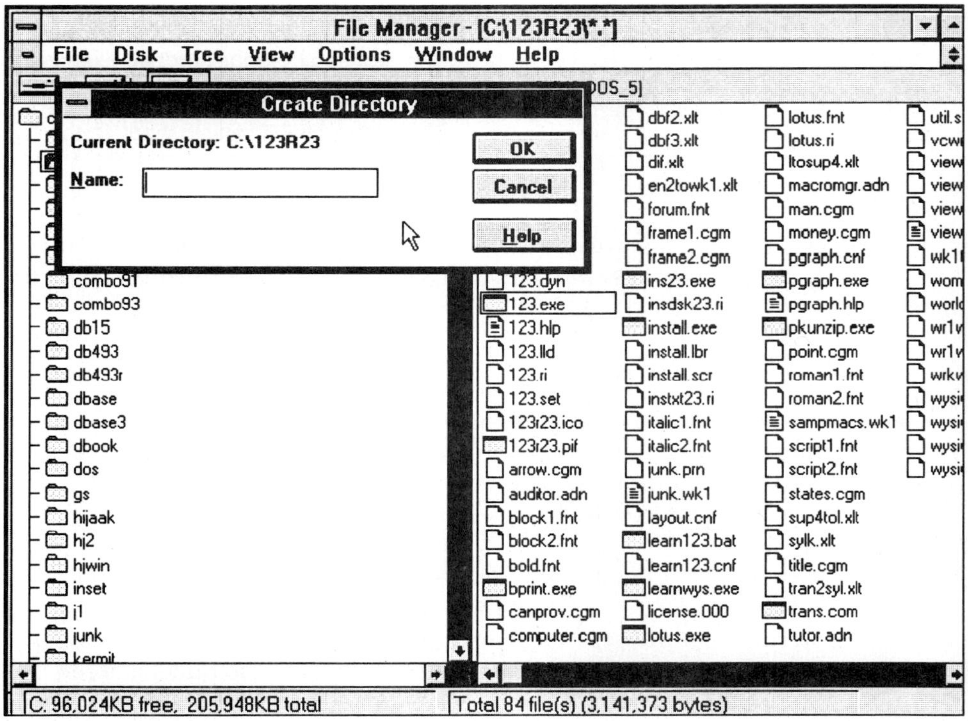

Figure 11-7
Create Directory dialog box

Chapter 11 Managing Files and Floppy Disks Using the File Manager

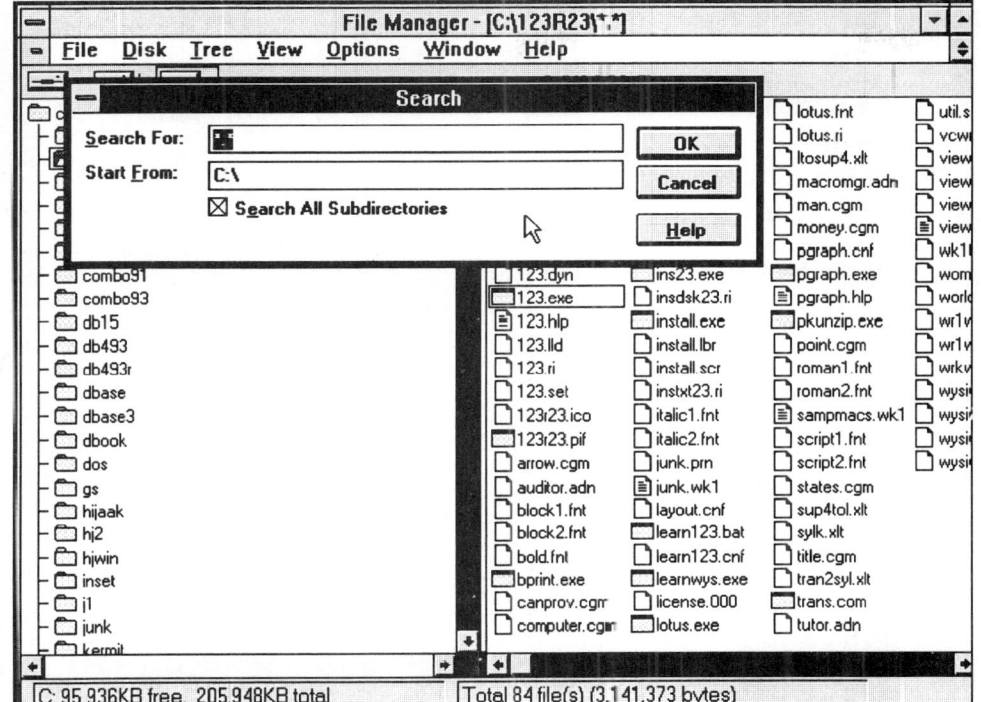

Figure 11-8
Search dialog box

To search for a file or directory, follow these steps:

1. Select the drive and directory from which you want to start the search.
2. From the File menu select Search. You will be presented with a screen similar to the one in Figure 11-8.
3. Type the desired file name. You can also use wildcards, for example, *.PIC to search for all the Lotus 1-2-3 graphic files.
4. The Start From box displays the default directory. If this is not the directory that you want, type in the desired directory name.
5. Select OK to finalize the process.

As an example, we requested a search of all directories for WK1 files. As you can see in Figure 11-9, we typed *.WK1 in the Search For box and typed C:\ in the Start From box. This means we are telling the File Manager to search the entire C drive. All of the WK1 files are displayed in the Search Results window (Figure 11-10). To see the rest of the .WK1 files, move the cursor down.

11-10
SEARCHING FOR A FILE OR A DIRECTORY

If a file or a directory is no longer needed, you can erase it, thereby freeing disk space for other use. To delete a file or a directory, follow these steps:

1. Select the file or the directory that you want to delete.
2. From the File menu, select Delete or press the Del key. You will be presented with a screen similar to the one in Figure 11-11.

11-11
DELETING A FILE OR A DIRECTORY

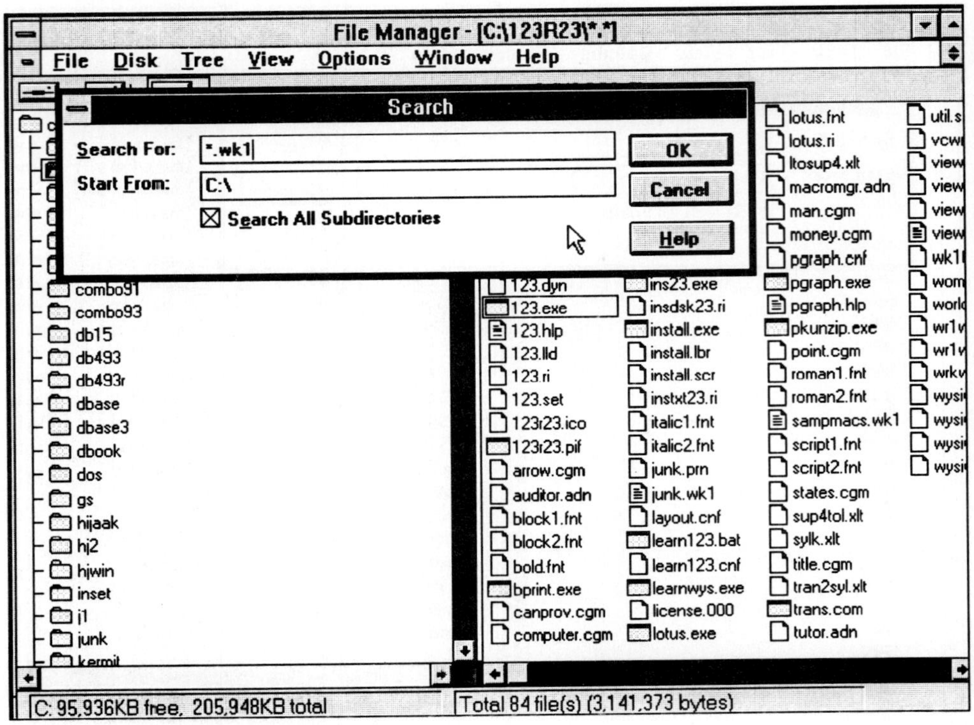

Figure 11-9
Search dialog box for WK1 files

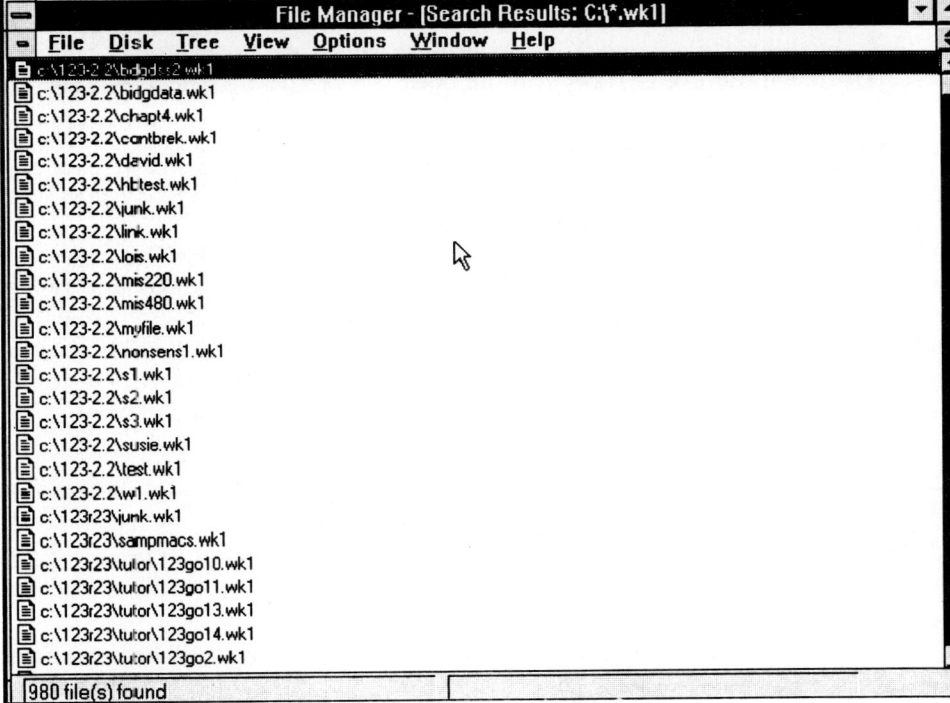

Figure 11-10
Search Results window

Chapter 11 Managing Files and Floppy Disks Using the File Manager

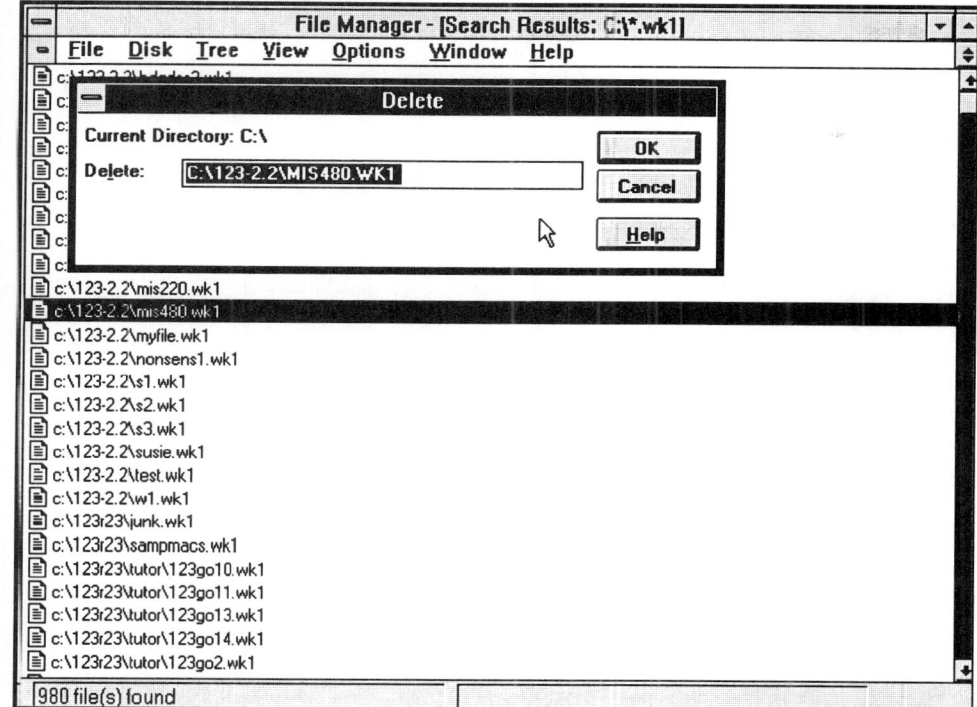

Figure 11-11
Delete dialog box

3. Select OK to erase the highlighted file or directory.
4. Respond Yes to the confirmation message. If you are deleting a subdirectory or more than one file, select the Yes to All option as required to delete all of the specified files.

Remember, when you delete a file or a directory, the file or directory is gone for good. Be careful; make sure this is what you want to do.

11-12 RENAMING A FILE OR A DIRECTORY

To rename a file or a directory, follow these steps:

1. Select the file or directory that you want to rename.
2. From the File menu select the Rename command. You will be presented with a screen similar to the one in Figure 11-12.
3. Type the desired file name (if it is not already displayed) in the From box. You can also use wildcard characters to rename a series of files at once. For example, if you want to rename all your DOC files to LTR, type *.DOC.
4. Type in the new name in the To box and click left on OK.

11-13 COPYING OR MOVING A FILE OR DIRECTORY

To copy a file or a directory, highlight it first and follow these steps:

1. From the File menu select the Copy command (press F8 as a shortcut).
2. You will be presented with a screen similar to the one in Figure 11-13.

Figure 11–12
Rename dialog box

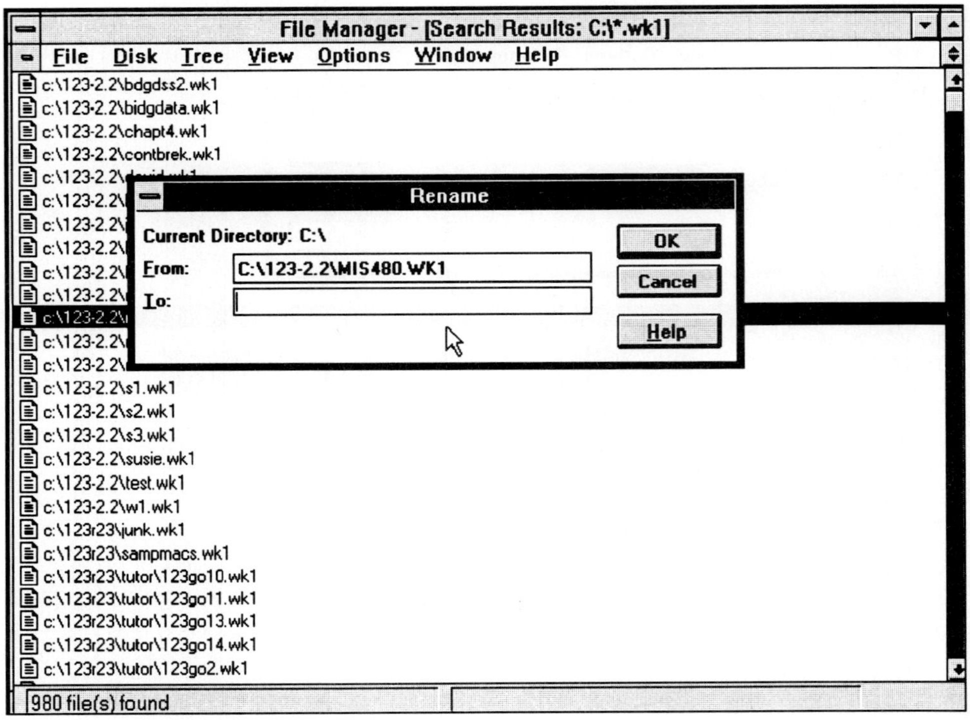

Figure 11–13
Copy dialog box

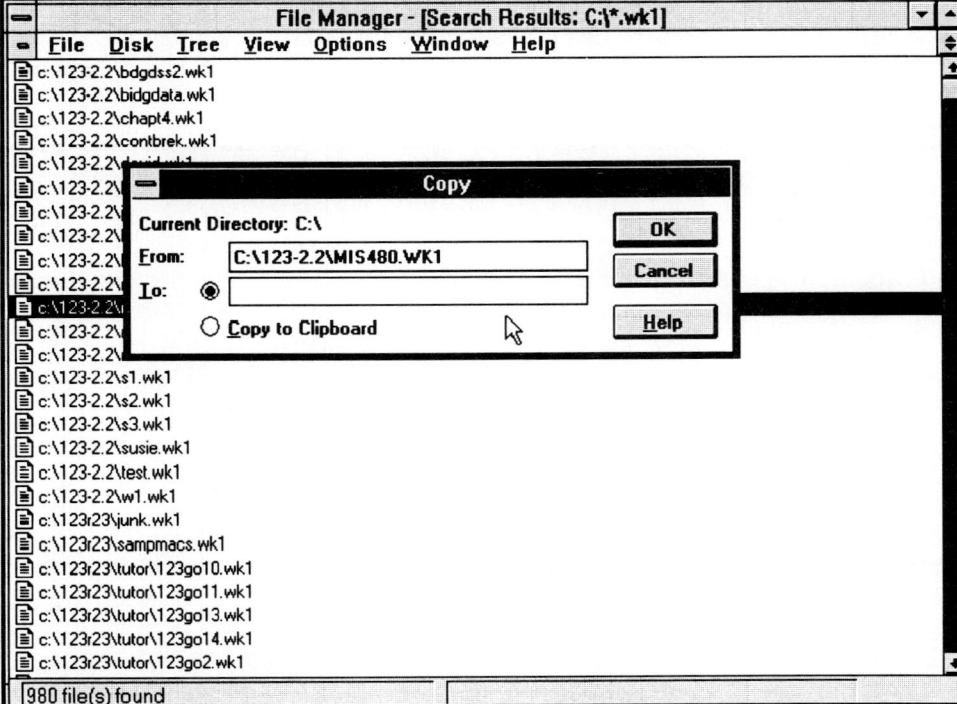

Chapter 11 Managing Files and Floppy Disks Using the File Manager

3. In the From box type in the file name that you want to copy (if you do not want to copy the current file or directory). In the To box type in the new name. You must specify the complete path in both the From and To boxes if the file or the directory is not located in the current drive or directory.
4. Click left on OK. (Wildcard characters allow you to copy a series of files or directories.)

You can also copy a file or directory to the Clipboard to be used by other Windows applications.

The Move (F7 for a shortcut) command is similar to the Copy command. The only difference is that when you use the Move command your original file is moved (cut) from its original location.

With either the Copy or Move command, if you highlight a directory, the entire directory and all of its contents (including all of its subdirectories) is copied or moved to the specified location.

11-14 USING MULTIPLE WINDOWS IN FILE MANAGER

Windows allows you to view more than one directory or drive at the same time and to copy or move the files contained within one window to the drive and/or directory displayed in another window. To copy a file while viewing multiple windows in the File Manager, follow the steps outlined next:

1. Open the File Manager.
2. Click left on the maximize button at the upper right of the File Manager screen to allow File Manager to fill the entire screen.
3. Click left on Window.
4. Click left on New Window. A second window displayed on the screen will show the same directory tree and files as the first window.
5. Click left on Window; then select Tile to display the windows in a tiled format. You will see a screen similar to the one in Figure 11-14. As you can see, both windows display the same information.
6. Place a formatted disk in drive A. To look at the contents of the disk, change the lower window by clicking on the drive A icon in the drive bar area at the top of the bottom window. Windows will automatically change the directory tree and file windows at the bottom of the screen to show the directories and files contained on the disk in drive A.
7. Next, click left on any file name in the file name area of the upper window; then, using the mouse, drag the file name down to the file name area of the window representing drive A at the bottom of the screen. Once you have the file name in this area, release the left button of the mouse. Windows will ask you to verify that you really want to copy the file to the disk. Click left on Yes and the file will be copied for you.

11-15 ASSOCIATING FILES WITH A SOFTWARE APPLICATION

File association is an interesting feature of Windows. (This feature is also available in DOS 5.) By means of this feature, you can select a file from your directory, and the related software application will be automatically started with the

Figure 11-14
Two File Manager windows in tile mode

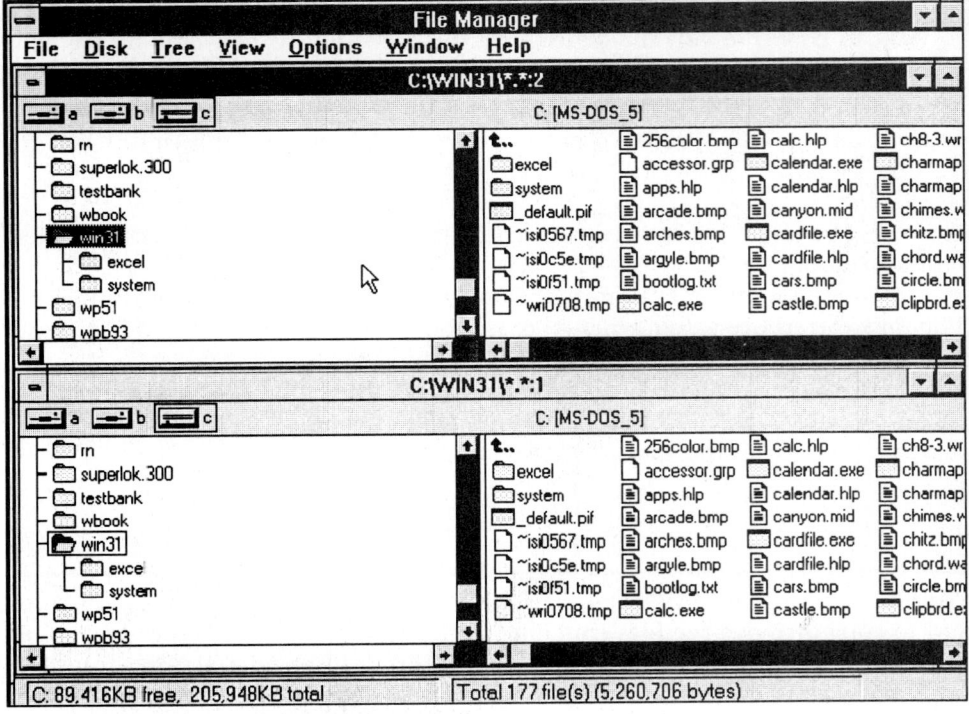

selected file loaded and ready for editing. Without this feature, you must start a particular software application, then load your desired file manually.

For some Windows programs file association takes place automatically during the installation process. For other programs the File Manager can establish an association between applications and a particular type of file. For example, you may want to associate all of your WK1 files with Lotus 1-2-3. To associate a file with an application, follow these steps:

1. Select Associate from the File menu. You will be presented with a screen similar to the one in Figure 11-15.

2. Type in the extension of the desired file in the Files with Extension box. For example, type *WK1* for Lotus 1-2-3 worksheet files.

3. In the Associate With box, type the name of the application file with which you wish to associate the data file. For example, type *123.EXE* (with a complete path). You can also select your application from the box displayed. If your application is not listed in the Associate With box, you can click on Browse and search for the desired application. When you click on Browse, you will see a screen similar to the one in Figure 11-16. Remember, to see the application program, you must be in the correct directory. If you are not in the correct directory, select the correct directory and proceed with the Browse command.

4. Click on OK. From now on, if you select any file with the WK1 extension, Lotus 1-2-3 will be started automatically with the selected file opened.

To remove the file association, invoke the Associate dialog box. Type in the extension of the desired file in the Files with Extension box. In the Associate With box, click left on [None]; then click on OK.

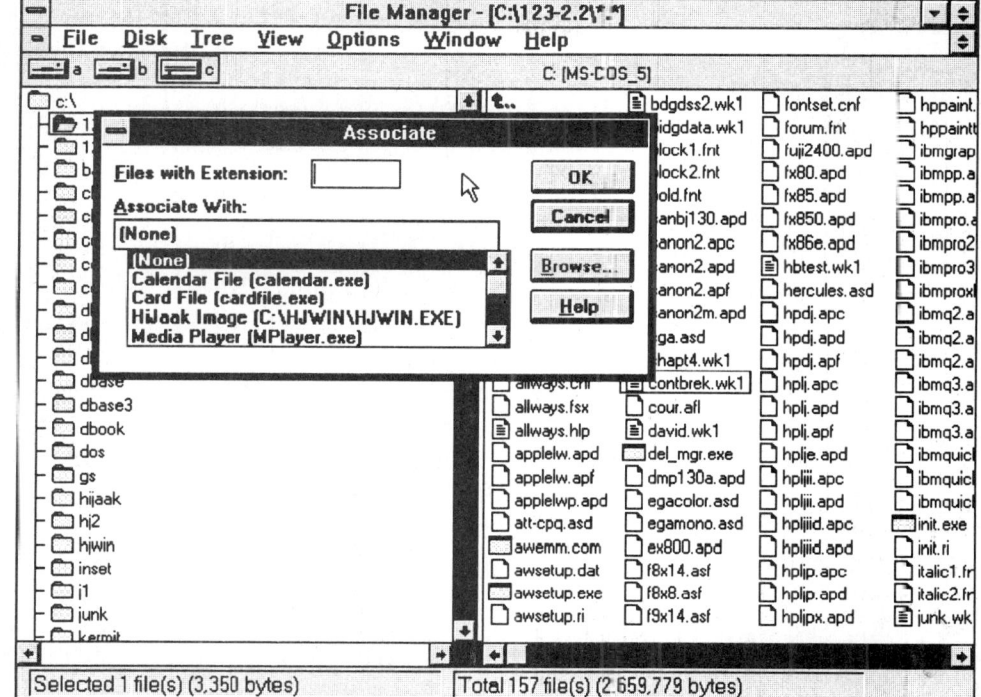

Figure 11-15
Associate dialog box

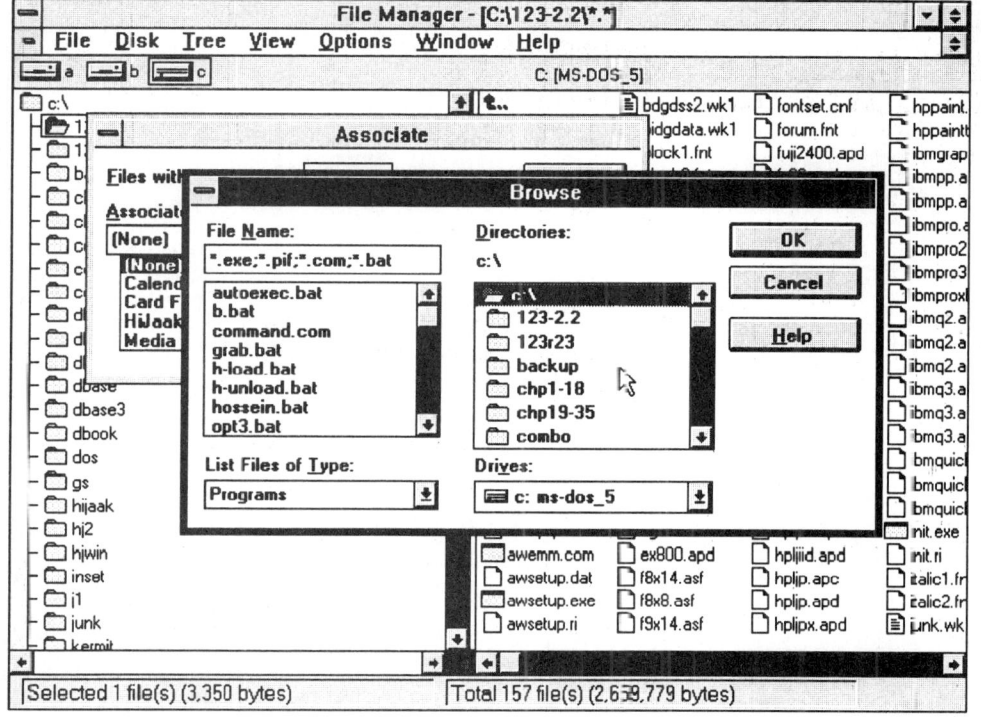

Figure 11-16
Browse dialog box

11-16
PRINTING A FILE

The Print command prints a file that is associated with an application program. For example, a WRI (Write application) file can be printed by using the Print command. To print a document, follow these steps:

1. Select the desired file.
2. From the File menu select Print. You will be presented with a screen similar to the one in Figure 11-17.
3. Click on OK. If you do not want to print the highlighted file, type in the complete path (if the file is not in the current directory) and the name of the desired file in the Print box; then click left on OK.
4. The application in which the document was created will be opened with the file already loaded. A Print dialog box also will be displayed (Figure 11-18). Click left on OK to print the selected file.

11-17
FORMATTING A DISK

Formatting a disk means preparing it for use. When you purchase a new disk, you cannot use it until you format it. During the formatting process, the File Manager checks the disk for possible damage, erases existing data from the disk, and creates the File Allocation Table (FAT) on the disk. The FAT reserves space on the disk for you to save information on it. To format a disk, follow these steps:

1. Insert a disk into a drive.
2. From the Disk menu select the Format Disk option.

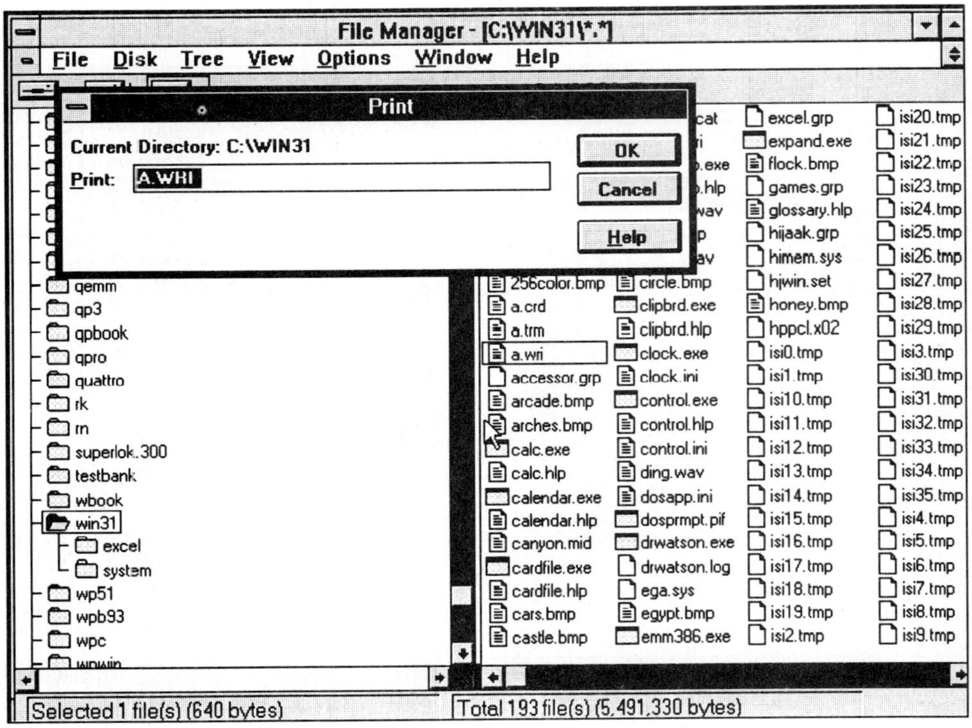

Figure 11-17
Print dialog box

Chapter 11 Managing Files and Floppy Disks Using the File Manager

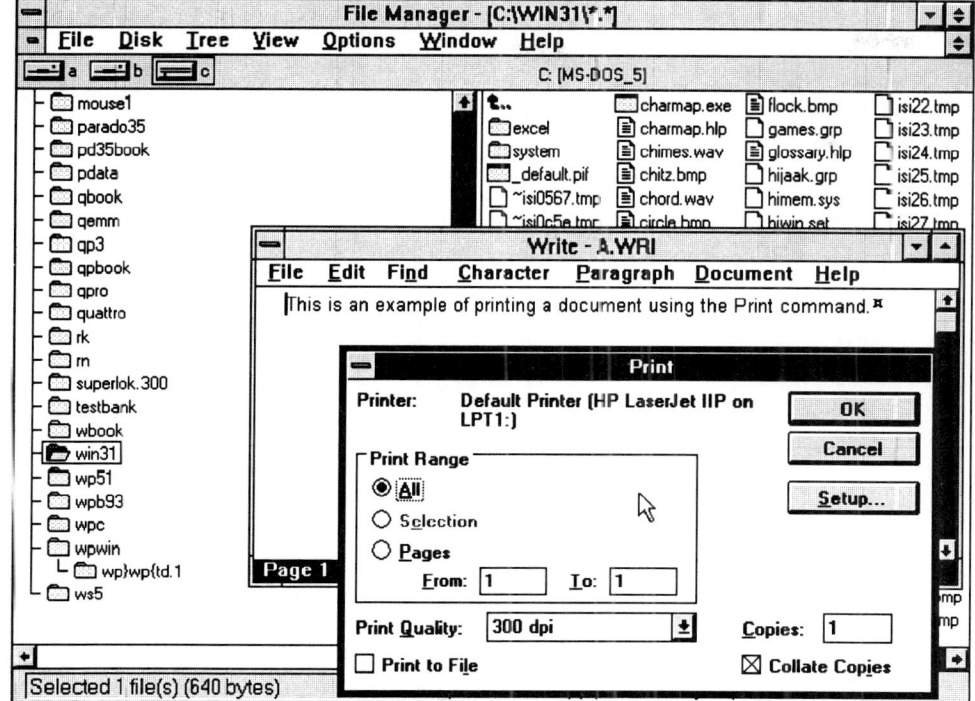

Figure 11-18

File for printing and the Print dialog box

3. You will be presented with a screen similar to the one in Figure 11-19. As you can see in this figure, the default drive is A. If this is not the drive you want, click on the down arrow in the Disk In box to select another drive.

4. In the Capacity box select the desired capacity. In our example the default is 1.2 MB. By clicking anywhere in the capacity box, you can select another capacity if 1.2 MB is not what you want.

5. Click on OK. You will be presented with the Confirm Format Disk dialog box. Click on Yes to confirm. In a few moments your disk will be formatted. When you are done, the File Manager asks you if you want to format another disk. Select Yes or No.

The Quick Format option (see Figure 11-19) erases the directory information from the disk (the FAT and root directory of the disk); however, the disk will not be checked for bad sectors. Use the Quick Format option only on disks that have been previously formatted.

11-18 LABELING A DISK

As you can see in Figure 11-19, one of the options in the Format Disk dialog box is the **Label option.** A label, which can consist of up to 11 characters, is an internal name for a disk. So if you accidentally lose the external sticker on your disk, this internal name (label) would help you to identify your disk. After you type the label name, click on OK. If you decide to change the label, select the Label option again and type the new name.

Windows 3.1

Figure 11-19
Format Disk dialog box

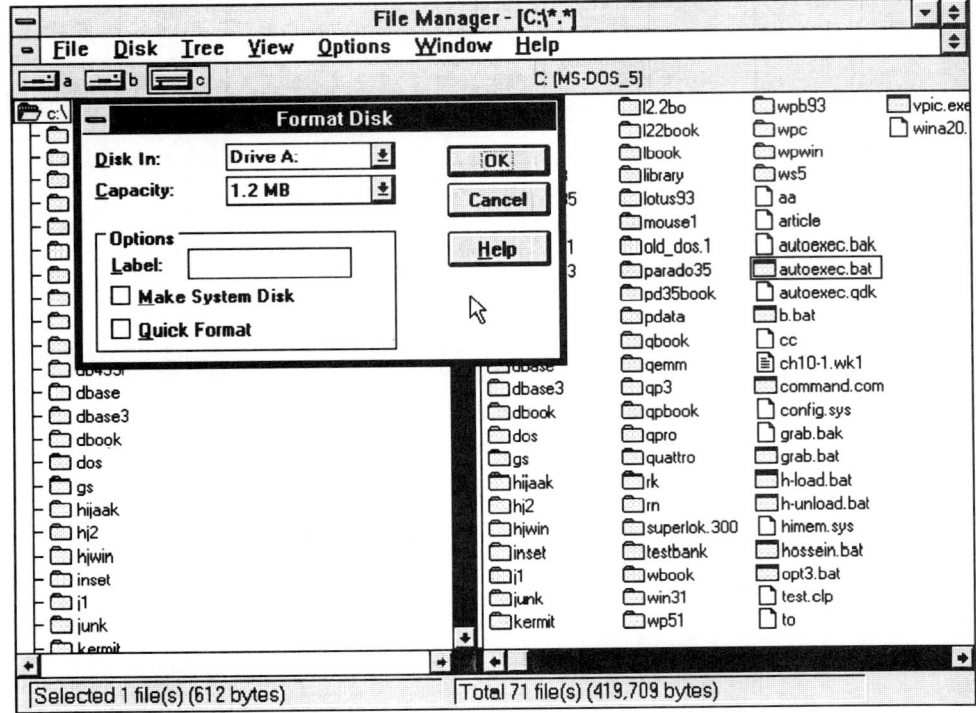

11-19
COPYING A DISK

By selecting the Copy Disk option from the Disk menu, you can create a duplicate copy of a disk. To do so, follow these steps:

1. Insert the source disk in the drive from which you want to copy. If your system has two drives of the same size, you can insert the blank disk (the destination disk) into the other drive.
2. From the Disk menu select Copy Disk. A dialog box will appear (Figure 11-20). Identify your source and destination by selecting the appropriate drive names, for example, A and B. To do this, click left on the down arrow in the Source In or Destination In boxes; then click left on the desired drive. If your system has only one drive, this dialog box will not appear. Your one drive will serve as both A and B.
3. Click on OK. The Confirm Copy Disk dialog box will appear. Select Yes, but be careful. Selecting Yes means that any files that were on your destination disk before the copy operation will be completely erased.

11-20
CREATING A SYSTEM DISK

By means of the File Manager you can create a **system disk.** When you create a system disk, the File Manager places a copy of COMMAND.COM and the two hidden system files that must be present to make the disk capable of booting up another computer. Such a disk can serve as a backup boot disk in the event that your original boot disk fails. Follow these steps:

Chapter 11 Managing Files and Floppy Disks Using the File Manager

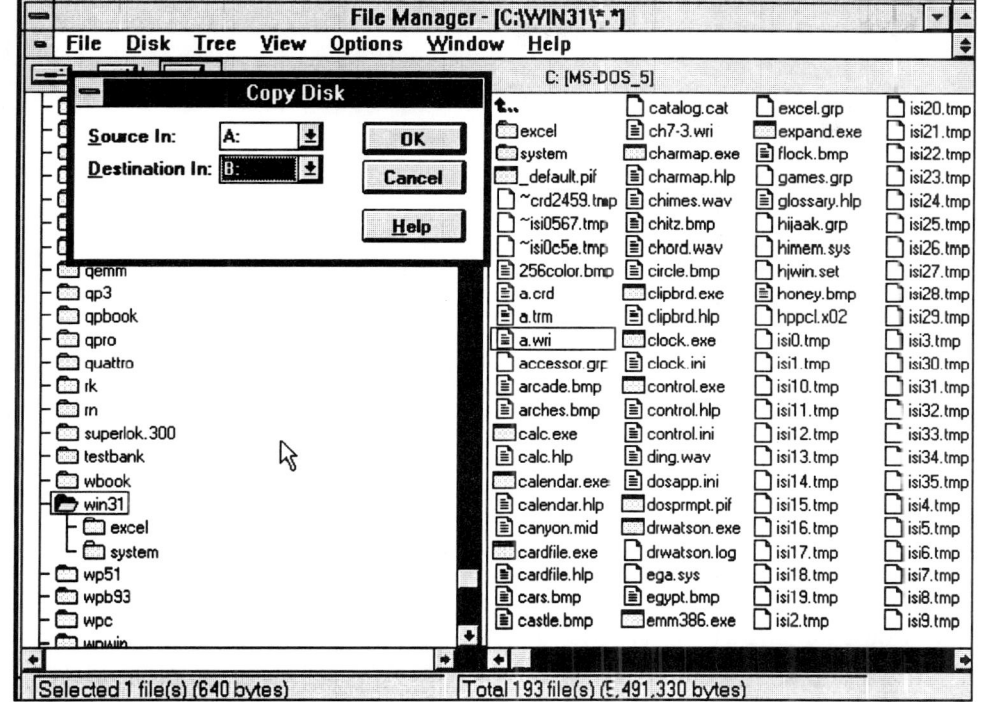

Figure 11-20
Copy Disk dialog box

1. Insert a formatted disk into a drive.
2. From the Disk menu, select the Make System Disk option.
3. Identify the correct drive and click on OK.

SUMMARY

This chapter focused on the important operations of the File Manager. After explaining the process of getting in and getting out of the File Manager, it showed you how to select, create, rename, copy, move, and change files and directories. The chapter also presented the steps for sorting the contents of a directory window and described the file association feature of Windows. The chapter concluded with guidelines for formatting, labeling, and copying a disk and creating a system disk.

REVIEW QUESTIONS

*These questions are answered in Appendix A.
1. What is the File Manager?
2. What are some of the tasks performed by the File Manager?
*3. How do you start the File Manager? How do you exit from the File Manager?
4. What is a directory window? What is included in a directory window?
5. How do you select a file by means of the mouse?
6. What are file types in Windows?
7. What are some of the parts of a directory window?
*8. How do you select several files that are in sequence?
9. How do you select several files that are not in sequence?
10. How do you deselect a file?

11. How do you sort the contents of a directory by name, size, and the last modification date?
*12. How do you specify the type of a file to be displayed?
13. What are wildcards? How are they used in the File Manager?
14. What are some of the rules for naming a file or a directory?
*15. What are reserved words? Why can't you use the reserved words for naming a file or a directory?
16. How do you create a directory?
17. How do you search a directory?
18. How do you use wildcards for searching a directory?
19. How do you erase a file from a directory?
*20. How do you rename a file?
21. How do you copy the entire contents of one directory to another directory?
22. What is the file association feature?
23. What are some of the advantages of associating files with a software application?
*24. How do you remove file association?
25. What kind of files can be printed through the File Manager?
26. How do you format a disk? What are some of the options for capacity?
*27. How many characters can be included in a disk label?
28. How do you copy a disk?
29. What is a system disk? How can you create a system disk?

HANDS-ON EXPERIENCE

1. Start the File Manager and do the following:
   a. Check the contents of the directory window. What is available?
   b. Check to see how many drives are displayed.
   c. Select three files that are in sequence (if you have any).
   d. Select a directory.
   e. Select three files that are not in sequence (if you have any).
   f. Deselect one of the selected files.
   g. Change your drive from C to A. Change it back from A to C.
2. Exit the File Manager and start it again. Then do the following:
   a. Select a directory and sort its contents first by file name, then by file size, and finally by the last date of modification.
   b. Display only one group of your files, for example, all your EXE, WK1, or BAK files.
   c. Create two directories on a disk in drive A under the names FIRST and SECOND.
   d. Select one file from your C drive and copy it to both the FIRST and SECOND directories under TEST1 and TEST2.
   e. Rename TEST1 to TRY1.
   f. Erase TEST2.
3. Using the file association capability of Windows do the following:
   a. Make sure that all your WRI files are associated with Write. Now to test the association, double-click on a file with the WRI extension. At this time Write should be started and your selected file opened.
   b. Print one of the WRI files by means of the Print option from the File menu.

Chapter 11 Managing Files and Floppy Disks Using the File Manager

    c. Associate another file with a software application that you have and print it using the Print command from the File menu in the File Manager.

    d. Remove the association created in step c.

4. Start the File Manager again (if it is not already started) and do the following:

    a. Format a disk in drive A with 360 K, 720 K, 1.2 MB, or 1.44 MB capacity.

    b. Format a disk in drive A with one of the above capacities and label it as TEST.

    c. Create a system disk.

    d. Copy the contents of one diskette in drive A to a disk in drive B. If you have only one drive, A serves as both A and B.

    e. Exit the File Manager.

KEY TERMS

Directory window   Label option   System disk

File association

KEY COMMANDS

Disk (to invoke the Disk pull-down menu)

File (to invoke the File pull-down menu)

View (to invoke the View pull-down menu)

Window (to invoke the Window pull-down menu)

MISCONCEPTIONS AND SOLUTIONS

Misconception The split window is the default view for a directory window. This is not always what you want.

    Solution By using the View command from the File Manager, you can change the view to display tree only (by selecting Tree Only) or to display directory only (by selecting Directory Only).

Misconception You want to select all your files for certain operations but using a wildcard is time consuming.

    Solution You can select all files in a directory by clicking on the first one then pressing Ctrl-/ (forward slash).

Misconception You decide to cancel the selection of a file, but going through the Select Files dialog box is time consuming.

    Solution Press Ctrl-\ (back slash) to cancel a selection.

Misconception Changing drives by means of the Disk menu is time consuming.

    Solution Press and hold down the Ctrl key while typing the letter of the drive that you want to select, for example, Ctrl-A for selecting the A drive. You can also click on the desired drive in the drive icon just below the menu bar.

Misconception When you change drives, File Manager searches the drive and displays its contents—a long process.

    Solution You can stop this process by pressing the Esc key. If you stop the process, however, only a partial directory tree is displayed, as indicated by the status bar at the bottom of the File Manager window.

Misconception You change one or several settings of Windows. When you start Windows again later, you do not see your changes.

    Solution Check the Save Settings on Exit in the Options menu of the File Manager or Program Manager. There must be a check mark next to it. If there is no check mark, your settings will not be saved for future use.

Misconception   You are moving files or directories to a destination on the same drive by pressing and holding down the Shift key and dragging the mouse.

> **Solution**   If your source and destination are on the same drive, you do not need to press and hold down the Shift key. Just drag the mouse.

Misconception   You are copying files or directories to a destination on another drive by pressing and holding down the Ctrl key and dragging the mouse.

> **Solution**   If your source and destination are on different drives, you do not need to press and hold down the Ctrl key, just drag the mouse.

Misconception   You are trying to print a file through the File Manager, but your attempt has not been successful.

> **Solution**   Some applications do not support printing though the File Manager. If this is the case, or if a file is not associated with an application, you must open the appropriate application and print the file from there.

Misconception   You have tried unsuccessfully to use the Quick Format option from the Format Disk dialog box.

> **Solution**   The Quick Format option works only for disks that have been formatted previously.

Misconception   You want to rename a file after it has been copied or moved from another directory. So you move or copy it and use the Rename command to change its name to a new name. You are frustrated by the time spent doing this.

> **Solution**   You can rename a file at the same time you copy or move it. Use the File menu's Copy or Move command and supply a new name in the To box.

ARE YOU READY TO MOVE ON?

Multiple Choice

1. Which of the following cannot be done through the File Manager?
   a. viewing files and directories
   b. creating directories
   c. removing directories
   d. copying and moving directories
   e. they all can be done

2. To exit the File Manager, from the File menu select
   a. Move
   b. Leave
   c. Exit
   d. Terminate
   e. none of the above

3. Which of the following is not included in the menu bar of the File Manager?
   a. Copy
   b. File
   c. Options
   d. Window
   e. Help

4. A directory window includes
   a. the drive icons on your computer
   b. a listing of all the directories on your computer
   c. navigation arrows to display more files and directories

Chapter 11 Managing Files and Floppy Disks Using the File Manager

   d. all of the above
   e. only a and b
5. What is the maximum number of characters a file or directory name can be?
   a. 5
   b. 10
   c. 12
   d. 11
   e. 8
6. To change the current drive to another drive, you can either use the mouse or choose the Select Drive option from which menu?
   a. Tree
   b. Disk
   c. File
   d. Options
   e. View
7. By means of the File Manager you can sort the contents of a directory based on
   a. name
   b. type
   c. size
   d. all of the above
   e. only a and c
8. The File Type menu box in the File Type dialog box includes all of the following except
   a. directories
   b. programs
   c. specific spreadsheet programs such as Lotus 1-2-3
   d. documents
   e. all of the above
9. For naming a file or a directory, which option from the following choices is *not* correct?
   a. The reserved words such as COM1 and COM2 can be used.
   b. The name can be up to eight characters.
   c. The name cannot include a period (.).
   d. The name cannot include an equal sign (=).
   e. The name cannot include spaces.
10. Using the File menu, you can do all of the following except
    a. copy a file
    b. graph a file
    c. delete a file
    d. rename a file
    e. print a file

True/False

1. The File Manager allows you to move or copy a file or a directory.
2. Generally speaking, file association makes it slower to use an application with an associated file.
3. To establish file association, you first must select the application software, then select a given extension.

4. If the desired application is not listed in the Associate With box, you can use the Browse option to find it.
5. The Print command prints a file that is associated with an application.
6. Using the Format option from the Disk menu, you can only format a 1.2 MB disk.
7. A label for the internal name of a disk can only be up to eight characters long.
8. When you copy the contents of a disk by using the Copy Disk Command onto another disk, the original contents of the second disk (destination disk) is lost.
9. You cannot generate a system disk using the Disk menu.
10. The File Manager shares several features with MS-DOS and PC-DOS.

ANSWERS

Multiple Choice	True/False
1. e	1. T
2. c	2. F
3. a	3. F
4. d	4. T
5. e	5. T
6. b	6. F
7. d	7. F
8. c	8. T
9. a	9. F
10. b	10. T

Additional Windows Accessories

12-1   Introduction
12-2   Calculator: An Overview
      12-2-1   Performing Simple Calculations
      12-2-2   Correcting Mistakes
      12-2-3   Using Operators and Symbols
      12-2-4   Conducting Simple Operations
12-3   Calendar: An Overview
      12-3-1   Layout of the Calendar Screen
      12-3-2   Performing a Simple Task
      12-3-3   Using Cursor-Movement Keys
      12-3-4   Setting an Alarm for an Event
      12-3-5   Calendar File Menu
      12-3-6   Calendar Edit Menu
      12-3-7   Calendar View Menu
      12-3-8   Calendar Show Menu
      12-3-9   Calendar Alarm Menu
      12-3-10 Calendar Options Menu
      12-3-11 Calendar Help Menu
12-4   Clock: An Overview
12-5   Cardfile: An Overview
      12-5-1   An Application of the Cardfile
12-6   Notepad: An Overview
12-7   Terminal: An Overview
      12-7-1   Components Required to Use Terminal
      12-7-2   Starting the Terminal Application
      12-7-3   Terminal Application
12-8   Character Map, Media Player, Recorder, and Sound Recorder

12-1
INTRODUCTION

In this chapter we consider six additional applications available in Windows 3.1 Accessories: Calculator, Calendar, Clock, Cardfile, Notepad, and Terminal. The chapter provides instructions for getting in and getting out of these very popular applications and a working knowledge for using them. For a detailed discussion of the applications, consult the Windows 3.1 manual. The chapter also introduces the accessories Character Map, Media Player, Recorder, and Sound Recorder.

12-2
CALCULATOR: AN OVERVIEW

The **Calculator** option in the Accessories group can be operated in either Standard or Scientific mode. In Standard mode, the Calculator can be used for simple calculations. In Scientific mode, the Calculator can be used for sophisticated scientific and statistical calculations such as average, standard deviation, sum of the squares, and much more. Now let us become familiar with the Calculator.

First, make sure that the Program Manager screen is displayed. Then, if necessary, double-click on the Accessories icon to open the Accessories group window. Position the mouse pointer on the Calculator icon in the window and double-click the left button of the mouse to execute the Calculator application. After a few seconds, the Calculator will be displayed; see Figure 12–1. Note that the Calculator cannot be maximized to the full size of the screen.

By default, the Calculator is in Standard mode when it is first started. To view the Scientific Calculator, put the mouse pointer on the View option in the Calculator main menu and click the left button of the mouse; then click the left button again on the Scientific option. Figure 12–2 displays the Scientific mode. The two calculators have many differences in appearance and performance. We will be working with the Calculator in Standard mode, so click left on the View option again; then click left on the Standard option.

Figure 12–1
Calculator screen in Standard mode

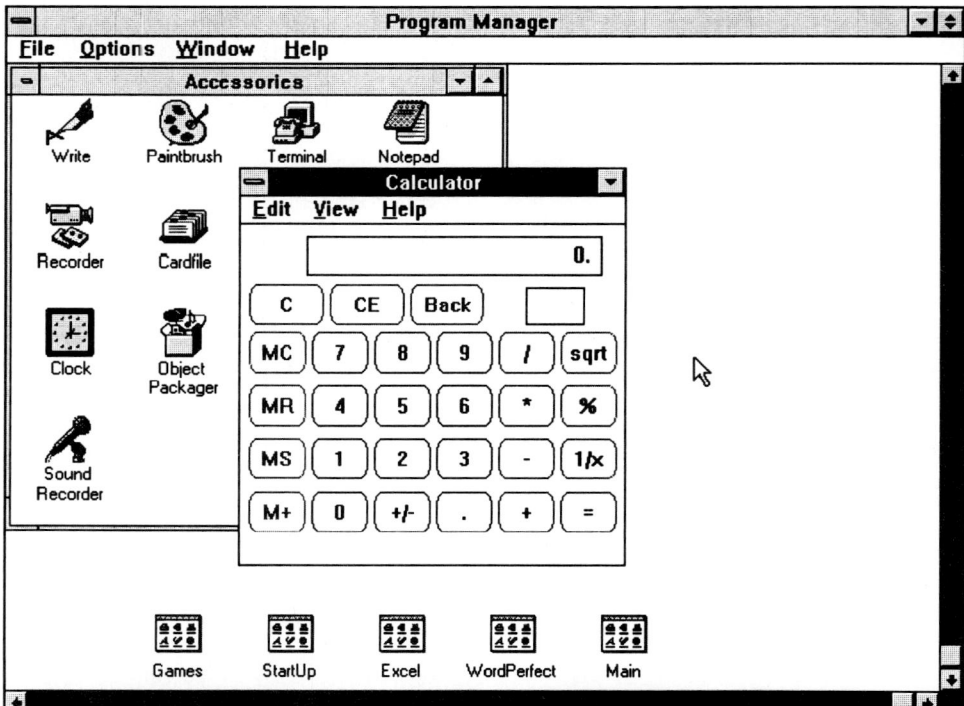

Chapter 12   Additional Windows Accessories

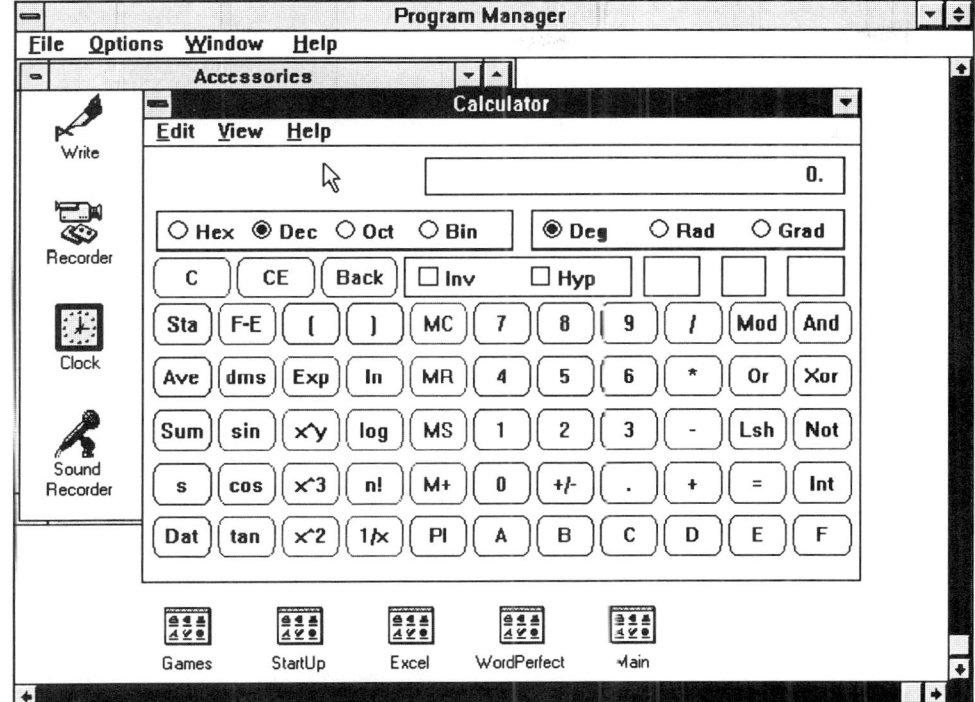

Figure 12-2
Calculator screen in Scientific mode

Performing Simple Calculations   12-2-1

Let us say you would like to use the Calculator to multiply 10 by 2. Follow these steps:

1. Enter the first number in the Calculator. Do this by manually entering the number at the keyboard or by clicking on the appropriate number using the mouse. We typed *10*.
2. Either type or click on the desired operator (+, −, *, /, and so forth) for your calculation. We typed * for multiplication.
3. Enter the second number in the Calculator. We typed *2*.
4. Press the Enter key, or type = (equal sign), or click on the = button in the Calculator. Windows instantly displays the result of your calculation in the display window. In this case, you will see 20.

   Whether you type the operator or click on it, the operator will *not* be displayed. You will see only a quick blink on the operator that you are using.

Correcting Mistakes   12-2-2

There are several ways to correct a number or calculation. Use the following buttons on the Calculator to make editing corrections:

      Back   Backspace—to erase the right-most digit of the current numeric entry. The Backspace key on the keyboard preforms the same function.

	CE	Clear entry—to clear the displayed number. If you have entered an incorrect number into a formula or calculation, click on the CE button to clear it.
	C	Clear—to clear the current calculation. If you have constructed a formula incorrectly, click on the C button to clear it.

12-2-3 Using Operators and Symbols

The Calculator has standard **arithmetic operators** for constructing formulas:

+	Addition
−	Subtraction
/	Division
*	Multiplication

Other **arithmetic symbols** and buttons on the Calculator include the following:

sqrt	Square root—to calculate the square root of a number (e.g., the square root of 25 is 5)
%	Percent—to calculate percentages
1/x	Invert—to calculate the reciprocal of the displayed number
=	Equals—to perform or execute the desired calculation
+/−	Plus/minus—to change the sign of the displayed number
.	Decimal—to enter a decimal point in numeric entries

Finally, the Calculator has several built-in memory functions:

MC	Memory clear—to clear any stored value from memory
MR	Memory recall—to recall any stored value from memory
MS	Memory store—to store any value in memory for later use
M+	Memory add—to add a value to the value stored in memory

12-2-4 Conducting Simple Operations

Working with the Calculator is simple. Follow the steps outlined next to learn how to use this powerful accessory:

1. Click on number 1, then click on 0 (zero), then click on the decimal point (.), then click on number 5. You should see the entry 10.5 in the Calculator display window.
2. Click on the * (asterisk) button to indicate multiplication.
3. Click on number 2. The number 2 will automatically replace the entry 10.5 in the display window.
4. Click on the = (equal sign) button to execute the calculation. Windows responds by displaying 21 in the display window.
5. Click on the / (forward slash) button to indicate division. Click on the number 7; then click on the = button. Windows responds by displaying the number 3 in the display window.
6. Click on the + (plus sign).

Chapter 12   Additional Windows Accessories

7. Click on the 1 (one).
8. Click on the = button. You should see 4 in the display window.
9. Click on the sqrt button. Windows displays the number 2 in the display window, which is the square root of 4.
10. Click on the MS button to store the number 2 in memory. The letter M will be displayed on the squared box underneath the display window.
11. Click on the C button to clear the current calculation.
12. Enter the number 8 either by typing the number from the keyboard or by clicking on the 8 button.
13. Click on the + button to indicate addition.
14. Click on the MR (Memory recall) button. The stored memory value, 2, appears in the Calculator display window.
15. Click on the = button to execute the calculation. Windows displays the number 10.
16. Click on the C button to clear the current calculation.
17. Click on the MC (Memory clear) button to clear memory of the stored value (2). The letter M will be erased from the squared box underneath the display window.

You have now practiced with most of the buttons available in the Standard mode of the Calculator. As you have seen, the Calculator is a flexible tool that is easy to learn and use.

12-3 CALENDAR: AN OVERVIEW

The **Calendar** option in the Accessories group allows you to easily schedule and track daily events, view an entire month's activities at a glance, set an alarm to remind you of special events, and much more. To become familiar with the Calendar, let's practice.

First, make sure that the Accessories window is displayed. Position the mouse pointer on the Calendar icon in the Accessories window; then double-click the left button of the mouse to execute the Calendar application. Click left on the maximize button to let Calendar fill the entire screen. After a few seconds, the starting screen of Calendar will be displayed (Figure 12–3).

12-3-1 Layout of the Calendar Screen

As you can see in Figure 12–3, at this point the title bar at the top of the Calendar screen reads [Untitled]. Immediately below the title bar is the Calendar main menu, which contains the following options: File, Edit, View, Show, Alarm, Options, and Help. These menu options will be discussed later in this section.

The current system time and date are displayed below the menu options. They can be changed through DOS or the Windows Control Panel by means of the Date/Time option. The contents of the area below the time and date depends on what view mode the Calendar is in, that is, Day or Month. By default, the Calendar is in the **Day view mode**. To switch to **Month view mode**, press the F9 function key (you can also use the View menu).

The Calendar in Month view mode (Figure 12–4) displays the entire current month. Columns represent days of the week and rows represent weeks in the month. Notice that the current date is highlighted.

Figure 12-3
Starting screen of the Windows Calendar

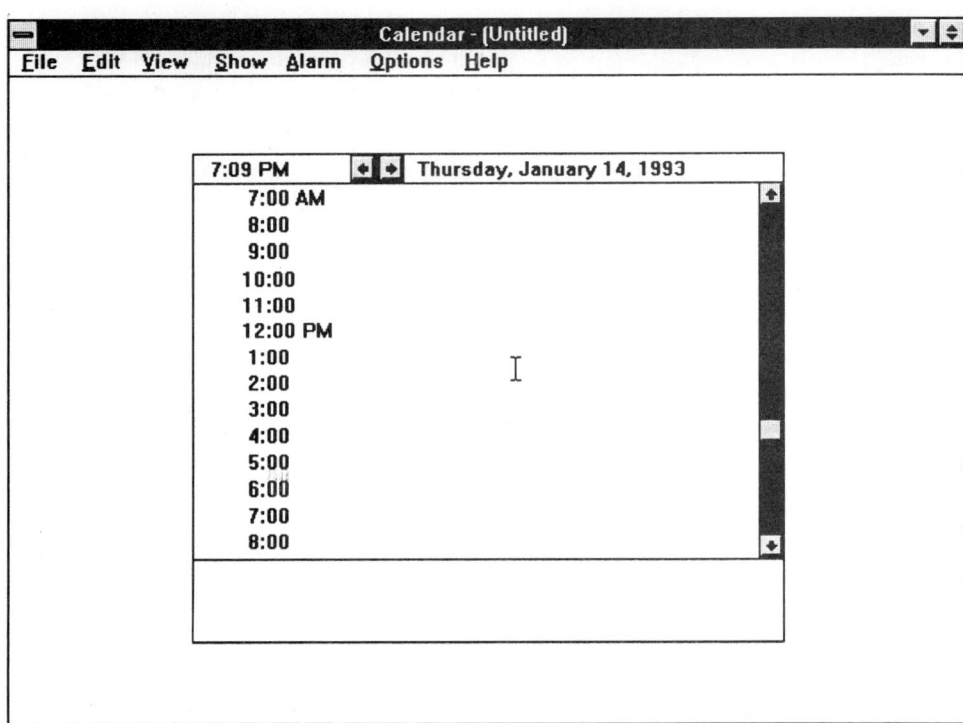

Figure 12-4
Calendar in Month view mode

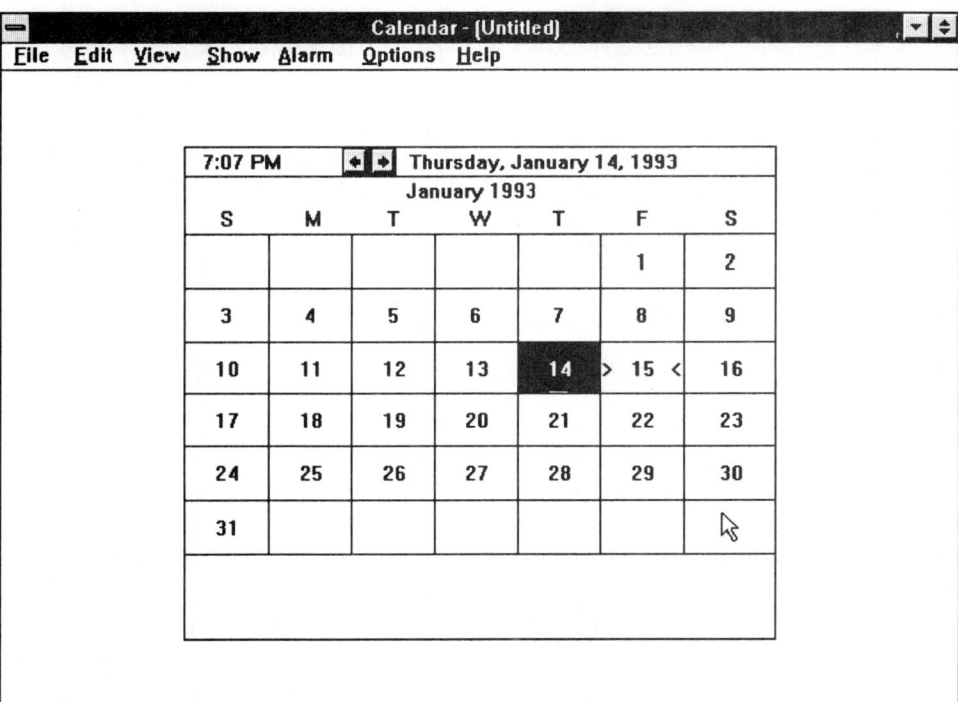

If you press the F8 function key, the Calendar automatically switches back to Day view mode. The cursor should be flashing next to the starting time (7:00 AM). Press the up-arrow key until the cursor stops at the top of the time readings. The earliest time for each day is 12:00 AM. Now press the down-arrow key until the cursor stops at the bottom of the time readings. The cursor should be flashing next to 11:00, the ending time for each day.

Performing a Simple Task

12-3-2

Let's try entering an appointment into the Calendar. You want to enter an appointment for the day after tomorrow. Assume today is January 14, 1993, as shown in Figure 12-4. To change the date that the Calendar is displaying, press the Ctrl-PgDn key combination twice. You can also click twice on the right arrow in the time/date display area. Notice that the date displayed in the Calendar now reflects the date two days from now (January 16, 1993, as shown in Figure 12-5), and that once again, the cursor is flashing next to 7:00 AM. Press the down-arrow key twice to move the cursor to the 9:00 entry. Now type *Meeting with accounting department to discuss cost increase*. Notice that as you type, the text scrolls off the screen to the right, so that you cannot see the entire entry.

Now let's mark this appointment with a special symbol to remind us of the meeting. To do this, press the F6 function key. The Calendar responds by displaying the Day Markings dialog box, which gives you five different mark symbols to choose from (Figure 12-5). Click left on Symbol 4 - x. The check box for symbol 4 will be filled with an x. Next, click on OK. You will not see the special symbol right away, but don't worry—you will see it later when you switch back to the Month view mode.

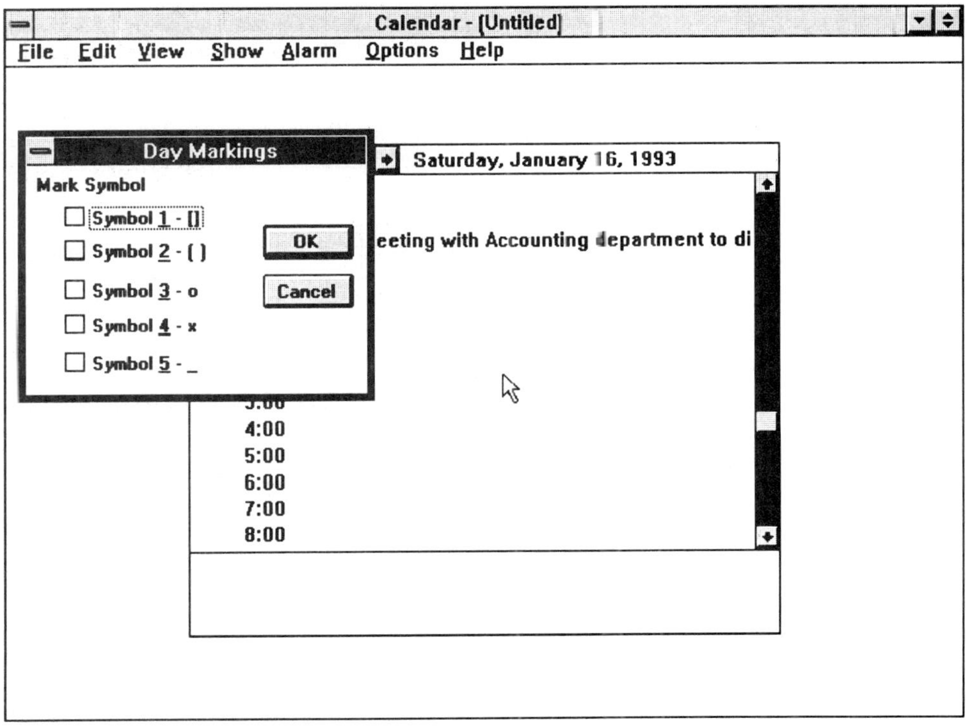

Figure 12-5
Day Markings symbols

Press the down-arrow key three more times to move the cursor to the 12:00 PM entry. Now type *Lunch with Dr. Prestage - Bistro*. To give this appointment a special marking, press the F6 key; then click left on the Symbol 1 – [] option. Notice that you now have have two symbols marked. Click left on OK to return to the Calendar. You now want to return to the previous day in the Calendar. One way to do this is to press the Ctrl-PgUp key combination, as you have already seen. However, let's try a different way of changing the date this time. Click left on the left-arrow icon in the time/date display area immediately below the title bar. Notice that the date automatically changes to reflect the day immediately prior to the date for which you were just making appointments. Press the F9 function key to switch the Calendar to Month view mode (Figure 12–6).

Several new pieces of information are now displayed in the Calendar. First, the current date in the Calendar has a less than symbol (<) to the right and a greater than symbol (>) to the left of the date (see Figure 12–6). Second, the date that you were in when you switched to Month view mode is highlighted in a color different from that of the rest of the days. Finally, the date for which you made your appointments has two further pieces of information (see Figure 12–6):

- The number of the date is surrounded by a box.
- A small "x" appears above and to the left of the date number.

The small marks on the appointment date represent the special symbols that you choose to remind you of your appointments. In another situation you might want to give some special symbol to birthdays, so that every time you are in the Month view mode you can easily spot the birthdays for that month. Or perhaps you'll decide to surround your anniversary with a box—you *know* you

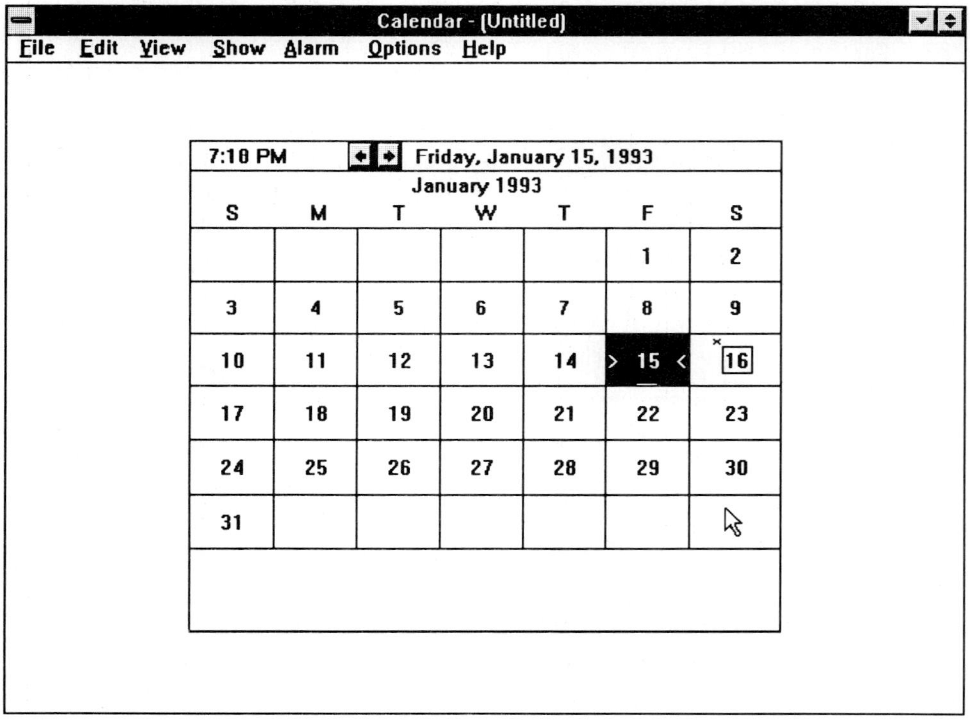

Figure 12–6
Calendar in the Month view mode with special markings

won't forget it again this year! These special symbols assign particular meanings to days, thereby giving you information about what is coming up.

Using Cursor-Movement Keys

12-3-3

While in the Month view mode, you can use the keys outlined in Table 12-1 to change to a different day or date. You can also use the options available in the Show menu to relocate the cursor to a different date in the Calendar. Click left on the Show option in the main menu. The Show menu (Figure 12-7) includes four options:

Today	Automatically relocates the cursor to the current date (the date matching the system date)
Previous	Same as PgUp
Next	Same as PgDn
Date	Prompts you to enter the desired date; allows quick movement to a specific date in the Calendar

Let's experiment with these cursor-movement methods. Display the Show menu and select Date. The Show Date dialog box appears on the screen and prompts you to enter the desired date. Type the date *01/01/95*. Press Enter or click left on OK. The Calendar instantly redisplays, highlighting the date requested. You can also press the F4 function key to request a new date. This method of switching dates is convenient because it allows you to quickly access a particular date. You can go as far back as 01/01/80 (which was a Tuesday, by the way) and as far forward as 12/31/2099 (a Thursday)!

In the next section, we will set an alarm to remind us of a new appointment. But first, let's save the Calendar to safeguard the changes that we have made so far. To do this, click left on File; then click left on Save. The Save As dialog box will be displayed; it allows you to enter a file name for the current calendar. Calendar files have the extension CAL. Type *CALENDAR* and click left on OK. Your calendar will be saved under the name CALENDAR.CAL, which you can verify by looking at the title bar of the Calendar after you have saved the file. There is no limit to the number of Calendars that you can create.

Key	Action
Right arrow (→)	Highlights the next date in the month. If you are on the last date of the month, the right-arrow key moves the highlight to the first date of the next month.
Left arrow (←)	Highlights the previous date in the month. If you are on the first date of the month, the left-arrow key moves the highlight to the last date of the previous month.
PgUp	Highlights the corresponding date in the previous month
PgDn	Highlights the corresponding date in the next month
Left-arrow icon	Same as PgUp
Right arrow icon	Same as PgDn

Table 12-1
Cursor-movement keys

Figure 12-7
Show menu

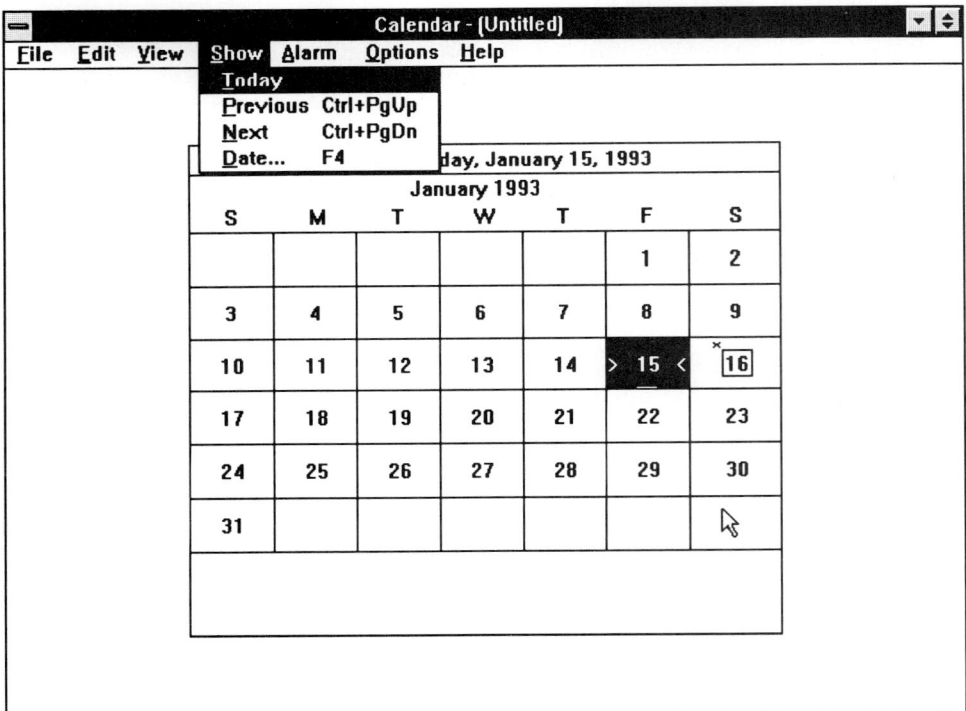

Every person in your family or office can maintain his or her own calendar, separate from everyone else's, just by giving their calendar a different file name.

12-3-4 Setting an Alarm for an Event

Let's try **setting an alarm** to remind you to go on vacation. The first thing you need to do is return to the current date in the Calendar. To do this, click left on Show; then click left on Today. Now that you are back on the current date, press the F8 function key to return to Day view mode. Look at the current time displayed at the upper left of the Calendar. We will set an alarm for 5 minutes from whatever time your Calendar is currently displaying. Press the F7 function key; the Calendar responds by displaying the Special Time dialog box. Type in a time that is 5 minutes past the time that the Calendar is displaying. Next, click left on the AM or the PM option, depending on which is appropriate for the special time that you are setting. Finally, click left on Insert to place the time into your Calendar. Your cursor should be flashing next to the new time. Press the F5 function key. You should see an alarm (small bell) symbol displayed to the left of the new time that you entered (Figure 12–8). Type *GO ON VACATION* and press the Enter key.

Now just sit back and wait for the alarm to go off. When the alarm does go off, you will hear a series of four beeps. Also, the Calendar will display a dialog box with the message "Please remember . . ." at the top, the time of the alarm, the message that you typed next to the time, and finally, an OK button at the bottom. Press the Enter key or click left on the OK button to return to the main Calendar screen.

If your computer is off, or if Windows is not running, or if you are running Windows but the Calendar application is not running at the time that

Chapter 12 Additional Windows Accessories

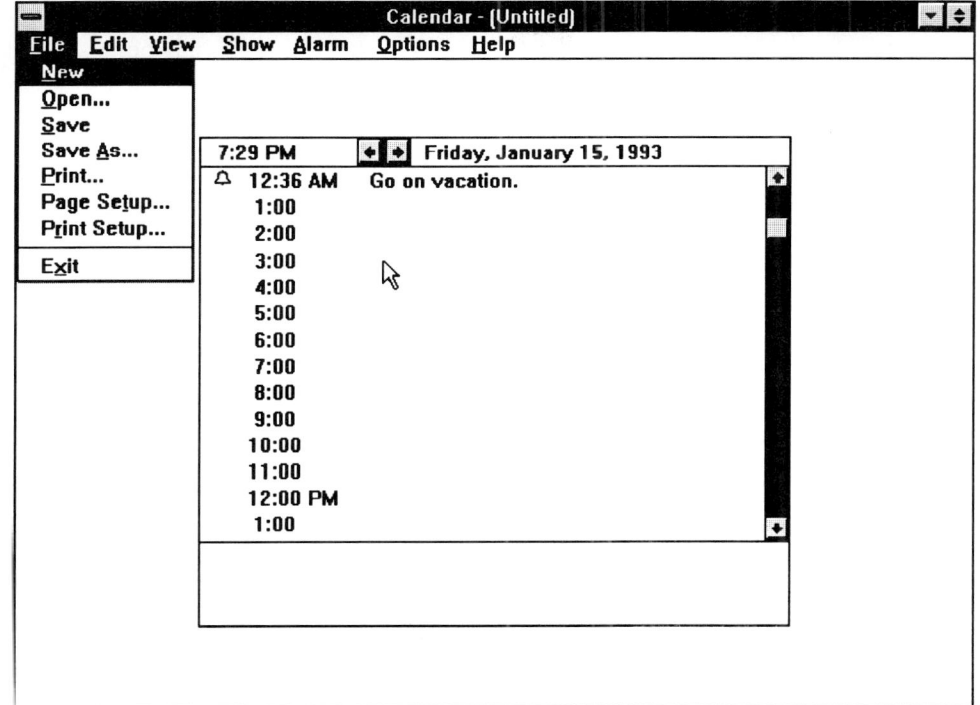

Figure 12-8
Calendar File menu

the alarm is set to go off, no alarm will go off. In the next sections, we discuss the contents of each menu option shown at the top of the Calendar screen.

Calendar File Menu 12-3-5

The File menu includes eight commands, or options (refer to Figure 12-8). Let us briefly discuss each.

The New option allows you to begin a brand new Calendar that has not been modified in any way. The Open option allows you to open (retrieve) a Calendar that has already been created so that you can continue to work with it, check appointments and upcoming events, and so forth.

The Save option allows you to save your Calendar. If it is the first time the Calendar has been saved, you will be prompted to enter a file name. If it is not the first time, your Calendar is saved automatically with the current file name, without further prompting. The Save As option also allows you to save your Calendar. It differs from the Save option, however, in that even if the Calendar has been saved previously, you are prompted to enter a file name. By means of this option, you can save a previously created Calendar under a different file name without altering the original Calendar.

The Print option allows you to print a Calendar. In the Print dialog box that is displayed, you can specify a single date or a date range to be printed. All of your entries will be printed for the specified date range with appropriate date and time headings. The Page Setup option displays the Page Setup dialog box, which allows you to specify a header, footer, and margins for a printed Calendar. The Print Setup option enables you to select the printer on which you would like to have a Calendar printed, the page orientation, the paper size, print quality, and so forth.

Windows 3.1

The Exit option should be used when you are finished working with a Calendar. If you have made changes to the Calendar that have not been saved, you will be notified that changes to the Calendar file have been made and will be asked if you want to save the changes. The options available in response to this prompt are Yes, No, and Cancel. Selecting Yes saves your changes and selecting No does not save your changes; both options allow you to exit. Selecting Cancel aborts the Exit command and returns you to the Calendar.

12-3-6 Calendar Edit Menu

As Figure 12-9 illustrates, the Edit menu has four options. Let us briefly explain each.

The Cut option, also accessed by pressing the Ctrl-X key combination, allows you to cut (erase) an appointment from the Calendar. The text to be cut must first be blocked (highlighted) by means of the click and drag method of selecting text. If desired, the appointment can be pasted to another time or date using the Paste option.

The Copy option, which can also be accessed by pressing the Ctrl-C key combination, allows you to copy an appointment to another spot in the Calendar. The text to be copied must first be blocked (highlighted) by means of the click and drag method of selecting text. The Paste option can then be used to place the copied text into its new location.

The Paste option, also accessed by pressing the Ctrl-V key combination is used together with the Cut and Copy options to move or copy text from other areas of the Calendar. The selected text must have already been cut or copied.

The Remove option allows you to remove all the appointments for a particular date or a range of dates. Use this option to prevent old appointments from cluttering up your Calendar.

Figure 12-9
Calendar Edit menu

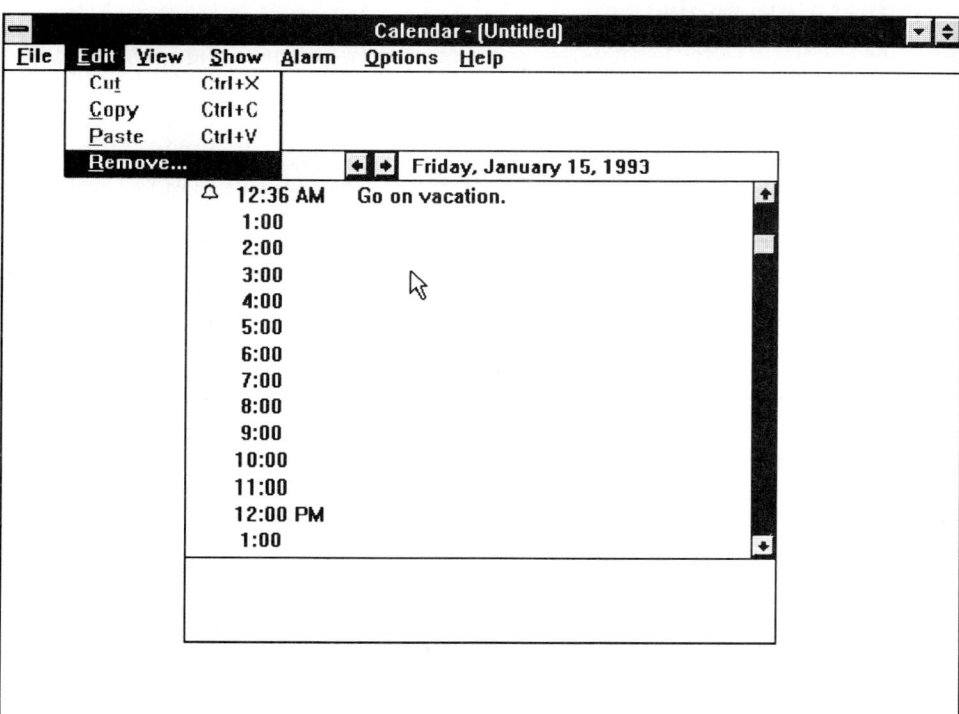

Chapter 12 Additional Windows Accessories

Calendar View Menu

12-3-7

As Figure 12–10 illustrates, the View menu includes two options: Day and Month. The Day option, also accessed by pressing the F8 function key, switches your Calendar into Day view mode. Month, also accessed by pressing the F9 function key, switches your Calendar into Month view mode.

Calendar Show Menu

12-3-8

The Show menu (see Figure 12–7) has four options. The Today option returns you to the current date in the Calendar. The previous option displays the previous day if you are in Day view mode and displays the corresponding date of the previous month if you are in Month view mode. This option can also be accessed by pressing the Ctrl-PgUp key combination if you are in Day view mode. The next option displays the next day if you are in Day view mode and displays the corresponding date of the next month if you are in Month view mode. This option can also be accessed by pressing Ctrl-PgDn if you are in Day view mode.

The Date option, also accessed by pressing the F4 function key, allows you to specify a particular date to view. Valid dates range from 01/01/80 through 12/31/2099.

Calendar Alarm Menu

12-3-9

As Figure 12–11 illustrates, the Alarm menu has two options: Set and Controls. The Set option sets an alarm on the time by which the cursor is flashing. In Day view mode, you can access this option by pressing the F5 function key. The Controls option allows you to specify whether the alarm should beep and

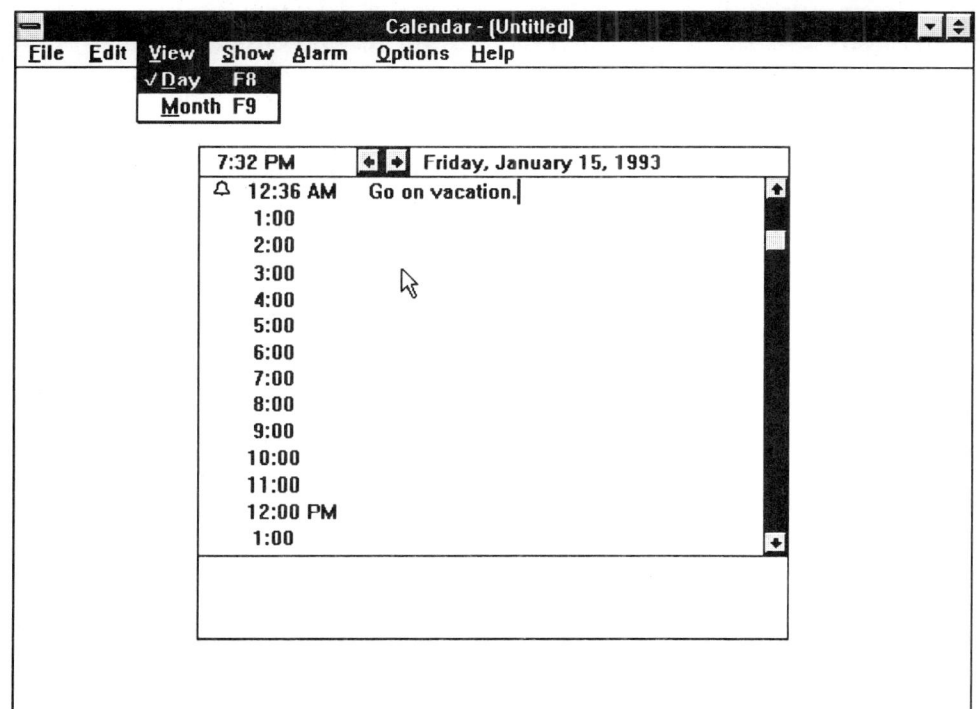

Figure 12–10
Calendar View menu

Figure 12–11
Calendar Alarm menu

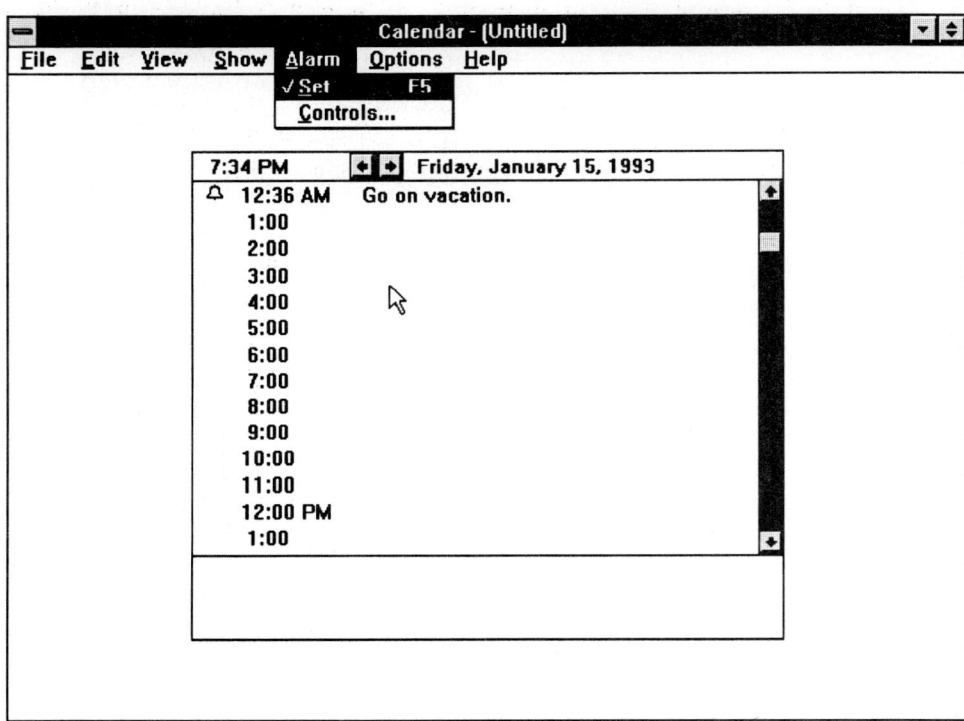

whether it should beep early. Using the Early Ring option, you can set the alarm to go off up to 10 minutes before the specified alarm time.

12–3–10 Calendar Options Menu

Figure 12–12 illustrates the three choices in the Options menu. The Mark option allows you to place up to five different special marks into your calendar to add meaning to particular dates. The marks, which also can be accessed by pressing the F6 function key, can only be seen in Month view mode.

The Special Time option, also accessed by pressing the F7 function key, allows you to insert or delete special times (a time not displayed in the time list) into your calendar. The Special Time option can only be accessed in Day view mode.

The Day Settings option allows you to change the interval between times in the Day view mode from 60 minutes to 15 or 30 minutes. By means of this option, you can also set your Calendar to display times using the 12-hour or 24-hour display format and indicate a different starting time if 7:00 AM is not appropriate to your needs.

12–3–11 Calendar Help Menu

The Help menu (Figure 12–13) explains how to use the Calendar and provides additional information on all of the Calendar's features. One of the limitations of the Calendar is that it is not capable of scheduling repeated events. For example, you cannot tell the Calendar to set a meeting for the first Wednesday of every month at 3:00 p.m. or a staff meeting every Tuesday at 7:00 a.m.

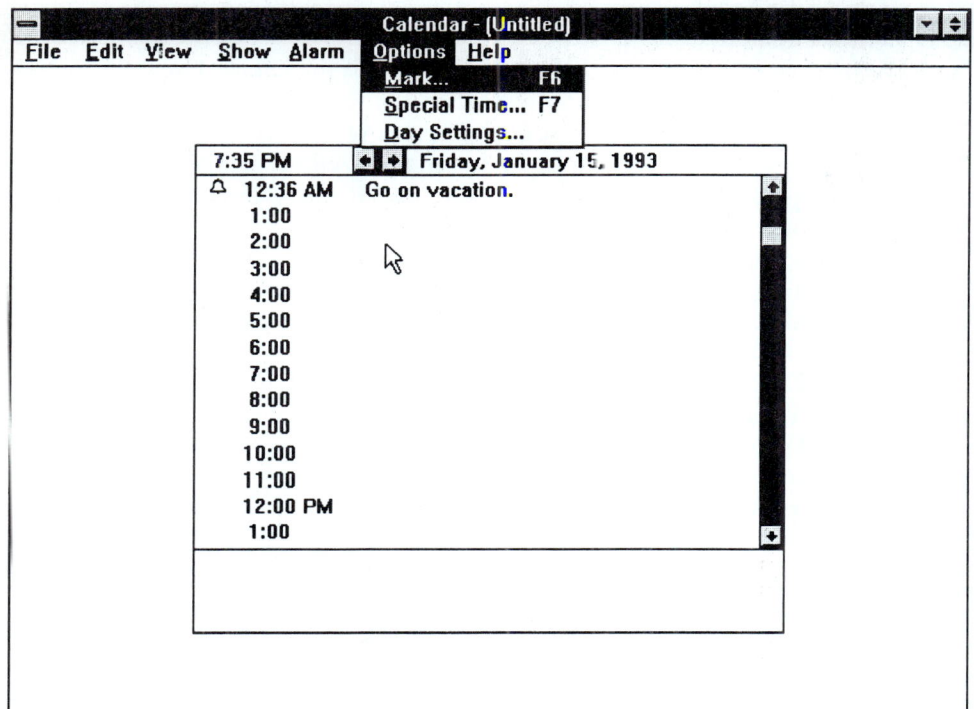

Figure 12-12
Calendar Options menu

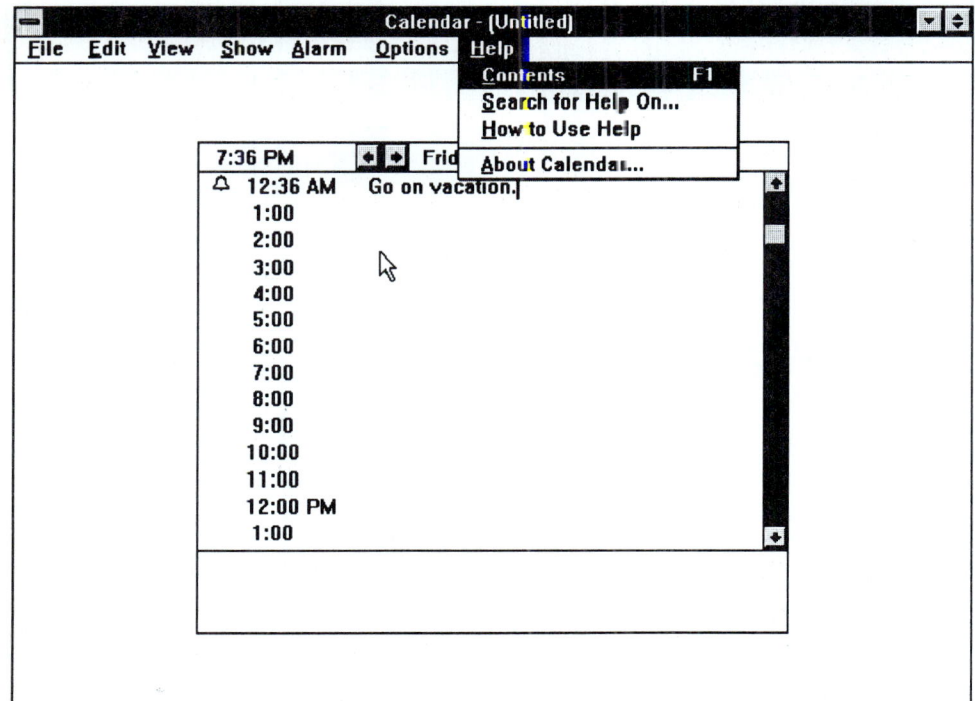

Figure 12-13
Calendar Help menu

12-4
CLOCK: AN OVERVIEW

Another important utility in the Accessories group is the **Clock**. Use the Clock to continuously display the current time and date on your screen. To run the Clock application, double-click on the Clock icon in the Accessories group; a Clock will appear on your screen. In Figure 12–14 we maximized the size of the clock. The Clock can display an analog or digital face, and it has some other interesting features, as you will soon see.

At the upper left of the Clock is the control-menu box. Just to the right of this is the title bar, and at the upper right are the minimize and maximize icons. Below this is the menu line, which has one only option: Settings. The middle of the Clock displays the current time and date.

If you click left on Settings, you will be presented with a screen similar to the one in Figure 12–15. Notice the seven options.

The Analog option switches the Clock into Analog display mode. In this mode, the Clock face has 12 dots representing the hours of 1 through 12, an hour hand, a minute hand, and a second hand. The Digital option switches the Clock into Digital display mode. In this mode, the Clock face displays the current time in the format of HH/MM/SS AM/PM format and the current date in this format: MM/DD/YY.

The Set Font option allows you to change the screen font that displays the time and date. It is available only in Digital display mode.

The No Title option is used to disable the display of the top two lines of the clock, thereby leaving only a square dialog box with the time/date display. Disabling the top two lines can also be done by double-clicking anywhere inside the Clock display. To bring the top two lines back, double-click again. The Seconds option is for disabling the display of seconds, and the Date option is for disabling the display of the date in Digital display mode.

Figure 12–14
Windows Clock starting screen

Chapter 12 Additional Windows Accessories   237

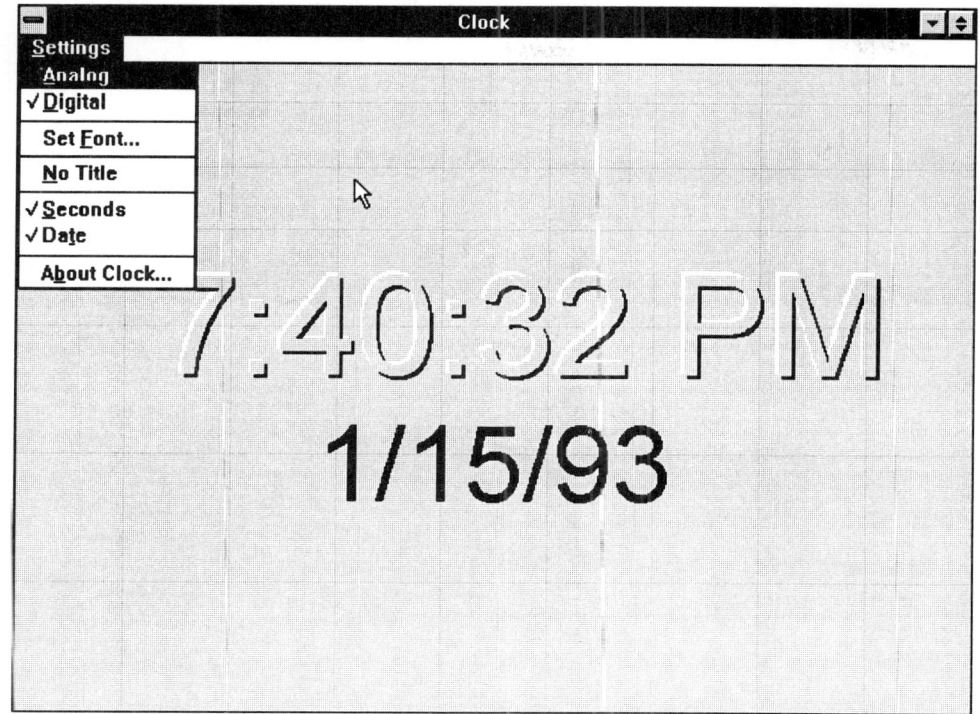

Figure 12-15
Options under settings of the Clock accessory

The About Clock option provides information such as the mode in which Windows is running, how much memory is available, amount of free system resources, and so forth.

The control-menu box at the upper left of the clock display contains one particular option (not shown) that is worth noting here: the Always on Top option. When you select this option, the Clock continues to display on your screen as long as you are running Windows applications. The advantage of placing the Clock in one of the corners of the screen is that you can keep track of time throughout the day while the active application occupies the larger portion of the desktop. The Clock will not, however, display over the top of non-Windows applications, even if you started the application from within Windows.

12-5 CARDFILE: AN OVERVIEW

The **Cardfile** can help you manage names, addresses, phone numbers, and other information critical to your daily activities. To run the Cardfile application, position the mouse pointer on the Cardfile icon in the Accessories group, and double-click the left button of the mouse. To maximize the Cardfile window so that it fills the entire screen, click left on the maximize (up-arrow) button at the upper right of the Cardfile window. You should see a screen similar to Figure 12-16.

The line below the menu shows that you are in Card View. To the right, notice the left- and right-arrow buttons; they can be used to scroll through the cards after you have established several cards in your Cardfile. To the right of these buttons, Cardfile indicates that there is only 1 card in the current Cardfile, and there is no information on that card.

Let's begin adding some new cards. First, click left on Edit; then click left on Index. The Index dialog box appears. Type *BRT Corporation* and press Enter. Cardfile instantly displays a card, with its name displayed above a double line and the cursor flashing below the double line. Next, type *General Information* and

Figure 12–16
Cardfile starting screen

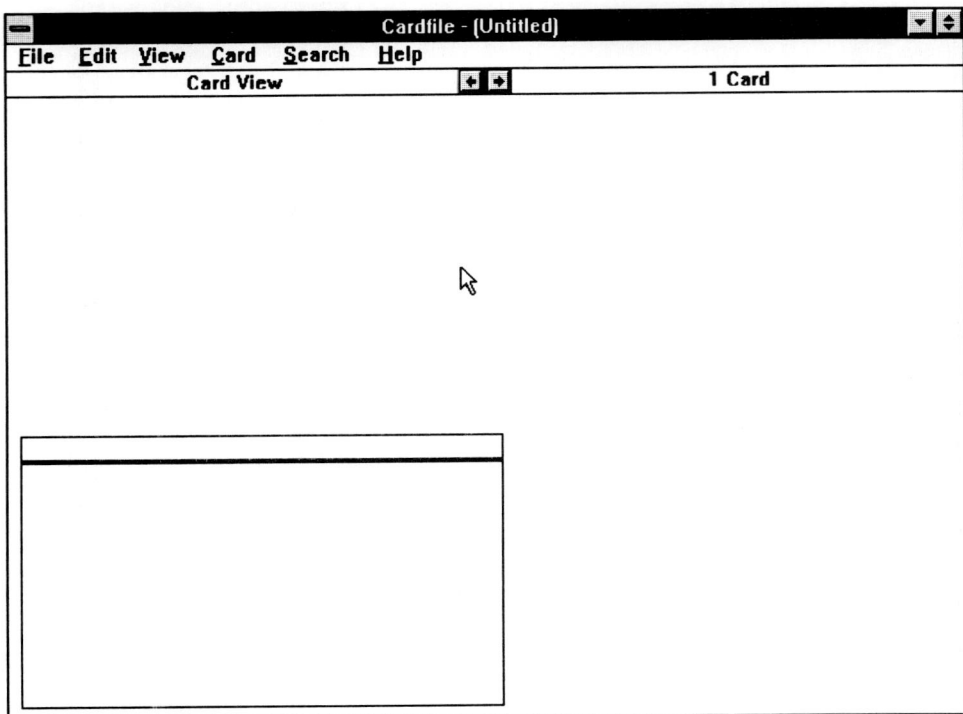

press the Tab key. Type *1-800-426-9400*. Now follow the steps outlined to add two more cards to the Cardfile:

1. Click left on Card and Add; then type *Brown, John* and press Enter.
2. Type *Engineer* and press Enter.
3. Type *123 Main Street* and press Enter.
4. Type *Portland, OR 97207* and press Enter.
5. Type *Phone: 501-456-7890*.
6. Click left on Card and Add; then type *Johnson, Barbara* and press Enter.
7. Type *Florist* and press Enter.
8. Type *768 Mt. Vernon Avenue* and press Enter.
9. Type *Portland, OR 97201* and press Enter.
10. Type *Phone: 503-111-2222*.

You have now a total of three cards in your cardfile; see Figure 12–17. The top line of each card is called the index line. This line is used to sort the Cardfile into alphabetical order. When you retrieve your cardfile, all your cards will be sorted in alphabetical order based on the first character in the index line. To edit an index line, double-click left anywhere in the index line of the card you wish to edit. Cardfile will display the Index dialog box, which allows you to add, change, or delete information contained within the index line. The index line may also be edited by selecting the Index option from the Edit menu, although the double-clicking method is much quicker.

When you press the PgUp key, notice that the previous card is displayed. Likewise, when you press the PgDn, key, the next card in the cardfile is displayed. You can move directly to a particular card in the cardfile by pointing the mouse pointer to the desired card and clicking left.

Chapter 12 Additional Windows Accessories

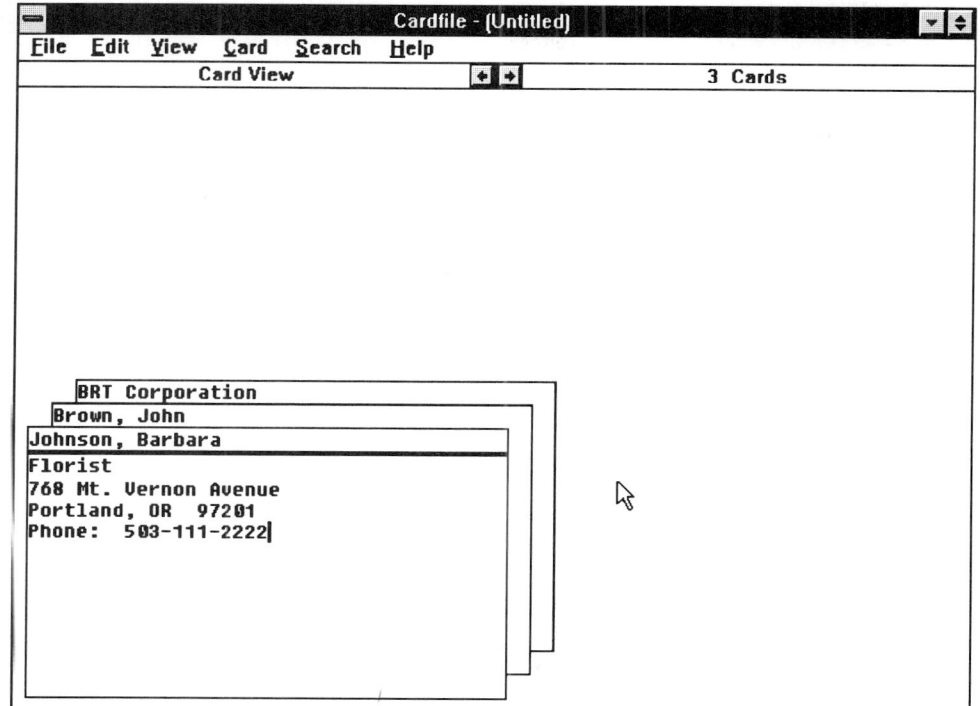

Figure 12-17
Three cards in the Cardfile

To print a card, click left on File; then click left on Print. Cardfile prints the card on top of the stack; it prints the name of the Cardfile at the top of the page and the page number at the bottom of the printout. You must be in Card View mode to print an individual card. The Print All option in the File menu can be used to print the contents of every card in the Cardfile (three cards per page). In List View mode, the Print All option prints the contents of the index area for every card in the Cardfile. Click left on View, then List, to switch the Cardfile to List View mode. You should see a screen similar to Figure 12–18.

To save a Cardfile, select File; then select Save As and specify a name of up to eight characters. We selected TEST. The new cardfile will be saved in the current drive and directory under the name TEST.CRD.

An Application of the Cardfile   12-5-1

We are going to add four more cards to the existing file and work with this file using Search and Copy and Paste commands. Follow these steps:

1. Select the Card option from the View menu to switch to Card view mode.
2. Press the F7 function key to display the Add dialog box.
3. Type *Spears, Betty* and press Enter.
4. Type the following entries for Betty Spears's card (press Enter after each line):

   Fancy Florist
   784 Fountain Drive
   Portland, OR 97127
   (503) 456-7890

Figure 12-18
Cardfile in List View mode

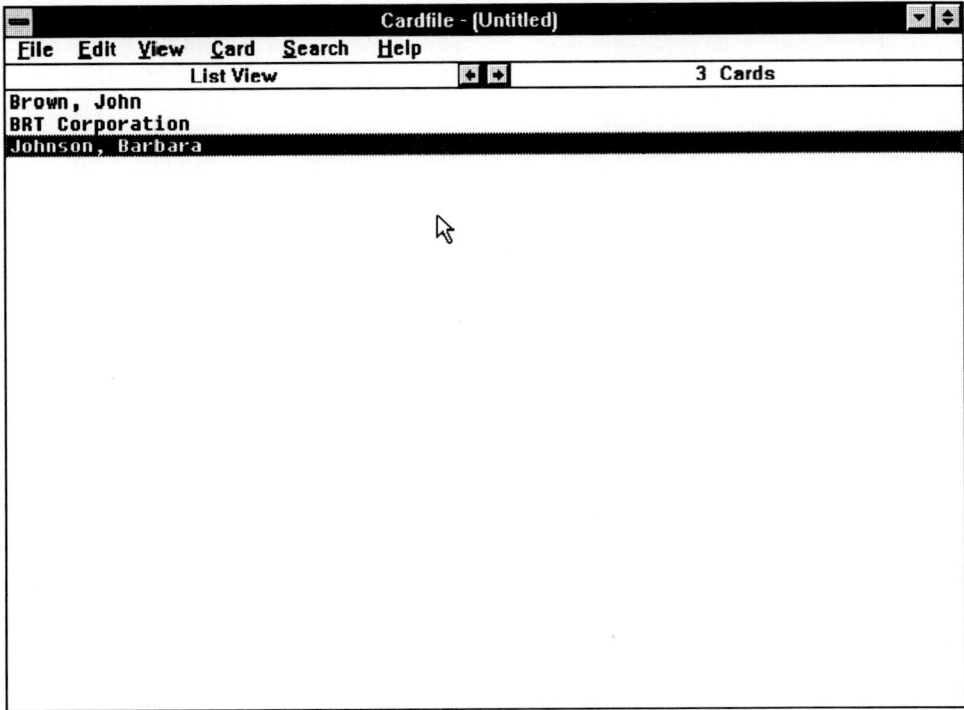

5. Press the F7 shortcut key to access the Add option from the Card menu.
6. Type *Vigen, Thomas* and press Enter.
7. Type the following entries for Thomas Vigen's card:

   Comsys Computing
   4242 El Tejon Drive
   San Diego, CA 93728
   (618) 222-3333

8. Press F7 to access the Add option from the Card menu.
9. Type *Graves, Teri* and press Enter.
10. Type the following entries for Teri Graves's card:

    573 Sulley Court
    Aspen, CO 58372
    (401) 888-7777

11. Press F7 to access the Add option from the Card menu.
12. Type *Wood, Connie* and press Enter.
13. Type the following entries for Connie Wood's card:

    926 Seashore Lane
    San Luis Obispo, CA 94838
    (987) 654-3210

Chapter 12 Additional Windows Accessories 241

You have created a file containing seven cards. Now we want to create a simple letter to Thomas Vigen using the Write application. To do so, we will use the search facility for the Cardfile to find Thomas Vigen's card in the file; then we'll copy the address information from the card into the letter in Write. Follow these steps:

1. Press Ctrl-Esc to display the Task List.
2. Double-click left on Program Manager.
3. Open Write.
4. Double-click left anywhere in the title bar of the Write application to maximize the size of the window.
5. Type *Thomas Vigen* and press Enter.
6. Press Ctrl-Esc to display the Task List.
7. Double-click left on Cardfile.
8. Select the Go To option from the Search menu. Cardfile will display the Go To dialog box.
9. Type *Vigen* and press Enter. (Uppercase or lowercase letters are okay.) Cardfile will instantly locate the first card in the cardfile that contains this text string in an index line.
10. Position the mouse pointer at the upper left of the address information; then click left and drag down and to the right so that the address area is highlighted.
11. Select the Copy option from the Edit menu. The highlighted text will be copied to the Clipboard.
12. Press Alt-Tab to switch back to the Write document that you have in progress.
13. Select the Paste option from the Edit menu. The address information will be pasted into the Write document at the cursor position. At this point, you are ready to complete the rest of the letter, generate a printout, and drop it into the mail!

This is just one example of how different Windows applications can work together. To make the task of creating a letter even easier, you could create a macro (discussed in the next chapter) to add the complimentary close and signature block at the bottom of the letter. Try to think of some other ways that you might use Windows to simplify the tasks you perform from day to day. When you have finished using Write, double-click left on the control-menu box at the upper left. Exit the Cardfile in the same manner.

12-6 NOTEPAD: AN OVERVIEW

The **Notepad** is a limited capability text editor that can be used to create and edit ASCII (American Standard Code for Information Interchange) format files such as AUTOEXEC.BAT and CONFIG.SYS. In addition, Notepad allows you to create to-do lists, reminders, and other information important for day-to-day activities. To execute the Notepad application, position the mouse pointer onto the Notepad icon in the Accessories group and double-click the left button of the mouse. To maximize the Notepad window so that it fills the entire display area, click left on the maximize icon at the upper right of the Notepad window. You should see a screen similar to Figure 12–19.

As you can see, the Notepad screen consists of a title bar, control-menu box, maximize button, minimize button (or restore button), and horizontal and vertical scroll bars. The main menu includes the following options: File, Edit, Search, and Help.

The File menu has several options. New is used for creating a new text file. The Open option allows you to edit a text file that you have already created. Save enables you to save the changes made to a text file. Save As is also used for saving changes made to a text file, but under a different name. The Print option allows you to print a text file. The Page Setup option adds a header or footer and changes page margins. Print Setup is used to specify the destination printer, paper size, and page orientation. Select the Exit option when you are finishing working with Notepad and wish to terminate the application.

The Edit menu has eight options. Use Undo (Ctrl-Z) to cancel your last action. For example, if you accidentally deleted a paragraph, Undo can bring it back. The Cut (Ctrl-X) option relocates text to another area in the text file or to another file and/or application by means of the Clipboard. The Copy (Ctrl-C) option copies text to another area in the text file or to another file and/ or application by means of the Clipboard. Paste (Ctrl-V) can be used to paste (insert) text that has been cut or copied back into a text file. Use the Delete (Del) option to delete highlighted text. Use the Select All option to highlight the entire text file. Select Time/Date (F5) option to insert the current time and date into the text file. The Word Wrap option enables or disables the word wrap feature. Some text files, such as AUTOEXEC.BAT and CONFIG.SYS, should be edited with word wrap disabled (because each command must be completely in one line), whereas other text files such as a to-do list should be edited with word wrap enabled. For examples of these two files see Appendix A.

Figure 12–19
Notepad starting screen

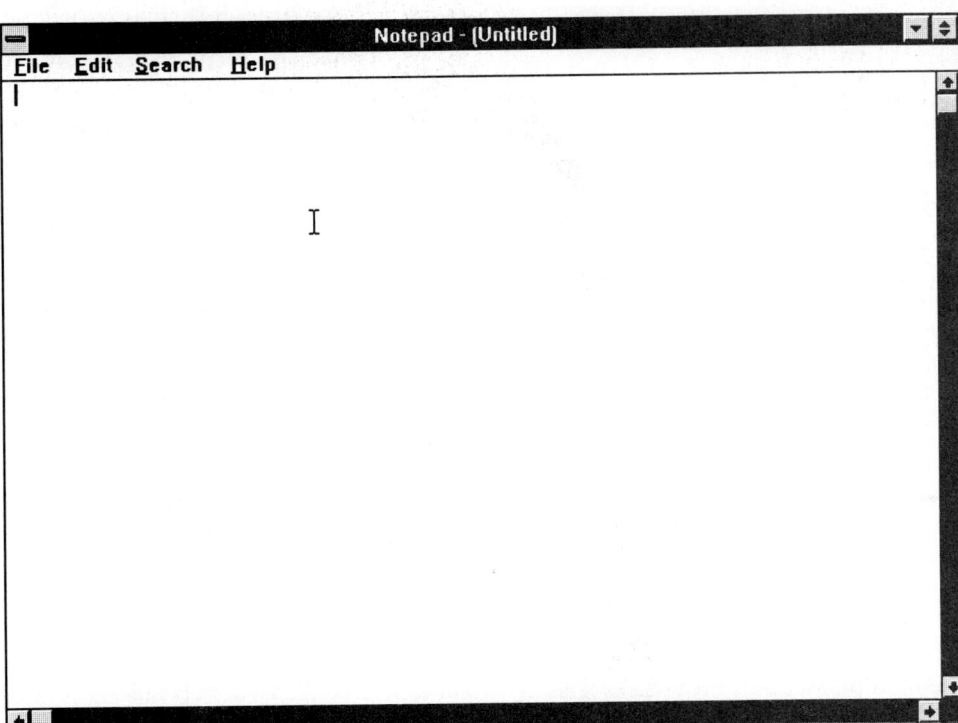

The Search menu has two options. The Find option allows you to search for a character string in the text file. The Find Next (F3) option locates the next occurrence of the specified search string.

The Help menu contains useful information on how to use Notepad and other Windows applications.

Now let's try using Notepad. Click the left button of the mouse on the Edit option in the main menu; then click left on the Time/Date option. Press the Enter key twice; then type *The Notepad is easy to use*. Next, click left on File, and Save As. Notepad displays the Save As dialog box. Type *SAMPLE* and press Enter. Your text file will be saved in the current drive and directory under the name SAMPLE.TXT. Make sure that your printer is on and online; then click left on the File menu and on Print. Notepad responds by printing a copy of your text file. The name of the file is at the top and the page number is at the bottom of the printout.

Notepad is easy to use and can serve a variety of purposes. To exit Notepad, click left on File and Exit or double-click on the control-menu box.

12-7 TERMINAL: AN OVERVIEW

Terminal is a communications program that allows you to connect your computer to another computer that might be in the same room, in the same building, across town, or even across the world. You can connect to a friend's PC and just chat or to a large online information retrieval system such as CompuServe where you can check the latest sports scores, weather, and stock prices.

Components Required to Use Terminal   12-7-1

Terminal requires the following communications hardware:

- A modem (modulator-demodulator)
- If you have an external modem, you will need an available serial port on your computer and a serial cable to attach your modem to the serial port
- A telephone line to connect to your modem

Connecting this hardware is easy. Once the equipment is in place, you are ready to use Terminal to connect to another computer. Before we begin our discussion of exactly how to do this, review the following communications terminology to familiarize yourself with some of the terms that you will encounter when using Terminal.

- Baud rate: The rate at which your computer communicates with another computer is called the baud rate. Typical transmission rates include 1,200, 2,400, 4,800, 9,600, 19,200, and so forth. The baud rate you choose is determined by the capabilities of the modem that you are using and the baud rate of the computer to which you are connecting. For example, if your modem is capable of 9,600 baud but the computer that you are connecting to is only capable of 2,400 baud, you must set your modem communications rate to 2,400 in order to establish a successful connection. Many modems available today automatically detect the baud rate capabilities of other modems. If your modem has this capability, then set your modem for its maximum baud rate. When it establishes a connection to another modem, it will automatically detect that modem's baud rate and, if necessary, reduce its own baud rate to the level required by the other modem.

- Data bits: The number of bits that make up 1 byte (character) of information varies in computers. Different computers establish different lengths for each character. Typically, the data bit setting is either 7 or 8—meaning that each character is either 7 or 8 bits in length. On our system we set data bits to 8.
- Parity: Parity, which can be none, odd, or even, is a method to ensure that what is received by the receiving computer is the same as the data being sent by the sending computer. On our system we set parity to none.
- Stop bits: Stop bits is a somewhat misleading term that indicates how much time (not bits) is inserted between bytes of data as the data is transmitted. On our system we set stop bits to 1.

12-7-2 Starting the Terminal Application

To run Terminal, position the mouse pointer on the Terminal icon in the Accessories group; then double-click the left button. To maximize the Terminal display area so that it fills the entire screen, double-click left anywhere in the title bar of the Terminal display window. You should see a screen similar to Figure 12–20.

The Terminal screen includes a title bar, control-menu box, maximize and minimize buttons, horizontal and vertical scroll bars, and the main menu options. The File option allows you to save the current Terminal settings to a file, open a new or existing settings file, print settings, and exit. By means of the Edit option, you can copy and paste text to and from the Terminal screen, send text to the system to which you are connected, select all text in the Terminal buffer, and clear the Terminal window and buffer of text.

Figure 12–20
Terminal starting screen

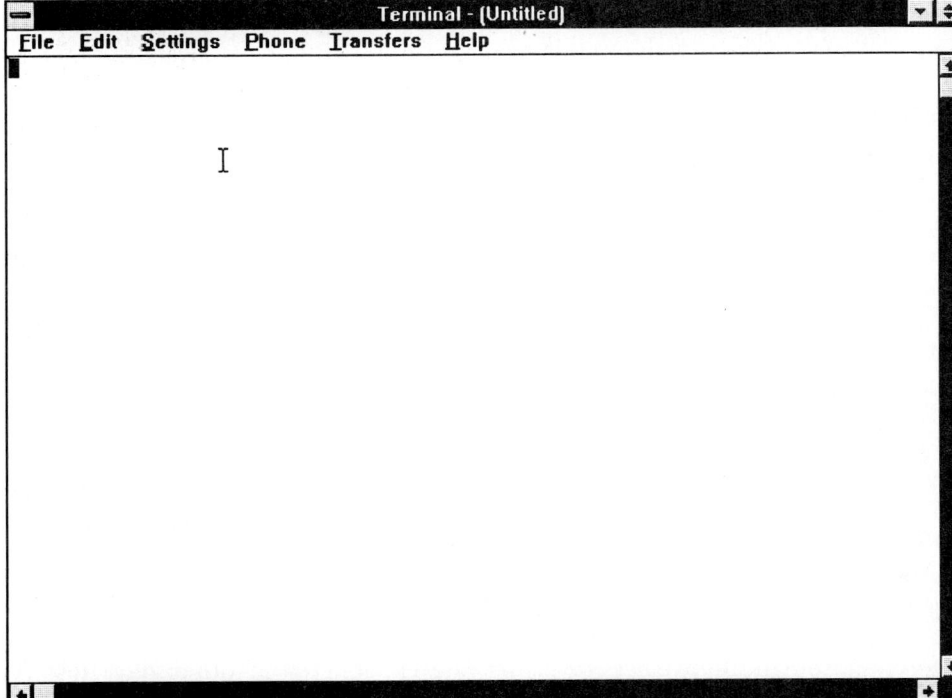

The Settings option allows you to specify a phone number, terminal emulation, terminal preferences, function key assignments, text and binary transfer options, communications settings, modem commands, printer echo, timer mode, and whether to show the function keys on the screen. The Phone option allows you to dial the specified phone number and hang up when you are finished communicating with the other computer. By choosing the Transfers option, you can send, receive, and view text files; send and receive binary files; and pause, resume, and stop the current modem operation. The Help option provides useful information on how to use Terminal as well as on other Windows topics.

Terminal Application

12-7-3

Now let's walk through an example of how to use Terminal. If necessary, make sure that the power to your modem is turned on. Next, click left on Settings; then click left on Communications. You should see a screen similar to Figure 12-21.

Use the mouse pointer and click left on the appropriate COM (serial) port in the Connector box; then set up the other options that are appropriate for your computer and modem. Click left on OK. Next, click left on Phone and on Dial. The Phone Number dialog box appears and prompts you to specify a phone number to be dialed. At this point, you should type the telephone number of the system with which you wish to connect. After entering a number into the Dial box, click left on OK. Terminal accesses your modem and begins dialing the specified phone number. If all of your settings are correct, you will establish a connection. If you do not establish a successful connection, check your communications settings and phone number and try again.

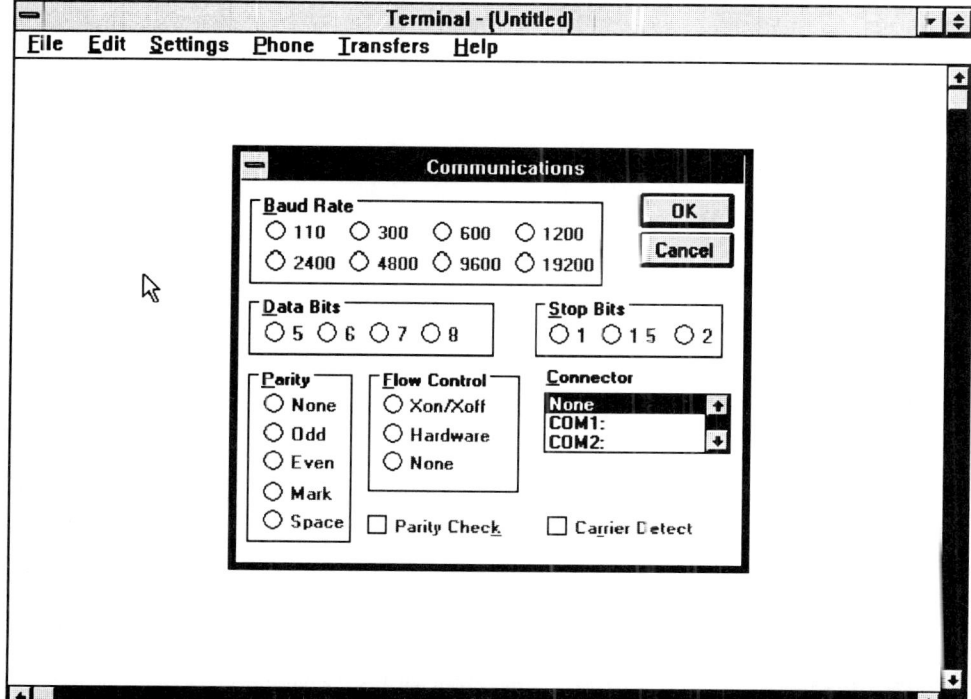

Figure 12-21
Communications dialog box

Let's say that you have successfully connected to an online information service. You will be prompted to log into the remote computer by entering your name and some password. If you have never logged into the system before, you will be prompted for your name, phone number, password, address, and other information that allows the "sysop" (system operator) of the remote computer to keep a list of all users that connect to the online service. After supplying the required information, further instructions will be displayed about how to proceed.

When you are ready to disconnect from the other computer, click left on Phone and on Hangup. Your connection to the remote computer will be terminated. To exit the Terminal application, click left on File and on Exit or double-click on the control-menu box.

12-8 CHARACTER MAP, MEDIA PLAYER, RECORDER, AND SOUND RECORDER

The Character Map, Media Player, Recorder, and Sound Recorder are the other accessories in Windows 3.1. (One final accessory—Object Packager—will be discussed in the next chapter.)

Character Map includes extended characters and special characters in symbol fonts that can be inserted into other applications. Each font contains a different set of characters. Character Map only works with Windows applications.

Media Player is used to play multimedia files and control hardware devices. Media Player can play sounds and musical instrument digital interface (MIDI) sounds and control any media control interface (MCI) multimedia device installed on your computer. For example, this feature allows you to play audio compact discs or videodiscs.

Recorder enables you to record a sequence of keystrokes and mouse actions—a macro—to play back at a later time. By means of this feature, you can simplify a series of repetitive steps by recording them once and playing them back as many times a you wish. We will talk about this feature more in the next chapter.

Sound Recorder can play, record, and edit sound files. Before using this feature, you must have the sound hardware installed in your system.

SUMMARY

This chapter provided an overview of six accessories available in Windows 3.1: Calculator, Calendar, Clock, Cardfile, Notepad, and Terminal. The discussion included the process of getting in and getting out of each application as well as a review of the menus and simple operations performed by them. For a detailed discussion of these applications, consult the Windows 3.1 User's Guide. The chapter also introduced Character Map, Media Player, Recorder, and Sound Recorder.

REVIEW QUESTIONS

*These questions are answered in Appendix A.

1. What are some of the tasks performed by the Windows Calculator?
2. How many modes does the Calculator have?
3. What are some of the buttons (keys) used for editing in Calculator?
*4. How do you correct your mistakes using Calculator?
5. What are some examples of symbols used by Calculator?
6. How do you clear the Calculator memory? How do you store a number in the memory?

Chapter 12 Additional Windows Accessories 247

7. What does Calendar do?
*8. How do you switch from Day view mode to Month view mode?
9. What happens if you press Ctrl-PgDn?
*10. How do you assign a special marking to an appointment?
11. How do you return to a previous date in the Calendar?
12. What are some of the cursor-movement keys in the Calendar environment?
*13. What does the Today option do in the Show menu?
14. How do you set an alarm for an appointment?
15. What are the options in the Calendar File menu?
16. What are the options in the Calendar Edit menu?
*17. What are the options in the Calendar View menu?
18. What does the Clock application do?
19. What are some of the options in the Clock menu?
20. What are some of the applications of the Cardfile?
*21. How do you add another card to your Cardfile?
22. How do you display the contents of a card?
23. How do you save in Cardfile?
24. What are some of the applications of the Notepad?
25. How do you exit from the Notepad?
26. Can you perform search operations using Notepad?
27. What are the applications of the Terminal component of Windows?
*28. What are the requirements for using the Terminal?
29. What is baud rate? What are some of the common baud rates?
30. What are Media Player, Character Map, and Recorder? Describe each.

HANDS-ON EXPERIENCE

1. Start Calculator and do the following:
   a. Switch to the Scientific mode.
   b. Switch back to the Standard mode.
   c. Add 5 and 10.
   d. Divide the result by 2.
   e. Multiply the result by 5.
   f. Store the result in memory.
   g. Add 100 to what you have in memory.
   h. Clear memory.
   i. Clear the data entry screen.
   j. Calculate the square root of 100.
   k. Clear the screen.
   l. Exit Calculator.
2. Start Calendar and do the following:
   a. Switch between Month and Day view mode.
   b. Set an appointment for tomorrow for lunch with Nooshin at 1:00 p.m.
   c. Set another appointment for the day after tomorrow at 2:00 p.m. for the dentist.
   d. Set an alarm for 10 minutes from now for an appointment with the chairman of the board.

e. By using the right-arrow icon, display the next date.

f. By using the left-arrow icon, display the previous date.

g. Practice with other cursor-movement keys outlined in Table 12–1.

h. Using the Save As option from the File menu, save your calendar.

i. Exit Calendar.

3. Start the Clock application and do the following:

    a. Switch from Digital display mode to Analog display mode.

    b. Switch back to digital.

    c. Select the Set Font option. What is available?

    d. By selecting the Seconds option, disable the display of seconds.

    e. Select the About Clock option. What is available here?

    f. What does the Always on Top option do?

    g. Exit the Clock.

4. Start the Cardfile application; answer or do the following:

    a. What are the menu options?

    b. What does the View option do?

    c. Create the following two cards:

    Dr. Morvareed
    2109 Sully St.
    Portland, OR 97201

    TRN International
    2122 South Broadway
    Los Angeles, CA 97206

    d. Press PgUp key to see your first card.

    e. Press PgDn key to see your second card.

    f. Save the card file under PERSONAL.

    g. What file extension does Cardfile attach to this file?

    h. Exit Cardfile.

5. Start the Notepad; answer or do the following:

    a. How many menu options are available in the starting screen?

    b. What are some of the uses of Notepad?

    c. What are the applications of the Page Setup option?

    d. How do you undo your last change?

    e. Can you perform cut and paste operations using Notepad?

    f. Type the following two lines:

    Using Notepad you can create AUTOEXEC files.
    Using Notepad you can also create Text files.

    g. Save this file under TEXT.

    h. Exit Notepad.

6. If you have access to a modem, start the Terminal application and transfer a message to a computer for which you have a number or access a bulletin board for which you have a number.

Chapter 12 Additional Windows Accessories

KEY TERMS

Arithmetic operator	Character Map	Notepad
Arithmetic symbol	Clock	Recorder
Calculator	Day view mode	Setting an alarm
Calendar	Media player	Sound Recorder
Cardfile	Month view mode	Terminal

KEY COMMANDS

Back (Backspace; in Calculator erases the right-most digit of a numeric entry)

C (in Calculator clears the current calculation)

CE (in Calculator clears the displayed number)

Calendar menu (see Figure 12–3)

Cardfile menu (see Figure 12–16)

Clock menu (see Figure 12–14)

Cursor-movement keys in Calendar (see Table 12–1)

Notepad menu (see Figure 12–19)

F8 (in Calendar switches from Day mode to Month mode)

F9 (in Calendar switches from Month mode to Day mode)

MISCONCEPTIONS AND SOLUTIONS

Misconception One way to switch between Day view mode and Month view mode in Calendar is to use the F9 and F8 function keys. F9 switches from Day to Month; F8 switches from Month to Day. You may not remember these keys.

    Solution You can double-click on the date in the status line to switch from one view to the other.

Misconception In Calendar, using the arrow keys to move from one date to another is time consuming.

    Solution Click the left-arrow icon in the Calendar status line to move to the previous date. To move to the next date, click the right arrow icon. You can also press Ctrl-PgDn.

Misconception You set an alarm for an event, but it does not work.

    Solution Probably the system sounds have been turned off by means of the Sound option in the Control Panel.

Misconception Using the Cardfile application, you bring a specific card to the front of a file by selecting the Go To option of the Search menu. This takes too much time.

    Solution If the card's index line is visible, point to the index line and click on it.

Misconception You are using Notepad and you see that the displayed date and time are not correct.

    Solution Use the Control Panel to reset date and time. This can also be done through DOS by using the Time and Date commands.

Misconception You are trying to change the basic communications settings of your system by using the Control Panel, but it doesn't work.

    Solution You must use the Communications command in Terminal to do this.

Misconception You are using your modem to connect to a remote computer but your attempt is not successful.

    Solution You probably have not specified the correct communications settings for the remote computer. Specify the new settings and retry.

ARE YOU READY TO MOVE ON?

Multiple Choice

1. The Calculator includes all of the following keys for editing except
   a. Back (Backspace)
   b. CE (Clear entry)
   c. C (Clear)
   d. all of the above are included
   e. only a and c are included
2. Which one of the following is *not* one of the built-in memory functions in the Calculator?
   a. MC
   b. MR
   c. TM
   d. MS
   e. M+
3. In Calendar, to switch from Month mode to Day mode press
   a. F8
   b. F9
   c. F7
   d. F6
   e. F5
4. In Calendar in Day view mode to switch to the next day press
   a. the down-arrow key
   b. Ctrl-PgDn
   c. Ctrl-PgUp
   d. PgDn
   e. PgUp
5. The Calendar File menu includes all of the following options except
   a. New
   b. Open
   c. Save
   d. Save As
   e. they are all included
6. The Clock menu includes all of the following options except
   a. Analog
   b. Digital
   c. Set Font
   d. No Title
   e. they are all included
7. Cardfile menu allows you to do all of the following except
   a. create a graph
   b. create a file
   c. view a file
   d. edit a file
   e. do a search operation
8. Using the Card option in the Cardfile menu, you can do all of the following except
   a. add a card

Chapter 12 Additional Windows Accessories

   b. delete a card
   c. duplicate a card
   d. you can do all of the above.
   e. only a and b
9. Notepad allows you to do all of the following except
   a. create a file
   b. save a file under a name
   c. graph a file
   d. edit a file
   e. print a file
10. To use the Terminal component of Windows, you need all of the following except
    a. a modem
    b. a computer with at least 8 MB of RAM
    c. a serial port
    d. a telephone
    e. a serial cable (for external modems)

True/False

1. A baud rate is the rate at which your computer communicates with another computer.
2. Parity can be either odd or even; there is no other option available.
3. The Calculator does not permit you to calculate the square root of a number.
4. Using the Calculator, you can store the result of a calculation in memory and add to it later.
5. Use the F9 function key while in Calendar to switch from Day view mode to Month view mode.
6. The Calendar offers five different marking symbols.
7. The PgUp key highlights the corresponding date in the previous year if you are in Day mode in Calendar.
8. When you save a file in Calendar, Windows attaches a BAT extension to the file name.
9. The Clock allows you to change from digital to analog.
10. Cardfile will *not* let you delete a card from your filing system.

Multiple Choice	True/False	ANSWERS
1. d	1. T	
2. c	2. F	
3. a	3. F	
4. b	4. T	
5. e	5. T	
6. e	6. T	
7. a	7. F	
8. d	8. F	
9. c	9. T	
10. b	10. F	

Advanced Features of Windows 3.1

13-1 Introduction
13-2 Recorder
    13-2-1 Starting the Recorder
    13-2-2 Example 1—A Macro for Typing a Centered Title
    13-2-3 Example 2—A Printing Macro
    13-2-4 Example 3—A Macro for Formatting a Disk
13-3 Object Linking and Embedding
    13-3-1 Embedding an Object Versus Linking an Object
    13-3-2 Example of Object Linking
    13-3-3 Hands-On Example of Object Embedding
    13-3-4 Hands-On Example of Object Linking
    13-3-5 Dynamic Data Exchange Versus OLE: What's the Difference?
13-4 Print Manager
13-5 PIF Editor
13-6 Object Packager

13-1
INTRODUCTION

This chapter introduces five advanced features of Windows 3.1. Recorder allows you to create macros. The Object Linking and Embedding feature enables you to embed and link various objects in Windows applications. Print Manager helps you to achieve effective management of different printers. The PIF Editor lets you run non-Windows applications more effectively. The chapter concludes with a discussion of the Object Packager as a tool for designing compact and interactive documents.

13-2
RECORDER

By means of Windows **Recorder,** you can record a sequence of keystrokes or mouse operations for later use. Such a collection of keystrokes or mouse operations is called a **macro.** Macros have a variety of purposes, for example, typing a company name, formatting a diskette, entering a closing in a business letter, or automating any repetitive task.

13-2-1 Starting the Recorder

Start the Recorder by double-clicking the left button of the mouse on the Recorder icon in the Accessories group. Click left on the maximize button at the upper right of the screen to allow Recorder to fill the entire screen. You should see a screen similar to the one in Figure 13–1. The title bar of the application shows Recorder [Untitled]. It is untitled until you save a macro through the File menu.

Note there are four options in the menu bar. The File option, similar to the File option of other applications, allows you to create a new macro, open an

Figure 13–1
Recorder screen

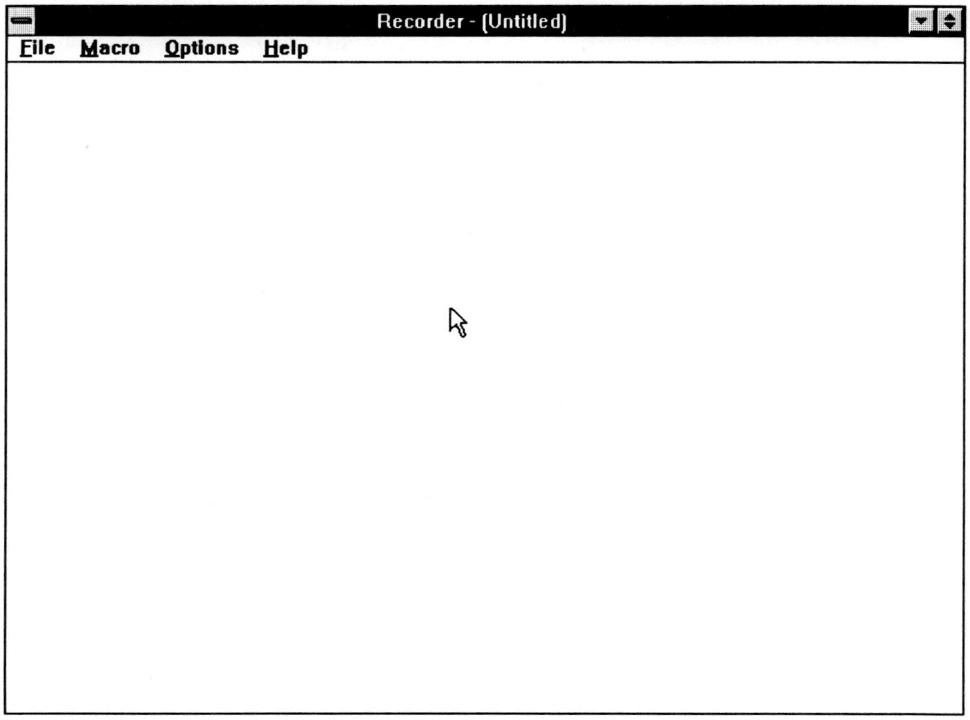

existing macro for editing, save a macro, perform merge operations, and exit the Recorder. The Merge option in the File menu can be used to combine two macros into one.

The Macro option has its own menu with options to run, record, delete, or change the properties of macros.

The Options menu gives you choices about settings that change how a macro runs. For example, you can control whether Ctrl-Break can be used to terminate a macro operation and whether a macro can work in any application or only in the application in which it was created.

The Help option contains terms, definitions, and other information about the use of Recorder. This option also permits access to a wealth of other topics contained within Windows.

Example 1 — A Macro for Typing a Centered Title 13-2-2

Our first macro will be one used to type a centered company name in a Write document. To create this macro, follow these steps:

1. Run the Write program by switching to the Accessories group and double-clicking left on the Write icon. Maximize the window by clicking left on the maximize button at the upper right of the screen.
2. Switch back to the Recorder by pressing the Ctrl-Esc key combination and double-clicking left on Recorder [Untitled].
3. Click left on Record in the Macro menu. You will see a screen similar to the one in Figure 13-2.
4. Type *Centered Company Title* in the Record Macro Name box. Macro names can consist of up to 40 characters.
5. Click left on Start (shown at the upper right of Figure 13-2). At this point, you will be returned to the Write screen. Recorder will now record any keystrokes or mouse operations that you execute. It is best not to use the mouse when creating macros because application windows can be in different locations on the screen when the macro is played back, thereby throwing off correct placement of the mouse pointer when making menu selections.
6. Press Alt-P to display the Paragraph menu; then press C to select the Centered option. As soon as you do this, the insertion point is moved to the center of the screen.
7. Type *ACME Glass Company* and press the Enter key two times.
8. Press Alt-P to display the Paragraph menu; then press L to select the Left option.
9. Press Ctrl-Break. You should see a screen similar to the one in Figure 13-3. Notice that the Recorder icon is flashing in the lower-left corner of the screen.
10. Click left on Save Macro; then click left on OK. Your macro is finished. Remember that the macro is saved only for the current working session. During your next session with Windows, this macro will not be available. To save the macro permanently so that it may be used in future sessions, you must highlight the macro name that you wish to save in the Recorder screen and select Save from the Recorder File menu. You will be presented with the Save As dialog box, which allows you to enter a permanent name for the highlighted macro. Recorder macro files have the extension .REC.

Figure 13-2
Recorder Macro screen

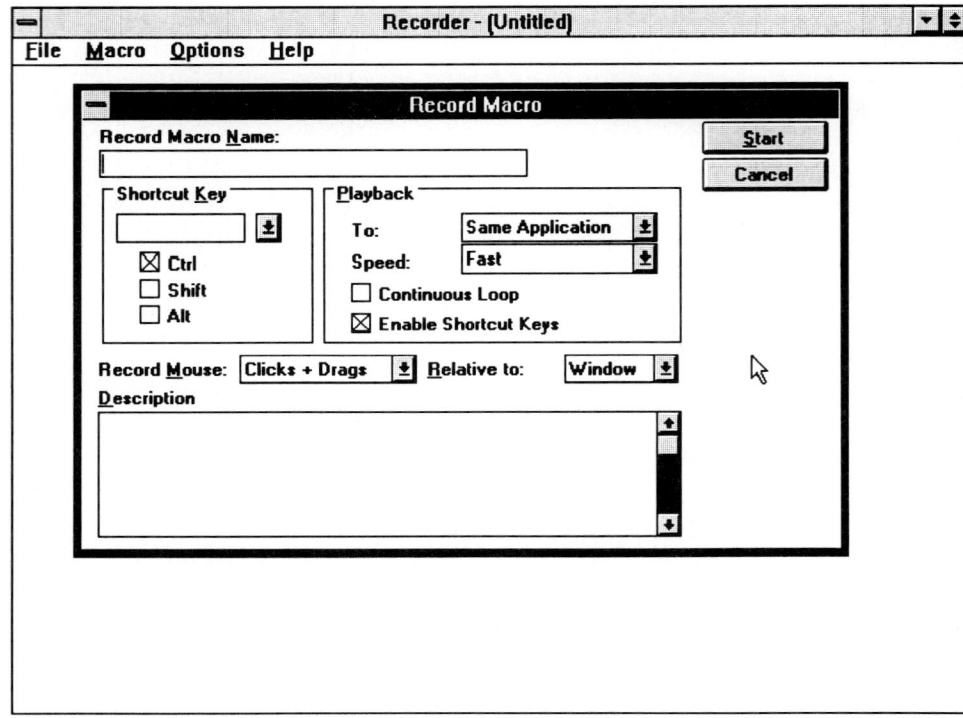

Figure 13-3
Recorder dialog box

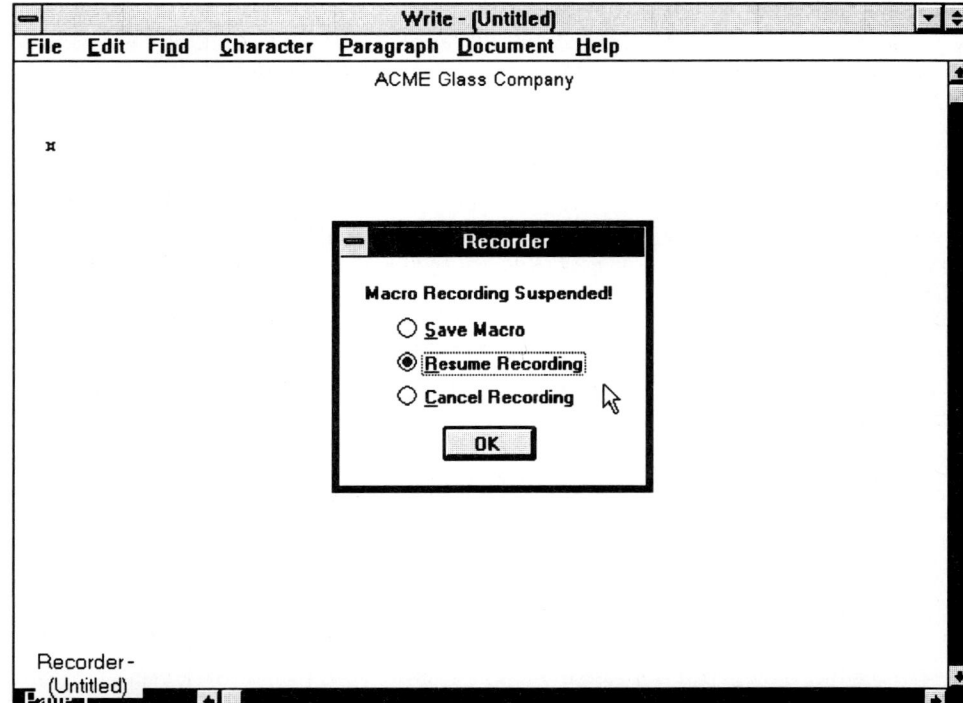

Chapter 13   Advanced Features of Windows 3.1

Now let's test the macro to make sure that it works properly.

1. Press the Enter key three times to move the cursor down a few lines.
2. Switch to the Recorder by pressing Ctrl-Esc and double-clicking on Recorder. Notice that the name of the macro that you created (Centered Company Title) is displayed in reverse video immediately below the Recorder menu bar.
3. Double-click left anywhere in the line occupied by the macro name. Your macro should run automatically, and a centered company title (ACME Glass Company) should be displayed on the screen. If it did, your macro is running properly. If it did not, repeat the steps outlined above to create your macro; then try it again.

Example 2 — A Printing Macro   13-2-3

Our second macro will be used to print the current Write document. In this macro, we will use a shortcut key. Follow these steps:

1. Switch back to the Recorder by pressing Ctrl-Esc and double-clicking on the Recorder option.
2. Click left on Record in the Macro menu.
3. Type *To Print a Write Document* in the Record Macro Name box.
4. Click left on the down-arrow icon in the Shortcut Key box; then click left on Backspace. Notice that the Ctrl, Shift, and Alt key boxes are displayed in this area. Leaving the Ctrl box marked means the Ctrl-Backspace shortcut key combination will be assigned to the macro.
5. Click left on Start. You will be returned to the Write document.
6. Press Alt-F to select the File menu. Then press P to select the Print option and press Enter. Write will print your document.
7. Press Ctrl-Break, click left on Save Macro, and then click left on OK to terminate macro recording. Your printing macro is finished.

   To test the macro, press Ctrl-Backspace. The File menu and Print dialog boxes will be displayed briefly; then your document should be printed. If your document is printed, your macro works properly. If your macro does not work, go back through the steps to create the macro and test it again. By the way, the macros that we have created so far will work only in the application in which the macro was created. For example, if you attempt to run the printing macro in any application other than Write, Recorder will display a dialog box explaining that an error has occurred in macro processing and that the macro cannot run. If this happens to you, just switch back to Write and press Ctrl-Backspace to execute the printing macro.

Example 3 — A Macro for Formatting a Disk   13-2-4

Our third macro will automatically format a high-density $5\frac{1}{4}$-inch disk in drive A. Follow these steps:

1. Exit Write without saving the file by selecting Exit from the File menu and responding N (for No).
2. If necessary, switch to the Program Manager by pressing Ctrl-Esc.

3. Run File Manager by double-clicking on the File Manager icon in the Main group. Maximize the size of the File Manager window by clicking left on the maximize button at the upper right of the screen.
4. Switch back to the Recorder using the Ctrl-Esc key combination.
5. Click left on Record in the Macro menu.
6. Type *To Format a High Density Disk in A:* in the Record Macro Name box.
7. Click left on Ctrl to disable this key.
8. Click left on the down-arrow icon in the Shortcut Key box; then click left on Caps Lock.
9. Click left on Shift and on Alt in the Shortcut Key box. Notice that both the Shift and Alt key boxes are checked, which indicates that to run this macro, you will have to press Shift-Alt-Caps Lock.
10. Click left on the down-arrow icon in the Speed box; then click left on Recorded Speed. This forces the keystrokes that are recorded in the macro to be executed at specific intervals, thereby eliminating potential problems (such as a time-out error that may occur during the execution of the macro later.)
11. Click left on Start. You will be returned to the File Manager.
12. Place a blank high density disk into drive A and close the drive door.
13. Press Alt-D to display the Disk menu and press F to select the Format Disk option from the Disk menu; then press Enter. You may need to alter the format parameters to fit your particular system configuration. Windows will display the Confirm Format Disk dialog box (including the warning that formatting the disk will erase all data on the disk) and ask for verification that you really want to perform the format operation.
14. Press Enter to select the Yes option. File Manager will begin formatting the disk. When the format operation is complete, File Manager will display the Format Complete dialog box, which displays disk capacity information and asks if you would like to format another data disk.
15. Press Enter to select the No option, which tells File Manager that you do not want to format another data disk.
16. Press Ctrl-Break, click left on Save Macro, and press Enter to terminate macro recording. Your Format macro is now finished.

To test the macro, place another blank high density disk into drive A and press Shift-Alt-Caps Lock. File Manager should immediately begin formatting the disk in drive A. If it does, your macro works properly. If the macro refuses to work or you get an error message, make sure that you are in the File Manager when you execute the macro. If the macro still will not work, try creating the macro from scratch and test it again.

As you can see, the Recorder feature can make any task easier and more efficient. The number of macros that you can create and the purposes that they serve is limited only by your imagination. Try practicing with some macros of your own to become more familiar with the Recorder.

13-3 OBJECT LINKING AND EMBEDDING

Windows 3.1 offers a powerful tool in the form of Object Linking and Embedding (OLE—pronounced "oh-lay"). Windows has always allowed users to copy graphics or other objects between applications. However, with earlier versions of

Windows, if you decided that you wanted to change a Paintbrush graphic that had been copied into a Write document, you had to delete it from your Write document, reload Paintbrush, load and edit the graphic to make the desired changes, save the graphic, and then copy it back into the Write document. Now, by means of OLE, you can create the graphic using Paintbrush, embed the graphic into your Write document, and edit the graphic from within the Write document—you don't have to delete it!

To be more specific, you can open the Paintbrush application automatically from within the Write document by double-clicking on the graphic. In this scenario, Paintbrush appears on the screen with the graphic already loaded and ready for editing. Any changes that you make to the graphic in Paintbrush are automatically made to the graphic in the Write document, because a dynamic link exists between the Paintbrush application and the graphic that is embedded in the Write document.

Several terms are important for understanding OLE:

- Object—any graphic or item of information. For example, a spreadsheet, a range or a single cell from within a spreadsheet, a table, and a graph are all examples of objects.
- Server—any application whose objects can be linked or embedded into other applications. Paintbrush and Sound Recorder are examples of server applications.
- Client—any application capable of accepting objects that are created by a server application. Write and Cardfile are examples of client applications.
- Source document—the document in which the object was created.
- Destination document—the document into which the object is embedded or linked.

Embedding an Object Versus Linking an Object 13-3-1

There is an important distinction between **embedding an object** and **linking an object.** When you embed an object, you are actually making a copy of the object from the server application and placing the copy into the client application. As discussed earlier, you may then make editing changes to the object from within the client application simply by double-clicking on the object. The server application that was used to create the object is automatically loaded, with the object ready for editing.

Now here is the distinction. Any changes that you make to an embedded object do *not* change the original object that was copied from the source document in the server application. Any editing changes appear only in the destination document of the client application; the source document object is left in its original form. On the other hand, linking an object involves creating a link, or reference, to the original object in the source document. Once an object is linked into the destination document, simply double-clicking on the object automatically loads the server application that was used to create the object, with the object ready for editing. At this point, changes made to the linked (client) object *do* change the source object in the source document.

Example of Object Linking 13-3-2

Let's say that you are the business office manager for a school district and you maintain budget data using a spreadsheet application. At some point during the year, you must send a budget report containing a copy of the spreadsheet to your school district board, the county office of education, and the state department of education. The three reports contain the same spreadsheet data, but each report also contains other pieces of information relevant only to the respective entity.

You create the three reports using Write, and in each of the reports (destination documents) you create a link to the spreadsheet (source document). You finish the reports and suddenly remember that you forgot to add a budget item into the spreadsheet (source document). No problem! Retrieve any one of the three reports (destination documents) into Write (the client application) and double-click on the spreadsheet (object); automatically the spreadsheet application (server) appears with the spreadsheet (source document) loaded on the screen. Make your editing changes, save the spreadsheet (source document), and exit the spreadsheet application (server). The links automatically update each of the three spreadsheets contained within the reports with the missing piece of information, and you can print reports and send them on their way.

13-3-3 Hands-On Example of Object Embedding

We will now walk through an example of how to embed a graphic created in Paintbrush into a Write document. Follow these steps:

1. Open Paintbrush.
2. Click on the maximize button at the upper right of the screen to allow Paintbrush to fill the entire screen.
3. Select the hollow circle tool from the toolbox and create a circle in the upper-left corner of the drawing area.
4. To save the drawing, select Save from the File menu and specify TEST as the name; then click left on OK.
5. Using the pick tool from the toolbox, select the drawing by clicking left above and to the left of the drawing; then drag the mouse down and to the right so that a dashed box surrounds the circle.
6. From the Edit menu, select Copy. This places a copy of the drawing in the Clipboard.
7. Exit Paintbrush by selecting the Exit option from the File menu.
8. Open Write.
9. Click on the maximize button at the upper right of the screen to allow Write to fill the entire screen.
10. Move the insertion point to the location where you would like to position the embedded object.
11. From the Edit menu, select Paste. A copy of the drawing is placed (or embedded) into your Write document.

Now let's say that you want to jazz up the drawing a little. To do this, double-click left anywhere on the object (the circle). Paintbrush will open with a copy of the drawing already displayed and ready for editing. Follow the steps outlined next to modify the object:

1. Click left on the Paint roller tool in the toolbox.
2. Click left on a different color in the color palette at the bottom of the screen.

Chapter 13 Advanced Features of Windows 3.1

3. Click left anywhere inside of the circle. Your circle should fill with the selected color.
4. Select Update from the Paintbrush File menu. The circle in the Write document should instantly fill with the selected color. As mentioned earlier, editing an embedded object does not change the appearance of the object in the source application. Editing changes made to an embedded object change only the appearance of the object in the destination application.
5. Select Exit & Return to [Untitled] from the Paintbrush File menu. Paintbrush will close, and you will be returned to your Write document so that you can continue working. Click left anywhere outside of the circle to deselect it; then you may continue editing your Write document. When you are finished editing, save your document under TEST and exit the Write application.

Hands-On Example of Object Linking 13-3-4

Follow the steps outlined next to link an object from Paintbrush to a card in Cardfile and a document in Write.

1. Open Paintbrush.
2. Click on the maximize button at the upper right of the screen to allow Paintbrush to fill the entire screen.
3. Select the hollow square tool from the toolbox and create a square in the upper-left corner of the drawing area.
4. Save the drawing by selecting the Save option from the File menu; then specify TRY as the name and click left on OK.
5. Using the pick tool from the toolbox, select the drawing by clicking left above and to the left of the drawing; then drag the mouse down and to the right so that a dashed box surrounds the square.
6. From the Edit menu, select Copy. This places a copy of the drawing in the Clipboard.
7. Switch back to the Program Manager by means of the Ctrl-Esc key combination.
8. Open Cardfile.
9. Click on the maximize button at the upper right of the screen to allow Cardfile to fill the entire screen.
10. Select Picture from the Edit menu.
11. Select Paste Link from the Edit menu. A copy of the drawing will be placed in the upper-left corner of the card.
12. Exit Cardfile by selecting the Exit option from the File menu; then click left on Yes to save your changes. Cardfile will respond by displaying the Save As dialog box.
13. Type *LINKTEST* and click left on OK to give the file a name. After saving the file, you will be returned to the Program Manager.
14. Open Write.
15. Click on the maximize button at the upper right of the screen to allow Write to fill the entire screen.
16. Select Paste Link from the Edit menu. A linked copy of the drawing will be placed in the upper-left corner of the document.

17. Exit Write by selecting the Exit option from the File menu; then click left on Yes to save the changes. Write will respond by displaying the Save As dialog box.
18. Type *LINKTEST* and click left on OK to give the document a name. Don't worry about the document having the same name as in the Cardfile—the extensions are different. After saving the file, you will be returned to the Program Manager. You have now created and saved an object in the source application (Paintbrush) and placed a linked copy of the object into a Cardfile card and a Write document. In addition to placing a copy of the drawing into the Cardfile card and write document, Windows also created a direct link between these two drawings and the application that created the drawing (Paintbrush). We will now test the links by making a change to the original object in Paintbrush, and opening the LINKTEST.CRD card file and LINKTEST.WRI document to see if the objects in these two files are updated with the changes.
19. Switch to Paintbrush by using the Ctrl-Esc key combination.
20. Select the Paint roller tool from the toolbox.
21. Click left on a different color in the color palette at the bottom of the screen.
22. Click left anywhere inside the box that you created. The box should be filled with the specified color.
23. Select Exit from the File menu, then click left on Yes to save your changes. You will be returned to the Program Manager.
24. Open Cardfile.
25. Click on the maximize button at the upper right of the screen to allow Cardfile to fill the entire screen.
26. Select Open from the File menu. Cardfile will display the Open dialog box.
27. Double click left on LINKTEST.CRD to open this file. Cardfile will display a screen similar to Figure 13-4 to alert you that this card file contains links to other documents and that the links may need updating.
28. Click left on OK. Your Cardfile with the object inside the card will be displayed. Notice that the change we made to the original object in Paintbrush has not appeared.
29. Select Picture from the Edit menu.
30. Select Link from the Edit menu. Cardfile will display the Link dialog box (Figure 13-5). This screen allows you to update your links, change or cancel your links, and view link information.
31. Click left on Update Now, then click left on OK. The link will be updated, and you should now see the changes that you made to the original object in Paintbrush.
32. Select the Exit option from the File menu, then click left on Yes to save your changes. You will be returned to the Program Manager.
33. Open Write.
34. Click on the maximize button at the upper right of the screen to allow Write to fill the entire screen.
35. Select Open from the File menu. Write will display the Open dialog box.
36. Double click left on LINKTEST.WRI to open this file. Write will display a screen similar to Figure 13-6 to alert you that this file contains links to other documents and to prompt you about whether to update the links now.

Chapter 13 Advanced Features of Windows 3.1

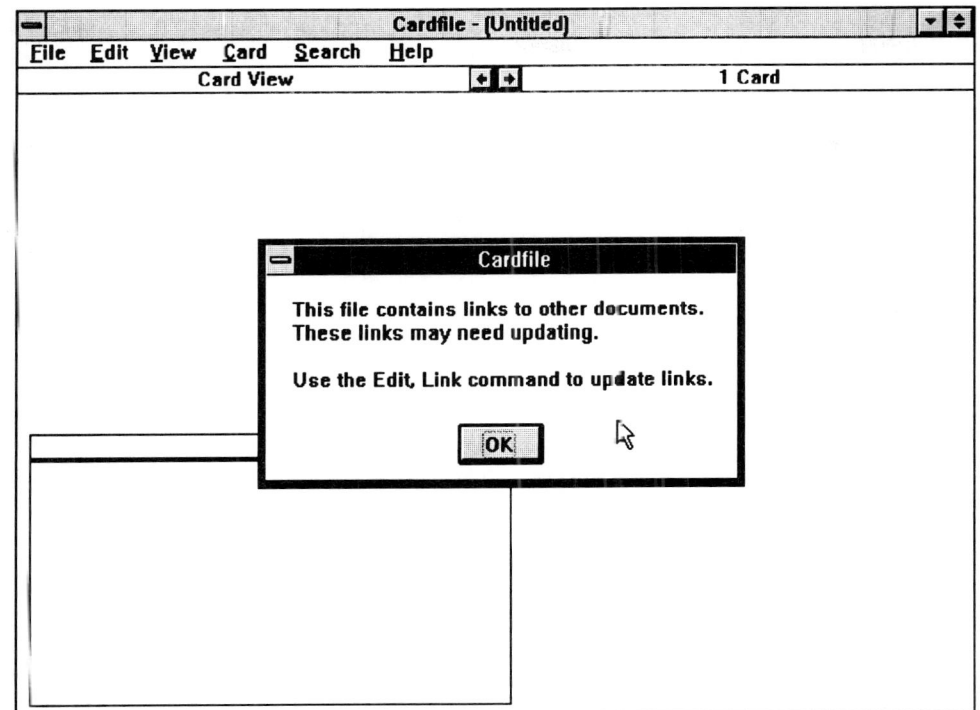

Figure 13-4
Cardfile link warning dialog box

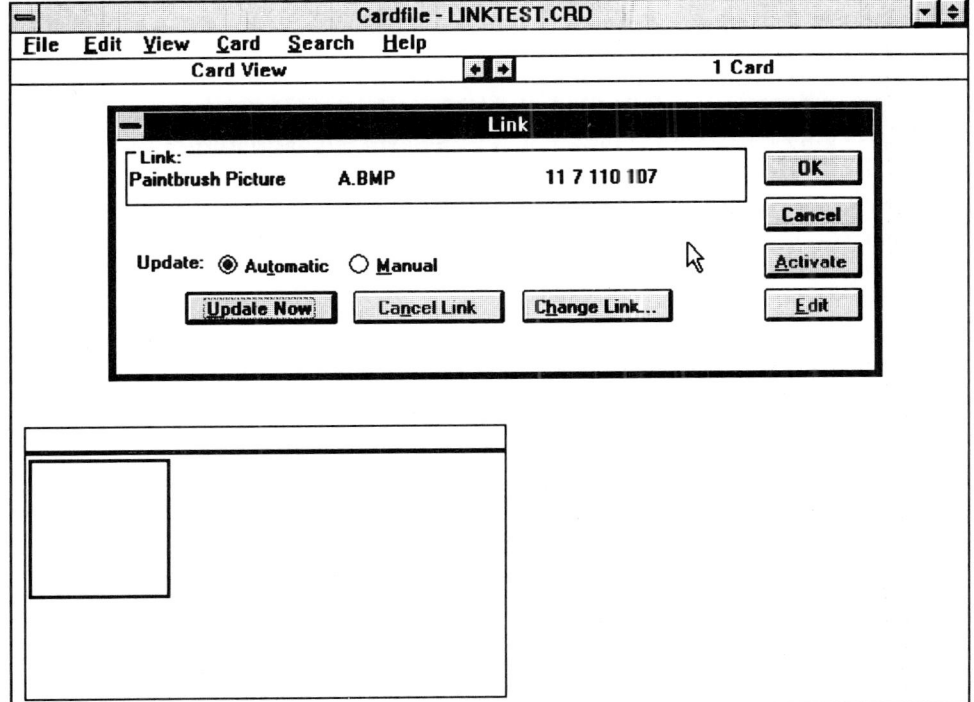

Figure 13-5
Cardfile Link dialog box

Figure 13-6
Write link dialog box

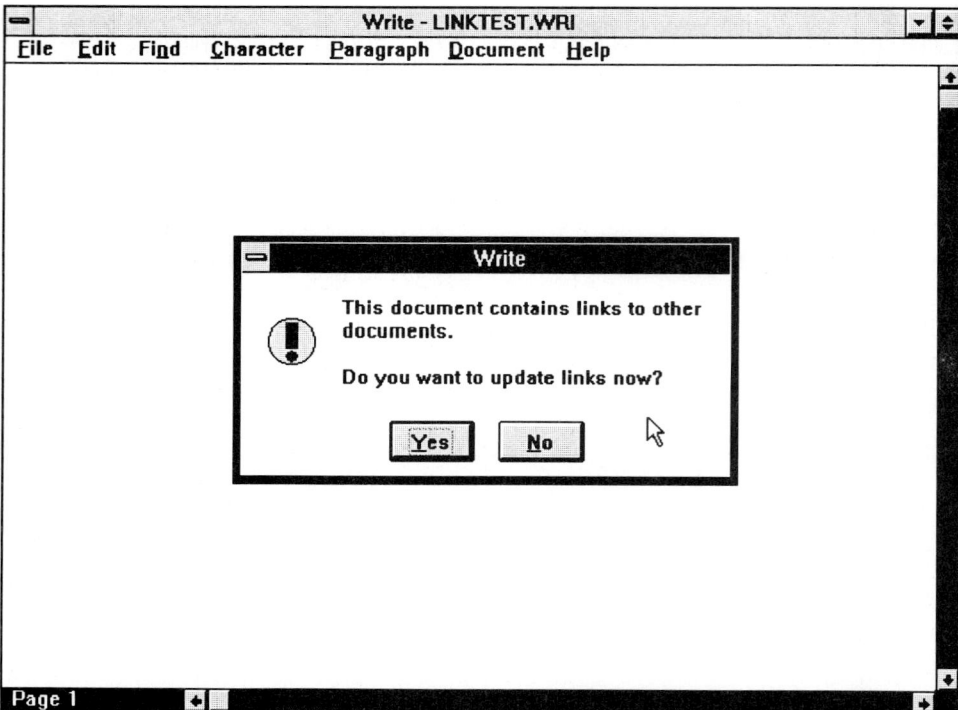

37. Click left on Yes. Your document will be displayed on the screen with your changes already displayed.
38. Select the Exit option from the File menu; then click left on Yes to save your changes. You will be returned to the Program Manager.

At this point, you may not be sure about the difference between linking an object (as we just did) and embedding an object as we did in the first example. When would you use one method and not the other? As you already know, double-clicking on the drawing automatically loads the application that created the drawing (Paintbrush) with the drawing ready for editing. If the drawing is *linked* in the destination application, any changes that you make to the drawing using the server application alter both the original object and all linked copies of the graphic in any client application (Cardfile, in this case). Alternatively, if the drawing were *embedded*, any changes that you make to the embedded drawing in the Cardfile do not alter the original file in the server application. In any case, you may edit the linked object using the same sequence of steps used to edit an embedded object.

13-3-5 Dynamic Data Exchange Versus OLE: What's the Difference?

The OLE feature of Windows 3.1 represents a significant improvement over the way that previous versions of Windows allowed the exchange of data between applications. In versions of Windows prior to 3.1, the capability to move objects among applications as we have been discussing was called **dynamic data exchange** (DDE).

To share information among different applications using DDE, all the applications must be running on the Windows desktop and the related files must be opened. And more important, the updating process occurs only one way: from the server to the client. The data can only be edited in the server application. So, OLE is the next logical step in technological progress beyond the DDE capabilities. By means of OLE, sharing information among different applications becomes document driven rather than application driven. Updating can take place in either direction.

The OLE feature also represents an improvement over DDE in its use of dynamic link libraries to maintain the link information used between applications. In previous versions of Windows, DDE link information was stored within the linking (server) application itself. This created overhead for each server application and opened the door to problems because such a wide variety of linking protocols existed between the various server application programs. With OLE, linking information is stored within dynamic link libraries, thereby freeing the various server application programs from having to store the information. Instead of many applications each storing link information, all link information is now stored under the single umbrella of dynamic link libraries. The application programs are free of the overhead and simply refer to the libraries as necessary to gain access to the link information they require. Thus, OLE is more application independent and flexible and forms a more reliable platform for using its powerful capabilities.

13–4 PRINT MANAGER

Windows **Print Manager** helps manage printers and print jobs. By means of the Print Manager, you can delete, pause, and resume print jobs; change the speed at which your system prints; add, delete, or change printer settings; and otherwise directly control the operation of your printer(s). When you create a print job in Windows, the file that is to be printed is sent to the print queue in Print Manager.

To start the Print Manager, double-click left on the Print Manager icon in the Main group; then click left on the maximize button at the upper right of the Print Manager window to allow Print Manager to fill the entire screen. You should see a screen similar to the one in Figure 13–7. At the top of the screen, you can see the title Print Manager. Below this, the menu bar is displayed. Explanations of some of the entries in the menu bar follow.

The View option controls what information is displayed on the Print Manager screen. Options included within View include Time/Date Sent, Print File Size, Refresh (also available by pressing the F5 function key, used in a network environment), Selected Net Queue, Other Net Queue, and Exit. As with most other Windows applications, a check mark next to the option indicates that the option is enabled, and options that are "grayed out" are not available.

The Options option contains the following items:

- Low Priority: This option allocates a minimum amount of processor time to the task of printing, thereby giving more processor time to the other applications that are running.
- Medium Priority: This option distributes processor time as equally as possible between the Print Manager and other applications that are running.
- High Priority: This option allocates more processor time to the printing task, thereby reducing printing time and slowing down any other applications that are running.

Figure 13-7
Print Manager screen

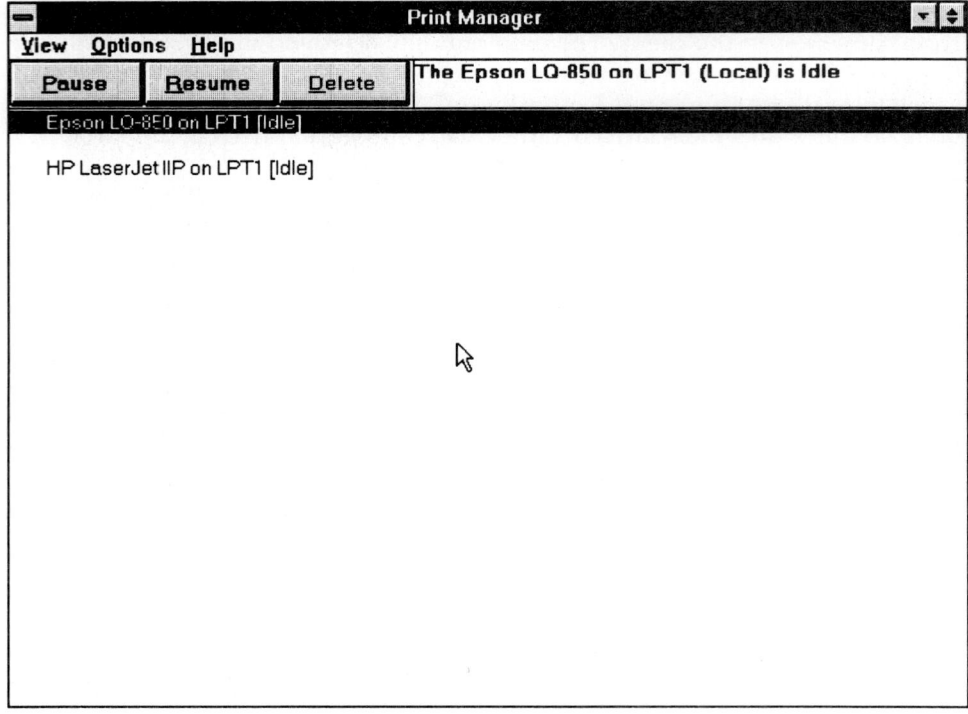

- Alert Always: This option tells Print Manager to display any message that requires user intervention.
- Flash if Inactive: This option tells Print Manager to flash the Print Manager icon or the title bar of the Print Manager window until the user maximizes the icon or makes the window active. Print Manager then displays its message.
- Ignore if Inactive: This option tells Print Manager to suppress the display of messages requiring user interaction if Print Manager is an icon or the Print Manager window is inactive.
- Network Settings and Network Connections: These options can be used to control network printers and network print queues (e.g., what port and network resource or path to use for printing across a network).
- Printer Setup: This option displays the Printers dialog box (Figure 13-8), which allows you to add and delete printers and change printer settings (e.g., the port used with printers, default page orientation, output quality, and so forth).

The area immediately below the main menu (refer to Figure 13-7) shows the pause, resume, and delete buttons. If you wish to delete a file that is in the print queue, simply click left on the file to be deleted; then click left on Delete. Windows prompts you to verify that you really want to delete the highlighted file. When you select Yes, the file is removed from the print queue. The pause and resume buttons can also be used to control printer operation. The Pause option interrupts the printing process temporarily. The Resume option resumes the printing process.

To the right of these buttons, the default printer name is displayed, along with a message indicating its status (either active or idle). Below the buttons, the print queue names are displayed. Information in this area includes the

Chapter 13 Advanced Features of Windows 3.1

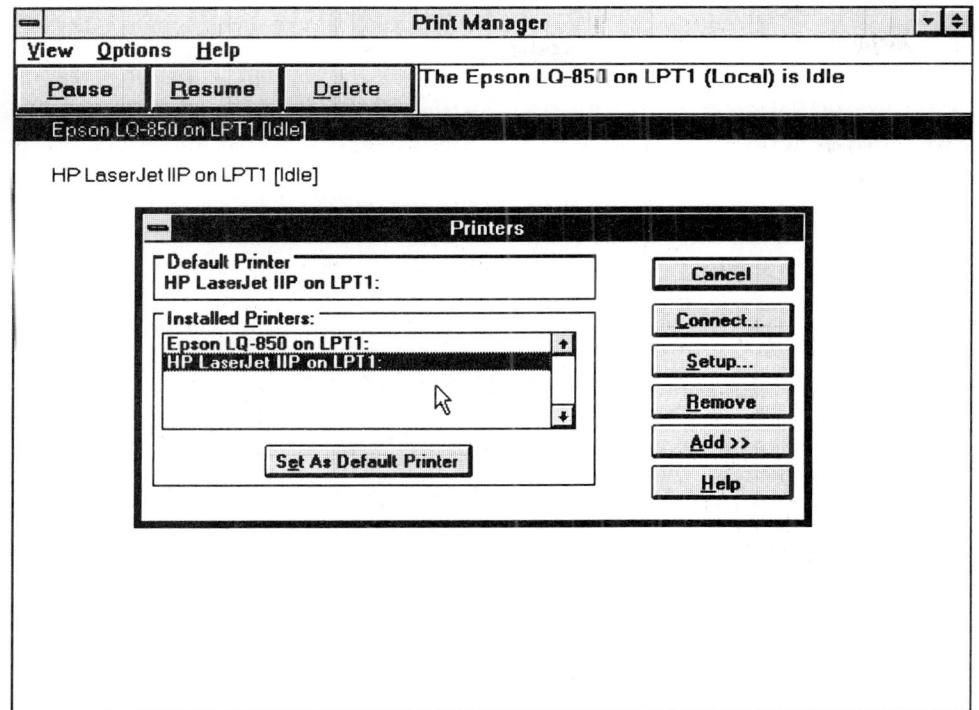

Figure 13-8
Printers dialog box

name of the printer, the port or network resource that the printer is using to print through, and the status of the printer. When a file is printing, the status of the print job is displayed under the appropriate print queue name. Information displayed in this area includes the title of the print job, the position of the file in the print queue, file size, time and date the file was sent to the queue, and, if the file is printing, the percentage of the file that has printed.

As you can see, the Print Manager offers a variety of tools to help you manage your print jobs effectively. It allows you to directly control the operation of your printer(s).

13-5
PIF Editor

A **program information file** (PIF) tells Windows how to run a specific non-Windows application. Windows 3.1 comes with more than 200 PIFs for common non-Windows applications. One way to get a listing of the PIF files in your system is to use the DOS command DIR *.PIF/W at the DOS prompt in your Windows subdirectory. This command displays all of the PIF files in the Windows subdirectory in wide format. Don't be worried if your system has only a few PIFs. PIF file information is stored in a file called APPS.INF, and Windows accesses the PIF information stored within this file as it is needed.

You may also use the File Manager to see all of the PIF files: First select the Windows subdirectory; then choose the By File Type option from the View menu. The File Manager displays the By File Type dialog box for you to enter the desired file specification. Type *.PIF* and press Enter; File Manager displays all of the PIF files in your Windows subdirectory.

The **PIF Editor** allows you to edit any of the PIFs to your particular needs. You can also use the PIF Editor to create your own custom PIFs. Basically, a PIF is a file that tells Windows how to allocate memory to the application with which that PIF is associated. You should either choose an existing PIF or create a new PIF for every non-Windows application that you use within Windows. If you run a non-Windows application that does not have a specific PIF associated with it, Windows automatically uses one called DEFAULT.PIF. Remember, in addition to selecting an existing PIF or creating a brand new PIF for use with an application, you may edit an existing PIF to fit your needs.

Two kinds of PIFs can be established and used with applications: Standard mode and 386 Enhanced mode. Windows automatically detects the mode in which your PIFs should be created; it depends on the mode in which your computer is running (Standard or Enhanced).

To learn more about how to create and use PIFs, double-click left on the PIF icon in the Main group of the Program Manager, or move the highlight to the PIF icon and press Enter to run the program. You will see a screen similar to the one in Figure 13–9. The main menu includes the following options:

- File: This option allows you to create a new PIF, open an existing PIF for editing, save the current PIF, and exit.
- Mode: This option allows you to specify whether the application for which you are creating a PIF should be executed in Standard mode or in 386 Enhanced mode. As mentioned earlier, in most cases just accept the default mode.
- Help: This option gives you access to the general help facility of Windows and specific information on the PIF Editor.

Figure 13–9
PIF Editor screen

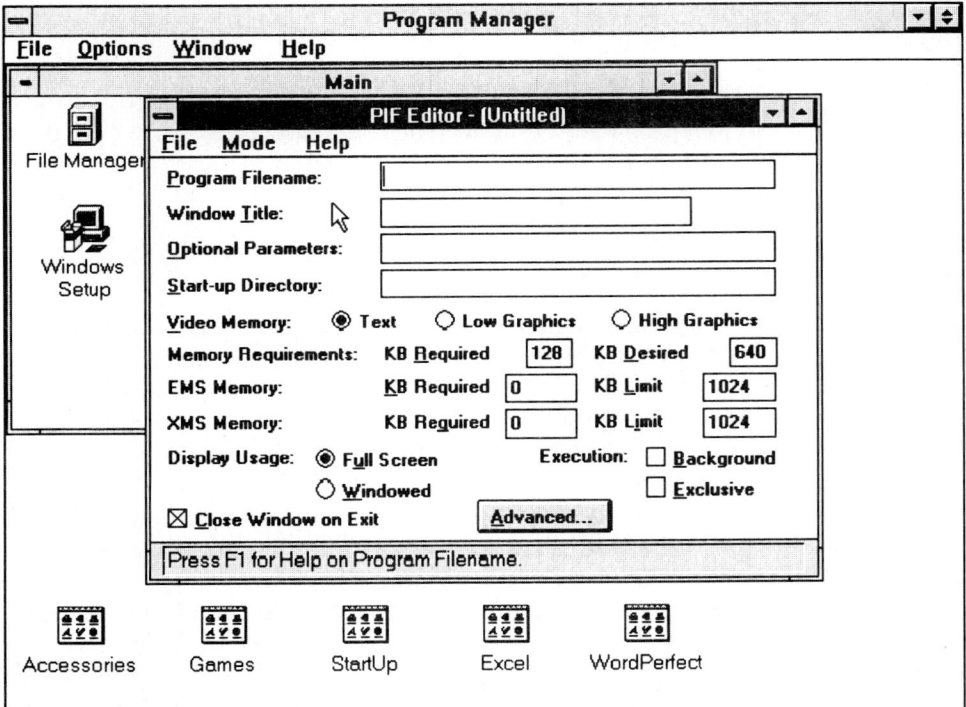

Below the menu line are all of the options that tell Windows how to handle memory for the application for which you are creating a PIF. Let us briefly discuss the options:

- Program Filename: This is the name of the application itself. For example, if you are creating a PIF for WordPerfect, the program file name would be C:\WP51\WP.EXE (assuming that WordPerfect is installed in the WP51 directory of drive C).

- Window Title: This is the application title that appears in the Task List when you run the application. For example, if you run WordPerfect for DOS using the PIF that is supplied with the program, the application name WordPerfect will be displayed in the Task List when you press the Ctrl-Esc key combination.

- Optional Parameters: These parameters can be used to alter the operation of the application. If the application has optional parameters, they should be entered in this box. For example, assume that you are using a network version of WordPerfect. On starting the application, you must supply your three-letter user access code. If you type /u=xxx (where "xxx" is your three-letter user access code) into the Optional Parameters field, WordPerfect will read that setting on start-up and *not* prompt you to manually enter the use code every time the application is run.

- Start-up Directory: This is the directory to which you want the application to have immediate access after it is running. For example, if you want WordPerfect to have immediate access to the files that are stored in C:\WP51\WP51DATA, enter this in the Start-up Directory box.

- Video Memory: This option asks you to check the type of video memory that you want your application to use (refer to Figure 13–9). Text uses the least amount of memory and is the fastest. Low Graphics is associated with CGA monitors and requires more memory than the Text option. High Graphics uses the most memory and should be used with EGA and/or VGA or higher-type monitors.

- Memory Requirements: This option tells Windows how much conventional memory to allocate to the application. Conventional memory is the first 640 K of memory on the system. The KB Required option tells Windows how much conventional memory to initially allocate to the application, and the KB Desired option tells Windows what the maximum amount of conventional memory allocated to the application should be. Most of the time, you leave the KB Required setting at 128 and the KB Desired at 640.

- EMS Memory: This option tells Windows how much expanded memory to allocate to the application. Some applications run better if they have access to expanded memory. The KB Required option tells Windows how much expanded memory to initially allocate to the application, and the KB Limit option tells Windows what the maximum amount of expanded memory allocated to the application should be. To prevent access to expanded memory, set both KB Required and KB Limit to 0.

- XMS Memory: This option tells Windows how much extended memory to allocate to the application. Some applications run better if they have access to extended memory. The KB Required option tells Windows how much extended memory to initially allocate to the application, and the KB Limit option tells Windows what the maximum amount of extended memory allocated to the application should be. To prevent access to extended memory, set both KB Required and KB Limit to 0.

- Display Usage: This option tells Windows whether you want to run the application in Full Screen mode or in a window.
- Execution: If this option is set to Exclusive, Windows will dedicate CPU operations strictly to this application while the application is in use. Alternatively, if this option is set to Background, Windows will allow the application to run simultaneously in the background while another application is running in the foreground. In this mode, for example, your communications software could continue sending and receiving information in the background while you work in another software application in the foreground.
- Close Window on Exit: This option tells Windows you want to keep the application window open and displayed on screen even after you have exited the application. This is particularly useful for applications that generate output to the screen, then terminate. Usually, after program termination, the application window closes. With this option enabled, the window remains open until you have had an opportunity to view the output. You can then close the window by clicking on the control menu box icon in the upper-left corner, and choosing Close.
- Advanced: This option gives access to more memory allocation and display settings. For example, in the Advanced screen, you can set Background and Foreground Priority, which tells the CPU how to allocate CPU resources to the application, how to handle video memory, and what keys to use for fast application switching.

The PIF Editor allows you to tell Windows exactly how to handle the application for which you are establishing the PIF. In most cases, the default settings in the PIF screen are appropriate. However, if you are having difficulty getting an application to run properly, or if you simply want to change the way that Windows interacts with an application, use the PIF Editor to make necessary changes.

13-6 OBJECT PACKAGER

The **Object Packager** adds icon-based information or recorded messages to documents and spreadsheets, thereby making them interactive. A double-click on the icon(s) will display the hidden note or play the recorded message.

Let's say that you have created an annual budget report using Write. You then link a spreadsheet created in Excel into the document by using OLE capabilities. After finishing the report, you decide that the meaning of the data in the spreadsheet would be clearer if you could somehow attach a note to help explain it. If you add the note into the spreadsheet, the spreadsheet will be cluttered, and besides, not everyone who will look at the spreadsheet requires additional clarification. The solution is simple: use the Object Packager. You can insert an icon into the report so that if the reader is interested, he or she can double-click on the icon to display the note or play the recorded message!

First create your note by typing it into a blank Write document; then save the note (be sure to remember the name!). Then, open the budget report, position the cursor in the document at the point where you want to insert the additional information, and select Insert Package from the Edit menu. Windows opens the Object Packager dialog box (Figure 13-10) so you can select an icon and associate the contents of a file with the selected icon. Select an icon that is

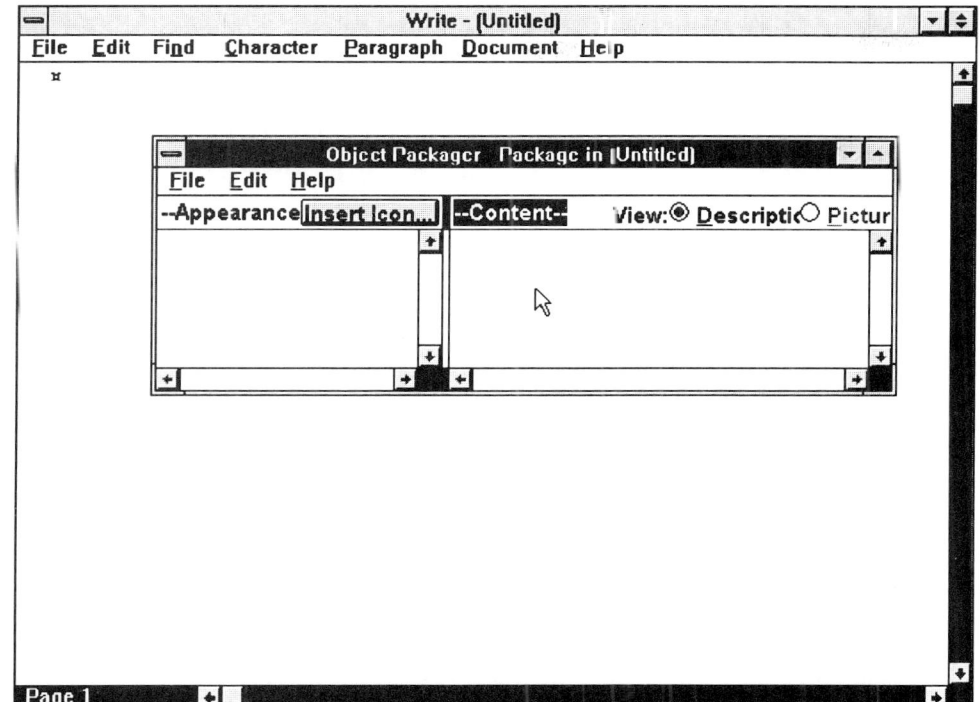

Figure 13-10
Object Packager dialog box

appropriate to the type of information that you wish to convey. Associate it with the note that you created in Write by selecting the Import option from the File menu. Double-click on the name of the Write file that contains your note. Select Exit from the File menu, and when the Object Packager prompts you about whether to perform the update, select Yes. You will be returned to your Write document and the icon you selected will be displayed on the screen.

You may view the information contained within the note by double-clicking on the icon. Likewise, other users who view this document on their screen can double-click on the icon. Windows responds by opening a Write window with the note that you created already displayed. The user can then add, change, or delete information contained within the note and save the changes so that the icon contains different information for the next user to view.

The Object Packager is also capable of recording a spoken message. If your system is equipped with a microphone, speakers, and the appropriate drivers, you can record a message of up to 60 seconds into a file and associate the file with an icon by means of the Object Packager. When another user double-clicks on the icon, he or she will hear your voice in the recorded message! Experiment with the Object Packager on your own to create more interesting and interactive documents.

SUMMARY

This chapter provided a working knowledge of five of the advanced features of Windows 3.1: Recorder, Object Linking and Embedding, Print Manager, PIF Editor, and Object Packager. This knowledge should assist you in using the Windows environment more effectively.

REVIEW QUESTIONS

*These questions are answered in Appendix A.

1. What is the Recorder? What are the applications of the Recorder?
2. How do you start the Recorder? How do you stop it?
*3. How many options are available in the Recorder menu?
4. What are the options under the Macro option of Recorder?
5. How long can a macro name be?
6. How do you know that a macro that you have designed will work properly?
7. What are some examples of shortcut keys used in macros?
*8. Can you run your macro from any application or must it be run from the application in which it was created? Discuss.
9. What is object linking? What is object embedding?
10. What is the difference between object linking and object embedding?
11. What are some of the unique advantages of object linking?
12. What is an object? What is a server application? What is a client?
13. Describe an application of object linking that might save you a lot of time.
*14. How do you modify an object that has been linked?
15. Give a couple of examples of applications that can use object linking.
*16. What is dynamic data exchange?
17. What is the difference between DDE and OLE?
18. What are some of the applications of the Print Manager?
19. What are some of the options in the Print Manager screen?
20. What is the role of the High Priority option in the Print Manager screen?
21. What does Pause do? What does Resume do?
*22. How can you use the PIF Editor?
23. How many types of PIFs can be established?
24. What are some of the options on the PIF Editor screen?
25. What is the role of the Start-up Directory in the PIF Editor screen?
26. What is the Object Packager? What are some of its applications?

HANDS-ON EXPERIENCE

1. Using the Recorder, create a macro in Write that will produce the following centered and bold entry (notice that the company title is in italics). When you are finished, test your macro to make sure that it works properly.

   ACME GLASS COMPANY
   123 Main Street
   Portland, OR 97207

2. Create a simple drawing using Paintbrush and save the drawing. Use the Copy option from the Edit menu to place a copy of the drawing into the Clipboard. Next, close Paintbrush and create a link by placing the copy of the drawing into the Write document that you created in exercise 1. Be sure to place the drawing a few lines below the company name and address. Test the link by editing the drawing. (Hint: to edit the drawing, double-click left on it). Make sure that the changes that you make to the drawing show up in the Write document.

3. Load the Print Manager; then change your printer port mapping to a port other than the one your computer is using. Be sure to write down what the port is supposed to

Chapter 13 Advanced Features of Windows 3.1

be before making any changes! Switch back to the Write document created in exercises 1 and 2 and print the document. Switch back to the Print Manager and study the effect of your change on the status of the print job. Delete the print job, set the printer port mapping back to the original setting, and print the document again. What happens this time?

4. Switch to the Program Manager and double-click left on the MS-DOS Prompt icon. Type *EXIT* and press Enter to return to the Windows Program Manager. Next, load the PIF Editor and open the PIF called DOSPRMPT.PIF (Hint: use the Open option in the File menu). Change the Display Usage setting from Full Screen to Windowed. Save the edited PIF; then close the PIF Editor. Once again, double-click left on the MS-DOS Prompt icon. How did the appearance of the MS-DOS Prompt screen change? How can you set it back to the way that it was at the beginning?

5. Start Write and type three lines of text. Save the document under the name TEST; then exit Write. Start Cardfile and type your address. Select the Picture option from the Edit menu. Use the Insert Object command from the Edit menu to access the Object Packager. Insert an icon just below the address that represents your TEST document. Now double-click on this icon. You should see the contents of the TEST document (three lines of text).

KEY TERMS

Dynamic data exchange
Macro
Embedding an object
Linking an object
Object Packager
PIF Editor
Print Manager
Program information file
Recorder

KEY COMMANDS

For options in the PIF Editor, see Figure 13–9.
For Print Manager commands, see Figure 13–7.
For Recorder commands, see Figure 13–1.

MISCONCEPTIONS AND SOLUTIONS

Misconception None of the macros that you created using the Recorder work.

> **Solution** Make sure you didn't create the macros using the mouse. As you know, the position of windows can change, thereby making mouse pointer positioning useless when making menu selections. Use the keyboard to select menu commands when creating macros.

Misconception You created a PIF for your non-Windows application, but when you run the PIF, Windows displays an error message stating that you do not have enough memory to run the application.

> **Solution** Open the PIF Editor and open the PIF that you created. Reduce the KB Required setting in the Memory Requirements section of the PIF Editor screen. Save the PIF and run the application again

Misconception You cannot edit the object that you embedded in one of your applications.

> **Solution** Are you double-clicking on the object? Is the application that you used to create the object still available on hard disk? If you have met both of these conditions, delete the object from the client application and embed it again according to the steps outlined in this chapter. It is possible (though unlikely) that the link information stored within the appropriate dynamic link library has become corrupted or lost. Embedding the object again will refresh the link

information within the dynamic link library. Now double-clicking on the object should automatically load the source application with the object ready for editing.

Misconception You send a print job to the printer; then you decide that you do not want to print it after all. You attempt to switch to the Print Manager but find that it is either not running or your print job is not displayed in it.

Solution Several conditions might be causing the problem. When you send a print job to the Print Manager, the job is immediately passed through the appropriate output port to the specified printer. If all of the data has been passed to the printer already, Print Manager will have already shut down and you will not be able to switch to it as an active application. Alternatively, you may switch to the Print Manager while it is still active, but the data is almost finished being transmitted to the printer. As soon as all of the data has been sent to the printer, the print job disappears from the Print Manager screen. Finally, if Print Manager is not running at all, you should check the Use Print Manager setting in the Printers dialog box of the Printers option contained in the Control Panel. If this setting is not selected, the Print Manager has been disabled. Selecting this option will enable the Print Manager again.

ARE YOU READY TO MOVE ON?

Multiple Choice

1. Which of the following is *not* an application of a macro?
    a. typing a closing
    b. typing a header
    c. formatting a disk
    d. creating a graph in Paintbrush
    e. they all are
2. Which of the following is *not* included in the Recorder menu bar?
    a. Draw
    b. Help
    c. Options
    d. Macro
    e. File
3. To switch from the Recorder to Write, one method is to press
    a. Ctrl-Caps Lock
    b. Ctrl-Esc
    c. Ctrl-Shift
    d. Shift-A
    e. none of the above
4. What is the maximum number of characters for a macro name?
    a. 10
    b. 20
    c. 30
    d. 40
    e. 50
5. Which of the following keys cannot be included in a macro name?
    a. Ctrl
    b. Shift

Chapter 13 Advanced Features of Windows 3.1 275

    c. Backspace
    d. Alt
    e. they all can be included

6. An object in Windows can be all of the following except
    a. a graph
    b. a Write document
    c. a menu bar
    d. a Paintbrush chart
    e. all of them

7. To bring a graph from Paintbrush to a document in Write, what should you select?
    a. Paste from the Edit menu
    b. Copy from the File menu
    c. New from the File menu
    d. File from the Paste menu
    e. none of the above

8. Which of the following options is not included in the Print Manager screen?
    a. View
    b. Options
    c. Save
    d. Pause
    e. Resume

9. If you run a non-Windows application that does not have a specific PIF associated with it, Windows automatically uses one called
    a. AUTO.PIF
    b. DEFAULT.PIF
    c. SAVE.PIF
    d. COMMON.PIF
    e. none of the above

10. The main menu of the PIF Editor includes all of the following options except
    a. File
    b. Mode
    c. Help
    d. they all are included
    e. only a and c are included

True/False

1. The Mode option in the PIF Editor allows you to specify whether the application for which you are creating a PIF should be executed in Standard mode or in 386 Enhanced mode.
2. In the PIF Editor, the Window Title and the Program Filename are the same.
3. In the PIF Editor, the EMS Memory option allocates the extended memory.
4. Using the Object Packager you can create interactive documents.
5. To start the recording procedure, you must select Record from the Macro menu in the Recorder application.
6. The Ctrl key cannot be used as a part of a macro name.
7. The embedding feature is new to Windows 3.1; earlier versions of Windows did not have such a capability.

8. In Windows, a graph or a table can be called an object.
9. The destination document is the document into which you intend to embed an object.
10. A macro can be executed from any application regardless of where it was created.

Answers	Multiple Choice	True/False
	1. e	1. T
	2. a	2. F
	3. b	3. F
	4. d	4. T
	5. e	5. T
	6. c	6. F
	7. a	7. F
	8. c	8. T
	9. b	9. T
	10. d	10. F

Appendix A
Answers to Selected Review Questions and Review of System Files

A–1
ANSWERS TO SELECTED REVIEW QUESTIONS

Chapter 1

2. Disk drive and keyboard.
6. Floppy and hard disks.
12. It varies; it starts at 640 K, 1 MB, 4 MB or higher.
16. Keep it in a dust-free environment. Protect it against excessive heat and humidity. Provide a constant electrical current.
21. Every application program provides an editing feature so you can correct your mistakes. In the worst case, you can retype your mistakes.
26. Priority of operations, or precedence of operations, refers to the order in which a computer handles calculations. The order is as follows: Expressions inside parentheses have the highest priority. Exponentiation (raising to power) has the next highest priority. Multiplication and division have the third highest priority. Addition and subtraction have the fourth highest priority. When there are two or more operations with the same priority, operations proceed from left to right.

Chapter 2

4. Always enter the correct date and time at boot-up time. If you do so, whenever you save a file it will be timed and dated correctly. Later, you can easily find out which version of the file is the most or the least recent version. To bypass the date and time, press Enter twice.
8. The DIR/W command generates a wide directory in a horizontal format. You see only the file names and their extensions. The DIR/P command generates a directory in a vertical format; you see one screen at a time. To see the next screen, press any key.
11. Press Ctrl-C or Ctrl-Break.
17. Type *VER* and press Enter.

Chapter 3

2. FORMATA:/S.
5. To generate an exact duplicate of a disk, use the DISKCOPY command. The target disk does not need to be formatted because the DISKCOPY command formats and copies at the same time.
10. The SYS command copies the DOS hidden files from the DOS disk to another disk.
13. COPY FileA.ABC+FileB.ABC FileC.ABC.

Appendices

16. DISKCOPY erases the target disk; COPY *.* does not. With DISKCOPY the target disk does not need to be formatted; with COPY *.* the target disk must be formatted. DISKCOPY transfers the hidden files; COPY *.* does not.

Chapter 4

3. Subdirectories improve the efficiency and effectiveness of secondary storage devices significantly. Subdirectories allow you to store different files in certain electronic folders for easy retrieval. Subdirectories are even more important in a hard disk environment because a hard disk has much more storage space than a floppy disk.
8. To move up one directory level, type *CD..* To move up two directory levels, type *CD..\..*
12. To erase a directory, first you must erase all the files and subsequent directories in that directory by using the DEL command. Then you can erase the empty directory by typing the RD command followed by the directory name.
15. You must run the FDISK program.
20. You must use the "A" parameter. For example,

   C>BACKUP C:*.* A:/S/A/D 10/10/92

   backs up all the files created since 10/10/92 and adds them to the disk in drive A without erasing any of the files in drive A.

Chapter 5

3. Windows uses a computer's memory more efficiently because it does not restrict itself to 640 K of conventional memory. If it cannot load an application completely to RAM, it spills over to the hard disk.
6. One method is to double-click the left button of the mouse while on the control-menu box.
12. Alt, Ctrl, and Shift.
16. Click the left button of the mouse while on the Help option in the Program Manager menu.
20. Window title, title bar, scroll bars, and so forth.

Chapter 6

5. The toolbox is a collection of tools for drawing various shapes. Altogether there are 18 tools.
8. To select the background color.
11. Select Image Attributes from the Options menu; then click the left button of the mouse on Black and White and on OK.
16. Select Undo from the Edit menu or press Ctrl-Z.
20. Invoke the File menu and select the Print Partial commands; then select the desired area.
24. Select File Save or File Save As.

Chapter 7

3. The Save command saves a document under its current name. The Save As command allows you to save a document under a different name.

Appendix A Answers to Selected Review Questions and Review of System Files

7. Yes. Select the Save File As Type from the Save As dialog box; then select the desired type.
12. Yes.
17. Copying does not change the selected text. Moving deletes the selected text from its original location.
24. Select Regular from the Character menu.

Chapter 8

3. Key combinations are shortcuts for performing a menu option without going through the menu.
6. Click left on the control-menu box.
9. To move a window from one location to another one using the keyboard.
14. Position the mouse pointer to one of the edges of the window and while pressing the left button of the mouse drag the edge in any direction.
17. Position the mouse pointer on one of the scroll arrows then click and hold it there.
22. The Task List is a window that shows all the applications that you are running and enables you to switch between them.

Chapter 9

4. Type or select its program name; then press Enter or click on OK.
7. Program files identify an application as an executable file. Typical extensions are .EXE .COM, .BAT, and .PIF.
12. Type *EXIT* and press Enter.
16. Select Copy or Copy To or Cut from the Edit menu of the application.
22. CLP.
25. Double-click on the control-menu box.
30. You can use a mouse or the keyboard.

Chapter 10

3. Double-click on its icon.
8. See section 10-2-6.
14. Three methods: Program Manager, File Manager, and Windows Setup program.
18. Yes.
24. Copy the application icon into the StartUp group.
32. There are several options, including Flying Windows, Mystify, Marquee, and so forth.

Chapter 11

3. To start, double-click on the File Manager icon from the Main group. To exit, double-click on the control-menu box.
8. Click left on the first file; move to the last file and press and hold down the Shift key; then click left.
12. From the View menu select by Sort by Type; then specify the type.
15. Reserved words used by Windows. If you try to use them, you will confuse Windows.
20. Select the File Rename command.

Appendices

24. Type the desired file extension in the Files with Extension box and in the Associate With box, click left on (None) and on OK.
27. Eleven.

Chapter 12

4. Use the Back (Backspace) key.
8. Press the F9 function key.
10. First press the F6 function key; then select the desired marking from the dialog box provided.
13. Displays the system's date.
17. Day (F8) and month (F9).
21. Select the Card option and click left on Add.
28. You have to have a modem, a serial port, a serial cable, and a telephone line. If you have an external modem, you will also need a serial port and a serial cable.

Chapter 13

3. Four.
8. You must run it from the application in which you generated the macro.
14. Double-click on the object in the destination document (client document).
16. Dynamic data exchange means changing the data in one place and having the change reflected in other places.
22. Use the PIF Editor to create program information files for non-Windows applications.

A–2
REVIEW OF SYSTEM FILES

When Windows is started, the computer system refers to the information contained within two very important files to control the operation and behavior of Windows after the application is running. These two files are called WIN.INI and SYSTEM.INI.

The INI extension identifies the files as *Ini*tialization files. The files are in ASCII format and can be edited directly using any application capable of editing standard text files. Knowledge of the contents and purpose of these files is important to gain a full understanding of how Windows works. In addition to these two files, Windows uses two other files in the system for initial system setup: AUTOEXEC.BAT and CONFIG.SYS.

In the next section, we discuss a special utility provided with Windows to display and allow editing of these files. This utility is called SYSEDIT.EXE.

Starting the SYSEDIT File

To run SYSEDIT, switch to the Program Manager and select the Run option from the File menu. Windows responds by displaying the Run dialog box. Type the word *SYSEDIT* and press Enter. At this point, a new window opens on your screen with the words "System Configuration Editor" displayed inside the title bar (Figure A–1). Within this window are four cascaded windows, each displaying the contents of a different file. As you can see, the title bars of the four smaller windows display the names SYSTEM.INI, WIN.INI, CONFIG.SYS, and

Appendix A Answers to Selected Review Questions and Review of System Files

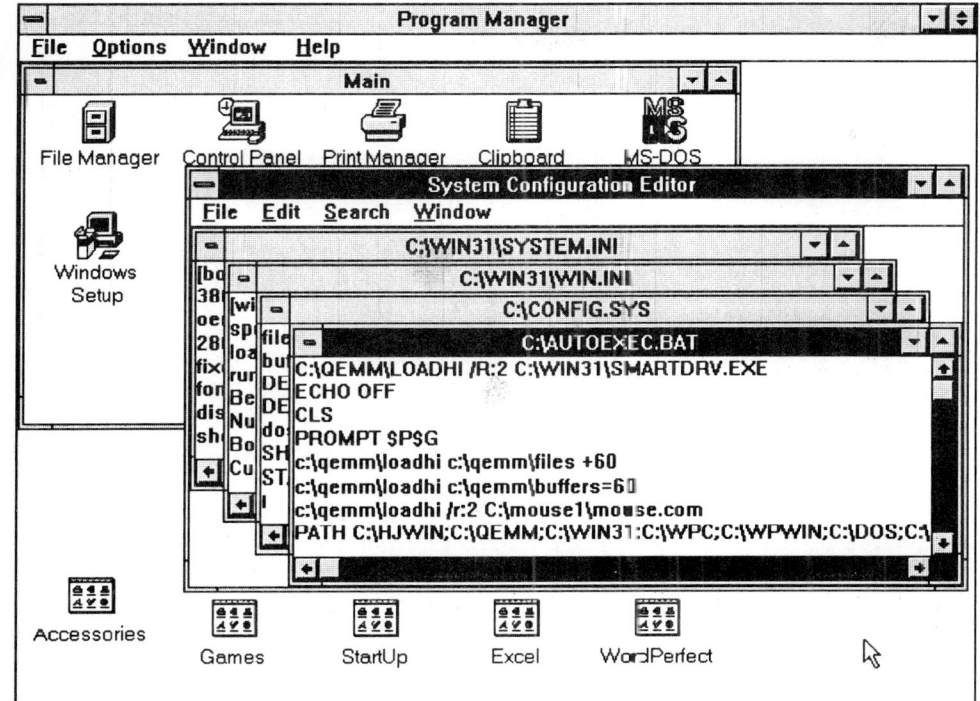

Figure A-1
System Configuration Editor screen

AUTOEXEC.BAT, respectively. Double-click anywhere in the title bar of the System Configuration Editor window to maximize the size of the window. Your screen should be similar to the one in Figure A-2.

The System Configuration Editor is a utility that allows you to quickly retrieve the contents of four of the most important files on your system. Once displayed, these files can be individually viewed, edited, searched for text strings, saved, and so forth.

The menu bar of System Configuration Editor contains the following options:

- File: This menu contains options that allow you to save your changes, print the contents of the current window, change the printer setup, and exit the System Configuration Editor.

- Edit: This menu contains options that allow you to Undo (Ctrl-Z) your last change, Cut (Ctrl-X) the highlighted text out of the window, Copy (Ctrl-C) the highlighted text, Paste (Ctrl-V) text that has been cut or copied into the window, Clear (Del) the character at the cursor position or the highlighted text, and Select All text to highlight all of the text in the window in preparation for cutting, copying, deleting, and so forth.

- Search: This menu contains options that allow you to find text that matches your specified text string, search for the next occurrence (F3) of the specified text string, and search for the previous occurrence (F4) of the specified text string.

- Window: This menu contains options that allow you to tile the windows in side-by-side display format, cascade the windows in an overlapping display format, arrange icons, and change to another window contained within the System Configuration Editor screen.

Figure A-2
Enlarged System Configuration Editor screen

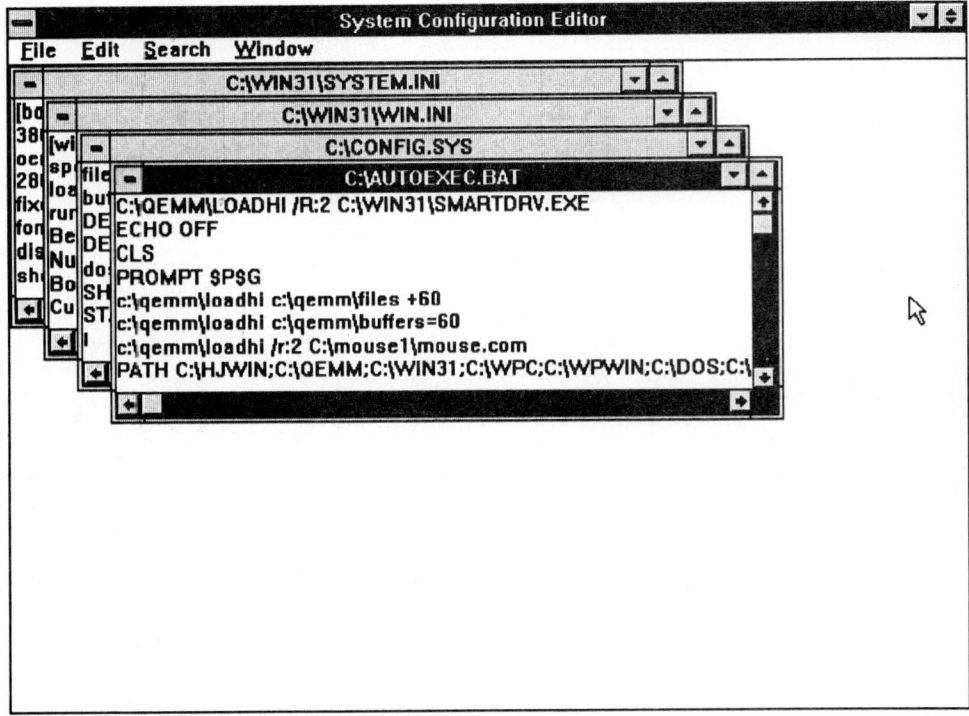

To exit from the System Configuration Editor, select the Exit option from the File menu.

The contents of the four smaller windows with examples are discussed in the next four sections.

Example of a Typical AUTOEXEC.BAT File

When the computer is turned on (booted), DOS searches the root directory of the boot drive for a file called AUTOEXEC.BAT. If DOS finds this batch file, the statements and instructions contained within the file are executed automatically. That is why it is called AUTOEXEC. However, if DOS does not find AUTOEXEC.BAT at the time of boot-up, the computer prompts the user to enter the date and time.

The AUTOEXEC.BAT file can be used to process instructions that you want executed every time you start your computer. The following example shows the contents of a typical AUTOEXEC.BAT file:

```
ECHO OFF
CLS
PROMPT $P$G
PATH C:\;C:\DOS
CD MENU
MENU
```

The six instructions contained within this file will be executed every time the computer is started. An explanation of each instruction follows:

Appendix A Answers to Selected Review Questions and Review of System Files

- ECHO OFF: This instruction tells DOS to suppress the display of the commands contained within AUTOEXEC.BAT as the batch file is executed.
- CLS: This instruction clears the screen.
- PROMPT PG: This instruction alters the display of the DOS system prompt to include the name of the current directory followed by a greater than symbol (>). For example, if you change your directory to \LOTUS\FORECAST, your DOS prompt will be C:\LOTUS\ FORECAST>. This is a helpful instruction, especially if you work with multilayer directories.
- PATH C:\;C:\DOS: This instruction sets a path to the root directory and to the DOS subdirectory of drive C. This allows you to execute instructions contained within these two directories regardless of your current subdirectory location.
- CD MENU: This instruction changes the current directory to the MENU subdirectory in preparation for the last instruction.
- MENU: This instruction executes the MENU program, thereby providing easy access to the application program options contained within the MENU.

As you can see, AUTOEXEC.BAT is nothing more than a DOS batch file that is executed automatically every time your computer is started, provided that DOS finds the file name in the root directory of your boot disk. AUTOEXEC.BAT takes all of the work out of getting your computer started. You can use a word processing program such as Write or NotePad to create the AUTOEXEC.BAT file.

Example of a Typical CONFIG.SYS File

At boot-up time, DOS searches the root directory of the boot drive for another file called CONFIG.SYS. If DOS finds the file, its contents are processed automatically. CONFIG.SYS is a DOS batch file just like AUTOEXEC.BAT; however, its function and purpose are very different. Whereas AUTOEXEC.BAT executes initial instructions at boot-up time, CONFIG.SYS establishes certain system parameters within which your system operates. The following example contains some typical CONFIG.SYS instructions:

```
FILES=40
BUFFERS=25
DEVICE=C:\MOUSE\MOUSE.SYS
```

The three instructions contained within this file will be executed every time the computer is started. An explanation of each instruction follows:

- FILES: This parameter defines how many files can be open at any one time. The example statement allows for 40 files to be open simultaneously. The number of files that should be specified on your computer depends on the type of applications that you are using. In a non-Windows environment, 25 files would probably be sufficient. Windows, however, operates by opening, running, and using many small files and programs simultaneously. Therefore, a larger number of files should be specified to allow Windows to operate smoothly and enable you to exercise the multitasking capabilities that Windows offers.

- BUFFERS: Buffers are small amounts of memory used by DOS to hold data that is being transferred during disk read and write operations. Each buffer is 528 bytes in size. The number of buffers specified depends on the applications that you are using, but in most cases 25 is sufficient.
- DEVICE=C:\MOUSE\MOUSE.SYS: Device drivers, like the one shown in this statement, are used to tell DOS how to communicate with the device itself. Other types of device drivers include PRINTER.SYS and CLOCK.SYS. The device driver that we included in this CONFIG.SYS file simply informs DOS that a mouse is connected to the computer and tells it where to look to find instructions about how to communicate with the mouse.

The same procedure for creating AUTOEXEC.BAT files applies to creating CONFIG.SYS files.

WIN.INI File

The WIN.INI file is the third window down in the stack of four windows (refer to Figure A–1). This initialization file serves a variety of purposes, from what colors and Wallpaper should be used to what printers have been set up for Windows. Double-click left on the title bar of this window to maximize it to the full size of the screen. Your screen should be similar to Figure A–3. Click on the down arrow at the bottom of the vertical scroll bar to scroll through this file.

As you can see, the WIN.INI file is divided into sections. Each section is preceded by the title of the section enclosed within brackets. Typical sections include [windows], [Desktop], and [Extensions]. Each section serves a different purpose relative to the overall function of Windows. For example, the windows section defines which applications should be loaded upon start-up, the current printer, and whether the screen saver is enabled. The Desktop section contains

Figure A–3
Partial listing of WIN.INI File

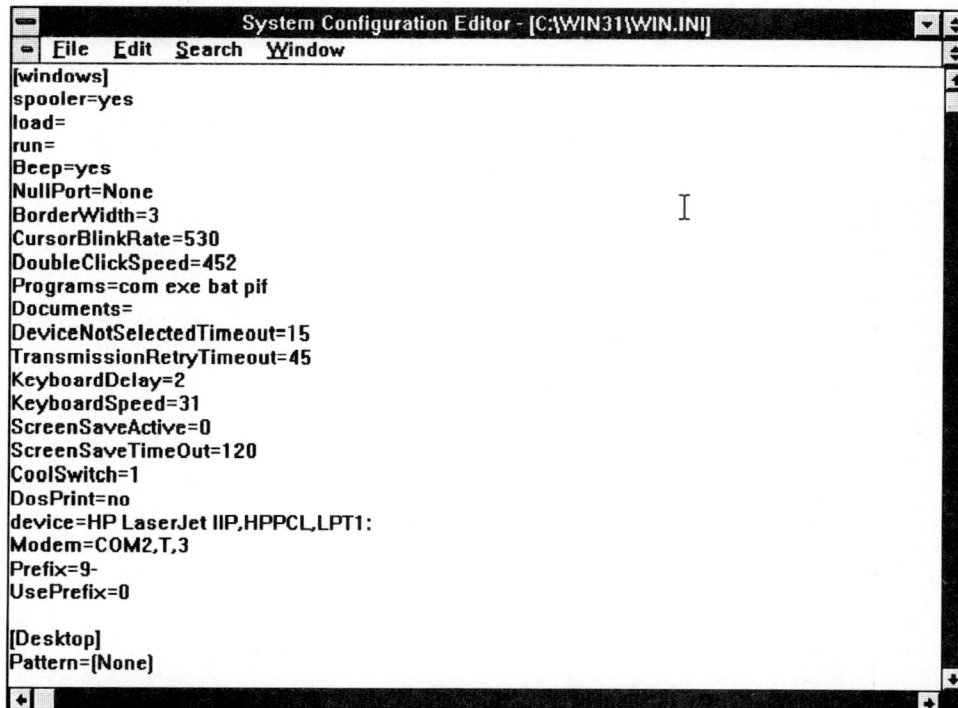

Appendix A Answers to Selected Review Questions and Review of System Files

settings for Wallpaper, icon spacing, and icon title size (among other things). Other sections define the type of printer(s) you are using, what output ports are available on your system, and so forth.

Making a change to one of these sections alters the performance or display characteristics of Windows. For example, scroll to the IconTitleSize setting within the Desktop section. Change the number that is displayed after the equal sign (=) to a higher number; then select the Exit option from the File menu. Choose Yes when you are prompted about whether to save the changes to your file. Exit Windows and start it again. You should see that the size of the text under the icons in the Program Manager screen has grown to accommodate the setting that you specified in the WIN.INI file. To change the setting back to its original size, run SYSEDIT again, change the IconTitleSize line back to its original setting, save the file, exit, and restart Windows. Remember, most changes that you make to this file will not show up until the next time you run Windows.

One final note: changes that you make using the Control Panel show up as changes to the settings contained within the WIN.INI file. For now, you may feel more comfortable using the Control Panel to make desired changes. However, the Control Panel does not allow all of the changes that are possible through direct editing of the WIN.INI file. Therefore, as you become more familiar with the capabilities of Windows, you may want to edit the contents of WIN.INI directly rather than through the Control Panel to achieve greater flexibility and more control over the Windows environment.

SYSTEM.INI File

The SYSTEM.INI file, which is at the bottom of the stack of four windows, contains all of the device drivers that define the keyboard, video, network, type of computer, and other peripheral device definitions. See Figure A–4.

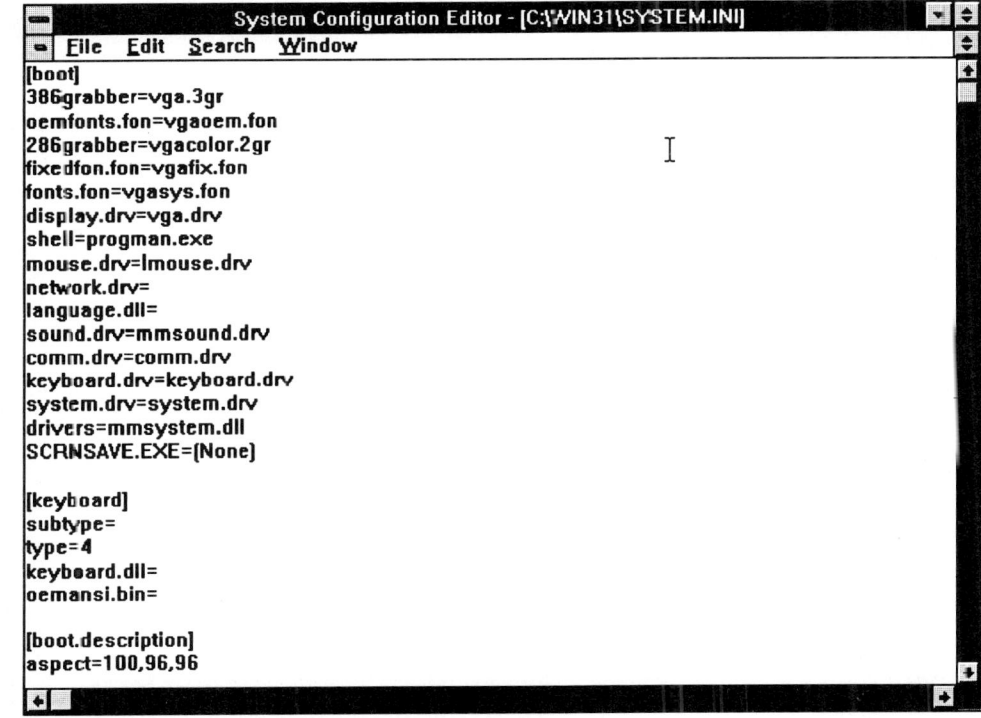

Figure A–4
Partial Listing of SYSTEM.INI File

Appendices

The four files that we have discussed can be edited, as you have seen, to alter the display and behavior characteristics of Windows. Take a few minutes to view all of the settings in the WIN.INI and SYSTEM.INI files. The time that you spend studying the contents of these files will help you better understand how Windows works and how you can customize Windows to your particular needs.

Appendix B
File Transfer Among Popular Software Packages

B-1
INTRODUCTION

This appendix presents guidelines for importing and exporting files to and from selected software, thereby enabling you to utilize the best features of each software package. By importing files from other software you also save time and frustration because you do not duplicate the same data file. The guidelines cover file transfer among DOS, WordPerfect 5.1, Lotus 1-2-3, dBASE III Plus/dBASE IV, Quattro Pro, Paradox, and BASICA.

Some software applications such as Quattro Pro and Paradox provide extensive support for file transfer. Other packages such as Lotus 1-2-3 provide a translate utility that enables you to translate one file format to another. The guidelines in this appendix involve exporting and importing ASCII files. For extensive information about the availability and use of the built-in file transfer facilities of each software application, consult the package's documentation.

B-2
WHY USE FILE TRANSFER?

File transfer allows the movement of a file generated by one software application program to another. There are three good reasons for performing such a task:

1. Utilizing a capability of one software package that is not available in another. For example, you might transfer a Lotus 1-2-3 spreadsheet to a report generated by a word processing program thereby creating a factual and comprehensive report. You may also want to import dBASE data into 1-2-3 for graphing—a feature that is not available in dBASE.
2. Utilizing the enhanced power in one package for the same basic tasks that can be performed by two software applications. For example, database operations performed by 1-2-3 are much faster than those performed by dBASE; therefore, you might want to translate a dBASE file into a 1-2-3 spreadsheet for faster processing.
3. Converting data files from earlier software application programs to more recent versions. This is a common practice. Consider converting VisiCalc (the most popular spreadsheet program before 1-2-3) files into 1-2-3 files. Without data transfer facilities, you would have to enter all the data again, a very time-consuming, error-prone, and tedious task.

B–3
WHAT IS AN ASCII FILE?

Probably the easiest and most straightforward method for file transfer is to use ASCII files. ASCII (American Standard Code for Information Interchange) is a data format generated and accepted by most software application packages.

An ASCII file, or simply a "print image" file (sometimes called a DOS text file), is a file composed of standard keyboard characters. To verify whether a file is in ASCII format or not is a simple task. At the DOS prompt type *TYPE file name.extension* and press Enter, for example, *TYPE SAMPLE.TXT* (press Enter). If the file is displayed on the screen in standard keyboard characters, it is in ASCII format; otherwise it is not. In other words, you should be able to read an ASCII file. For example, 1-2-3 files generated by the /Print File command (files with the PRN extension) are ASCII files.

As mentioned earlier, different software packages include specific capabilities for file transfer. For example, 1-2-3 includes the translate utility, which is able to translate from and to several different file formats. The next few sections provide specific guidelines for file transfer among selected software applications.

B–4
FILE TRANSFER AND DOS

Files created by the COPY CON, EDLIN, and EDIT (in DOS 5) commands are automatically in ASCII format. If you are using EDLIN, enter the following command to load and edit an ASCII file:

```
EDLIN SAMPLE.BAT (press Enter)
```

In this case both EDLIN and SAMPLE.BAT are assumed to be in your default directory and drive. If they are not, you must include the drive identifier and/or the exact path. SAMPLE is the name of the file and BAT is its extension. After you have loaded the file, it is available for editing. When you save a file in EDLIN or EDIT, the file is automatically saved in ASCII file format.

B–5
FILE TRANSFER AND WORDPERFECT 5.1

Creating ASCII Files

To generate an ASCII file in WordPerfect press Ctrl-F5 (Text In/Out). You are presented with the following menu:

```
1 DOS Text; 2 Password; 3 Save As; 4 Comment; 5 Spreadsheet: 0
```

From this menu select option 1 (DOS Text). You are presented with the following menu:

```
1 Save; 2 Retrieve (CR/LF to [HRt]); 3 Retrieve (CR/LF to [SRt] in HZone): 0
```

Appendix B File Transfer Among Popular Software Packages

From this menu select option 1 (Save). At this point WordPerfect responds with

```
Document to be saved (DOS Text):
```

Type in a name (for example SAMPLE) and press Enter. The file extension is optional. You must also specify the drive identifier and/or the correct path if you are not saving into the default drive and directory.

It is a good idea to save your file in WordPerfect format as well. To do this use either F10 or F7. If you do save your file in WordPerfect format, be sure to use a different name; otherwise, the file created in ASCII format will be overwritten by the file with the same name in WordPerfect format!

Importing ASCII Files

To import an ASCII file into WordPerfect press Ctrl-F5 (Text In/Out). From this menu select option 1 (DOS Text). From this menu select either option 2, Retrieve (CR/LF to [HRt]) or option 3, Retrieve (CR/LF to [SRt] in HZone). Type the name of the file and press Enter. The file will be imported into the WordPerfect document at the cursor position.

The "CR/LF" refers to the carriage return/line feed codes in the ASCII file. These codes are used to end one line and move the cursor to the next line.

Using the CR/LF to [SRt] option enables the imported file to closely match the WordPerfect format. If you use this option, you should set the margin width of your WordPerfect document to closely match that used by the ASCII file. If you use the CR/LF [HRt] option, set the WordPerfect document margin wider than the margin of the ASCII file that is being imported.

B–6
IMPORTING FILES INTO WORDPERFECT: A SECOND METHOD

Another method of importing ASCII format files into WordPerfect is through the F5 (List Files) key. To use this method, press F5. WordPerfect responds by displaying the name of the default directory in the lower left corner of the screen. If this drive/directory path is correct, press the Enter key; otherwise, type the desired drive and directory path and press Enter. WordPerfect displays the listing of files contained in the displayed directory. To import an ASCII file from this screen, you have two options.

1. You can highlight the file that you want to import and select 1 or R (Retrieve) from the List Files menu. WordPerfect briefly displays

```
Document Conversion in Progress
```

in the lower-left corner of the screen as the file is being imported. The imported file is converted into standard WordPerfect format and displayed on the screen.

2. Highlight the file that you want to import, then press Ctrl-F5 (Text In/Out). WordPerfect responds by displaying

```
(DOS) Retrieve [drive:\path\file name.extension]? No (Yes)
```

If you press Y, WordPerfect retrieves the specified file without further prompting.

Note that using this method does not trigger the "Document Conversion in Progress" message that a normal retrieve request generates. This is so because WordPerfect does not need to convert the document into WordPerfect file format. The file is imported in its simple ASCII format with no additional format codes.

B-7
FILE TRANSFER AND LOTUS 1-2-3

Creating ASCII Files

To create ASCII files in 1-2-3, use the /Print File command. After selecting /Print File, you must specify the desired range (press Enter), then select Align, Go, and Quit. When you print to a file, the file is saved with a PRN extension. Remember that when you generate an ASCII file from your spreadsheet, the converted file is no longer a true worksheet. To maintain this spreadsheet in its original form, you must use the /File Save command before conversion and save your file in WK1 format. However, if you forget to save in standard format first, 1-2-3 offers the /Data Parse command which enables you to convert this ASCII file back to its original form. After issuing the /Print File command you must specify the Range, then choose Align, then Go, and finally Quit. The Quit command closes the file and finalizes the file creation process.

Importing ASCII Files

To import an ASCII file into 1-2-3, use the /File Import command. After issuing this command specify the file name and then press Enter. You are prompted to select Formulas or Values. Select Values. The file is imported into the spreadsheet at the position of the cellpointer, and as many rows down and columns to the right as necessary are used to accommodate the entire file.

B-8
FILE TRANSFER AND dBASE

Creating ASCII Files

In dBASE, to create an ASCII file you use the COPY command. The syntax of this command is:

COPY TO {file name}/{scope}/FIELDS {field list}/FOR {condition}/
WHILE {condition}/TYPE {file type}

The scope, FIELDS, FOR, and WHILE entries are optional. These options provide more control over the final results. The TYPE option indicates the type of file to be created. Three file types are most commonly generated by dBASE:

Appendix B File Transfer Among Popular Software Packages

1. WKS (worksheet): This file extension generates spreadsheet files accepted by 1-2-3. For example, to generate a 1-2-3 WK1 file in dBASE, at the dot prompt type *COPY TO SAMPLE.WK1/TYPE WKS*. Now in 1-2-3, by using the /File Retrieve command, you can bring this file into 1-2-3 and perform any operations on it.
2. SDF (system data format ASCII file): This file type copies database fields using the same format as the fields in the database file structure. It does not contain field separators; therefore, there is no space between fields. An example is *COPY TO SAMPLE/TYPE SDF*.
3. DIF (Visicalc worksheet): This format was originally used by VisiCalc—the first commercial spreadsheet. It now can be read by 1-2-3 also. An example is *COPY TO SAMPLE.TXT/TYPE DIF*.

Importing ASCII Files

To import an ASCII file into dBASE, at the dot prompt issue the APPEND FROM command. For example,

APPEND FROM SAMPLE.TXT

As usual you can use the FOR condition to append selected records. In this example, the SAMPLE.TXT file will be appended to your current file.
    Export and import facilities are also available through the dBASE III Plus assist menu and dBASE IV Control Center.

B-9
FILE TRANSFER AND 1-2-3 PIC FILES

1-2-3 generates PIC files when you issue the /Graph Save command. By integrating graphs into your reports, you can significantly improve the quality of your documents. In the past, graphs were manually cut and pasted into reports. By using the procedure described below, you can electronically include any of your 1-2-3 graphs in WordPerfect documents. Follow these steps:

1. Start with 1-2-3 and create the graph of your choice.
2. By using the /Graph Save command, save your graph. This procedure generates a file with a PIC extension.
3. Exit 1-2-3 and start WordPerfect. Press Alt-F9. This invokes the graphics menu:

    ```
    1 Figure; 2 Table Box; 3 Text Box; 4 User Box; 5 Line; 6 Equation: 0
    ```

4. Press 1 or F for Figure. The following menu is displayed:

    ```
    Figure: 1 Create; 2 Edit; 3 New Number; 4 Options: 0
    ```

5. Options 2, 3, and 4 are used when the graph has already been imported into the document. In our case, select 1 or C for Create. The following menu is displayed:

```
Definition: Figure
1 - Filename
2 - Contents                 Empty
3 - Caption
4 - Anchor Type              Paragraph
5 - Vertical Position        0"
6 - Horizontal Position      Right
7 - Size                     3.25" wide × 3.25" (high)
8 - Wrap Text Around Box     Yes
9 - Edit
```

The Filename option indicates the name of the graphics file to be imported into your WordPerfect document.

The Contents option will be modified after a file has been retrieved into the memory of the computer through the use of option 1. In our case, after loading a PIC file, Contents will be set to "Graphic."

The Caption option allows you to enter a caption to appear with your graph.

The Anchor Type option allows you to specify how the graph should appear in relation to the text that surrounds it. If you select option 4 (Anchor Type), you receive the following menu:

```
Anchor Type: 1 Paragraph; 2 Page; 3 Character: 0
```

If you select the Paragraph option, the graph stays with the text that surrounds it even if the surrounding text is moved to a new position in the document. If you select Page, the graphics box stays at a fixed location on the page even if the surrounding text is moved to a new position in the document. If you select the Character option, the graph is treated as part of the text.

The Vertical Position and Horizontal Position options allow you to specify where the graph will appear on the page. If you select option 5 (Vertical Position), WordPerfect responds:

```
Offset from top of paragraph: 0"
```

If you select option 6 (Horizontal Position), WordPerfect displays the following menu:

```
Horizontal Position: 1 Left; 2 Right; 3 Center; 4 Full: 0
```

It is up to you to decide the exact position of your graph.

The Size option allows you to specify the exact height and width of the graph on the page.

The Wrap Text Around Box option allows Yes or No alternatives. If you select Yes, the text wraps around the graphics box. If you select No, the text is allowed to print over the top of the graph. Usually, you should select the Yes option.

The Edit option brings the graph to the screen.

6. After selecting the Create option, select F (for File name). Enter the drive, path, name, and extension of your file (if the file is not on the default drive) and press Enter.

7. Exit this menu by pressing the space bar; then press Shift-F7 and select option 6 (View Document). Your graph is displayed on the screen. To print the graph, press the space bar and select option 1 (Full Document).

Appendix B File Transfer Among Popular Software Packages

B-10

FILE TRANSFER AND QUATTRO PRO

Creating ASCII Files

Follow the steps outlined next to create an ASCII file using Quattro Pro. For this exercise we assume that the spreadsheet you are saving occupies the range of cells A1 through F5 (A1 .. F5).

1. Press the / (forward slash) key to access the main menu.
2. Press P (Print).
3. Press B (Block). Assuming that your cellpointer is located in cell A1, Quattro Pro responds with the following prompt:

   `[Enter] [Esc] The block of the spreadsheet to print: A1`

4. Type *A1 .. F5* and press Enter.
5. Press D (Destination). Quattro Pro displays the Destination menu.
6. Press F (File). Quattro Pro prompts you with the following message:

   `Enter print file name:`

7. Type a name for your file (up to eight characters) and press Enter. We typed SALES and pressed Enter. Quattro Pro now returns you to the main Print menu.

   Quattro Pro saves the spreadsheet data, using the file name you specified, with the extension PRN.
   To verify that the ASCII file was created successfully, use the left-arrow key to display the File menu, then select the Utilities option, then select the DOS Shell option. Quattro Pro responds with the following message:

`Enter DOS Command, Press Enter for full DOS Shell`

Press the Enter key; you will be presented with a DOS prompt. Type the following command to view the ASCII file:

   TYPE SALES.PRN (press Enter)

Note: If you entered a different file name, replace the word "SALES" with the name you specified.) The data from cells A1 .. F5 will be displayed on screen. Type the DOS command EXIT and press Enter to return to Quattro Pro.

Importing ASCII Files

Make sure you have a blank spreadsheet, then follow the steps outlined to import an ASCII file into Quattro Pro. We assume that you have generated an ASCII file using another application, in this case, 1-2-3.

1. Press the / (forward slash) key to access the main menu.
2. Press T (Tools).
3. Press I (Import).

Appendices

4. Press A (ASCII Text File). Quattro Pro responds with the following prompt:

   ```
   Enter name of file to import:
   ```

A listing of all files in the default directory with the extension PRN is displayed for you. You may highlight the desired file name and press Enter, or you may type the drive, path, and file name of the desired file and then press Enter. Quattro Pro imports the specified ASCII file and displays its contents on screen for you.

B–11

FILE TRANSFER AND PARADOX

Creating ASCII Files

Follow these steps to create an ASCII file using Paradox. We assume that you have already created a table consisting of 10 records.

1. If necessary, press the F10 key to display the main menu.
2. Press T (Tools) to select the Tools option from the main menu.
3. Press E (ExportImport) to select the ExportImport option.
4. Press E (Export) to select the Export option. Paradox responds by displaying the various output file formats that are available to you.
5. Press A (ASCII) to select the ASCII option.
6. Press D (Delimited) to select the Delimited option. Paradox prompts you to enter the name of the table that will be used to create the ASCII file.
7. Press the Enter key and Paradox responds by displaying the names of tables that are available to be selected.
8. Highlight the desired table name and press Enter, or type the name of the table from which you want to create an ASCII file and press Enter. We highlighted the table name CUSTOMER and pressed Enter. Paradox responds with a prompt requesting the name of the converted file.
9. Type a name for your output ASCII file, then press Enter. We typed CUSTLIST then pressed Enter. Paradox responds in the lower right corner with the message

   ```
   Converting Customer to custlist.TXT...
   ```

The ASCII file is created on the default drive, in the default directory, under the file name that was specified during the ASCII file creation process. When the message in the lower right corner of the screen stops flashing, ASCII file creation is finished.

Follow these steps to verify that the ASCII file has been successfully created:

1. If necessary, press the F10 key to display the main menu.
2. Press T (Tools).
3. Press M (More).

Appendix B   File Transfer Among Popular Software Packages

4. Press T (ToDOS). Paradox will clear the screen and display a DOS prompt for you.
5. Type the following command to send the contents of the ASCII file to the printer:

   TYPE CUSTLIST.TXT > LPT1

   (Note: If you used a name other than CUSTLIST for your ASCII file, specify that name instead of CUSTLIST. Also, if LPT1 is not the port you are using for printed output, specify the correct output port instead of LPT1.)

Your output will be sent to the printer. Each record in the file will be printed on a separate line with commas separating each field and quotation marks surrounding the contents of each field. View the ASCII data output to make sure that it is correct, then type *EXIT* and press Enter to return to Paradox.

Importing ASCII Files

Follow the steps outlined next to import an ASCII file into Paradox. We assume that you have already created a comma delimited ASCII file using another application program.

1. If necessary, press the F10 key to display the main menu.
2. Press T (Tools) to select the Tools option.
3. Press E (ExportImport) to select the ExportImport option.
4. Press I (Import) to select the Import option. Paradox responds by displaying various application program file formats that are available to you.
5. Press A (ASCII) to select the ASCII option.
6. Press D (Delimited) to select the Delimited option. Paradox prompts you to enter the name of the file to be imported.
7. Press Enter to view the names of available ASCII files from which you can select.
8. You may highlight the desired import file and press Enter, or type the name of the desired import file and press Enter. We typed SALESMAN.TXT and pressed Enter. Paradox responds by prompting you for the name of the new Paradox table that will be created as a result of the import operation.
9. Type the name of the new Paradox table that will be used to hold the incoming ASCII data and press Enter. We typed TEST and pressed Enter. Paradox imports the ASCII file data; it displays the imported data from left to right on the screen with the name of the new table in the upper left corner and Field-1, Field-2, and so forth displayed at the top of each column of data.

B–12

FILE TRANSFER AND BASICA

BASICA can generate ASCII files in several ways. The following program is one that can be used to generate a sequential ASCII file. The resulting file can easily be imported to any software that accepts ASCII files.

```
10      REM TO CREATE ASCII FILE CALLED STUREC
20      OPEN "STUREC" FOR OUTPUT AS #1
30      FOR I=1 TO 3
40          READ A$,B$,C
50          WRITE #1,A$,B$,C
60      NEXT I
70      CLOSE
80      DATA SUSAN SHAY, BUSINESS, 3.85
90      DATA KIM BROWN, COMPUTER, 2.60
100     DATA ED STRONG, MATH, 4.00
110     END
```

To see the contents of the ASCII file STUREC, type these instructions:

>RUN (press Enter)   (program will run)
>SYSTEM (press Enter)   (exit from BASICA to DOS prompt)
>A > TYPE STUREC (press Enter)
>"SUSAN SHAY","BUSINESS",3.85
>"KIM BROWN","COMPUTER",2.60
>"ED STRONG","MATH",4.00

Also, if a file is saved using the SAVE "File name",A command, the file is saved in ASCII format with the BAS extension automatically supplied.

BASICA can read an ASCII file by using the LINE INPUT #1 command. For example, you can read an ASCII file line by line into a one-dimensional array in a BASICA program. The following routine reads a 1-2-3 ASCII file (PRN file) called MYFILE.PRN into array X$(100):

```
10      DIM X$(100)
20      OPEN "MYFILE.PRN" FOR INPUT AS #1
30      J=1
40      WHILE NOT EOF(1)
50          LINE INPUT #1,X$(I)
60          J=J+1
70      WEND
80      END
```

The following routine prints the contents of array X$:

```
10      FOR I=1 TO J
20          PRINT "X$(I)=",X$(I)
30      NEXT I
40      END
```

SUMMARY

This appendix reviewed ASCII files and the advantages of file transfer among different software. Specific guidelines for file transfer using DOS, WordPerfect, Lotus 1-2-3, dBASE, Quattro Pro, Paradox, and BASICA were presented. To become familiar with this important topic, you have to practice by creating a sample file in one software package and exporting or importing it into the other packages.

Appendix B File Transfer Among Popular Software Packages

REVIEW QUESTIONS

1. What is file transfer? Why should it be done in some cases?
2. What is an ASCII file?
3. How do you know if a file is in ASCII format?
4. How do you create an ASCII file using DOS?
5. How do you create an ASCII file using WordPerfect?
6. How is an ASCII file imported into WordPerfect?
7. How do you import a PIC file into WordPerfect?
8. What are the advantages of importing a PIC file into a WordPerfect document?
9. How do you create an ASCII file using 1-2-3?
10. How is an ASCII file imported into 1-2-3?
11. How do you create an ASCII file using dBASE?
12. How is an ASCII file imported into dBASE?
13. What are some of the file transfer features of Quattro Pro?
14. How is an ASCII file imported into Quattro Pro?
15. How do you create an ASCII file using Paradox?
16. How is an ASCII file imported into Paradox?
17. How do you read the contents of an ASCII file into a BASICA array?
18. How do you create an ASCII file using BASICA?

Index

About Clock option, 237
Accessories group, 179
Accounting software, 16–17
Adapter cards, 6
Advanced option, 270
Airbrush, 108
Alarm menu (Calendar), 233–34
Alarms, 230–31
Alert Always option, 266
Always on Top option, 237
Analog option, 236
Applications
   Calculator, 222–25
   Calendar, 225–35
   Cardfile, 237–41
   Clock, 236–37
   exiting, 169
   file association, 209–11
   Notepad, 241–43
   Recorder, 246, 254–58
   running two or more, 164
   starting, 162–64, 188
   switching between, 164–65
   Terminal, 243–46
Applications group, 179
APPS.INF file, 267
Arithmetic operations, 23–24, 224
ASCII file transfer, 288–91, 293–95
Associate With box, 210
ATTRIB command, 53
AUTOEXEC.BAT file, 280, 282–83
Auxiliary devices, 5–6
Auxiliary memory, 6, 9–11

Background color, 98–99
Backup, 66–67
BACKUP command, 65
Backup files, 31, 66–67
Backup option, 124
Bank switching, 8–9
BASICA file transfer, 295–96
Batch files, 31
Baud rate, 243–44
Bernoulli box, 9
Bitmaps, 190
Booting up, 30–31

Boxes, 106–7
Built-in formulas, 23

CAD (computer-aided design)
   software, 17
Calculator application, 222–25
Calendar application, 225–35
   Alarm menu, 233–34
   alarms, 230–31
   Copy option, 232
   cursor-movement keys, 229–30
   Cut option, 232
   Date option, 233
   Edit menu, 232
   events, 227–29
   Exit option, 232
   File menu, 231–32
   Help menu, 234–35
   New option, 231
   Open option, 231
   Options menu, 234
   Page Setup option, 231
   Paste option, 232
   Print option, 231
   Print Setup option, 231
   Save As option, 231
   Save option, 231
   screen layout, 225–27
   setting alarms, 230–31
   Show menu, 233
   View menu, 233
Cancel option, 76
Cardfile application, 237–41
Cascade command, 179
CD command, 61
CD ROM (compact disk read-only
   memory), 11
Central processing unit (CPU), 4
Character Map, 246
CHDIR command, 61
CHKDSK command, 48–50
Circles, 107
Click and drag, 79–80
Client, 259
Clipboard, 110, 129–31, 166–69
Clipboard Viewer, 167

Clock application, 236–37
   Date option, 236
Close Window on Exit option, 270
Closing windows, 150
CLS command, 31
Cold boot, 30
Color monitors, 4
Color option, 188
Command files, 31
Commands
   control-menu, 144–46
   for directories, 61–62
   DOS (disk operating system),
     44–53
   external, 31
   internal, 31
   memory-resident, 31
   nonmemory-resident, 31
Communications software, 15
Comparing
   disks, 48, 65
   files, 52
COMP command, 52
Computer-aided design (CAD)
   software, 17
Computer files. *See* Files
Computers. *See* Mainframe
   computers; Microcomputers
Computer virus, 20
CONFIG.SYS file, 280, 283–84
Constants, 23
Control menu, 142–44
Control-menu box, 88–89
Control-menu commands, 144–46
Control Panel, 188–91
Controls option, 233–34
Conventional memory, 6–9
Copy command, 110
COPY command (DOS), 50–51
   versus DISKCOPY command,
     51–52
Copy Disk option, 214
Copying
   directories, 63–64, 207–9
   disks, 47, 51–52, 65, 214
   files, 50–52, 207–9

299

Copying, *continued*
 program items, 186
 subdirectories, 64
 text, 166
Copy option
 Calendar, 232
 Notepad, 242
Copy To command, 110
Correcting mistakes, 171
CPU (central processing unit), 4
Crash, 65, 67–68
Creating
 directories, 62–63, 204
 documents, 121–22
 groups, 181–83
 program items, 184–86
 system disk, 214–15
Cursor-movement keys (Calendar), 229–30
Cursor Position option, 112
Curved lines, 106
Custom Wallpaper, 190
Cut and paste, 129–31
Cut command, 110
Cut option
 Calendar, 232
 Notepad, 242
Cutout, 99
Cutout tools, 103–4

Database software, 14
Data bits, 244
Data types, 22–23
DATE command, 30
Date option
 Calendar, 233
 Clock, 236
Date/Time option, 189
Day option, 233
Day Settings option, 234
Day view mode, 225
dBASE file transfer, 290–91
DDE (dynamic data exchange), 264–65
DEFAULT.PIF file, 268
DELETE command, 53
Delete option, 242
Deleting
 directories, 64–65, 205–7
 files, 205–7
 groups, 183
 program items, 186
 text, 126
Deselecting
 directories, 201
 files, 201

Desktop, 75
Desktop option, 189
Desktop publishing software, 15
Destination document, 259
Dialog box, 75, 144
Digital option, 236
DIR command, 31–34
Directories, 60–61, 198
 commands for, 61–62
 copying, 63–64, 207–9
 creating, 62–63, 204
 deleting, 64–65, 205–7
 deselecting, 201
 moving, 207–9
 naming, 203–4
 removing, 64–65, 205–7
 renaming, 207
 searching for, 205
 selecting, 200–1
 sorting contents, 201–2
Directory window, 198–99
DISKCOMP command, 48, 65
DISKCOPY command, 47, 65
 versus COPY command (DOS), 51–52
Disk drives, 6, 201
Diskettes. *See* Disks
Disk operating system. *See* DOS
Disks, 6, 9–11. *See also* Hard disk
 comparing, 48, 65
 copying, 47, 51–52, 65, 214
 formatting, 34–35, 44–46, 212–13, 257–58
 labeling, 46, 213–14
Display Usage option, 270
Documents, 169–71, 259
 creating, 121–22
 moving within, 125–26
 retrieving, 124–25
 saving, 122–24
 switching between, 170
Document window, 144
DOS (disk operating system), 30–31
 commands, 44–53
 file specifications, 31
 file transfer, 288
 hidden files, 50
 keys, 34
 prompts, 30–31, 61, 163–64
Double-clicking, 79
Draft option, 102
Drag and drop, 90
Drawing, 98, 105–8
Drawings
 entering text into, 101–2
 printing, 102–3

Drivers option, 189
Drives, 6, 201
Dynamic data exchange (DDE), 264–65

Edit menu
 Calendar, 232
 Paintbrush, 110
Edit option, 244
Ellipses, 107
Embedding objects, 90, 258–65
EMM (expanded memory manager), 8
EMS (expanded memory specification), 8
EMS Memory option, 269
Enhanced mode, 82–83
Enhancing text, 132–33
Enlarging windows, 148
EPROM (erasable programmable read-only memory), 6
Erasable optical disk, 11
ERASE command, 53
Events, 227–29
Executable files, 31
Execution option, 270
Exiting
 applications, 169
 Paintbrush, 96–97
 Windows 3.1, 75–78
Exit option
 Calendar, 232
 Notepad, 242
 Paintbrush, 110
Expanded memory, 7–9
Expanded memory manager (EMM), 8
Expanded memory specification (EMS), 8
Expansion slots, 6
Exporting files, 287–96
Extended memory, 7–9
External commands, 31

FAT (file allocation table), 35, 44, 212
FDISK command, 65–66
File allocation table (FAT), 35, 44, 212
File association, 209–11
File extensions, 31
File Manager, 90, 198
 changing drives, 201
 copying disks, 214
 copying files and directories, 207–9
 creating directories, 204
 creating system disk, 214–15

Index

File Manager, *continued*
  deleting files and directories, 205–7
  directory window, 198–99
  file association, 209–11
  file types, 202–3
  formatting disks, 212–13
  labeling disks, 213–14
  moving files and directories, 207–9
  multiple windows in, 209
  naming files and directories, 203–4
  printing files, 212
  renaming files and directories, 207
  searching for files and directories, 205
  selecting files and directories, 200–1
  sorting directory contents, 201–2
  starting applications from, 162
File menu
  Calendar, 231–32
  Paintbrush, 108–10
File option
  Paintbrush, 108
  PIF Editor, 268
  Recorder, 254–55
  Terminal, 244
Files, 22, 198. *See also* File transfer
  backup, 31, 66–67
  batch, 31
  command, 31
  comparing, 52
  copying, 50–52, 207–9
  deleting, 205–7
  deselecting, 201
  DOS specifications, 31
  executable, 31
  exporting, 287–96
  hidden, 50
  importing, 287–96
  moving, 207–9
  naming, 31, 203–4
  opening, 169–70
  printing, 212
  program, 163
  read-only, 53
  renaming, 52, 207
  saving, 170
  searching for, 205
  selecting, 200–1
  system, 31, 280–86
  types, 202–3
File transfer, 287
  ASCII files, 288–91, 293–95
  BASICA files, 295–96

File transfer, *continued*
  dBASE files, 290–91
  DOS files, 288
  Lotus 1-2-3 files, 290
  1-2-3 PIC files, 291–92
  Paradox files, 294–95
  Quattro Pro files, 293–94
  WordPerfect 5.1 files, 288–90
Financial planning software, 15–16
Find and replace operation, 127–29
Find Next option, 243
Find option, 243
Flash if Inactive option, 266
Floppy diskettes. *See* Disks
Fonts, 90, 132–33
Fonts option, 188
Foreground color, 98–99
FORMAT command, 34–35, 44–46
Formatting
  disks, 34–35, 44–46, 212–13, 257–58
  hard disk, 66
Formula types, 23
Function keys, 5
Functions, 23

Games group, 179
Games software, 18
Grammar checker software, 13–14
Graphical user interface (GUI), 74
Graphics software, 14–15
Group icons, 162, 180
Groups, 178–83
  changing description of, 183
  creating, 181–83
  deleting, 183
Group windows, 160
  opening, 179
  rearranging, 179–80
  reducing to icons, 179
GUI (graphical user interface), 74

Hard disk, 30. *See also* Disks
  backing up, 66–67
  crash, 65, 67–68
  formatting, 66
  managing, 65
  partitioning, 65–66
  restoring, 65, 67–68
Help facility
  for specific topics, 85
  tutorial facility, 85–88, 90
  Windows 3.1, 83–88
Help menu
  Calendar, 234–35
  Paintbrush, 112–13

Hidden files, 50
High Priority option, 265
Horizontal scroll bar, 89

I-beam, 125–26
Icons, 75
  changing, 187–88
  group, 162, 180
  moving, 147
  program-item, 178–83, 188
  reducing group windows to, 179
  reducing windows to, 148
  restoring to windows, 148
Ignore if Inactive option, 266
Image Attributes option, 112–13
Importing files, 287–96
Input devices, 2
Inserting text, 126
Insertion point, 88–89
Internal commands, 31
International option, 189
Investment analysis software, 17–18

Keyboard, 2–3, 5
  Calendar, 229–30
  DOS keys, 34
  function keys, 5
  Windows 3.1, 81–82
  Write, 125
Keyboard option, 189
Key combinations, 82

LABEL command, 46
Labeling disks, 46, 213–14
Label option, 213–14
Line drawing, 105–8
Linesize box, 97
Line spacing, 131–32
Line width, 98–99
Linking objects, 90, 258–65
Lotus 1-2-3, 14
  file transfer, 290
Low Priority option, 265

Macro, 254–58
Macro option, 255
Magnetic storage devices, 9–10
Mainframe computers, 21
Main memory, 6–9
Mark option, 234
Maximize button, 89
MD command, 61
Media Player, 246
Medium Priority option, 265
Memory, 6–13
  auxiliary, 6, 9–11
  conventional, 6–9

Memory, *continued*
   expanded, 7–9
   extended, 7–9
   main, 6–9
   primary, 6–9
   processor speed and, 11–13
   random-access (RAM), 6–9
   read-only (ROM), 6
   secondary, 6, 9–11
Memory Requirements option, 269
Memory-resident commands, 31
Menu bar, 88–89
Menus
   conventions, 142
   Paintbrush, 108–13
Merge option, 255
Microcomputers, 2–4. *See also* Files; Software
   auxiliary devices, 5–6
   booting up, 30–31
   care of, 20
   data types, 22–23
   formula types, 23
   hands-on session, 21–22
   mainframes, compared with, 21
   memory, 6–13
   selection guidelines, 18–20
   value types, 23
Microprocessor, 4, 11–13
Minimize button, 88–89
Mistakes, 171
MKDIR command, 61
Modem, 15, 243–44
Mode option, 268
Modes, 82–83, 225, 268
Monitors, 3–4
Month option, 233
Month view mode, 225
MORICONS.DLL file, 187–88
Mouse, 75, 78–80, 88, 90
   Paintbrush, 98
   Write, 125–26
Mouse option, 189
Mouse pointer, 78, 89
Moving
   directories, 207–9
   documents, 125–26
   files, 207–9
   icons, 147
   program items, 186–87
   text, 131, 166
   in text, 171
   windows, 146–47
MS-DOS, 36–38. *See also* DOS (disk operating system)
MS-DOS prompt, starting applications from, 163–64

Multimedia, 90
Multitasking, 74

Naming
   directories, 203–4
   files, 31, 203–4
Network Connections option, 266
Network Settings option, 266
New option
   Calendar, 231
   Notepad, 242
   Paintbrush, 108
Next option, 233
Nonmemory-resident commands, 31
Nonnumeric data, 23
Notepad application, 241–43
   Copy option, 242
   Cut option, 242
   Exit option, 242
   New option, 242
   Open option, 242
   Page Setup option, 242
   Paste option, 242
   Print option, 242
   Save As option, 242
   Save option, 242
   Undo option, 242
No Title option, 236
Numeric data, 22

Object, 259
Object linking and embedding (OLE), 90, 258–65
Object Packager, 270–71
OK option, 76
OLE (object linking and embedding), 90, 258–65
1-2-3 PIC file transfer, 291–92
Online tutorial, 85–88, 90
Opening
   files, 169–70
   group windows, 179
Open option, 108
   Calendar, 231
   Notepad, 242
Optical technology devices, 10–11
Optional Parameters option, 269
Options menu
   Calendar, 234
   Paintbrush, 112–13
Output devices, 2–4

Page breaks, 134–36
Page Setup option
   Calendar, 231
   Notepad, 242
   Paintbrush, 110

Paintbrush, 96
   background color, 98–99
   cutout tools, 103–4
   drawing with, 98, 105–8
   Edit menu, 110
   entering text into drawings, 101–2
   exiting, 96–97
   Exit option, 110
   File menu, 108–10
   File option, 108
   foreground color, 98–99
   Help menu, 112–13
   line width, 98–99
   menus, 108–13
   mouse, 98
   New option, 108
   Options menu, 112–13
   Page Setup option, 110
   Pick menu, 112
   printing drawings, 102–3
   Print option, 110
   Print Setup option, 110
   Save As option, 108
   Save option, 108
   screen, 97–98
   starting, 96–97
   Text menu, 112
   text tool, 101–2
   toolbox, 97, 99–101, 105–8
   Undo command, 110
   Undo option, 101
   View menu, 110–12
Palette, 97
Paradox file transfer, 294–95
Parity, 244
PARK.COM program, 65
Partial option, 102–3
Partitioning hard disk, 65–66
Paste command, 110
Paste From command, 110
Paste option
   Calendar, 232
   Notepad, 242
PATH command, 62
PC. *See* Microcomputers
PC-DOS, 36–38. *See also* DOS (disk operating system)
Permanent area, 21
Personal computers. *See* Microcomputers
Phone option, 245
PIC file transfer, 291–92
Pick menu (Paintbrush), 112
Pick tool, 103
PIF Editor, 267–70
   File option, 268

Index

PIF (program information file), 267–70
Polygons, 107–8
Ports, 6
Ports option, 188
Previous option, 233
Primary memory, 6–9
Printers, 191
Printer Setup option, 266
Printers option, 189, 191
Printing
  drawings, 102–3
  files, 212
  text, 126–27
Print Manager, 265–67
Print option
  Calendar, 231
  Notepad, 242
  Paintbrush, 110
Print Setup option
  Calendar, 231
  Paintbrush, 110
Priority of operations, 23–24
Processor speed, 11–13
PROGMAN.EXE file, 187–88
Program Filename option, 269
Program files, 163
Program information file (PIF), 267–70
Program-item icons, 178–83, 188
Program items, 184–88
  copying, 186
  creating, 184–86
  deleting, 186
  moving, 186–87
Programmable read-only memory (PROM), 6
Program Manager, 160–62
  starting applications from, 162
Program Manager window, 76
Project management software, 17
PROM (programmable read-only memory), 6
PROMPT PG command, 61
Prompts, 30–31, 61, 163–64
Proof option, 102
Properties command, 188

Quattro Pro file transfer, 293–94
Quick Format option, 213

RAM (random-access memory), 6–9
RD command, 61
Read-only files, 53
Read-only memory (ROM), 6

Recorder application, 246, 254–58
  File option, 254–55
Reducing
  group windows to icons, 179
  windows to icons, 148
Remove option, 232
Removing directories, 64–65, 205–7
RENAME command, 52
Renaming
  directories, 207
  files, 52, 207
Reserved names, 203
RESTORE command, 65, 67–68
Restoring
  hard disk, 65, 67–68
  icons to windows, 148
Retrieving documents, 124–25
RMDIR command, 61
ROM BIOS (Basic Input/Output System), 8
ROM (read-only memory), 6
Root directory, 60, 198
Run command, starting applications with, 162–63
Run Minimized box, 163, 188

Save As command, 170
Save As option
  Calendar, 231
  Notepad, 242
  Paintbrush, 108
Save Colors option, 112–13
Save command, 170
Save option
  Calendar, 231
  Notepad, 242
  Paintbrush, 108
Saving
  documents, 122–24
  files, 170
Scissors tool, 103
Screens
  Calendar, 225–27
  Paintbrush, 97–98
  parts of, 88–89
Screen Saver, 191
Scroll bars, 89, 148–50
Searching
  for directories, 205
  for files, 205
Secondary memory, 6, 9–11
Seconds option, 236
Select All option, 242
Selecting
  directories, 200–1
  files, 200–1
  text, 127, 165–66

Server, 259
Set Font option, 236
Set option, 233
Setting alarms, 230–31
Settings option, 245
SHIPDISK.COM program, 65
Shortcut keys, 82
Show menu (Calendar), 233
Software, 13–18
  accounting, 16–17
  communications, 15
  computer-aided design (CAD), 17
  database, 14
  desktop publishing, 15
  financial planning, 15–16
  games, 18
  grammar checker, 13–14
  graphics, 14–15
  investment analysis, 17–18
  project management, 17
  selection of, 19
  spreadsheet, 14
  tax preparation, 18
  terminate and stay resident (TSR), 17
  utility, 17
  word processing, 13
Sorting directory contents, 201–2
Sound option, 190
Sound Recorder, 246
Source document, 259
Special Time option, 234
Spreadsheet software, 14
Standard mode, 82–83
Starting up
  applications, 162–64, 188
  Paintbrush, 96–97
  Windows 3.1, 75–78
  Write, 120–21
Start-up Directory option, 269
StartUp group, 179, 188
Stop bits, 244
Straight lines, 105–6
Subdirectories, 60
  copying, 64
Switching
  applications, 164–65
  documents, 170
SYS command, 50
SYSEDIT file, 280–82
System date, 30
System disk, 214–15
System files, 31, 280–86
SYSTEM.INI file, 280, 285
System time, 30

Task List, 151–52
Tax preparation software, 18
Terminal application, 243–46
  File option, 244
Terminate and stay resident (TSR) software, 17
Text, 170–71
  copying, 166
  correcting mistakes, 171
  deleting, 126
  enhancing, 132–33
  entering into drawings, 101–2
  inserting, 126
  moving, 131, 166
  moving around in, 171
  printing, 126–27
  selecting, 127, 165–66
Text menu (Paintbrush), 112
Text tool, 101–2
386 Enhanced option, 189
Tile command, 179–80
TIME command, 30
Today option, 233
Toolbox, 97, 99–101, 105–8
Transferring files. *See* File transfer
Transfers option, 245
TREE command, 62
TrueType fonts, 90
Tutorial facility, 85–88, 90
Typefaces, 90, 132–33

Undo command
  Paintbrush, 110
  Write, 131
Undo option
  Notepad, 242
  Paintbrush, 101
Upgrading to Windows 3.1, 89–90
User-defined formulas, 23
Utility software, 17

Value types, 23
Variables, 23
VER command, 38
Vertical scroll bar, 89

Video Memory option, 269
View menu
  Calendar, 233
  Paintbrush, 110–12
View Picture option, 112
Virus, 20
VOL command, 46
Volume label, 45–46

Warm boot, 30
Wildcards, 22, 32–33, 202, 205
Window border, 89
Window corner, 89
Windows, 75
  closing, 150
  enlarging, 148
  modifying size, 147–48
  moving, 146–47
  multiple windows in File Manager, 209
  parts of, 151
  reducing to icons, 148
  restoring icons to, 148
Windows Paintbrush. *See* Paintbrush
Windows 3.1. *See also* Applications
  advantages, 74–75
  closing windows, 150
  control menu, 142–44
  control-menu commands, 144–46
  documents, 169–71
  enlarging windows, 148
  exiting, 75–78
  Help facility, 83–88
  keyboard, 81–82
  menu conventions, 142
  modes, 82–83
  modifying window size, 147–48
  mouse, 78–80
  moving icons, 147
  moving windows, 146–47
  Program Manager, 160–62
  reducing windows to icons, 148
  restoring icons to windows, 148
  screens, 88–89

Windows 3.1, *continued*
  scroll bars, 89, 148–50
  starting, 75–78
  Task List, 151–52
  terminology, 75
  upgrading to, 89–90
  window parts, 151
Windows Write. *See* Write
Window title, 88–89
Window Title option, 269
WIN.INI file, 188, 280, 284–85
WordPerfect 5.1 file transfer, 288–90
Word processing software, 13
Word size, 11–13
Word Wrap option, 242
WORM (write once, read many) disk, 11
Write, 241
  creating documents, 121–22
  cut and paste, 129–31
  deleting text, 126
  enhancing text, 132–33
  find and replace, 127–29
  inserting text, 126
  keyboard, 125
  line spacing, 131–32
  mouse, 125–26
  moving text, 131, 166
  moving within documents, 125–26
  page breaks, 134–36
  printing text, 126–27
  retrieving documents, 124–25
  saving documents, 122–24
  selecting text, 127
  starting, 120–21
  Undo command, 131
Write once, read many (WORM) disk, 11

XCOPY command, 62
XMS Memory option, 269

Zoom In command, 110–12
Zoom Out command, 110–12

ISBN 0-02-309533-4